Building Medallion Architectures
Designing with Delta Lake and Spark

Piethein Strengholt

O'REILLY®

Building Medallion Architectures

by Piethein Strengholt

Published by O'Reilly Media, Inc., 141 Stony Circle, Suite 195, Santa Rosa, CA 95401.

O'Reilly books may be purchased for educational, business, or sales promotional use. Online editions are also available for most titles (*http://oreilly.com*). For more information, contact our corporate/institutional sales department: 800-998-9938 or *corporate@oreilly.com*.

Acquisitions Editor: Michelle Smith
Development Editor: Shira Evans
Production Editor: Katherine Tozer
Copyeditor: Liz Wheeler
Proofreader: Heather Walley

Indexer: nSight, Inc.
Interior Designer: David Futato
Cover Designer: José Marzan Jr.
Illustrator: Kate Dullea

April 2025:   First Edition

Revision History for the First Edition
2025-03-28:   First Release
2025-08-08:   Second Release

See *http://oreilly.com/catalog/errata.csp?isbn=9781098178833* for release details.

978-1-098-17883-3

[LSI]

Table of Contents

Part II.   Crafting the Medallion Layers

Part III.   Real-World Case Studies

Part IV.   Scaling, Governance, and the Future of Medallion Architectures

Foreword

Medallion architectures—I have a love/hate relationship with them. How could something so bluntly simple cause so much confusion and debate in our industry? Why does everyone have a differing definition for them? Why do we even need such concepts? And most importantly—why should you care?

I had spent nearly a decade as an in-house business intelligence developer before I turned external consultant, just in time to catch the wave of Europe's early Azure adoption for analytics. Wrestling with single-box SQL Server to create cloud-friendly architectures, and seeing how it simply did not fit, led me to embrace the explosive rise of data lakes and distributed compute back in 2015.

Since then, my mission has been clear: unify our approaches, learn from the past, and evolve without clinging to outdated traditions. Medallion architectures are a great tool for communicating that vision. At Advancing Analytics, I help companies world-wide unlock the true potential of their data—going beyond "faster and cheaper" so evolving businesses can work in new ways, enabled by the data they already have. I advise industry giants like Microsoft and Databricks, shaping the tools and strategies of tomorrow, and spend a lot of time talking about data architectures at worldwide conferences, events, and on our own Advancing Analytics YouTube channel (*https:// youtube.com/c/AdvancingAnalytics*).

I've designed architectures for gigantic global retailers, tech-savvy digital startups, monolithic regulated financial services, and everything in between, and I can happily tell you that there is a huge amount of commonality in those designs. After all, they're all extracting data, cleaning data, and performing analytics. So, if you're transitioning from traditional warehousing, or navigating from the chaos of big data, don't worry—the journey you're beginning is well-trod and understood, and there are a wealth of experts like myself and Piethein here to help.

We fought tooth and claw to have any kind of standards in the world of lakes. Medallion architectures are exactly that—a design standard for building platforms using data lakes. These emerging concepts can seem esoteric, the purview of highly specialized technicians. But make no mistake: they've become central to how we build modern data platforms. Even Microsoft, once strongly associated with relational databases, has thrown its weight behind the lakehouse vision with Microsoft Fabric. If you work in data and analytics, understanding Medallion architectures isn't optional—it's essential.

In fact, Medallion architectures are a fantastic concept that is widely misunderstood. Too often, they're treated as a rigid, step-by-step framework, when they are actually a flexible approach to making sense of an evolving landscape. They are an attempt to simplify a decade of organic evolution and technical innovation into concepts that can be presented to nontechnical users. But simplification comes at a cost: it leaves huge gaps for debate, misinterpretation, and frustration.

This book serves as your guide to adopting a Medallion architecture, cutting through the hype and hyperbole and explaining why we use certain patterns and how to implement them. But where did this confusion come from, and why do we need Medallion architectures? To understand this, we need to peek into the history.

It started in the era of big data, with an explosion of innovation around distributed storage and compute. The early days of big data saw data lakes adopted for serious-scale analytics and deep innovation—we could run queries at previously unimaginable scale and unlock a world of data analysis. But this innovation came at a price. Fast forward several years and data lakes are getting bad press; they're in the trough of disillusionment, turns out. They won't solve all of the worlds problems. We saw the emergence of the dreaded term—"data swamp."

Now, this isn't a failing of the technology itself, it's simply the nature of early adoption and innovation. The world of big data and early lakes was being run on invention—each individual data pipeline could be incredibly robust, but there was no overall architecture or operating model guiding design. Meanwhile, the relational database world thrived on discipline. Decades of practice-honed architectural frameworks like Kimball's created predictable, effective analytics systems. It is a very, very well-understood architectural space, almost to the point where it is too rooted in tradition. As data lakes matured, the challenge became to adapt the rigor of the warehouse to the scale and flexibility of the lake without falling foul of dogmatic tradition.

Then came the breakthrough. Accessible distributed compute technologies like Apache Spark, underpinned by new data layouts such as Delta Lake, Iceberg, and Hudi, turned data lakes into manageable, high-performance platforms. The lakehouse was born—a unifying vision that combined the best of lakes and warehouses. Medallion architectures emerged as the bridge to guide organizations through the lakehouse era. Instead of being the domain of niche companies with unique technical challenges, data lakes have become the de facto technology for data platforms; the doors have been thrown wide open—come on in, the water's lovely.

Medallion architectures are a simple Bronze–Silver–Gold conceptualization of the operating model for running a data lakehouse. An attempt to make a set of complex, flexible technical decisions, an easy-to-understand process to prevent organizations from falling into the data swamps of old. But that's the problem with boiling a complex problem down to a simple illustration—everyone begins to fill in the gaps and apply their own deeper meanings and definitions. That's where we are currently, and likely where you're starting with this book.

Implementing a Medallion architecture isn't about following a checklist set of instructions. It's not about taking the exact, fixed process and trying to fit your unique organization around it. Instead, focus on providing your data consumers with context—organize your data so they understand when it has been cleaned, when it is ready for consumption. Help them find the data to empower their work as fast and easily as possible. Once you have that, you can fit the processes to your design.

That's where this book shines. Piethein has gathered the history, context, processes, and nuance of these design patterns and distilled them. You'll gain a much richer understanding of why we follow certain processes and the value we get from them—which you can then use to fit these processes to your own unique organizational culture. If you're coming to this from the world of data warehousing, many of these concepts will be incredibly familiar—tweaked and adjusted for the changing technology stack.

There's an important word above: *context*. It's easy to document some processes and technical implementations and put it out into the world as the "right" way to do things, but that rapidly loses value if we forget the "why." Throughout this book, Piethein gives you that important piece of the puzzle—not just how to implement certain processes, but why we need those processes and the decisions we have made along the way. You'll be equipped with the ability to decide for yourself which processes and methods to adopt, and which, frankly, aren't required for your specific implementation.

This book isn't just a guide; it's a companion. You'll return to its insights and techniques as you navigate your journey, dipping back into implementation chapters and refining your approach. By the end, you won't just understand Medallion architectures—you'll master them.

So, go on, dive in and start your journey in the world of lakes and lakehouses.

— Simon Whiteley
CTO and founder of
Advancing Analytics (https://advancinganalytics.co.uk)

Preface

About a year ago, in early 2024, I was prepping up for my third architecture design workshop of the week. As I stood in front of the eager participants, the conversation naturally turned to Medallion architecture. Participants started firing off questions: "What are the best practices?" "What do other enterprises do?" "Is this architecture a valid pattern for larger organizations operating across multiple domains?" "Does data mesh replace a lakehouse architecture?" "How do we implement the Silver layer in practice?"

Every time I discuss the concept of Medallion architecture, it feels like I'm unraveling a complex puzzle. Despite its simplified layered approach to addressing various architectural concerns, the persistent lack of clear definitions and descriptive guidelines often leads to a flurry of questions, sparking confusion and inefficiency within organizations. This recurring theme prompted me to take decisive action: I decided to write a book that would provide a comprehensive guide to Medallion architecture, offering clarity and direction to professionals navigating this complex landscape.

Over the years, I've dedicated myself to studying Medallion architecture extensively. My research and practical experience have revealed its significant overlap with data warehousing, governance, metadata management, and data modeling. These elements are not isolated; they are interconnected, each impacting the other profoundly. Aware of the ongoing challenges and recognizing the need for clarity among professionals, I was driven to create a resource that could light the way to understanding. I also learned that, like many things in life, good designs come with nuances.

Building Medallion Architectures is my effort to demystify a complex subject. Before I started writing, I surveyed professionals to understand what readers might expect from this book. Most practitioners were looking for a hands-on guide and insights into complex topics like data mesh and generative AI, with many emphasizing the importance of governance and security. They also expressed a strong desire to learn from the experiences of other real-world organizations. I've kept all this feedback in mind while writing this book.

I cover a wide range of topics related to Medallion architecture. However, based on the feedback I received, I had to prioritize some areas over others. As a result, you won't find in-depth discussions on continuous integration and deployment, DataOps, machine learning, data lineage, or business data modeling here. These topics are indeed valuable, but they require their own detailed exploration, which is beyond the scope of this book. Instead, I chose to focus on the most pressing and impactful areas to ensure the insights you gain are practical and actionable.

My goal is to meet your expectations and provide clear, straightforward guidelines and definitions to help you effectively implement Medallion architectures. Whether you're a newcomer, still wrapping your head around lakehouse architecture, or gearing up for your first project, let's navigate this complex terrain together.

This book is structured to cater to a diverse audience, with each section designed to address different aspects of Medallion architecture. It begins by exploring the evolution of data architecture, highlighting key practices from the past and present. It then introduces the core concepts of Medallion architecture with clarity and without bias. Moving from theory to practice, the book offers detailed tutorials for hands-on engagement and learning. Additionally, it features case studies that illustrate successful implementations of Medallion architecture across various enterprises, providing insights into best practices and common pitfalls. Finally, the book discusses the latest trends such as data mesh, data governance, data contracts, security, and artificial intelligence (AI), offering valuable perspectives for those looking to enhance and scale their data architectures.

Having said this, I hope that *Building Medallion Architectures* proves to be an invaluable resource for everyone from novices to seasoned professionals. Whether you're seeking a solid introduction, hands-on practice, real-world applications, or advanced knowledge, this book has something to offer.

Who Should Read This Book

If you've picked up this book, chances are you're deeply involved in the world of data. Maybe you're planning to set up a new data platform, looking to enhance an existing one, or simply curious about what Medallion architecture is all about. You might be wondering how it operates, how to implement it effectively, and whether it can be tailored to meet your specific needs.

You could be a member of a data engineering team, part of an enterprise architecture group, or hold a key role as a chief data officer. Perhaps you're a data engineer, a data scientist, or a data manager. Maybe you're even part of a broader data-focused team. Whatever your role, this book is designed to help you grasp the essentials of Medallion architecture and discover how it can transform data into valuable insights.

This guide is here to demystify the complexities and equip you with the knowledge to make informed decisions in the ever-evolving landscape of data management. Let's dive in and explore how Medallion architecture can be a game-changer for your organization.

Navigating This Book

This book is a practical guide for understanding and implementing one or multiple Medallion architectures. It's also a reference guide for those who are already familiar with the concept and want to deepen their understanding. The book dives into the Azure technology stack to explore how to implement a real Medallion architecture. We'll look at services like Microsoft Fabric, but not for promotional purposes or to compare them directly with other services. The main goal is to deepen your understanding of Medallion architecture and demonstrate its practical applications.

As technology evolves rapidly, I've chosen to focus on well-established services and features that are less likely to undergo significant changes soon. For instance, tools like Apache Airflow, (Azure) Data Factory, PySpark, and methods driven by metadata are robust and adaptable to various settings. The skills you develop here using Microsoft Fabric will also equip you to work effectively with other Spark- and Delta Lake-based platforms.

The book is divided into four parts, moving from theory to practice:

- In Part I, "Understanding the Medallion Framework", we begin with an introduction to the evolution of data architecture. We'll start by looking at both the historical and current best practices to understand how data architecture has evolved. Recognizing the relevance of old concepts and seeing their transformation is crucial for grasping today's data complexities. Next, we'll dive deep into Medallion architecture, breaking down its core concepts and implementation stages.

- In Part II, "Crafting the Medallion Layers", we transition to a more hands-on approach. Here, you'll be guided through the complete process of building a Medallion architecture using Microsoft Fabric. For readers interested in using Azure Databricks instead, an external blog post provides complementary content that offers an alternative learning path. This part of the book is filled with a range of material, from fundamental concepts to sophisticated strategies, all presented in a vendor-neutral manner. This ensures that you can apply these insights across any lakehouse architecture effectively.

- Moving to Part III, "Real-World Case Studies", we'll bridge the gap between theory and practice by featuring interviews with professionals who have successfully implemented Medallion architectures in their organizations. We'll explore how AP Pension, Amadeus, and ZEISS have leveraged Medallion architecture to enhance their data handling and analytics capabilities.

- In Part IV, "Scaling, Governance, and the Future of Medallion Architectures", we'll wrap up the book by discussing how to scale Medallion architectures for larger enterprises and delve into advanced topics like data mesh and data contracts. Furthermore, we'll explore the future of Medallion architecture by examining generative artificial intelligence.

Conventions Used in This Book

The following typographical conventions are used in this book:

Italic
> Indicates new terms, URLs, email addresses, filenames, and file extensions.

`Constant width`
> Used for program listings, as well as within paragraphs to refer to program elements such as variable or function names, databases, data types, environment variables, statements, and keywords.

This element signifies a tip or suggestion.

This element signifies a general note.

This element indicates a warning or caution.

Using Code Examples

This book is packed with essential code snippets and configuration parameters that are crucial for both understanding the concepts and building the end-to-end tutorial. All of these resources are freely available for download from my GitHub page at *https://github.com/pietheinstrengholt/building-medallion-architectures-book*.

If you have a technical question or a problem using the code examples, please send email to *support@oreilly.com*.

This book is here to help you get your job done. In general, if example code is offered with this book, you may use it in your programs and documentation. You do not need to contact us for permission unless you're reproducing a significant portion of the code. For example, writing a program that uses several chunks of code from this book does not require permission. Selling or distributing examples from O'Reilly books does require permission. Answering a question by citing this book and quoting example code does not require permission. Incorporating a significant amount of example code from this book into your product's documentation does require permission.

We appreciate, but generally do not require, attribution. An attribution usually includes the title, author, publisher, and ISBN. For example: "*Building Medallion Architectures* by Piethein Strengholt (O'Reilly). Copyright 2025 Piethein Strengholt, 978-1-098-17883-3."

If you feel your use of code examples falls outside fair use or the permission given above, feel free to contact us at *permissions@oreilly.com*.

O'Reilly Online Learning

O'REILLY® For more than 40 years, *O'Reilly Media* has provided technology and business training, knowledge, and insight to help companies succeed.

Our unique network of experts and innovators share their knowledge and expertise through books, articles, and our online learning platform. O'Reilly's online learning platform gives you on-demand access to live training courses, in-depth learning paths, interactive coding environments, and a vast collection of text and video from O'Reilly and 200+ other publishers. For more information, visit *https://oreilly.com*.

How to Contact Us

Please address comments and questions concerning this book to the publisher:

O'Reilly Media, Inc.
141 Stony Circle, Suite 195
Santa Rosa, CA 95401
800-889-8969 (in the United States or Canada)
707-827-7019 (international or local)
707-829-0104 (fax)
support@oreilly.com
https://oreilly.com/about/contact.html

We have a web page for this book, where we list errata, examples, and any additional information. You can access this page at *https://oreil.ly/building-medallion-architecture*.

For news and information about our books and courses, visit *https://oreilly.com*.

Find us on LinkedIn: *https://linkedin.com/company/oreilly-media*.

Watch us on YouTube: *https://youtube.com/oreillymedia*.

Acknowledgments

Data practitioners, data engineers, and other experts have significantly enhanced this book. I aimed to create a solid, enjoyable read, and if you find it so, it is largely due to the wonderful and intelligent individuals who supported me throughout this journey. Raising a child takes a village, and writing a book certainly takes a supportive community. Thank you to everyone who contributed to bringing this project to life.

I would like to specifically highlight several individuals for their invaluable feedback and suggestions: Ole Olesen-Bagneux, Christopher Mendyk, Aitor Murguzur, James Serra, Mayank Srivastava, Jaimi Sasikumar, Henri Kornegoor, Francesco Fava, Paul Andrew, Kristof Van de Loock, Jaco van Gelder, Corné Potgieter, Simon Oster, Bart van der Hulst, Daan Humble, Batuhan Tüter, Prajnan Sharma, Jonas De Keuster, René Bremer, Ben Kuzey, Remy Ursem, Mark Benson, Sanjeev Mohan, Henri Heijltjes, and Sarath Sasidharan. Your insights and support have truly shaped this book, and I am deeply thankful for your contributions.

Thanks to the Databricks team, including Isaac Gritz, Michael Davison, and Franco Patano, for your supportive and insightful feedback. I am grateful for your assistance.

A special thanks to Jacob Rønnow Jensen for your assistance with the AP Pension chapter. Your transparency and insights have been crucial, and I appreciate your valuable suggestions.

Many kudos to Amadeus, especially Joel Singer and Bertrand Cognard. Your insights and shared experiences have been invaluable, and I am grateful for your support.

A big shoutout to the team at Carl Zeiss, including Markus Morgner, Sascha Saumer, and Gert Christen. I value your insights and appreciate your transparency.

A big thanks to Scott Haines, coauthor of *Delta Lake: The Definitive Guide* (O'Reilly), for sharing your insights and feedback. You've been of great support bringing in nuances to the book.

A huge thanks to Simon Whiteley, who has been a great source of inspiration and support. I see you as an example of how to be a great community leader.

I'd also like to extend my gratitude to the O'Reilly Media team, specifically to Michelle Smith for your support, and to my fantastic editors, Shira Evans and Katherine Tozer. Your guidance and support have been instrumental in shaping this book, and I am grateful for working with such a fantastic team.

Finally, I must express my deepest gratitude to my wife, Jessica, and our three daughters, Julia, Valerie, and Maxime, for their constant support and encouragement. Your love and understanding have illuminated my path throughout this journey.

## PART I

Understanding the Medallion Framework

This first part of the book is your gateway to mastering the complexities of data architectures, beginning with a comprehensive overview of their evolution and extending into an in-depth theoretical analysis of the Medallion architecture. Designed to provide a solid theoretical foundation, this part delves into the historical developments and layer-specific insights of the Medallion model, preparing you for the practical applications discussed in later chapters.

Chapter 1 takes you on a journey through the historical development of data architectures. It discusses the origins of these systems, the enduring design principles that continue to influence modern architectures, and the lessons learned over decades of data management. This chapter is crucial for anyone looking to grasp the foundational concepts that will recur throughout the study of Medallion architecture and other data systems.

In Chapter 2, we'll explore the foundational preconditions that underpin the Medallion architecture. This chapter sets the stage by introducing key concepts and patterns that we will frequently refer to in our detailed discussion of other chapters.

In Chapter 3, the focus shifts to a thorough exploration of the Medallion architecture itself. This chapter breaks down each layer of the Medallion model, providing insights into their functions, interactions, and the strategic importance of each component. While still theoretical, this chapter aims to bridge the gap between abstract concepts and their practical implications, setting the stage for the detailed application-based discussions in later chapters.

Together, these chapters form a comprehensive introduction to the themes and concepts that will be developed throughout *Building Medallion Architectures*. They are essential for anyone looking to deeply understand the structure and utility of advanced data architectures in modern enterprises.

## CHAPTER 1

The Evolution of Data Architecture

Creating a robust data architecture is one of the most challenging aspects of data management. The process of handling data—ranging from its collection to transformation, distribution, and final consumption—differs widely depending on a variety of factors. These factors include governance, tools used, the organization's risk profile, size, and maturity, the requirements of the use cases, and other needs, such as performance, flexibility, and cost management.

Despite these differences, every data architecture comprises several fundamental components. I frequently discuss these components using the metaphor of a three-layered architecture design, a concept I introduced in my previous work: *Data Management at Scale* (O'Reilly). This design has proven instrumental for organizations in conceptualizing and structuring their data management strategies. It features three layers: the first includes various data providers; the second serves as the distribution platform; and the third consists of data consumers. Additionally, an overarching metadata and governance layer is crucial for managing and overseeing the entire data architecture. You can see a reflection of this design in Figure 1-1.

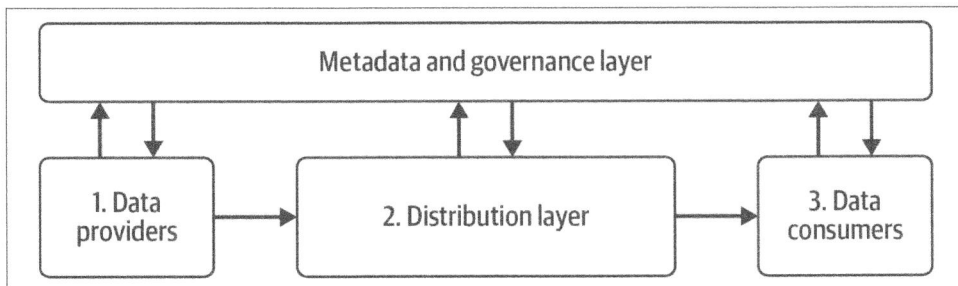

Figure 1-1. The three-layered architecture design

From left to right, here's a brief overview of each layer:

The first layer
> This layer consists of various data providers, which represent the diverse sources from which data is extracted. This extracted data is characterized by a mixture of data types, formats, and locations spread across different organizations.

The second layer
> This layer represents the distribution platform and is complex due to the vast array of tools and technologies available. Organizations face the challenging task of selecting from hundreds, if not thousands, of products and open source solutions for integration.

The third layer
> This layer comprises data consumers, characterized by consuming data services. Data services leverage business intelligence, machine learning, and artificial intelligence (AI) to provide predictions, automation, and real-time insights. Other services manage basic storage and data processing. This layer includes a wide variety of technologies and application types, as each business problem demands a customized solution, making both types of services essential in modern data architectures.

To round off the high-level architecture, I typically draw an overarching layer in discussions, referred to as the metadata and governance layer. This layer plays a crucial role in overseeing and managing the entire data architecture.

The three-tiered diagram, with a particular focus on the inner architecture of the middle layer, illustrates the evolution of data platform management within organizations. It showcases a significant shift from traditional proprietary data warehouse systems to more adaptable, open source, and distributed data architectures. This transformation is driven by a collection of open source tools and frameworks, collectively known as the *modern data stack*.

The challenge is that the modern data stack does not represent a complete data platform on its own. It requires the integration of many independent services and tools, each designed to tackle specific elements of data processing and management. Each service or tool brings its own set of standards for data exchange, security protocols, and metadata management. Furthermore, the overlapping functionalities of many services complicate the deployment and usage. Therefore, to effectively leverage the modern data stack, one must carefully select the appropriate services and then meticulously integrate each component. This integration process poses a significant barrier to entry.

This issue isn't a failing of any one vendor; it's a failing of the market.[1]

—Benn Stancil

Technology providers see this issue too. They have recognized the complexity of integrating and managing infrastructure, data storage, and computation. They've made significant progress in development and standardization, particularly in Apache Spark (*https://spark.apache.org*) and open source table formats, such as Delta Lake (*https://docs.delta.io/latest/index.html*). This has led to the creation of comprehensive software platforms, simplifying the way data can be handled. Many data engineers prefer these platforms due to their innovative features. In addition, organizations that leverage Spark and Delta Lake find the *Medallion architecture* (which I'll define in the next section) particularly advantageous as it fully exploits the strengths of a robust, scalable, and efficient framework for end-to-end data management and analytics.

What Is a Medallion Architecture?

A Medallion architecture is a data design pattern used to logically organize data, most often in a lakehouse, using three layers for the data platform, with the goal of incrementally and progressively improving the structure and quality of data as it flows through each layer of the data architecture (from Bronze ⇒ Silver ⇒ Gold layer). In Chapter 3, we delve into the details of each layer. For now, here's a brief overview of each layer:

Bronze layer

The Bronze layer stores raw data from various sources in its native structure, serving as a historical record and a reliable initial storage.

Silver layer

The Silver layer refines and standardizes raw data for complex analytics through quality checks, standardization, deduplication, and other transformations. It acts as a transitional stage for processed, granular data with improved quality and consistency.

Gold layer

The Gold layer optimizes refined data for specific business insights and decisions. It aggregates, summarizes, and enriches data for high-level reporting and analytics, emphasizing performance and scalability to provide fast access to key metrics and insights.

Such a design, as seen in Figure 1-2, offers an excellent opportunity for implementing applications or use cases for business growth and development.

---

1 This quote is from Benn Stancil's article, "Microsoft Builds the Bomb" (*https://oreil.ly/FMlrI*), which discusses market-wide challenges in data platform solutions.

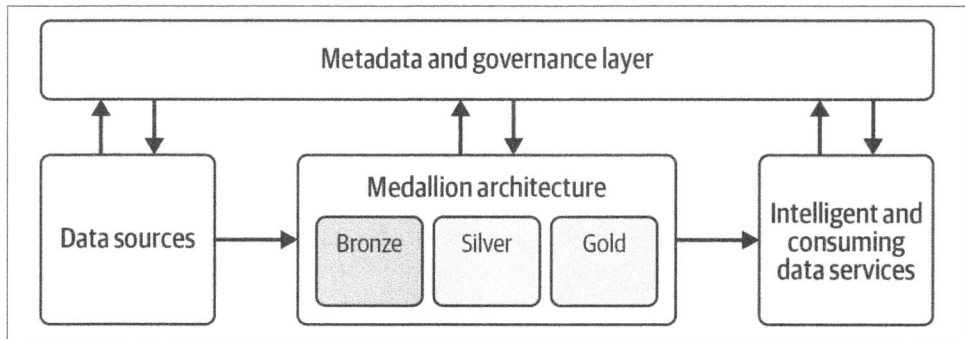

Figure 1-2. A Medallion architecture, which arranges data into three layers, enhancing the data's structure and quality as it progresses through the layers

The Medallion architecture offers business-friendly labels for different layers. However, many enterprises fail to grasp how to effectively layer and model their data, spending countless hours discussing issues such as selection, integration, overlapping features, and so on. They struggle with fitting objectives into different zones or understanding the meaning of "Bronze," "Silver," and "Gold". Questions also arise about governance and scaling strategies. For instance, what parts of the architecture can be made metadata-driven with flexible configuration and automation? Choosing a comprehensive platform does not automatically answer these questions or solve these issues.

Before diving into the specifics of answering these questions and designing a Medallion architecture, it's crucial to first comprehend the evolution of data architectures. Where did these platforms originate? What design principles persist and still must be applied today? Understanding the history and fundamental principles of data architectures will provide a solid foundation for effectively utilizing these end-to-end platforms. This chapter aims to provide an introduction by exploring past developments, observations, patterns, best practices, and principles. By equipping you with the necessary background information, reasoning, and lessons learned, you'll be better prepared for Part II, when you learn how to design and implement your own data architecture.

If you feel you're already well-versed in the fundamentals of data architecture, feel free to skip ahead to Chapter 3 on the detailed discussion of the Medallion architecture and its layers. If not, join me as we start by examining traditional data warehouses. Then we'll move on to explore the patterns behind the emergence of data lakes, including Hadoop. We'll discuss the pros, cons, and lessons learned from each architecture, and how these developments relate to modern best practices. Lastly, we'll delve into the lakehouse and Medallion architectures, which are closely intertwined. In that section, we'll also discuss different technology providers.

A Brief History of Data Warehouse Architecture

Let's take a journey back to the 1990s. Back then, data warehousing emerged as a common practice for collecting and integrating data into a unified collection. The aim was to create a consistent version of the truth for an organization, serving as key source for business decision making within the company.

This process of delivering data insights involves many steps, such as collecting data from various sources, transforming it into a consistent format, and loading it into a central repository. This process is covered in more detail in Chapter 3. For the moment, let's concentrate on the architecture of a data warehouse, as shown in Figure 1-3, which also includes sources and consuming services, such as reporting tools.

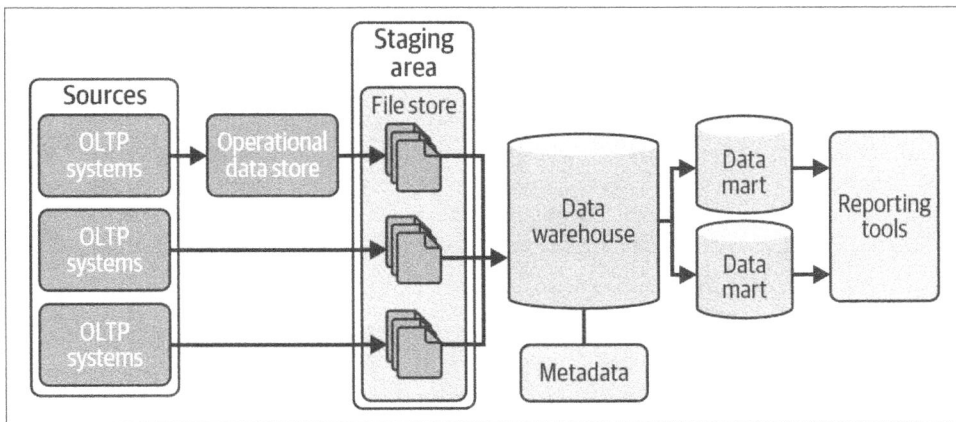

Figure 1-3. Typical data warehouse architecture

I'll start the analysis by exploring the various layers, beginning with OLTP systems on the left, then moving into the data warehouse in the middle. The data marts on the right are introduced and discussed in "Inmon Methodology" on page 11.

OLTP Systems

Most of the source systems were designed for transactional or operational purposes, reflecting the early computing needs to manage transactions and maintain records. These sources, as seen in Figure 1-3 on the left, are often referred to as *online transaction processing* (OLTP) systems, reflecting their vital operational role.

If you look into an OLTP system, you'll observe that operational workloads are usually quite predictable. You should understand how OLTP systems are used and what typical loads are expected. Queries are relatively straightforward, and the data retrieved is relatively low in volume: reading a record, updating a record, deleting a record, etc. The underlying physical data model is designed (optimized) to facilitate these predictable queries. The result is that OLTP systems are usually normalized, aiming to store each attribute only once.

Database Normalization Versus Denormalization

In the context of relational databases, normalization is a process that restructures data to reduce redundancy and improve data integrity. It is usually performed using a set of rules known as *normal forms*, each addressing specific anomalies or redundancies. The 3NF, or third normal form, is the most commonly used in practice. Normalization allows data to be stored more efficiently and consistently, facilitating easier maintenance and retrieval of data. Thus, when we talk about normalized data, we refer to data that has been organized in a way that enhances its storage efficiency and integrity.

Denormalization is the process of reversing the effects of normalization, intentionally introducing redundancy into a database for the purpose of improving query performance and data retrieval speeds. Denormalization is often used in data warehousing and analytics to optimize data retrieval and processing. By denormalizing data, we can reduce the number of joins required to retrieve data, which can significantly improve query performance. However, denormalization can also introduce data integrity issues, as redundant data can become inconsistent if not properly managed.

Many OLTP systems prioritize maintaining integrity and stability. To achieve this, most OLTP systems use database management systems that adhere to the ACID properties—atomicity, consistency, isolation, and durability.[2] These properties are crucial for running business transactions effectively, as they help in managing and safeguarding data during operations. However, the OLTP design leads to several implications that are important to understand, especially during discussions with organizations.

First, operational systems are not designed to easily provide a complete and consolidated analytical view of what's happening in the business or specific domains. This is because extracting data from highly normalized data models for complex queries is often challenging because it puts a lot of strain on OLTP systems. To get the insights needed, complex queries are required. These queries involve more data and combinations of data, meaning that many tables must be joined or grouped together. Unfortunately, these types of queries are typically quite resource-intensive and can hit performance limits if executed too frequently, especially when dealing with large

---

2 ACID principles ensure reliable database transactions by making them indivisible, consistent, isolated, and durable, which is crucial for maintaining data integrity, especially in critical systems like finance and operations.

datasets.[3] If an operational system becomes unpredictable due to these issues, it could negatively impact the business. Therefore, it's essential to consider the potential implications of a normalized design carefully. While it may work well for certain purposes, it's not always the best approach for providing comprehensive analytical views.

Secondly, the stringent requirements for high integrity, performance, and availability often make OLTP systems costly. To optimize these systems, a typical strategy includes shifting unused data out and/or designing the systems to handle only the most recent data. This approach means updates to the data occur instantly without keeping older record versions. Engineers sometimes, in the context of data virtualization,[4] argue for keeping all historical data within these OLTP systems instead of moving it to a data warehouse, data lake, or lakehouse. However, this is often impractical due to the inherent design of OLTP systems. In some instances, storing vast amounts of historical data can bog down these systems, resulting in slower transaction processing and update times. Additionally, maintenance and adaptability challenges can arise.

Thirdly, OLTP systems were originally designed to be specifically optimized for particular businesses, isolated and independent. Each system stores its data differently. This isolation and diversity make it difficult for any single system to offer a unified view without significant data integration efforts.

By separating analytical loads from operational systems, organizations address many of these issues. This separation not only preserves the integrity of the historical data but also optimizes systems for better analytical processing. Furthermore, storing and processing data from various sources in a universal format offers a more cohesive view than a single system could provide. The standard practice is to move this data to a middle layer, such as a data warehouse.

Data Warehouses

The data warehouse serves as a central hub where everything converges. It is used to gather and organize data from various source systems, transforming it into a consistent format for *online analytical processing* (OLAP), which involves complex processing specific to the needs of analytical processing. As offline analyses are typically less business-critical, the integrity and availability requirements for those systems can be less stringent. While data in OLTP systems is stored and optimized for integrity and redundancy, in OLAP, you optimize for analytical performance. Given that, in OLAP,

---

3 Applications, such as web services, that retrieve extensive data for a single observation do not always necessarily pose a problem.

4 Data virtualization is a technology that allows you to manage and manipulate data without needing to copy and export the data. Essentially, it creates a virtual layer that separates users from the technical details of data, such as its location, structure, or origin.

mainly repeated reads are performed, and few writes, it's common to optimize for more intensive data reading. Data can be duplicated to facilitate different read patterns for various analytical scenarios. Tables in OLAP databases are generally not heavily normalized, but preprocessed into denormalized data structures: tables are usually large, flattened, sparse copies of data.

> *Deciphering Data Architectures* by James Serra (O'Reilly) provides a comprehensive overview of data architectures, including data warehousing, data lakes, and lakehouses. It's a valuable resource on the evolution of data architectures and the principles behind them.

To load data into the data warehouse, you need to extract it from the different source systems. The extraction process is the first step. This process involves understanding the source data and reading and copying the necessary data into an intermediate location, often called the staging area, for further downstream manipulation. The staging area, as you can see in Figure 1-3, lies between the operational source systems and the data integration and presentation areas. This area of the data warehouse is often both a storage area and a set of processes commonly referred to as extract, transform, and load (ETL).

The Staging Area

The staging area, sometimes called the *landing area* or *staging layer*, can be implemented in different ways, varying from relational databases and file stores. Relational databases are more flexible, but more expensive. File stores are cheap, but offer limited features. Staging areas are also typically used to retain historical copies. This is useful for reprocessing scenarios in cases where the data warehouse gets corrupted and needs to be rebuilt. The number of older data deliveries (historical copies) can vary between staging areas across organizations. I have seen use cases where all the data deliveries, including corrections, had to be kept for audits for several years. In other use cases, I have seen the staging area emptied (nonpersistent) after successful processing or after a fixed period of time. In this context, cleaning is done to reduce storage costs or may be required from a governance perspective.

The complexity with extracting and staging is that different source systems may each have a different type of data format. Therefore, the actual ingestion process will vary significantly depending on the data source type. Some systems allow direct database access, while others permit data to be ingested through APIs. Despite advancements, many data collection processes continue to depend on extracting files because extracting files is proven to be more cost-effective and simpler to implement for large volumes of data.

Once the technical data is extracted to the staging area, various potential transformations will be applied, such as data cleansing, enriching data, applying master data management, and assigning warehouse keys. These transformations are all preliminary steps before data from multiple sources is combined, transformed, and loaded into the data warehouse integration and presentation areas. In most cases, you need to rework heavily normalized and complex data structures. As you learned in the OLTP section, these structures come directly from our transactional source systems.

It's crucial to understand that data transformation issues persist when constructing modern data architectures. There is no escaping this data transformation dilemma. The data must be cleaned and integrated to be useful for analytical processing.

So, the question remains: how do you model data in the integration and presentation areas? Let's discuss two common methodologies: Inmon and Kimball.

Inmon Methodology

Unfortunately, there remains some confusion among data engineers about whether, after extraction and transformation, the data should be modeled in physical normalized structures before being loaded into the presentation area for querying and reporting. The confusion stems from the different approaches to handling data.

Traditionally, data warehouses were expensive systems. Emerging in the early 1990s, the Inmon approach, named after its creator Bill Inmon and illustrated in Figure 1-4, was a widely used method based on a normalized data model, generally modeled in the third normal form.

This 3NF model structures data into tables with minimal redundancy, ensuring that each piece of data is stored only once and eliminating duplicate data. It also ensures referential integrity by ensuring that every nonprime attribute of the table is dependent on only the primary key. This method substantially reduces the required storage space. Furthermore, it involves creating a centralized and highly structured data warehouse, known as an enterprise data warehouse (EDW), which serves the entire organization.

For querying and better performance, the Inmon approach also incorporates a presentation layer: data marts. These are created after data has been efficiently stored in the integration layer. These additional data marts typically contain only a subset of the integration layer's data. They are designed to cater to a specific use case, group, or set of users. The data in these data marts is usually organized in star schemas, as it has been optimized for reading performance. The simplicity and denormalization of data structures in star schemas are the key reasons why they are well-suited for read-intensive operations. Consequently, it might be argued that data in data marts is stored less efficiently compared to the integration layer. Additionally, substantial effort is required to transform the data from the 3NF in the integration layer to a denormalized model in the data marts. This process often involves complex joins to reassemble the data, thereby restoring its full meaning for more effective analysis and querying.

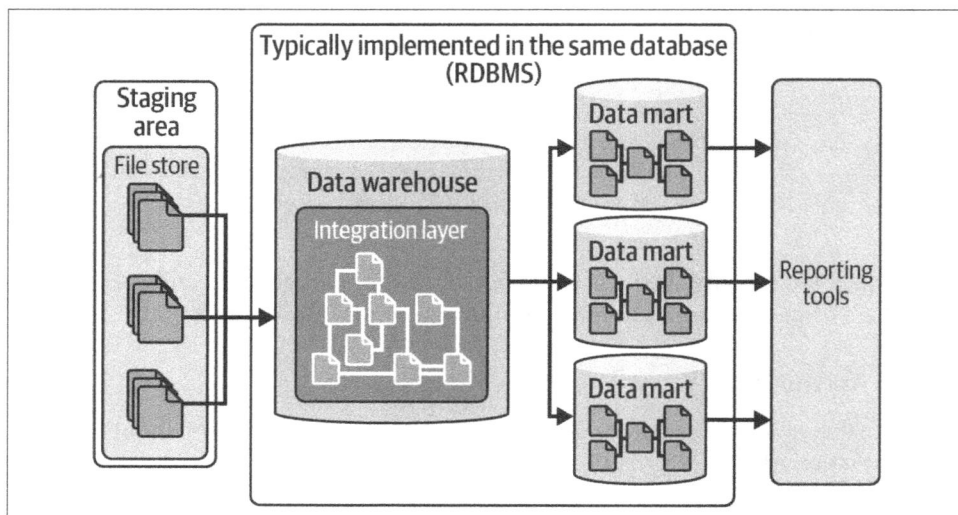

Figure 1-4. The Inmon approach; a top-down design where a centralized data warehouse is built first, and then data marts are created from this central warehouse

Many practitioners have reservations about the approach of using normalized structures in the integration layer and dimensional structures for presentation purposes. This is because data is extracted, transformed, and loaded twice. First, you extract, transform, and load the data into the normalized integration layer. Then, you do it all over again to ultimately load the data into the dimensional model. Obviously, this two-step process requires more time and resources for the development effort, more time for the periodic loading or updating of data, and more capacity to store the copies of the data. Another drawback is that if new data has to be added to a data mart, data always has to be added to the integration layer first. Since the development takes time and changes to the integration layer have to be made carefully, users requiring new data have to wait (longer).

Moreover, data redundancy—unnecessary duplication of data—is frequently pointed out as an issue in the Inmon integration layer. However, this argument carries little weight in the era of cloud computing. Cloud storage has become quite cost-effective, though computation costs can remain high. Because of this high costs, many experts now advocate for the Kimball data modeling approach.

Kimball Methodology

Kimball methodology, named after its creator Ralph Kimball, was introduced in 1996 as a data modeling technique, and is often used in data warehousing.[5] It focuses on the creation of dimension tables for efficient analytical processing. In this approach, dimensional data marts are built first to respond to business needs. For this, Kimball recommends a dimensional modeling technique using a star schema.

An abstract representation of the Kimball methodology is shown in Figure 1-5.

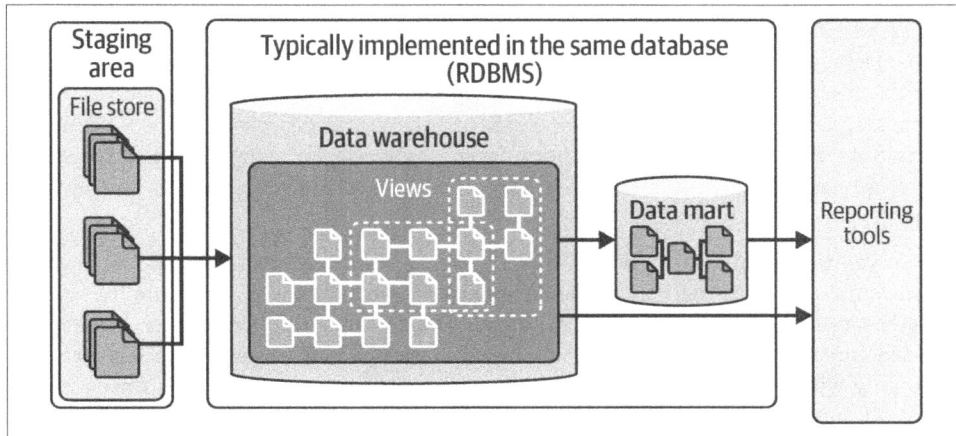

Figure 1-5. The Kimball methodology; a bottom-up approach to building the data warehouse

In this approach to data modeling, the integration layer of the data warehouse is seen as a conglomerate or collection of dimension tables, which are derived copies of transaction data from the source systems. Once data is transferred into the integration layer, it's already optimized for read performance. This data, being more flattened and sparse, closely resembles the data mart structures in the Inmon approach. Yet, unlike the Inmon model, Kimball's integration layer comprises dimension tables, which form the foundation for the data marts. Therefore, not only does Kimball recognize data marts, it also sees them as vital for enhancing performance and making subselects. Data marts permit aggregation or modification of persistent data copies based on user group requirements. Intriguingly, data marts can also be virtual. These are logical, dimensionally modeled views built on top of the existing dimension and fact tables in the integration layer, offering flexibility and efficiency in data handling.

---

5 Ralph Kimball introduced the data warehouse/business intelligence industry to dimensional modeling in 1996 with his seminal book, *The Data Warehouse Toolkit: Practical Techniques for Building Dimensional Data Warehouses* (John Wiley & Sons).

Confusion About the Functions of Data Warehouse Layers

It's crucial to clarify that there can be confusion about the functions of data warehouse layers, which correlates to the same confusion that can arise when layering a Medallion architecture. These different layers, which form the middle part of the larger overall architecture, are designed to assign contrasting responsibilities to various stages, mirroring common practices in software architecture. Typically, there's a staging or ingestion layer where raw data is stored, effectively separating the source systems from the data warehouse. Following this is an integration or transformation layer, where data is integrated after meeting all the acceptance criteria of the staging area. Here, cleansed, corrected, enriched, and transformed data is stored in a unified model. It's harmonized, meaning formats, types, names, structures, and relations have been standardized. This layer also contains historical data processed to show changes over time. Finally, there's a presentation layer where relevant data is selected for specific use cases. The data is remodeled to meet the specific requirements of the use case.

However, it's essential to note that there could be valid reasons to deviate from this traditional three-layered data warehouse design. For auditability or flexibility, some organizations implement additional layers. For instance, an extra layer might be added for auditability, where sources are first mapped to the target model before merging with other sources. Alternatively, the staging area could be split into a low-cost file store holding all data deliveries and a relational database only containing the most recent validated data. The key takeaway is that the number of layers or zones depends on your requirements. There's no universally correct answer. It's about making the right trade-offs to meet your specific needs.

To facilitate this approach to dimensional modeling, Kimball introduces the concept of *conformed dimensions*. These are key dimensions that are shared across and used by various user groups. Additionally, Kimball introduces the technique of historizing data through *slowly changing dimensions* (SCDs).

SCDs are tables that capture all historical changes slowly and predictably. In other words, an SCD is a type of dimension that has attributes to show change over time. SCD1, SCD2, and SCD3 are the most commonly used methods for handling these changes:

SCD1 (https://oreil.ly/yjJ8c)
> This type, also known as "overwrite," involves simply updating the existing record in the data warehouse with the new information. This method works well when historical data is not important and only the most current data is needed. However, SCD type 1 does not allow for tracking historical changes, as the old data is overwritten with the new data.

SCD2 (https://oreil.ly/XfL43)

> This type, also known as "add new row," involves creating a new record in the data warehouse for each change that occurs, while still retaining the original record. This method is useful when historical data is important and needs to be preserved. SCD2 allows for tracking changes over time by creating a new record with a new primary key value, but retaining the original record with a separate primary key value. This way, the data warehouse can maintain a complete history of changes over time.

SCD3 (https://oreil.ly/3IFm9)

> This type, also known as "add new attribute," involves adding a new attribute to the existing record in the data warehouse to track changes. This method is useful when only a few attributes need to be tracked over time. However, SCD3 has limitations, primarily that it only tracks a limited amount of history (typically just one previous state).

In the era of modern data architectures, data modeling, such as the Inmon and Kimball methodologies, continues to play a vital role in managing and harnessing the power of data effectively. It aids in understanding and utilizing complex data efficiently by separating the concerns of ingestion, integration and harmonization, and consumption. By creating solid representations of data and its interrelationships, data usage becomes easier for both technical and nontechnical stakeholders. Additionally, data modeling facilitates better performance and query optimization. With a well-structured data model, it's easier to locate and retrieve specific data, thereby improving the system's speed and performance. Finally, it supports better data governance and security. With clear data models, organizations can implement better data management policies, ensuring the right access control and data usage.

Key Takeaways from Traditional Data Warehouses

This brings us to the end of our discussion on traditional data warehouses. We've explored the Inmon and Kimball methodologies, which are still relevant today. As a review, we'll cover the key takeaways from traditional data warehouses that you can apply moving forward.

Firstly, the concept of layering data isn't new. It's been proven to be an effective strategy for separating different concerns, which helps in organizing and managing data more efficiently.

Secondly, data modeling is crucial. It plays a significant role in flexibility, reducing data redundancy, boosting performance, and serving as an interface for the business. Getting data modeling right is essential for any data management system to be effective.

Lastly, traditional data warehousing highlights the tight integration between software and hardware. Typically hosted on-premises, these systems integrate compute and storage tightly, making data handling quick and efficient. They include sophisticated pieces of software that maximize the performance of the hardware they run on. You can scale these systems vertically by boosting the physical infrastructure. Despite their potential costliness and limitations, these systems were once the preferred choice for many organizations and still hold value for specific use cases today.

Data warehouses are invaluable to businesses because they deliver high-quality, standardized data, essential for informed decision making. The key to their effectiveness lies in their expert data modeling and the tight integration of hardware and storage, ensuring fast and efficient data retrieval. This makes them an essential tool for business operations.

However, traditional data warehouse architectures that rely on relational database management systems (RDBMSs) face difficulties in handling rapidly increasing data volumes. They encounter storage and scalability issues that can lead to substantial costs. The main issue is that scaling vertically (adding more power to a single machine) has limits and can get expensive. Apart from cost, other issues preventing the scalability of data warehouse architecture to meet current demands include a lack of flexibility in supporting various types of workloads, such as handling unstructured data and performing machine learning tasks. Therefore, engineers have begun to explore other architectures that can address these challenges. This leads us nicely into the next section where we'll explore data lake architectures.

A Brief History of Data Lakes

Data lakes emerged as a solution to the shortcomings of traditional data warehouses. They started gaining traction in the mid-2000s, alongside the rise of open source software. Unlike their predecessors, data lakes introduced a new distributed architecture that could manage vast amounts of data in various states: unstructured, semi-structured, and structured. This flexibility expanded the usability of data.

Data lakes use open source software and, therefore, can run on any standard or affordable commodity hardware. This shift away from proprietary RDBMSs marked a significant change in how big data solutions were built, away from costly hardware clusters. Additionally, the integration of machine learning technologies into data lakes provides them with capabilities beyond the traditional reporting uses of data warehouses. For a visual understanding of how a data lake is structured, refer to the diagram in Figure 1-6.

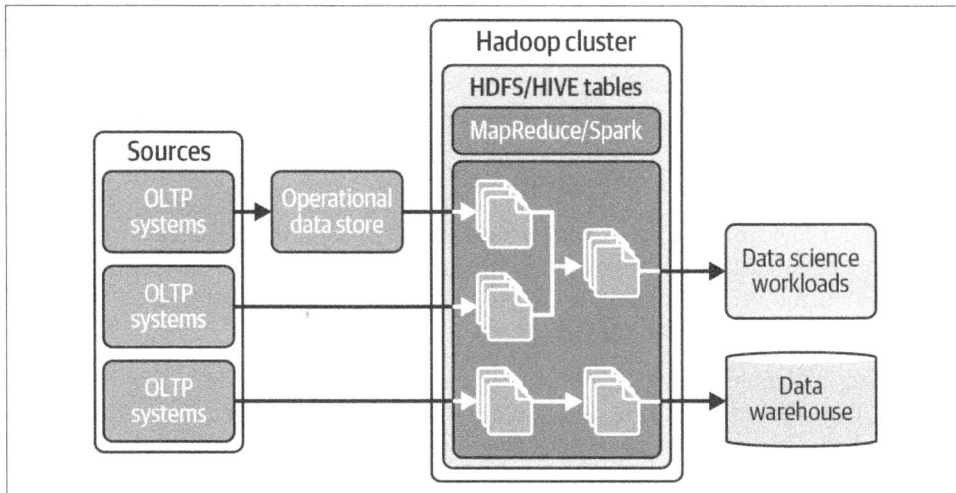

Figure 1-6. Typical data lake architecture with raw copies of data

The first generation of data lakes primarily used Hadoop, a well-known open source software framework that includes a variety of tools and services. At the heart of Hadoop are the MapReduce programming framework and Hadoop Distributed File System (HDFS),[6] which enables the processing of large datasets using a distributed algorithm across a cluster. Additionally, Hadoop comes with several other utilities that enhance its capability to store, process, and analyze massive amounts of data.

A key component worth mentioning is Apache Hive.[7] Developed on top of Hadoop, Hive is a data warehouse system that offers a SQL-like interface for querying and analyzing large datasets stored in the HDFS. One of Hadoop's strengths in the context of data lakes is its flexibility with data formats. Unlike traditional databases that demand a predefined schema, Hadoop with Hive supports a schema-on-read approach. This approach allows you to ingest and store data without a fixed structure and only define the schema when you read the data. This flexibility is invaluable for handling various types of data. We explore Hive in more detail in the section "Apache Hive" on page 19.

Understanding Hadoop is crucial when comprehending modern data architectures because many Hadoop components, or at least concepts, are still present today. In the

---

6 Hadoop originated from Sanjay Ghemawat, Howard Gobioff, and Shun-Tak Leung's paper, "The Google File System" (*https://oreil.ly/rLCCa*), published in 2003. This was followed by a second influential paper, "Map-Reduce: Simplified Data Processing on Large Clusters" (*https://oreil.ly/lqVkL*), by Jeffrey Dean and Sanjay Ghemawat.

7 Apache Hive was developed by Facebook based on the ideas presented in the research paper by Ashish Thusoo et al. titled "Hive: A Warehousing Solution Over a Map-Reduce Framework" (*https://oreil.ly/VUqMc*).

upcoming sections, we will cover the most relevant essentials. We'll start with the HDFS, move on to MapReduce, and then dive into Hive. We'll also discuss the limitations of using the HDFS and MapReduce. Lastly, we will discuss the emergence of Apache Spark, as it forms the backbone of many modern lakehouse architectures.

Hadoop's Distributed File System

The Hadoop Distributed File System is renowned for its fault tolerance and capacity to handle large datasets. It's important to note that the HDFS scales horizontally,[8] contrasting with the vertical scaling required by RDBMSs, thereby addressing issues of load and separating compute from storage.

Unlike the data management of RDBMS in data warehouses, the HDFS operates differently. It divides data into large chunks (blocks), which are then distributed and replicated across nodes within a network of computers. Each block is typically 128 MB or 256 MB in size, and the default replication factor is three. Consequently, reading and writing data (input/output, I/O, operations) in the HDFS can be time-consuming, especially if the data is not appropriately aligned and distributed across the nodes. Additionally, processing data in these files can present challenges; numerous small files can lead to excessive processing tasks, causing significant overhead. Because Hadoop is optimized for large files, logically grouping data enhances the efficiency of storage and processing. So, yes, it's advisable to use (denormalized) data models with Hadoop. Its data distribution process is very powerful but can be extremely inefficient if not managed properly.

In the HDFS, blocks are immutable, meaning you can only insert and append records, not directly update data. This differs from how data warehouse systems process individual mutations. Hadoop systems store all changes to data in an immutable write-ahead log before an asynchronous process updates the data in the data files. Then, how does this affect historic data within our data models? You may recall the concept of slowly changing dimensions from our discussion of the Kimball methodology. SCDs optionally preserve the history of changes to attributes, allowing us to query data at a specific point in time. If you would like to achieve this with Hadoop, you must develop a workaround that physically (re)creates a new version of the dimension table, including all the historic changes. You can do this by loading all data and creating a new table with the updated data. This process is resource-intensive and can be complex to manage. Therefore, it's crucial to consider the implications of using Hadoop for traditional data warehouse workloads.

---

8 Horizontal scaling involves adding more machines or nodes to a system to handle increased load, distributing the workload across multiple servers. Vertical scaling involves adding more resources (such as CPUs, RAM, or storage) to an existing machine to enhance its capacity and performance.

Now, transitioning from how the HDFS manages data to how it's processed, let's talk about MapReduce.

MapReduce

MapReduce is a programming model designed to process data in parallel across a distributed cluster of computers. For many years, it served as the primary engine for big data processing in Hadoop. MapReduce uses three phases—map, shuffle, and reduce—to process jobs:

Map phase
> During the map phase, the input data is divided into smaller chunks, which are processed in parallel across the nodes in the cluster. However, if the data is not evenly distributed across the nodes, some nodes may complete their tasks faster than others, potentially reducing overall performance.

Shuffle phase
> During the shuffle phase, the output data from the map phase is sorted and partitioned before being transferred to the reduce phase. If the output data is voluminous and needs to be transferred across the network, this phase can be time-consuming.

Reduce phase
> During the reduce phase, the previously shuffled data is aggregated and further processed in parallel across the nodes in the cluster. Similar to the map phase, if the reduce tasks are not evenly distributed across the nodes, some nodes may finish processing faster than others, which can lead to slower overall performance.

The map, shuffle, and reduce processes can lead to performance issues in Hadoop if the data is not evenly distributed across the nodes. Since data needs to be transferred across the network, it is crucial that tasks run efficiently. While MapReduce may not be directly used in the latest modern platforms, its concepts and approach to big data computation still form the basis for many of today's modern data architectures. Next, let's explore Apache Hive, which was originally built on the foundation laid by MapReduce.

Apache Hive

Initially developed by Facebook, Apache Hive (*https://hive.apache.org*) provides a SQL layer over Hadoop, enabling users to query and analyze large datasets stored in Hadoop using a SQL-like language known as HiveQL. Hive employs MapReduce as its underlying execution engine to process queries and analyze data. It stores its data in the HDFS. For data querying, Hive translates HiveQL queries into MapReduce jobs, which are then executed on the Hadoop cluster. These jobs read data from the

HDFS, process it, and write the output back to the HDFS, a process that involves significant disk I/O and network data transfer.

Hive differs significantly from traditional data warehouses in terms of data storage and querying. Unlike traditional data warehouses, where data is stored in a proprietary format and queries are executed directly on this data, Hive stores data on the HDFS and executes queries using MapReduce jobs. Additionally, the file formats in Hive use open formats that are available under open source licenses. To better understand how Hive stores and manages data, let's discuss the pattern of external and internal tables, followed by the Hive Metastore.

External and internal tables

In Apache Hive, a key distinction exists between external and internal tables. External tables link to data stored outside of Hive, typically in CSV or Parquet files on the HDFS. Parquet files on the HDFS. Hive does not control this data; it merely provides direct file-level access, allowing you to analyze the files. For example, you can mount a CSV (comma-separated values) file as an external table and query it directly.

> When you drop an external table in Hive, it only removes the metadata, leaving the underlying data intact. In contrast, dropping a managed table results in the deletion of both the table's metadata and its underlying data.

On the other hand, internal tables, also known as managed tables, are fully controlled by Hive. These tables often use columnar storage formats like ORC (Optimized Row Columnar) and Parquet, which are prevalent in many modern Medallion architectures. These formats are particularly beneficial for analytical queries involving aggregations, filtering, and sorting of large datasets. They enhance performance and efficiency by drastically reducing I/O operations and the amount of data loaded into memory. Additionally, columnar formats offer better data compression, which saves storage space and reduces the costs associated with managing large volumes of data.

Hive Metastore

A key component in Hive is the Hive Metastore, a central repository that stores metadata about the tables, columns, and partitions in an HDFS cluster. This metadata includes the data schema, the data location in the HDFS, and other information necessary for querying and processing the data. This component is still present in many of today's Medallion architectures.

Hive, through its metastore, allows for data to be ingested without the strict requirement of first defining a schema. Instead, the schema is applied dynamically when the data is accessed for reading. This method is also known as "schema on read." This flexibility is in stark contrast to the "schema-on-write" methodology prevalent in traditional databases, where data must conform to a predefined schema at the time of writing.

> The schema-on-read approach, still present in modern data architectures, often leads to misunderstandings. Some engineers mistakenly believe that schema on read eliminates the need for data modeling. This is a significant misconception! Without proper data modeling, data will be incomplete or of low quality, and integrating data from multiple sources becomes challenging. Inadequate data modeling can also lead to poor performance. While the schema-on-read approach is helpful for quickly storing and discovering raw data, it's still necessary to ensure data quality, integration, and performance.

Hive, along with its metadata, the HDFS, and MapReduce, initially faced some challenges. The first issue concerned the efficient handling of many small files. In the HDFS, data is spread across multiple machines and is replicated to enhance parallel processing. Each file, regardless of its size, occupies a minimum default block size in memory because data and metadata are stored separately. Small files, which are smaller than one HDFS block size (typically 128 MB), can place excessive pressure on the NameNode.[9] For instance, if you are dealing with 128 MB blocks, you would have around 8,000 files for 1 TB of data, requiring 1.6 MB for metadata. However, if that 1 TB were stored as 1 KB files, you would need 200 GB for metadata, placing a load on the system that is 1,280 times greater. Such issues can drastically reduce the read performance of the entire data lake if not managed correctly.

Second, the first version of Hive didn't support ACID transactions and full-table updates, risking that the database would get into an inconsistent state. Fortunately, this issue has been addressed in later versions. In "Emergence of Open Table Formats" on page 25, I'll come back to this point when covering the Delta table format.

Third, MapReduce can be quite slow. At every stage of processing, data is read from and written back to the disk. This process of disk seeking is time-consuming and significantly slows down the overall operation. This performance issue brings us to Apache Spark,[10] which tries to overcome this performance challenge.

---

9 The NameNode in Hadoop is responsible for managing the filesystem namespace, storing metadata for all files and directories, and regulating access to files by clients. It also manages the mapping of file blocks to DataNodes, ensuring data reliability and availability.

10 Modern Spark runtimes have features that carefully handle the small files problem. Miles Cole has posted an optimization guide for Microsoft Fabric (*https://oreil.ly/AmdYE*), providing more background information.

Spark Project

MapReduce, despite its benefits, presented certain inefficiencies, particularly when it came to large-scale applications. For instance, a typical machine learning algorithm might need to make multiple passes over the same dataset, and each pass had to be written as a unique MapReduce job. These jobs had to be individually launched on the cluster, requiring the data to be loaded from scratch each time.

To address these challenges, researchers at UC Berkeley, specifically from the AMPLab (*https://amplab.cs.berkeley.edu*), initiated a research project in 2009 to explore ways to speed up processing jobs in Hadoop systems. They developed an in-memory computing framework known as Spark. This framework was designed to facilitate large-scale data processing more efficiently by storing data in memory rather than reading it from disk for every operation. This team also developed Shark, [11] an extension of Spark designed to handle SQL queries, thereby enabling more interactive use by data scientists and analysts. Shark's architecture was based on Hive. It converted the physical plan generated by Hive into an in-memory program, enabling SQL queries to run significantly faster (up to 100 times) than they would on Hive using MapReduce.

As Spark evolved, it became apparent that incorporating new libraries could greatly enhance its capabilities. Consequently, the project began to adopt a "standard library" approach.[12] Around this time, the team began to phase out Shark in favor of Spark SQL, a new component that maintained compatibility with Hive by using the Hive Metastore.

However, the speed improvements offered by Spark come with certain preconditions. For instance, Spark needs to read data from the disks to bring it into memory, and this is not an instantaneous process. So, after data is written to the HDFS, an additional loading process is required to read it from the disks and bring it into Spark's memory. This principle still holds true today. For example, when restarting the Spark cluster, all in-memory data is lost, and the data must be reloaded to regain the speed benefits. For building modern architectures, this means that there's typically a startup time before resources become available,[13] and during this period, data isn't immediately present in Spark. The data only becomes readily available for quick usage when querying and/or caching processes are initiated.

---

11 See the research document from AMPLab at UC Berkeley on Apache Shark (*https://oreil.ly/JUlEw*).

12 See the 2014 post by Reynold Xin, "Shark, Spark SQL, Hive on Spark, and the Future of SQL on Apache Spark" (*https://oreil.ly/13nUf*).

13 In modern lakehouse architectures, the cold start time for querying or processing data can be significantly reduced by using sidecar files (*https://oreil.ly/4mYIQ*). These files contain metadata such as schema information, statistics, and indexing data, enabling more efficient data management and query execution.

Let's park the discussion on Spark for now and move on to the learnings from data lakes and their evolution. We'll pick up the Spark discussion again when we delve into lakehouse architecture in the next section.

Moving Forward with Data Lakes

What can you learn from data lakes and their evolution? Let's consider a few key points.

Data lakes, powered by Hadoop, are robust solutions for storing massive volumes of raw data in various formats, both structured and unstructured. This data is readily available for processing in data science and machine learning applications, accommodating data formats that a traditional data warehouse cannot handle. Unlike traditional data warehouses, data lakes are not restricted to specific formats. They rely on open source formats like Parquet, which are widely recognized by numerous tools, drivers, and libraries, ensuring seamless interoperability. Moreover, many of the core concepts, such as external and managed tables, still exist in modern data architectures.

However, as data lakes gain popularity and broader usage, organizations have begun to notice some challenges. While ingesting raw data is straightforward, transforming it into a form that can deliver business value is quite complex. Traditional data lakes struggle with latency and query performance, necessitating a different approach to data modeling to take advantage of the distributed nature of data lakes and their ability to handle various data types flexibly.

Furthermore, traditional data lakes face their own set of challenges, such as handling large numbers of small files or providing transactional support. As a result, organizations have often relied on feeding data back into the traditional data warehouse, a two-tier architecture pattern in which a data lake stores data in a format compatible with common machine learning tools, from which subsets are loaded into the data warehouse.

To tackle these challenges, the industry has been shifting toward integrating the two-tier architecture into a single solution. This new architecture combines the best of both worlds, offering the scalability and flexibility of a data lake along with the reliability and performance of a data warehouse. To better understand how this integration has evolved, it's essential to explore the history and development of the lakehouse architecture.

A Brief History of Lakehouse Architecture

Now that we've discussed the history of data warehouses and data lakes, we've come to the last part of our discussion on the evolution of data architectures. Let's take a look at today's architectures that use lakehouses as the foundation with open source data table formats, such as Delta Lake. For this, we look at the evolution of Spark after it was launched. After that, we'll discuss the origin of Databricks, its role in the data space, and its relationship to other technology providers. Then, finally, we'll look at the Medallion architecture.

Founders of Spark

By 2013, the Spark project, with contributions from over 100 contributors across 30 organizations, had significantly grown in popularity. To ensure its long-term sustainability and vendor independence, the team decided to contribute Spark as open source to the Apache Software Foundation (*https://apache.org*). Accordingly, Spark became Apache Spark: an Apache top-level project.

In 2013, the creators of Spark founded a company named Databricks (*https://data bricks.com*) to support and monetize Spark's rapid growth. Databricks aims to simplify big data processing, making it more accessible to data engineers, data scientists, and business analysts. Following this, the Apache Spark (*https://spark.apache.org*) community launched several versions: Spark 1.0 in 2014, Spark 2.0 in 2016, Spark 3.0 in 2020, and Spark 4.0 in 2025. They continue to enhance Spark by regularly introducing new features.

Interestingly, Databricks adopted a different market strategy from its Hadoop competitors. Instead of focusing on on-premises deployments, like Cloudera and Hortonworks, Databricks opted for a cloud-only distribution called Databricks Cloud. At that time, there was even a free Community Edition. Databricks started first with Amazon Web Services, the most popular cloud service at that time, and later included Microsoft Azure and Google Cloud Platform. In November 2017, Databricks was announced as a first-party service on Microsoft Azure via its integration, Azure Databricks. Over the years, the pace of cloud adoption accelerated, and cloud-based solutions with decoupled storage and compute gained popularity, leading to the decline of traditional on-premises Hadoop deployments. Today, we can confidently say that Databricks made a smart strategic move.

What does this mean for Hadoop? Has Hadoop become obsolete? No, it's still alive in the cloud ecosystem, though it has undergone significant changes. Vendors replaced the HDFS with cloud-based object storage services. With object storage, the data blocks of a file are kept together as an object, together with its relevant metadata and a unique identifier. This differs from the HDFS, where data is stored in blocks across different nodes, and a separate metadata service (like the NameNode in the HDFS) tracks the location of these blocks.

The switch to cloud-based object storage brings several advantages. Not only is it generally less expensive for storing large volumes of data, but it also scales more efficiently, even up to petabytes. Every major cloud provider offers such services, complete with robust service-level agreements (SLAs) and options for geographical replication. For example, Microsoft has introduced Azure Data Lake Storage (*https://oreil.ly/uZmTa*), an object storage solution that maintains compatibility with the HDFS interface while modernizing the underlying storage architecture. To sum it up: while the HDFS interface is still in place, the underlying storage architecture has undergone a major overhaul.

The same evolution has happened with Spark. It received many contributions, predominantly from Databricks. Nowadays, it can operate independently in a cluster of virtual machines or within containers managed by Kubernetes. This flexibility means you aren't tied to a single, massive Hadoop cluster. Instead, you can create multiple Spark clusters, each with its own compute configuration and size. Depending on your needs, these clusters can all interact with the same object storage layer, making Spark both elastic and dynamic.

Databricks is the leading force behind Apache Spark's roadmap and development. It offers a managed platform, whereby users get the full benefits from Spark by not having to learn complex cluster management concepts or perform endless engineering tasks. Instead, users navigate through a user-friendly interface. Companies using Databricks will also benefit from its latest innovations.

Let's shift gears a little bit and move on to today's modern architectures, which have seen significant advancements thanks to the development of open source table format standards like Hudi, Iceberg, and Delta Lake.

Emergence of Open Table Formats

Recognizing the critical need for improved transactional guarantees, enhanced metadata handling, and stronger data integrity within columnar storage formats, several projects were developed and later became open source. Apache Hudi (*https://hudi.apache.org*), initiated by Uber, was one of the first to emerge in 2017. It was designed to simplify the management of large datasets on Hadoop-compatible filesystems, focusing on efficient upserts, deletes, and incremental processing. This project set the stage for further innovations in handling big data. Moreover, Hudi offers seamless integration with existing storage solutions and supports popular columnar file formats such as Parquet and ORC.

Following closely, in 2018, Netflix released Apache Iceberg (*https://iceberg.apache.org*) to tackle performance and complexity issues in large-scale analytics data systems.

Iceberg introduced a table format that improved slow operations and error-prone processes, enhancing data handling capabilities. It has gained popularity due to its rich feature set and ability to support Parquet, ORC, and Avro file formats.

In 2019, Databricks launched Delta Lake (*https://oreil.ly/Vg07Q*) to further address the challenges in traditional data lakes, such as the lack of transactional guarantees and consistency problems. Delta Lake brought ACID transactions, scalable metadata handling, and unified streaming and batch data processing, all while ensuring data integrity through schema enforcement and evolution. Delta Lake exclusively utilizes the Parquet file format for data storage and employs Snappy as the default compression algorithm.

Apache Hudi, Apache Iceberg, and Delta Lake

In 2024, Databricks made a strategic decision by acquiring Tabular, a company that supports the Apache Iceberg initiative, one of the leading open source lakehouse table formats. The main objective of this acquisition is to enable compatibility between various lakehouse platforms. To achieve this compatibility in the short term, Delta Lake has introduced UniForm (*https://oreil.ly/0dvyM*), which allows you to write data primarily to Delta Lake and then asynchronously generate the metadata for Apache Iceberg or Hudi. In the long run, Databricks is committed to developing a single, open, and common standard of interoperability across platforms, promising a more cohesive and streamlined approach to data management. Beside this development, there's also another initiative called Apache XTable. This originated from the founders of Apache Hudi, another lakehouse table format. Apache XTable provides true unidirectional conversion between the three formats (Delta, Hudi, and Iceberg).

Delta Lake provides ACID transactions through a transaction log (also known as the DeltaLog). Whenever a user performs an operation to modify a table (such as an insertion, update, or deletion), Delta Lake breaks that operation down into a series of discrete steps composed of one or more of the actions below. Those actions are then recorded in the transaction log as ordered, atomic units known as *commits*. The transaction log is automatically stored in a *_delta_log/* subdirectory among the Parquet files for a particular table. In Figure 1-7, you can see an example of the DeltaLog.

In Delta Lake, every commit is recorded in a JSON file, beginning with *000000.json* and continuing sequentially. As you update your tables, Delta Lake preserves all

---

previous versions.[14] This feature, known as "time travel," allows you to view the state of a table at any specific point in time. For instance, you can easily check how a table appeared before it was updated or see its state at a particular moment. To learn more, I encourage you to read "Diving Into Delta Lake: Unpacking the Transaction Log" (*https://oreil.ly/aDOQt*).

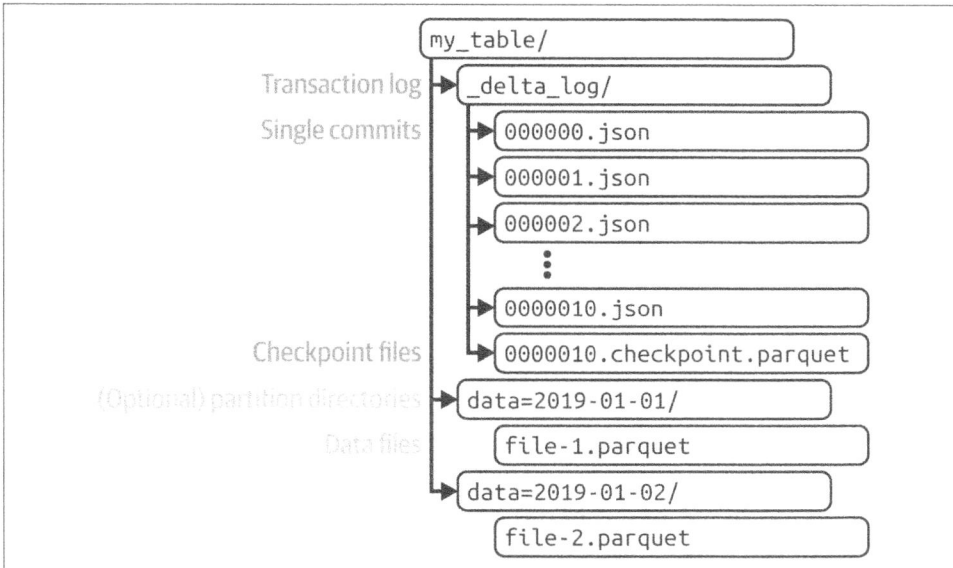

Figure 1-7. Example of how Delta Lake structures its data and transaction log

The Rise of Lakehouse Architectures

As Delta Lake made its debut, the *lakehouse architecture* concept began to gain traction. This innovative model combines the benefits of both data lakes and data warehouses. It allows organizations to operate on a unified data platform, primarily using open source software as its foundation. While the concept of the lakehouse is not inherently tied to any specific technology, the most popular implementations of the lakehouse architecture are built around Apache Spark and Delta Lake. So, Spark delivers the compute for big data processing, while Delta Lake provides an open source storage layer. Figure 1-8 offers an overview of what a lakehouse entails.

---

14 Every previous version is recorded in Delta Lake. However, when you perform an upsert or delete, the older versions stay put until the vacuum process kicks in. But Delta Lake isn't actually deleting any data immediately; it simply removes data that the current snapshot of the table no longer references. You can configure the intervals for both vacuuming and deleting. For a detailed explanation, check out Chapter 5 of *Delta Lake: The Definitive Guide* (*https://oreil.ly/TV-07*) (O'Reilly), titled "Maintaining your Delta Lake."

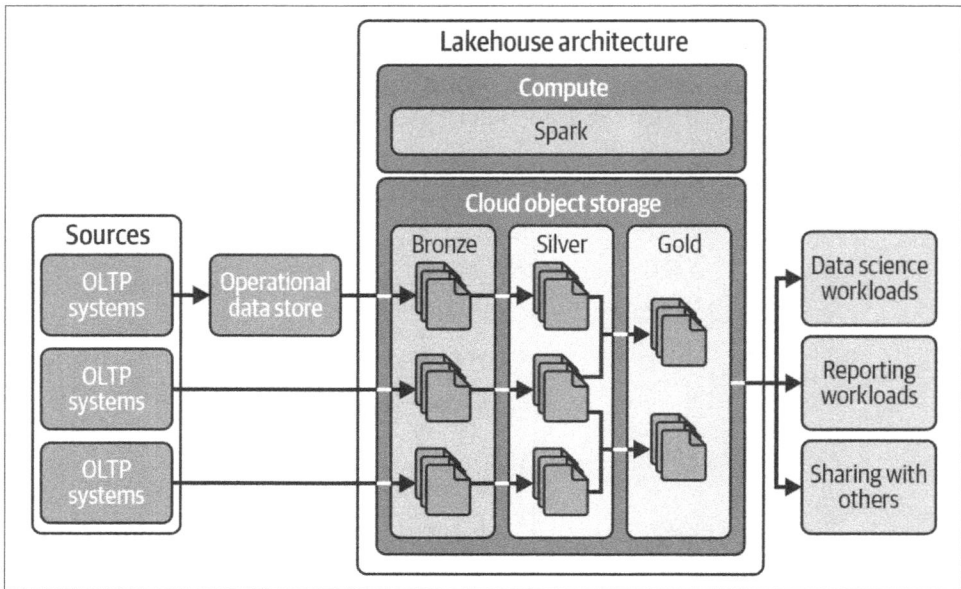

Figure 1-8. Typical lakehouse architecture, with a representation of the Bronze, Silver, and Gold layers included

The lakehouse architecture distinguishes itself from previous architectures by supporting low-cost cloud object storage while simultaneously providing ACID transactions. Moreover, it significantly enhances performance compared to traditional data lakes, largely due to innovations stemming from Apache Spark. Databricks was the pioneer in coining the term *lakehouse* and positioning itself within this product space. Subsequently, other major players followed quickly. Here is an overview of the current landscape as of 2025:

Databricks

As a strong advocate for lakehouse architecture, Databricks integrates Delta Lake, which supports ACID transactions and scalable metadata management. This table format pairs seamlessly with Apache Spark, enhancing big data processing and analytics for improved performance and reliability.

Azure HDInsight

Microsoft's cloud-based service, Azure HDInsight, offers a managed Apache Hadoop and Apache Spark service, providing a scalable and efficient environment for big data processing. It supports various table formats and integrates with other Azure services for enhanced data analytics.

Azure Synapse Analytics

A Microsoft service, Azure Synapse Analytics merges big data solutions with data warehousing into a unified analytics service. It offers flexible querying options through SQL serverless on-demand or provisioned resources, optimizing the management and analysis of extensive datasets.

Microsoft Fabric

This analytics and data platform is provided as a software as a service (SaaS) experience. Microsoft Fabric utilizes Apache Spark and Delta Lake, along with a suite of other services, to facilitate a wide range of data operations and analytics.

Cloudera

Cloudera provides a robust platform supporting various table formats and data processing frameworks. With strong integration capabilities for Apache Hadoop and Apache Spark, Cloudera offers a flexible environment suitable for constructing diverse lakehouse architectures.

Dremio

Leveraging Apache Arrow (*https://arrow.apache.org*), Dremio enhances in-memory data operations across multiple languages. This platform excels at efficient data retrieval and manipulation, making it ideal for direct data lake exploration and analysis.

Starburst

Specializing in Trino (*https://trino.io*), an open source distributed SQL query engine, Starburst delivers fast and scalable data analytics across numerous data sources. It supports a range of table formats and integrates seamlessly with other lakehouse technologies to boost query performance.

In addition to the vendors previously mentioned, other major players like Amazon Web Services, Google Cloud Platform, and Snowflake have also started to incorporate the term "lakehouse" within their offerings. This trend underscores the increasing recognition and adoption of lakehouse architecture within the data management industry. Tech giants recognize the value of blending the best aspects of data lakes and warehouses, leading to more comprehensive and efficient data solutions. As more organizations look to optimize their data handling and analytics capabilities, the lakehouse model continues to gain traction as a preferred architecture, shaping the future of data management.

Finally, Databricks and Microsoft have endorsed the Medallion architecture as a best practice for layering data within architectures based on Spark and Delta Lake. This approach is also the central theme of this book. This design pattern organizes data within a lakehouse, aiming to enhance the structure and quality of data incrementally as it moves through the architecture's layers—from Bronze to Silver to Gold. In the following section, we will delve deeper into the practical challenges encountered in implementing the Medallion architecture. After addressing these challenges, we will conclude this chapter and move on to explore the fundamentals of the Medallion architecture in Chapter 2 and design patterns in Chapter 3.

Medallion Architecture and Its Practical Challenges

The Medallion architecture, originally coined by Databricks, is not an evolution of any existing architectures. Instead, it is a data design pattern that offers a logical and structured approach to organizing data in a lakehouse. The term derives from its three distinct layers: Bronze, Silver, and Gold, which are user-friendly labels for managing data, similar to layering data in data warehouses or data lakes. The progression from Bronze to Gold signifies not only an improvement in data quality but also in structure and validation.

Despite the intuitive labels of the Medallion architecture—Bronze for raw data, Silver for cleaned data, and Gold for consumer-ready data—practical guidance is missing. This gap highlights a broader issue: there is no consensus on the specific roles of each layer, and the terms themselves lack descriptive precision. As we conclude that data modeling remains crucial, it's clear that while the naming convention offers a starting point, the real challenge lies in its practical application and the variability between theoretical guidance and actual execution, a central topic explored in this book.

In Chapter 2, we go over some of the foundational concepts that will help you navigate the Medallion architecture, including landing zones, raw data, batch processing, and ETL and orchestration tools. Then, in Chapter 3, we delve deeper into the Medallion architecture by discussing every layer in detail. This thorough examination will provide a clearer understanding of how data progresses through these layers and the challenges and considerations involved in effectively applying this architecture in real-world scenarios.

Conclusion

We began our exploration of the evolution of data architectures with traditional data warehouses and OLTP systems. From there, we moved on to the emergence of Hadoop and data lakes, and finally to the innovative lakehouse model. Each step in this evolution has been driven by the need to address specific limitations of the previous architectures, particularly in handling the scale, diversity, and complexity of modern data.

This evolution has also changed the way we can manage and control today's data architectures. With traditional data warehouses running on-premises, we had the ability to change the hardware configuration, the network, and the storage. However, with the rise of cloud computing, we have seen a shift toward fully distributed and managed services, which has made it easier to scale up and down but has also made it harder to control the underlying infrastructure. Proper configuration, layering, and data design are crucial in this context. For example, we have already emphasized the importance of data modeling in architecture design, and it remains a fundamental requirement for the successful design of modern data architectures. In the next chapters, we will delve deeper into these aspects.

Another important evolution is the speed at which business users expect new projects and insights to be delivered to them. This presents a challenge for the delivery of modern data architectures, as development teams face constant pressure to deliver rapid insights. Many organizations fail to recognize the indispensable need for data modeling. Data mesh approaches often overlook this necessity,[15] leading to a recurring problem where distributed teams repeatedly create slightly varied, incompatible models. These variations become entrenched in analytics models, ETL pipelines, data products, and application codes, turning what was once a clear and explicit design into something obscured and siloed.

The Medallion architecture within these platforms recognizes these issues but falls short of offering a definitive solution. The practical application of this design pattern exposes a gap between theoretical models and their real-world implementations and examples. This discrepancy underscores the ongoing need for precise data modeling and governance strategies tailored to the specific needs of organizations.

Moving forward, it is crucial for data architects and engineers to continue exploring these models, understanding their intricacies, and applying them thoughtfully to meet the increasing demands of big data environments. Chapter 2 will provide a detailed overview of the foundational preconditions required for building modern data architectures. By establishing a strong foundation, we prepare ourselves for more advanced discussions in Chapter 3, which will delve deeper into the Medallion architecture, providing more detailed insights into each layer.

---

15 Data mesh (*https://oreil.ly/ZVipF*) is a decentralized approach to data architecture and organizational design. It treats data as a product, focusing on domain-oriented ownership, data as a product, self-serve data infrastructure, and computational governance.

## CHAPTER 2

Laying the Groundwork

Before building a house, you need to first establish a solid foundation. The same idea applies to Medallion architecture. This chapter serves as a preparatory bridge, introducing key components and patterns that recur throughout our discussions of Medallion architectures. It also sets the stage for Chapter 3, in which we'll dive deeply into the Medallion architecture and its layers.

In this chapter, we cover several core areas:

Extra landing zones
> Preliminary areas where raw data is ingested before it lands in the Medallion architecture

Raw data
> The unprocessed data collected from various sources, which forms the basis for further transformations and analysis

Batch processing
> A method of data processing where data is collected, processed, and then output in batches at scheduled intervals

Real-time data processing
> In contrast to batch processing, this involves processing data as soon as it becomes available, enabling immediate analysis and decision making

ETL and orchestration tools
> Integral for extracting, transforming, and loading data, and play a crucial role in orchestrating and automating workflows within the data ecosystem

The inclusion of these components in the Medallion architecture varies. Some practitioners draw them directly within the main architectural framework, while others prefer to position them outside the diagrams or at the periphery, emphasizing their supportive role.

We will also explore the management of Delta tables. Understanding how to effectively manage these tables is crucial for maintaining the integrity and efficiency of your data processes across the different Medallion layers.

By the end of this chapter, you should have a solid foundational understanding of these key elements, preparing you for a deeper dive into the Medallion architecture and its operational layers in subsequent chapters.

Foundational Preconditions

Before you can dive into designing and implementing any architecture, you need data. Therefore, to kick off designing and implementing a new architecture, the first step always begins with pinpointing target source systems and figuring out the best way to gather data from them. In this context, a major challenge involves whether it's necessary to use intermediate landing zones for data ingestion, which can facilitate better organization and transformation before the data integrates into the Medallion architecture. Following that, you need to decide on the data ingestion methods—should you go with batch processing or real-time processing? This decision will influence the tools and techniques you choose for data integration, orchestration, and table management.

In the following sections, we'll explore these decisions in the order previously mentioned. This discussion will build a solid foundation for you to understand the Bronze, Silver, and Gold layers that we will cover in detail in Chapter 3. Let's start by discussing the potential need for additional landing zones.

Extra Landing Zones

A "landing zone" is often used as a preliminary area where raw data is ingested before it lands in the Medallion architecture. Various factors influence this choice, such as the characteristics of the data source.

For example, when dealing with external services or SaaS vendors, you might need a secure landing zone to initially store data before moving it to the Bronze layer. Similarly, certain application teams with strict data ingestion requirements may require their own dedicated landing zones. These teams manage the extraction process, ensuring there are no unexpected errors or data inconsistencies. They might also require specific ETL tools or deployments of integration runtimes (*https://oreil.ly/*

QIHbo) for this purpose. In such cases, it is common to have multiple landing areas between your sources and the lakehouse architecture.

Conversely, direct data ingestion into the Bronze layer is feasible depending on the requirements of the source system. For example, if the source system has robust security measures and stable direct ingestion techniques, it may be more efficient to bypass intermediate landing zones and feed data directly into the Bronze layer. In these instances, there is no need to stage the data before it is ingested into the Bronze layer. Consequently, the approach to data ingestion can differ significantly depending on the characteristics of the data sources and the particular needs of the data management teams.

Landing Zones Takeaway

While the Bronze layer mainly serves as the area for data collection, you may need an extra preliminary landing zone in larger or more complex environments. It's up to you to decide whether to label this layer as Bronze. Some organizations might call it a "tin layer," "pre-Bronze," "pre-refinement," "staging," or "landing area" and place it outside the typical Medallion architecture. Others might include it in the Bronze layer design. The important thing is to ingest and store data in a way that meets your organization's specific functional and nonfunctional requirements.

Let's now explore some more nuances, focusing on handling raw data, followed by the different types of ingestion methods.

Raw Data

When discussing data collection with the goal of having the data land in the Bronze layer, using terms like "raw" or "as-is," you need to be careful. Let's consider complex transactional systems that involve vendor packages with thousands of tables. In these cases, an engineer might need to step in and mediate during the data extraction process.

Take an example from my experience as an architect. I had to handle data extraction from Temenos T24, which is a core banking system. This system stores all its data in XML format, with each table having just two columns: RECID for the primary key and XMLRECORD for the data. Extracting this data directly would lead to a very complex and unmanageable dataset. To solve this, we used the T24 Data Extractor. This tool pulls the data from the T24 database and stores it in a more manageable data structure. At a later stage, we transitioned to using Apache Flink (*https:// flink.apache.org*) to decode and process the data in motion, allowing us to transform and enrich the XML records as they were streamed from T24 to other environments.

Similarly, complex enterprise resource planning systems, with their tens of thousands of specialized and interconnected tables, pose significant challenges for direct data extraction. Organizations often use extraction services or tap into semantic models provided by these commercial packages to mediate this process.

What can you learn from these examples? There could be mediation applied. The first step from technical system tables to ingestion sometimes involves a middleware or custom-built software component. Its job is to map complex system tables or proprietary data structures into a simpler and more manageable data model.

Raw Data Takeaway

Preprocessing complex data or applying mediation happens before the data reaches the the first layer. This is not considered a transformation within the Medallion architecture. Therefore, while the data in the first layer is typically "raw," preprocessing can be crucial for manageability and clarity in cases involving complex systems.

Now that we've covered the initial essentials, let's shift our focus to another crucial aspect of data management—whether to opt for batch or real-time ingestion. Understanding the differences between these methods will further enhance our approach to handling data efficiently. We'll start with batch processing, followed by a longer discussion on real-time data and streaming ingestion because of its complexity.

Batch Processing

Batch processing is a method in which data is collected over a period and then processed all at once. This approach remains popular today for several reasons. First, it's cost-effective because it allows you to process large datasets in a single operation. This reduces the need for continuous processing and keeps components from running nonstop. Additionally, many existing systems and infrastructures widely support batch processing. It's also particularly advantageous when building historical perspectives, as it processes all accumulated data in one go.

When setting up batch data ingestion within your Bronze layer, you need to keep a few key considerations in mind:

- Maintaining data integrity is crucial. Use validation methods like row counts, checksums, or hash totals to ensure data accuracy and completeness during transfers. Also, track auditing information such as file counts, data volume, copy duration, activity run IDs, and outcomes to facilitate monitoring and troubleshooting.

- Unlike continuous processing, batch data processing occurs at set intervals. Select these intervals carefully, considering data source availability, the processing sequence, and the urgency of data analysis.

- Despite best efforts, batch processes might face failures. Therefore, setting up robust error handling mechanisms is essential for the resilience of the Bronze layer. Consider creating an "error layer" or "data orphanage" dedicated to monitoring and managing these issues. This layer acts as a safety net, catching any problems that arise during batch processing, ensuring smooth and reliable data management.

- Selecting the right tools for data extraction and ingestion is crucial for effective data management. Consider the various tools and methods available to ensure seamless data integration and processing. For instance, Azure Data Factory (*https://oreil.ly/GBGoh*) is widely used for data extraction, workflow orchestration, and pipeline management, offering over 200 connectors. Evaluating and choosing the appropriate tools can significantly enhance the efficiency and reliability of your data collection processes. We'll connect back to tools and considerations in "ETL and Orchestration Tools" on page 42.

Before exploring modern data ingestion methods, it's important to acknowledge that data collection remains a significant dilemma for many organizations. This is because of source systems implications, the variety of formats and network designs, and the diversity of technologies and platforms. All of these challenges make it difficult to extract data in a consistent and standardized manner.

Batch Processing Takeaway

Data collection challenges are not new; historically, organizations collected data for data warehouses. Consequently, many organizations often reuse existing interfaces, such as custom data extraction scripts or traditional batch deliveries, to import data into their lakehouses. Although batch processing might seem straightforward, it often remains a complex task for enterprises because each source usually receives its own unique treatment.

As organizations advance, they may consider adopting more contemporary interfaces, such as real-time data ingestion. This versatility is where modern lakehouse architectures excel, as they efficiently manage both batch and real-time ingestion.

Real-Time Data Processing

As highlighted in Chapter 1, modern lakehouse architectures efficiently handle streaming or real-time data. By processing data the moment it's generated, you enable immediate insights and timely decisions, crucial for applications such as fraud detection, personalized customer interactions, and dynamic system adjustments. This ability significantly boosts the responsiveness and effectiveness of your applications, making it a potent tool for businesses in fast-paced environments.

To set up real-time data ingestion in your system, you'll usually need to add extra components or tweak your existing setup. This is because most applications don't automatically generate events. As a developer or engineer, you might have to modify your application's architecture to handle event distribution. For instance, if you're working with a Node.js application (*https://nodejs.org*) using Express (*https://expressjs.com*), you might install a library and write code to send events to a service like Azure Event Hubs (*https://oreil.ly/F07DH*).

In some situations, you might also need to add software or components to read transaction database logs or to make API calls. Once you've established a steady stream of events, your data platform can begin to capture and process this data using services or frameworks such as Spark.

> In data movements, it's essential to differentiate between state-carrying events and simple notifications. State-carrying events provide a snapshot of an application's state at a specific time, useful for processing, analysis, or triggering further events. They are crucial in data architectures for monitoring data changes or updates. Conversely, notifications are basic alerts that inform systems or users about occurrences, prompting immediate action, such as notifying a user of a new email or alerting a system administrator about a potential issue. They typically do not include detailed state information.

Technology providers support multiple approaches to managing real-time or streaming data. This variety is necessary due to the complexity and the wide range of integration options available. So, in the next sections we'll look at the most common options at the time of writing. We start by discussing Spark Structured Streaming, a stream processing engine that allows you to read streams and transform data while it's still flowing. After that we'll discuss change data feed and change data capture, followed by considerations and other learning resources.

Spark Structured Streaming

Robust support for Structured Streaming (*https://oreil.ly/PKzWU*) within the Apache Spark engine greatly improves real-time data processing. As an integral part of Spark, it facilitates the continuous processing of data streams, allowing data ingestion from diverse sources such as event log files, IoT devices, and real-time messaging systems like Apache Kafka. Spark Structured Streaming also excels in handling data in its raw, unstructured form, which is typical in many real-time data scenarios.

At this stage, transformations become critical as they convert raw data into a more usable format. For unstructured data, these transformation steps might include flattening nested JSON, extracting fields from XML, or applying complex functions to derive new columns. These operations are essential for cleansing and preparing data for downstream analytics and storage, ensuring that the data can be effectively processed and analyzed.

Once the data has been transformed, Structured Streaming provides the capability to perform various output operations. This includes writing the processed data to persistent storage systems for further analysis or future use. Supported destinations can vary widely depending on the application requirements and might include Delta Lake for ACID-compliant storage and versioning, traditional databases for relational storage, NoSQL databases for schema-less storage options, or even directly back into real-time message buses or event queues to enable further processing or real-time analytics.

> Real-time ingestion with Spark requires an "always on" compute cluster, which can result in higher costs. If latency is not a concern, consider triggering (every five minutes) and executing these workloads to lower the cost.

Additionally, Structured Streaming's integration with other components of the Spark ecosystem, such as MLlib (*https://spark.apache.org/mllib*) for machine learning, allows for the development of sophisticated analytical pipelines. This integration empowers organizations to derive real-time insights from their data, facilitating immediate decision making and enabling reactive and proactive business strategies. In summary, the support for Structured Streaming in Spark is a powerful feature for organizations looking to leverage real-time data processing.

Change Data Feed

Another pattern in the context streaming data processing worth discussing is change data feed (*https://oreil.ly/TzJWZ*). This feature allows you to capture changes to Delta tables as they occur, enabling you to process these changes in (near) real time.

To enable change data feed, you need to set the `delta.enableChangeDataFeed` property to true on the Delta table. Here's an example of how you can enable the change data feed on a Delta table:

```
ALTER TABLE myDeltaTable
SET TBLPROPERTIES (delta.enableChangeDataFeed = true)
```

The change data feed can serve as an input data source for Spark Structured Streaming. The combination of these two provides a powerful mechanism for processing real-time data. It allows you to process, for example, only the changes after an initial `MERGE` comparison, thereby accelerating and simplifying ETL/ELT operations. With this same pattern, you can also stream changes downstream to other systems like Kafka or an RDBMS, which can then use this incremental data for processing in later stages of data pipelines.

For a practical guide on how Delta Lake is integrated with Spark Structured Streaming, you can visit the Delta Lake documentation on "Table Streaming Reads and Writes" (*https://oreil.ly/H9-aT*). This resource provides detailed insights and examples to help you implement streaming data ingestion effectively.

Change Data Capture

Change data capture (CDC) is a technique employed to identify and capture changes made to data in real time. CDC tools actively monitor database modifications and record these changes as they occur, enabling the replication of data to other systems. This method is especially effective for real-time data capture of your source systems, facilitating the seamless integration of these changes into data platforms. We'll discuss CDC in more detail in Chapter 5. Let's conclude the section about real-time data processing with considerations and learning resources.

Considerations and Learning Resources

Spark Structured Streaming, change data feed, and CDC are integral components that enable powerful, real-time data integration and analytics pipelines. For a detailed comparison of how each component contributes to these processes, see Table 2-1.

Table 2-1. Overview of real-time data processing options

Option	Description
Spark Structured Streaming	Supports complex operations and integrates with various sources and sinks; handles continuous data processing.
Change data feed	Captures changes to Delta tables in real time; enables efficient data processing by streaming only the increments and difference between states (also known as deltas).
CDC	Tracks and captures changes in database transaction logs effectively, allowing for real-time data replication and integration.

When discussing real-time data replication, stream processing, and the design of your Bronze layer, nuances come into play. For instance, consider using Microsoft Fabric's mirroring capability (*https://oreil.ly/IXZ-U*) to replicate data in near real time from a cloud native Azure SQL application into the lakehouse. This replication technique uses the database's CDC technology, transforms it into appropriate Delta tables, and lands it in the lakehouse architecture (OneLake). The question of whether this data belongs to the Bronze layer depends on your specific needs.

If your primary goal is to stack full data extracts, the real-time replicated data might be better classified as part of an intermediate (or landing) area. This setup allows you to query the data directly, as if it were part of the source, without impacting the source application. However, it doesn't organize the Bronze layer to accumulate raw data copies for historical analysis effectively. In this scenario, the initial layer acts as a replication or pre-Bronze layer.

Conversely, if your aim is to maintain a queryable Bronze layer that mirrors the source data "as-is," then real-time replicated data can be considered part of the Bronze layer. Ultimately, the classification hinges on your specific needs and how you plan to utilize the replicated data within your lakehouse architecture.

Real-Time Data and Streaming Ingestion Takeaway

The key takeaway for streaming and real-time data ingestion is that the decision to implement real-time data ingestion or replication, and to classify this data within the Bronze layer or an intermediate area, is fundamentally driven by distinct usage requirements and strategic objectives.

It's also important to understand that with real-time data ingestion, updates often occur across multiple layers simultaneously. For instance, you might use Spark Structured Streaming to process streaming data from Azure Event Hubs (*https://oreil.ly/F_35_*) directly. Then, while processing, you can immediately perform transformations such as removing unwanted columns, aggregating data, or even adding preliminary sentiment scores. You could store the raw data in the Bronze layer but also send the transformed, cleaned data immediately to the Silver layer, or even the Gold layer. In such scenarios, the Bronze layer acts more like an archive zone rather than a layer from which to read. This approach of parallel processing is especially useful for real-time analytics and insights, enabling you to quickly access and analyze incoming data.

Streaming is a complex topic thoroughly explored in *Delta Lake: The Definitive Guide*. If you're interested in delving deeper into this subject, I also encourage you to follow the comprehensive guide, "Structured Spark Streaming with Delta Lake: A Comprehensive Guide" (*https://oreil.ly/wJ_SY*). These learning resources provide detailed insights and guidance on implementing streaming within the Delta Lake framework, enhancing your understanding and ability to manage real-time data effectively.

Ingestion management, whether dealing with batch or streaming data, is a complex subject that requires clear guidance to navigate effectively. Choosing the right methods is crucial to ensure efficient data handling. To implement these methods successfully, leveraging the right tools becomes essential, as they directly influence the efficiency and effectiveness of data ingestion processes.

ETL and Orchestration Tools

Discussing the tools for extracting, transforming, loading, and orchestration is crucial as it can significantly influence the design of the data pipeline. In Chapter 5, I'll come back with examples, but for now, know that the following popular tools are available, each with unique features that cater to different needs within data architectures:

Apache Airflow
> This is an open source platform that allows you to programmatically author, schedule, and monitor workflows. It's particularly useful for orchestrating complex data pipelines and managing dependencies between tasks. We discuss Apache Airflow further in Chapter 6.

Azure Data Factory
> This is widely used among organizations that have adopted Synapse Analytics, Azure Databricks, and Microsoft Fabric. It is effective at creating, scheduling, and orchestrating data workflows. Within Microsoft Fabric, Azure Data Factory (ADF) is simply referred to as Data Factory, but the functionality largely remains the same. Another important feature of ADF is its support for numerous connectors, which enable the extraction of data from a wide variety of sources.

Databricks Auto Loader
> This is specifically designed for the Databricks ecosystem. It excels at incrementally processing new files as they arrive in cloud object storage. One of its standout features is its handling of schema evolution. We discuss Auto Loader further in Chapter 5.

Databricks LakeFlow Connect
> This is another Databricks-specific service. It provides built-in connectors for various sources, including Salesforce and SQL Server, facilitating data ingestion.

Databricks Workflows
> This is a managed orchestration service as part of Databricks. It lets you define, manage, and monitor multitask workflows for ETL, analytics, and machine learning pipelines.

For broader compatibility and feature sets, third-party tools such as Fivetran (*https://fivetran.com*), Qlik (*https://qlik.com*), StreamSets (*https://docs.streamsets.com*), Syncsort (*https://precisely.com/product/precisely-syncsort/syncsort-mfx*), Informatica (*https://informatica.com*), and Stitch (*https://stitchdata.com*) are also popular choices. These tools offer extensive connectors and orchestration capabilities and are often used in conjunction with other tools to enhance functionality.

When designing your Medallion architecture, it is essential to consider the specific capabilities and limitations of the chosen ETL tools. The complexity of data loading steps enabled by these tools might necessitate more preprocessing steps within your architecture. Thus, the choice of ETL tools can dictate not only the design of the first layers but also influence the architecture as a whole. So, careful consideration is required to ensure that your data architecture adheres to the organizational requirements.

Assuming you have successfully captured the data through ingestion tools, it's time to shift our focus to managing those tables.

Managing Delta Tables

Table management is a concern across all layers, considering its effect performance, usability, and costs. Techniques such as *-ordering and liquid clustering are recommended methods for improving the way data is managed, making retrieval processes more efficient and effective. In the next sections, we'll look at these techniques in more detail. We'll start with Z-ordering and V-ordering, and then move on to partitioning. We close this section with a discussion on liquid clustering, table compaction and optimized writes, and the DeltaLog.

Z-Ordering

Z-ordering (*https://oreil.ly/nPgbD*) is a technique that boosts data retrieval efficiency by grouping related information within the same files. This method is particularly efficient because it improves locality, reduces I/O operations, and supports multidimensional data management—making it two to four times more efficient than regular data retrieval. Z-ordering, especially, performs better in scenarios that require efficient filtering and joins. While liquid clustering, which merges the advantages of Z-ordering and table partitioning, has taken over in some scenarios, you might still find Z-ordering relevant depending on your setup.

In practice, Delta Lake automatically takes advantage of this technique through its data-skipping algorithms. To implement Z-ordering, simply specify the columns you want to organize by using the ZORDER BY clause. This method ensures that your data is optimally arranged for quicker access and processing.

```
OPTIMIZE events
WHERE date >= current_timestamp() - INTERVAL 1 day
ZORDER BY (eventType)
```

This technique significantly reduces the volume of data that needs to be scanned, enhancing overall performance. However, Z-ordering is particularly beneficial for large tables, such as those spanning hundreds of gigabytes, terabytes, or more. This focus on large-scale datasets ensures that Z-ordering effectively optimizes data retrieval in environments where managing vast amounts of data is a challenge.

V-Ordering

V-ordering is another technique used to optimize the retrieval of data. Unlike Z-ordering, V-ordering is a write-time optimization for the Parquet file format. Basically, it's an optimization that logically organizes data based on the same storage algorithm used in Power BI's VertiPaq engine. This enables faster reads under Microsoft Fabric compute engines, such as Power BI and Warehouse. Note that V-ordering is 100% compliant with the open source Parquet format, so all Spark engines can read it as regular Parquet files.

According to Microsoft's Delta Lake table optimization and V-order documentation (*https://oreil.ly/WzkA2*), the performance gains with V-ordering depends on the engine and scenario. In summary, performance with V-ordered files could deliver an average of 10% faster read times, with some scenarios showing improvements of up to 50%. You can configure V-order using Delta table properties. Here's an example:

```
CREATE TABLE person (id INT, name STRING, age INT)
USING parquet TBLPROPERTIES("delta.parquet.vorder.enabled" = "true");
```

It's important to acknowledge that for V-ordering, there's a cost to performance optimization. Sorting can impact average write times by 15%.[1] However, this feature can be disabled if necessary. The reason for the negative impact on write times is the additional sorting step that occurs during the write process. This can become a concern when dealing with a large amount of data writes and limited data reads.

To ensure optimal performance, it is best to align V-ordering with the layers of your architecture or specific use case; for example, for use cases where the SQL endpoints are heavily used. This alignment will help you determine if the benefits of using V-order sorting outweigh the potential loss of performance.

Now that we have covered ordering, let's move on to data partitioning, which is another pattern that can improve performance.

---

[1] Miles Cole shares specific numbers on the performance gains for different workloads in his blog post: "To V-Order or Not: Making the Case for Selective Use of V-Order in Fabric Spark" (*https://oreil.ly/3iOeE*).

Table Partitioning

Table partitioning is an effective strategy for managing large datasets, typically those that are several hundred gigabytes (GBs) up to many terabytes (TBs) in size. It involves dividing a large table into smaller, more manageable segments, significantly enhancing query performance by reducing the volume of data that needs to be read during each query. Within Delta Lake, you can partition a table by a specific column. The date column is a common choice for partitioning, but you can select any column frequently used in queries. For example, if you often retrieve data based on country, partitioning by the country column would be beneficial. To implement partitioning, you specify the desired column in the PARTITIONED BY clause. This tailored approach ensures quicker access to relevant data, streamlining query processes. Here, you can see an example:

```
CREATE TABLE events
USING DELTA
PARTITIONED BY (date)
```

Both partitioning and Z-ordering are most effective with very large tables. While you can combine Z-ordering and partitioning, it's important to remember that Z-order clustering can only occur within a partition and cannot use the same field for both techniques.

Liquid Clustering

Optimally implementing Z-order and partitioning comes with challenges and trade-offs. These optimizations require a fixed data layout, demanding careful up-front planning. To address these challenges, the Delta Lake project introduced a new feature called *liquid clustering* in mid-2024. This feature is set to replace traditional Z-ordering and partitioning. Liquid clustering simplifies the decision-making process for data layout and significantly boosts query performance by automatically optimizing the data layout. This means you no longer need to manually fine-tune the data arrangement for optimal performance.

Liquid clustering adapts the data layout dynamically based on the clustering keys. Unlike the static data layout seen in Hive-style partitioning, this flexible, or "liquid," layout changes in response to evolving query patterns. This dynamic adjustment tackles issues like suboptimal partitioning and column cardinality. Moreover, you can apply incremental optimizations and recluster columns without the need to rewrite the data. For more detailed information, check out the official Delta Lake documentation on liquid clustering (*https://oreil.ly/b5COK*).

Compaction and Optimized Writes

Delta Lake offers an operation named OPTIMIZE, specifically engineered to address the small files problem, a common issue that we discussed in "Hadoop's Distributed File System" on page 18. As you update, delete, or add new data, Delta Lake stores these changes in smaller files. Over time, these smaller files accumulate and can slow down data retrieval processes. To tackle this issue, you can run an optimize job, which compacts the smaller files into larger, more manageable files, enhancing query performance. You can run the optimize job using the OPTIMIZE statement, as shown here:

```
OPTIMIZE delta_table_name;
```

Another way to increase performance is by optimizing writes. By default, this feature is turned off, but you can activate it in Delta Lake version 3.1 and later. Simply set the delta.autoOptimize.optimizeWrite table property to true. With this setting enabled,[2] Delta Lake automatically optimizes the data file layout during writes, leading to enhanced query performance. You can find more information on these features in the Delta Lake documentation (*https://oreil.ly/eo8ac*).

Now that we have explored several table optimization techniques, let's delve into the transaction log, as it plays a crucial role in safeguarding data integrity and facilitating data recovery.

DeltaLog

The Delta transaction log, also known as the DeltaLog, is a key feature of Delta Lake frequently used within all the layers of the Medallion architecture. DeltaLog, as mentioned earlier in Chapter 1, is a transaction log that carefully records every change made to data within a Delta table. This includes additions, alter statements, optimize jobs, modifications, and deletions of data. The log maintains a comprehensive history of the table and is stored as a series of JSON files in the *_delta_log* directory, located within the Delta table's directory.

Each transaction generates a new log file, capturing detailed information about the performed actions, the files added, the files removed, and other relevant transaction details. By default, the retention threshold for these files is set to seven days. However, you can modify this setting using the ALTER TABLE SET TBLPROPERTIES statement, allowing for greater flexibility in managing how long transaction logs are retained.

---

2 Similar to V-ordering, using the delta.autoOptimize.optimizeWrite feature introduces a bit of extra overhead. For moderate-sized jobs, handling between 2 and 5 million rows, you can expect an additional delay of about 5 to 10 seconds.

This feature ensures robust data management and enhances the ability to audit and roll back changes if necessary.

> The VACUUM statement cleans up a table directory by removing any files not managed by Delta and deleting data files that are not part of the table's latest transaction log state and are older than a specified retention threshold. This helps maintain an efficient and streamlined data storage environment, while also ensuring cost savings and compliance.

For the Medallion architecture, DeltaLog provides a robust safety measure. Should an error arise or data integrity be compromised, particularly in the Silver or Gold layers, you have the ability to quickly revert to a prior version of your Delta table. This rollback is facilitated through the use of the RESTORE command, enabling access to earlier versions of a table by time or version number. This feature supports crucial functions such as data auditing, rollbacks, and the replication of experiments or reports.

However, it is essential to note that DeltaLog's main purpose is geared toward data recovery and auditing rather than serving as a conventional historical database. For example, attempting to identify records changed over the last month through the transaction log would require extensive data processing, as all files must be read and compared for changes. A more efficient way to track these historical changes is to manage them directly within a table, using a method like a slowly changing dimension. This approach not only optimizes performance but also helps maintain data integrity over time. We'll come back to this topic in "Slowly changing dimensions" on page 69.

Table Management Takeaway

For optimal data management performance, align *-ordering methods like V-ordering and liquid clustering with your architecture's specific layers, focusing on the queries and access patterns of each layer. This alignment ensures efficient query processing and data retrieval. Additionally, setting thoughtful retention thresholds for Delta tables is critical. Choose thresholds that support your operational needs and data recovery scenarios, balancing data freshness with storage costs.

With this comprehensive understanding of the roles and considerations of the various ingestion and table management patterns, we are well-equipped to make informed decisions about the structure and methodologies of the Medallion architecture. Now, let's summarize the key insights gathered and consider how they inform the next stages of our architectural journey.

Conclusion

Laying the groundwork for the Medallion architecture is a meticulous process that begins with a comprehensive understanding of the initial preconditions, such as identifying source systems and determining the most efficient methods for data export and ingestion. Each source system may require a customized approach to effectively manage data extraction and loading, which underscores the importance of not underestimating this foundational phase. During this phase, it is crucial to engage in detailed planning and collaboration with the owners of the source systems. This collaboration will help you make informed decisions about whether to apply mediation, employ additional landing zones, and use integration runtime components, as well as how to choose between batch and real-time processing. These choices come with their own sets of nuances and can significantly impact the amount of work required for collecting data.

Moreover, the selection of ETL and orchestration tools is a critical factor that can dictate the design of the initial layers and influence the overall architecture. Careful consideration and standardization are required to ensure that these tools not only meet the current needs but also align with the broader organizational requirements. In the context of tools and services, standardization is key for effective governance, metadata management, lineage collection, consistent data quality reporting, and other aspects of data management. This decision will affect the flexibility and scalability of the Medallion architecture.

In addition, the management of tables and the approach to data modeling are closely linked and vital for optimizing performance. Effective table management strategies must be considered early in the design process to ensure that the architecture can handle the intended data loads efficiently.

With these fundamental aspects covered, we have set the stage for building a Medallion architecture. In Chapter 3, we will delve deeper into the specifics of each layer, discussing its detailed design, considerations, and established best practices.

## CHAPTER 3

Demystifying the Medallion Architecture

In Chapter 1, we explored the evolution of Spark and Delta Lake, and introduced you to the Medallion architecture. This design pattern helps organize data logically within modern lakehouse architectures. It utilizes three layers (Bronze, Silver, and Gold) to progressively refine datasets throughout the lifecycles of data ingestion, data transformation, and data loading into various destinations.

Explaining the Medallion architecture to organizations often feels like opening a can of worms, as each layer, meant to address different concerns, lacks clear definitions and descriptive guidelines. This ambiguity leads to more questions than answers, creating a cycle of confusion and inefficiency.

Despite the popularity of this three-layered design, there's significant debate about the scope, purpose, and best practices for each layer. Moreover, the gap between theory and practical application is substantial. In this chapter, I will share insights from my practical experiences on designing each layer of the Medallion architecture by using a theoretical viewpoint. In Part II, the focus shifts from theory to practice. The insights from this chapter are carried forward when engaging in a hands-on exercise where you'll be taught to build a real solution architecture.

The Three-Layered Design

Before discussing the specifics of each layer in the Medallion architecture, it's crucial to understand the high-level purposes and functions of the three primary layers: Bronze, Silver, and Gold. Figure 3-1 illustrates the flow of data from the Bronze layer through the Silver and into the Gold layer, highlighting key processes such as ingestion, processing, and usage for analytics.

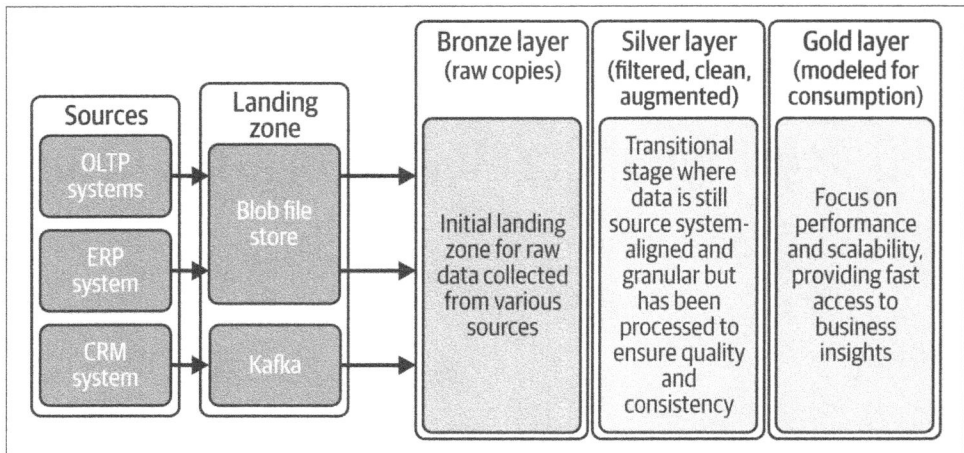

Figure 3-1. The Medallion architecture and its three layers: Bronze, Silver, and Gold

In Figure 3-1, each layer plays a distinct role in the transformation and refinement of data, facilitating a structured progression from raw data collection to data that can be used for data-driven value creation. I introduced the layers in Chapter 1, but this section will provide you with more details with key characteristics of each layer, setting the stage for a deeper exploration of the technologies and processes involved:

Bronze layer

Acts as the zone for raw data collected from various sources. Data in the Bronze layer is stored in its original structure without any transformation, serving as a historical record and a single source of truth. It ensures data is reliably captured and stored, making it available for further processing.

Its key characteristics are high volume, variety, and veracity. The data is immutable to maintain the integrity of its original state.

Silver layer

Refines, cleanses, and standardizes the raw data, preparing it for more complex operational and analytical tasks. In this layer, data undergoes quality checks, standardization, deduplication, and other enhancements that improve its reliability and usability. The Silver layer acts as a transitional stage where data is still granular but has been processed to ensure quality and consistency.

Its key characteristics are that data in the Silver layer is more structured and query-friendly, making it easier for analysts and data scientists to work with.

Gold layer

Delivers refined data optimized for specific business insights and decision making. The Gold layer involves aggregating, summarizing, and enriching data to support high-level reporting and analytics. This layer focuses on performance, usability, and scalability, providing fast access to key metrics and insights.

Its key characteristics are that it's highly curated and optimized for consumption, so the data in the Gold layer supports strategic business operations and decisions.

> While the shift from on-premises RDBMSs to decoupled and distributed architectures has transformed technology, the fundamental methodologies of data warehousing and data modeling are still relevant. If you're not confident with these skills, I recommend brushing up on the basics. Great resources include Kimball Group's books (*https://oreil.ly/ehuVU*) on data warehousing and dimensional modeling, as well as *Star Schema: The Complete Reference* by Christopher Adamson (McGraw Hill Osborne Media) (*https://oreil.ly/VZT3Q*). These great resources provide a solid foundation for understanding the principles of data modeling.

Before we dive into the specifics of each layer, let's start by getting our mindset right about the Medallion layers. It's crucial to think of these layers as logical, not physical. So, when talking about, for example, the Bronze layer, don't frame it as just one physical layer. Instead, view it as a logical layer that could span across several physical layers. This approach will help us stay flexible and make more sense of the structure. Having said that, let's get started.

Bronze Layer

The Medallion architecture starts with the Bronze layer. The main goal of this layer is to store data from various sources in its original state without any modifications. It ensures that the data is easily accessible for further processing and enables users to explore and analyze it instantly. Essentially, it serves as a queryable reservoir for raw data.

In the next couple of sections, we'll first discuss the processing hierarchy and how this influences the potential Bronze layer's overall design. After that, we'll focus on the archiving and control objectives by discussing processing full and incremental loads, historization, schema management, and technical validation checks. I'll conclude with usage and a summarization the key points about the Bronze layer before moving on to the Silver layer.

Processing Hierarchy

Whether the Bronze layer consists of a single physical layer or multiple sublayers depends on the complexity of the data sources and the organization's needs. In earlier discussions in Chapter 2, we touched on the possibility of having extra landing zones and whether these zones are part of the Bronze layer. Let's revisit this topic with an example scenario and draw some conclusions.

Traditional source systems often dictate the format in which data must be exported, typically using formats like CSV or JSON. Consider a legacy application that exports data only to a local file storage location. In this scenario, you would integrate the data into your Medallion architecture through batch processing.

Here's a typical process flow: the process begins by staging the data in a landing zone, where you perform minimal processing tasks such as decompressing zipped files, comparing checksums, and generating metadata. Following this, you copy the data to the Bronze layer, converting it into a format like Delta Lake to enhance performance. At this stage, you also carry out basic validations to ensure data integrity. Optionally, you might also classify or encrypt the data to protect sensitive information. Finally, you compare and integrate the data with your existing Bronze datasets to maintain consistency and completeness. We'll revisit these details when implementing the Bronze layer in Chapter 5 using external tables or Delta copies.

> Encrypting the raw data is essential to protect personally identifiable information (PII) from unauthorized access. Therefore, it's not uncommon to encrypt the data before it lands in the Bronze layer. This encryption can be done using open source encryption frameworks, such as Fernet (*https://oreil.ly/e5C_d*), or other encryption tools.

In the data processing hierarchy, the Bronze layer often includes multiple sublayers: an internal staging area, a processing and refinement area, and eventually storage in Delta format. Thus, whether the Bronze layer is a single physical layer or multiple sublayers depends on data source complexity, organizational requirements, and the decision on whether to include the landing zone as part of the Bronze layer.

With the processing hierarchy established, it's crucial to focus on how data is processed and managed over time because each data source is unique and the way data is delivered can vary significantly between source systems. Some systems provide full extracts, others deliver delta increments, and still others stream data continuously. Therefore, deciding on the appropriate processing pattern is essential. Let's explore these strategies in detail, starting with processing full data loads, followed by processing incremental loads.

Processing Full Data Loads

Full data loads involve transferring the entire dataset from the source system, rather than just changes, ensuring all data is available for downstream processing. When processing full data loads, large batches of data are typically handled at fixed intervals, often with the optional use of landing zones. After validation, the data is stored in its raw form and accumulated in folders alongside all previous data deliveries. At this stage, minimal transformations are usually performed; sometimes data is filtered, or sensitive columns are encrypted. After accumulating the data, the most recent delivery is typically either converted to the Delta Lake format or typically exposed as external tables for processing in the next layer. We will revisit these patterns in Chapter 5, where we explore the processing of full data loads in greater detail and demonstrate concrete examples.

Processing Incremental Data Loads

The pattern of loading increments, or "delta loads,"[1] is often employed in scenarios where only changes or updates to the data need to be processed, allowing for more efficient data handling and reduced processing time compared to full data loads. In this approach, you typically receive only the data that has changed, often in the form of events, for example. This data is usually staged in a preliminary layer, where you might first apply some lightweight transformations. These could include changing the file format (e.g., from JSON or Parquet) and converting the data to the Delta Lake format or making simple data type corrections. After these initial steps, you can utilize append mode (*https://oreil.ly/Kihgv*) or merge operations (*https://oreil.ly/VPIQE*) to integrate this incoming new data with the existing data already present in the Bronze layer. Let's explore these methods further:

Append mode
> In the context of Delta Lake, "append mode" means that new data is added to an existing Delta table without modifying or deleting the existing data. This is useful for scenarios where you want to continuously add new records to a dataset, such as logging or streaming data, without affecting the existing data.
>
> Here is an example where df represents a DataFrame, a structured collection of data with named columns. Using Spark, you can read data into the DataFrame and subsequently append it to a Delta table:
>
> ```
> df = spark.read.json(f"{filePath}/events/*.json")
> df.write.format("delta").mode("append").saveAsTable("events")
> ```
>
> Append mode does not address updates or deletions—it simply appends new data to the end of the dataset. Merge operations are more sophisticated than a simple append because they allow for both the insertion of new records and the updating of existing records based on some key.

---

1 Delta loads refer to the process of loading only the changes (newly added or modified data) since the last data load, rather than loading the entire dataset again.

Merge mode

In Delta Lake, the "merge mode" provides a way to perform upserts (a combination of updates and inserts) to a Delta table. This is particularly useful when you need to update existing records and insert new ones in a single operation, based on a specified condition.

Suppose you manage a table containing customer information, including a status flag labeled `is_current` for customers present in the source system within the last 180 days. You can use a `MERGE` operation on the Delta table, which efficiently allows for multiple changes simultaneously:

- Insert new customers.
- Update the status of customers who have recently returned.
- Modify the status of existing customers in the Delta table who are now inactive.

Delta Lake efficiently handles these operations behind the scenes, ensuring data integrity and streamlined processing. We'll connect back to this merge approach in Chapter 5.

Processing incremental loads is an efficient method to manage large datasets by processing only the changes since the last load instead of reprocessing the entire datasets. In scenarios with large source system tables, such as those containing millions of rows, this approach could be particularly useful. Furthermore, incremental loading is also essential for efficiently updating data in any layers, such as the Silver and Gold layers, without reprocessing the entire dataset. A consideration for incremental loading is to combine it with a change data feed to push incremental changes to your next layers.

> By implementing incremental processing with Delta Lake and Spark, and utilizing configurations like `trigger(Available Now=True)`, organizations can manage their data more effectively and economically.

For incremental loading to work effectively, your (source system) tables need to have unique incremental identifiers or `updated_at` columns. These markers allow you to detect any new or updated records since the last load. Furthermore, it's crucial to ensure that the source system does not update records that are older than the last fetched increment. If updates on older records are possible, standard incremental loading might miss these changes. In such cases, using CDC or similar tools might be necessary. These tools are designed to capture all data changes—inserts, updates, deletions—from the transaction logs and can be more reliable for ensuring complete data synchronization.

For streaming, you would typically specify the initial position's startingVersion (*https://oreil.ly/mdyg9*) by using the Delta (or Iceberg) transaction log. This allows you to pick up exactly where you left off without needing to run any additional commands.

Alternatively, you could use a max function (*https://oreil.ly/CBhY8*) on the identifier or *updated_at* column from your Bronze layer to determine the most recent entry processed. Once you have the highest value (max(updated_at)) from the Bronze layer, you can then query the source data for records with identifiers or timestamps greater than this value. This strategy ensures that only new or updated records since the last load are processed.

Maintaining a metadata control table that tracks processed records is another recommendation. This helps manage data flow and ensures consistency, particularly in complex systems.

For a deeper understanding of incremental delta loads and their practical usage, consider watching "Incremental Refresh with Your Warehouse Without a Date in Microsoft Fabric" (*https://oreil.ly/cNE8z*). This video on incremental delta loads provides comprehensive insights and examples to help you implement this technique effectively.

By capturing incoming data in its incremental form, you can integrate it with the complete historical dataset. This process of historization is crucial not only for building a comprehensive archive but also for ensuring that current data is readily accessible for further downstream processing. We'll explore this topic next.

Data Historization Within the Bronze Layer

The Bronze layer is designed primarily for storing complete snapshots or copies of data, similar to what you'd find in a staging environment in traditional data warehouse environments. This layer is especially useful if your method involves fully extracting and overwriting data, as it allows you to maintain a comprehensive history of all data deliveries. The Bronze layer usually also serves as a robust archive, preserving data for many years, which is vital for audit purposes. However, there may be instances where you need to clean up data that has been processed and is no longer required.

In a Medallion architecture, archiving data is straightforward when you use an efficient storage format like Parquet or Delta and organize it in folders.[2] By structuring your data in interval-partitioned tables and sorting them into folders labeled with a

---

2 Depending on the compression algorithm, you can expect a size reduction of nearly 75% for your data in Parquet files from other formats, such as CSV.

YYYY/MM/DD or datetime format, you keep your data well-organized and manageable. This systematic organization not only keeps your data tidy but also simplifies access and auditing. If you ever need to look back at data from a specific day, you can easily recreate its state, ensuring you can retrieve historical data accurately whenever needed.

However, it's important to note that the Bronze layer is not intended for historization of data in the sense of representing a fully processed SCD2 table. Data in the Bronze layer is often considered immutable, meaning it is read-only. While you may append or merge data to incrementally grow the dataset over time, updates or processing of the data are not typical practices at this stage.

> You can apply data versioning by using the Delta Lake time travel feature. It is primarily designed for data recovery, auditing, and reproducing experiments or reports, rather than for comprehensive long-term data archiving.

Historization is crucial, especially when dealing with Bronze-level datasets. This process enables the archiving of data iterations over time, which can be essential for auditing or debugging purposes. Furthermore, historization supports the ability to perform reloads and recoveries. This feature is vital for handling instances of poor-quality data or disruptive changes in schemas, allowing you to revert to a previous version of the dataset and reprocess it.

While delving into the complexities of processing historical data, you encounter a significant challenge: schema evolution. As businesses grow and data sources are frequently updated, the database structure (schema) can change. This evolution can lead to inconsistencies in data processing, making it essential to manage schema changes effectively. We'll explore this topic in the next section.

Schema Evolution and Management

The Bronze layer is crucial for managing widely varying and ever-changing data schemas as data enters the system. Effectively handling schema evolution at this stage sets the foundation for all the data processing and analytics that follow. You can tackle incoming schema changes either in the Bronze layer or wait until the data moves to the Silver layer. The timing of addressing these changes depends largely on your specific needs and the characteristics of your data.

When managing schemas, organizations face design choices, each with its own approach to schema evolution:

Schema-on-read

This method applies the schema dynamically as you read the data. With this, data is stored without a strict schema in place. The schema is only inferred or applied when the data is accessed during processing (reading). This flexible approach requires the system to recognize and possibly adapt to various data schemas right after the point of ingestion. This approach is particularly useful for semi-structured or unstructured data or structured data without any built-in schema enforcement, such as CSV or Parquet files.

Schema-on-write

This approach involves defining the schema—like the table and column names, the data types, and the primary keys—as you write the data into storage. With this method, you must define the schema up front, making sure that the data conforms to this schema right from the start, before writing. It's a more rigid approach compared to schema-on-read, as it enforces schema consistency from the beginning. When applied, it's generally used for structured data.

When using Delta Lake, if there is no predefined schema, the system will establish an initial schema by using the `StructType` from the DataFrame that is being converted to Delta format. In Apache Spark, `StructType` refers to a container that defines the structure and types of columns in a DataFrame.

In the Bronze layer, schema-on-read is a common approach where data is stored in its original format without enforcing a schema during ingestion. This method offers flexibility since it does not demand an up-front schema definition and can gracefully handle changes in data structure. For instance, imagine you partition your data daily using a YYYY/MM/DD time partitioning format, storing each day's data as Parquet files within corresponding folders labeled by date. With schema-on-read, you can immediately access and read this data across different days without needing to predefine how the data structure should look. This approach allows for easy integration and analysis of data collected over time. However, there are several important factors to consider.

Firstly, relying solely on schema-on-read does not allow for blind data processing. You may need to detect and log schema changes, handle failures, restore data using Delta Lake's time travel feature, and add schema-related metadata for more refined processing in later stages. We'll delve into these aspects and introduce tools like Auto Loader in the detailed discussion in "Databricks Auto Loader" on page 142.

Secondly, defining a data update method is essential, especially for historization and integration of data. Options include continuously appending to or merging with existing datasets, completely overwriting them, or applying time-based partitioning. The choice largely depends on the nature of the data, its usage, the specific system requirements, and performance considerations. For instance, appending is commonly used for transactional data because this type of data grows incrementally with each new transaction. Overwriting might be chosen for datasets that receive regular source corrections, or where only the most recent data snapshot is relevant. Time-based partitioning can be implemented to enhance query performance and manage large datasets effectively, especially when data access is time-sensitive.[3]

Therefore, the Bronze layer often combines schema-on-read and schema-on-write techniques. Initially, schema-on-read is applied in the landing or pre-Bronze layer. Hence, you first read data without explicitly declaring the data schema. Then, as you move the data to a layer where it becomes "queryable," you switch to schema-on-write. For this critical layer, it's wise to choose a storage format like Delta Lake that supports schema evolution. Delta Lake allows the data schema to adapt as it evolves, eliminating the need to overhaul or reload the entire dataset. This capability keeps the data current and usable, even as changes occur. We'll revisit this feature shortly.

However, be mindful that keeping schemas consistent can pose challenges, especially if the source systems are prone to frequent changes. This requires vigilance and possibly more sophisticated schema management strategies to ensure data integrity and system reliability. For this reason, to keep things running smoothly, it's essential to maintain a schema that consistently matches the source system as data enters this layer. You usually set up the schema during the data ingestion process to comply with specific standards, either through data definition languages (DDLs) or programmatically using tools like Spark SQL or Databricks Auto Loader. We'll revisit this subject in more detail in Part II.

MergeSchema and Schema Enforcement

Delta Lake offers a set of features for managing data schemas, such as handling schema evolution and schema enforcement. The features you apply depend on your system's specific needs and design, and you can see them across all layers of the Medallion architecture.

For example, as data evolves, there might be a need to modify the table schema to accommodate new types of data (e.g., adding new columns). mergeSchema simplifies this process. It's a feature designed to help manage and evolve the schema of Delta Lake tables over time. To enable this, add the following option in a write operation in Apache Spark: .option("mergeSchema", "true"). Delta Lake then takes care of adjusting the table schema in the following ways:

- If a column exists in the source DataFrame but not in the Delta table, Delta adds the new column. All existing rows will have a null value in this new column.

---

3 See "Table Partitioning" on page 45 for more on partitioning.

- If a column is in the Delta table but not in the source DataFrame, it remains unchanged. New records will have null values for these missing columns.

- Adding a `NullType` column sets all existing rows to null for that column.

- If a column with the same name but a different data type exists, Delta Lake tries to convert the data to the new type.[4] If the conversion fails, Delta Lake throws an error.

In case of errors or failures, you can roll back the table to a previous version using Delta Lake's table history. This rollback feature allows you to recover from schema evolution issues. After reverting, you can reprocess the corrected data using the appropriate schema. For more detailed information on how Delta Lake supports schema evolution, check out the blog posts at Delta Lake Schema Enforcement (*https://oreil.ly/8PtcS*) and Delta Lake Schema Evolution (*https://oreil.ly/lZLnp*).

To handle schema changes more strictly, you can use the Delta constraints (*https://oreil.ly/vFv6M*) feature, which is closely aligned with the schema-on-write approach. This method ensures that the data written to a Delta table strictly matches the table's schema, and it rejects any writes that do not conform. As data enters the system, Delta Lake verifies its adherence to the predefined schema. Any deviation results in an error, thereby maintaining the integrity and consistency of your data. However, this approach can make it challenging to handle persistent and disruptive changes in the source system's schema.

If you encounter changes that affect compatibility, for example, changes that cannot be handled via the `mergeSchema` option, you'll need to reconcile the schemas. When adjusting a Delta table's schema, you have several options:

Using `SQL ALTER COLUMN` *statements*

Updating schemas with `SQL ALTER COLUMN` statements involves making direct changes, which requires careful coordination between the source system owners and the data platform managers. One effective way to manage these modifications is by checking the operations or scripts into a repository. This method is very precise but can be labor-intensive and prone to errors due to the intricate coordination required.

Automated schema evolution

You can implement automated tools or scripts that can detect schema changes in the source system and automatically generate and apply the necessary `ALTER`

---

4 `TypeWidening` (*https://oreil.ly/bqCmp*) allows changes within the same type category. However, it doesn't permit changes from one type category to another, like converting a string to a bool. To make such a change, you must perform a table-wide overwrite and set `overwriteSchema: true`.

statements to the target system. We'll discuss this approach in more detail in "Handling Schema Evolution" on page 145.

Using a metadata-driven framework

This recommended approach not only helps maintain the original and new target schemas but also provides a robust way to manage changes systematically. By maintaining mappings between schemas, you create a scalable method that can handle complex transformations and schema evolution without extensive manual intervention. This ensures the metadata repository is always up-to-date and accurately reflects the schemas in use. It might be helpful to integrate this with your continuous integration and deployment (CI/CD) pipeline to automate updates and deployments. We'll connect back to this approach in Chapter 5.

Restricting disruptive changes

Sometimes, you might consider requiring source system teams to avoid making disruptive changes. Thus, you'd only allow backward-compatible changes to be made. While this places constraints on the source systems, it can significantly reduce the complexity and frequency of schema updates.

Alternatively, for very disruptive source system schema changes that cannot be reconciled with the previous version, you might consider creating a new version of the data pipeline. In this scenario, the new data would land in a new target location, allowing you to manage significant schema changes more effectively. This allows you to maintain multiple versions of the schema concurrently, and applications or processes can specify which version of the schema they need to interact with.

As we explore schema evolution and the strategies to adapt data structures to evolving business needs, it becomes evident that one of the essential aspects of managing these schema changes is the necessity to implement robust technical validation checks to detect errors and unknown changes. These processes are closely interlinked and, together, they significantly improve data management.

Technical Validation Checks

Technical validation checks are crucial, as issues with data integrity, accuracy, completeness, and consistency can have significant operational and strategic impacts on any organization. Within the lakehouse architecture, the Bronze layer acts as the initial repository for raw, typically unstructured data. Here, data is stored in its native format, which may include inconsistencies or errors.

Implementing validations, such as format, schema, and completeness checks, at this stage is essential for several reasons. First, it ensures that the data conforms to specified standards, which helps maintain consistency across the dataset. This is particularly important as data from various sources may not adhere to a stable structure. Moreover, early validation helps in identifying and addressing data integrity issues. In particular, it's useful when applying a schema-on-write approach. By catching errors at the onset, it prevents the propagation of inaccuracies to subsequent layers—Silver and Gold—where data is further processed and refined for analytical purposes.

The design of the Bronze layer centers on strong data validation controls because it acts as the primary shield for technical validation checks and observability. You have different options: perform these checks in one go, break them into segments, or integrate them during data transfer to the Silver layer. To validate data effectively, many companies use scripts and keep a metadata repository. This repository holds technical schema details from their source systems, enabling automatic enforcement of data validation rules, both declaratively and dynamically.

The design of your Bronze layer also hinges on your tolerance for data integrity issues. If you anticipated a failure in downstream processes or if data consumers cannot handle these issues, you should halt the pipeline. This approach, known as *intrusive data integrity processing*, involves storing validated and incorrect data in a separate folder or table. By doing this, you can easily identify and rectify the issues, ensuring these datasets do not enter your actual Bronze layer.

Conversely, if you can tolerate data integrity or completeness issues, you may opt to continue processing the data, a method referred to as *nonintrusive data quality processing*. In this scenario, both validated and incorrect data are stored directly in the target Bronze-layer folder or table. This allows you to proceed with data processing, but be mindful that you may need to address these issues in another layer (typically Silver) later on.

Most of the checks validate the technical aspects of the data source to prevent data from advancing to the next zone unless it meets the set of predefined standards. If data doesn't meet the next zone's standards, it's the responsibility of the data owners to rectify this in close collaboration with application teams and data engineers. These team members, who manage and source the data, must ensure that the data fulfills the integrity requirements stipulated by the consumers or users of the lakehouse.

In this way, the Bronze layer not only serves as a repository for raw data but also as a critical checkpoint for data integrity and accuracy, ensuring only data that meets predefined quality standards progresses further into the lakehouse architecture. This proactive approach to data management helps safeguard the integrity and usability of the data throughout its lifecycle in the lakehouse.

A variety of tools are available for managing data ingestion, validation, and orchestration processes, and ensuring that your data's integrity is intact:

- You can use Delta Lake's schema validation features for addressing compatibility and consistency issues. For instance, schema enforcement ensures that developers adhere to predefined standards, keeping the tables clean. When data is written to a table, Delta Lake performs schema validation to check if the data's schema matches the table's schema. If the schema is compatible, the validation passes, and the write succeeds. However, if the schema is incompatible, Delta Lake cancels the transaction, preventing any data from being written.

- You can use data quality frameworks or tools, such as Delta Live Tables, Great Expectations, data build tool (dbt), Ataccama, or Monte Carlo Data. We'll come back the differences between these tools in Chapter 6.

- You can use custom solutions with scripts, code, and schema metadata to validate data integrity. This approach is often used when organizations have specific requirements that are not met by existing tools or frameworks. Custom solutions can be tailored to the organization's unique needs, providing a more flexible and customizable way of working.

- Azure Data Factory supports schema drift detection (*https://oreil.ly/yOaM2*), which makes you less vulnerable to changes in upstream data sources.

Now that we've covered some design considerations, let's explore how the Bronze layer is used and its role in the broader context of data utilization. This will help us understand its importance and integration within the larger data management framework.

Usage and Governance

Some data practitioners argue that business users can benefit from querying or conducting ad hoc analyses on Bronze data. However, raw data poses significant challenges because it demands a deep understanding of the source system's design and the intricate business logic embedded within. The frequent presence of numerous small tables complicates usability. Being tightly coupled to the original source system presents significant challenges, especially when the source system undergoes changes. These complexities often discourage direct use of Bronze-layer data for business analysis.

To ensure proper governance, implement strict access controls to prevent unauthorized data access, manipulation, or deletion. The data in the Bronze layer is immutable, meaning it remains unaltered from its original state, although exceptions exist when handling overly technical data. This immutability requires maintaining detailed logs that record data ingestion times, sources, and any system interactions to enable accurate traceability.

It's crucial to set up alerts to monitor any anomalies in data size, format, or arrival times to maintain the integrity of data pipelines. Developing and regularly updating an incident response plan is vital for addressing issues related to incorrect data deliveries effectively. Implementing best practices, such as thoroughly documenting changes and maintaining a clear reference catalog, is also recommended.

In essence, the Bronze layer serves as a foundational staging area in the Medallion architecture. It collects raw data from diverse sources and processes it by validating and converting it into the preferred format, such as Parquet or Delta. Although data in this layer is typically immutable, there are exceptions, particularly when it involves enriching the data with metadata or applying filters and transformations to manage sensitive information effectively. Data in this layer may either be completely raw or slightly augmented.

The Bronze Layer in Practice

The Bronze layer serves as the foundation for capturing and storing raw data in its most authentic form. It functions as the base input layer that reliably ingests and preserves all source data in an unaltered state, safeguarding against data loss and corruption. This makes it a reliable foundation for (re)loading and further processing.

The Bronze data layer should not be viewed as rigid. It should be tailored to meet the specific needs of your organization. This could involve adding extra landing areas, preprocessing layers to handle incremental data deliveries, and data validation parking zones, as illustrated in Figure 3-2. Or, you can treat (parts of) the Bronze layer as a virtual layer, where data is not physically stored but is instead represented by a logical representation of the source systems. By adapting the design to your organization's needs, you can maximize the effectiveness of the Bronze layer.

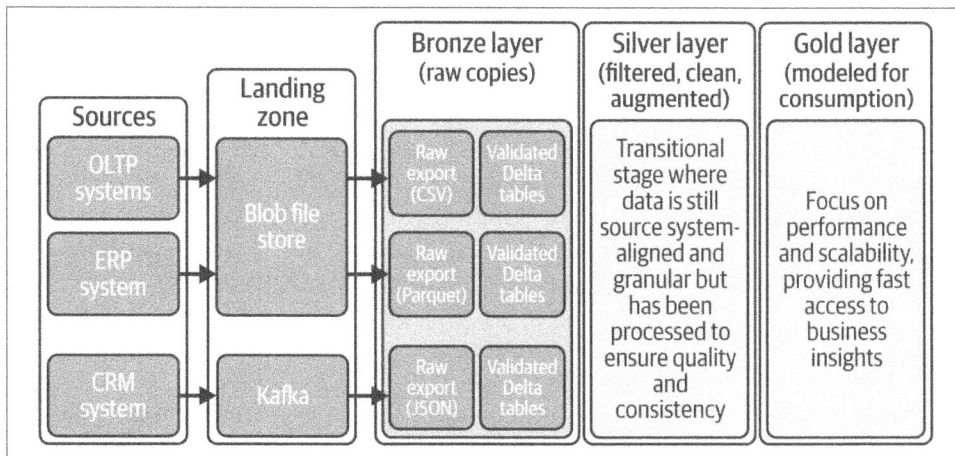

Figure 3-2. How the Bronze layer could look in practice

While the Bronze layer is indispensable for data integrity and historical accuracy, the rawness of the data limits its direct applicability for analytical purposes. Data in this state often contains inconsistencies, redundancies, and anomalies that can skew insights if not addressed. Furthermore, the Bronze layer is tightly coupled with source systems, which introduces risks and dependencies. Thus, transitioning to the Silver layer becomes essential.

Silver Layer

Having validated the data in our Bronze layer, where it now resides in a queryable state, we can progress to the Silver layer. This layer focuses on cleansing and enhancing the data. Here, formats are standardized for elements such as date and time, reference data is enforced, naming standards are conformed, duplicates are removed, and a series of functional data quality checks are conducted. Additionally, low-quality data rows are discarded and irrelevant data is filtered out. Most importantly, at this stage, data generally isn't yet merged or integrated with data from other sources.

Designing a Silver layer, similar to the Bronze layer, requires making complex decisions. Let's dive into these nuances and explore some common trade-offs. We'll start with data cleaning activities, then tackle a design consideration. Next, we'll discuss its usage, which includes operational querying and machine learning applications.

Cleaning Data Activities

Frequently, organizations encounter poor-quality source data, necessitating thorough cleansing. Many data cleansing tasks can be automated within the loading and processing phases, although some are more effectively addressed at the operational source. You want to avoid that these data quality issues pop up elsewhere. Source systems, for example, could also have interfaces to other applications. Therefore, it's recommended to fix data quality issues at the source of origination.

The data cleansing process can be governed by specific ETL rules or, in some cases, through mapping tables. It's also important to recognize that developing a cleaning process is complex and often requires multiple revisions. After loading data into the Gold layer, you may discover issues that necessitate a return to the Silver layer, and sometimes even to the Bronze layer, to resolve these issues effectively.

The following activities are examples of aspects of data cleaning:

Reducing noise and removing inauthentic data
> Eliminate irrelevant data, such as unnecessary columns or rows, to enhance data quality and reduce storage requirements. This step also involves removing inauthentic data, which does not accurately reflect the true (golden) source.

Handling missing values
> Assess missing data within your dataset and decide the approach for addressing it—options include removal, substitution with a default value, or employing imputation techniques to estimate missing values based on surrounding data.

Removing duplicates

Verify that your dataset is free of duplicate records unless specifically required (e.g., for retention compliance). Duplicates can distort analysis and lead to inaccurate models.

Trimming spaces

Remove unnecessary spaces in data entries, particularly in string data types where leading and trailing spaces could impact sorting, searching, and other string manipulation tasks.

Error corrections

Identify and rectify errors in data entry, such as typos, incorrect capitalization, or erroneous units. This category also covers the detection and correction of outliers—data points that deviate markedly from the norm.

Consistency checks

Confirm data consistency throughout your dataset. This includes standardizing abbreviations, terminologies, and units of measure (e.g., consistently using *NL* instead of alternating with *NETHERLANDS*).

Standardizing formats

Ensure date formats are consistent (e.g., using [YYYY]-[MM]-[DD]), recognizing that different locales may prefer alternative formats (like [DD]-[MM]-[YYYY]).

Correcting types

Ensure that columns are assigned correct data types, such as numeric, date, or floats, as appropriate.

Fixing ranges

Check that data in each column adheres to specified value ranges.

Fixing uniqueness

Ensure that data in each column maintains uniqueness, where required.

Fixing constraints

Validate that no column is orphaned; each child record must correspond to an existing parent record in the parent table.

Masking sensitive data

Conceal any PII appearing in clear text prior to data usage to protect privacy and comply with regulations.

Anomaly detection

Detect and fix anomalies that could indicate data quality issues. For instance, a sudden spike in sales data could be a sign of a data quality issue.

Applying master data management
> Process data to ensure the accuracy, uniformity, and consistency of an organization's shared critical data.

Standardizing data
> Process data like addresses, phone numbers, locations, and reference codes to ensure consistency and accuracy across systems.

Conforming data
> Conform data using a common data model to standardize and harmonize information across different systems.

This list is not meant to be exhaustive. Writing cleaning rules is a complex task that requires a deep understanding of the data and the business processes that generated the data. Remember, after cleaning, the table structures are generally the same as in the Bronze layer. It's important to note that incorrect or rejected data isn't typically deleted. Instead, it's flagged or filtered out and then stored in a sibling quarantine table within the Silver layer. We'll revisit this topic in more detail with code snippets and examples in Chapter 6.

Now that you have cleaned the data, what should you do next? Should you retain it in its original structure, or should you remodel it? Let's explore these questions in the following sections.

Designing the Silver Layer's Data Model

The design of the Silver layer's data model is a critical aspect of the Medallion architecture. This is often a hot topic, as there are many possibilities. It is significantly influenced by the number of data sources collected, the extent to which these sources share the same key elements or objects that can be matched, related, and combined across different source systems, and the need to harmonize these overlapping key elements for an integrated perspective.

We'll start with conforming and renaming columns, followed by denormalization. Next, we'll discuss SCDs, the use of surrogate keys, and harmonization with other sources. Finally, we'll discuss 3NF and data vault modeling techniques and close with a discussion on the Silver layer's usage and governance.

Conforming and renaming columns

In a Medallion architecture, it's common for the Silver and Bronze layers to align (straight one-to-one) in terms of their tables, though the way data is presented in these layers might slightly differ.

While it may not be a standard practice everywhere, many organizations I've worked with consider renaming columns to apply consistent naming conventions a best practice in the Silver layer, and I agree with this approach. By renaming and commenting on columns, data teams ensure these names are descriptive and truly reflective of the data they represent. This simplifies both the navigation and manipulation of datasets. Additionally, it enhances communication among team members who rely on the same data, thereby minimizing confusion and reducing errors during data processing. Here is an example of how to use SQL to create a table and rename columns with technical names to more user-friendly names in a query:

```sql
/** Create table with user-friendly comments **/
CREATE TABLE silver.customer (
    CustomerID BIGINT COMMENT 'Customer Identifier',
    FullName STRING COMMENT 'Customer Full Name',
    Region STRING COMMENT 'Region Code',
    SignupDate DATE COMMENT 'First Sign Up Date',
    LastLogin DATE  COMMENT 'Last Login Date'
);

/** Table and field names are easy to read **/
INSERT INTO silver.customer
(CustomerID, FullName, Region, SignupDate, LastLogin)
SELECT
    custID AS CustomerID,
    CONCAT(f_name, ' ', l_name) AS FullName,
    rgcd AS Region,
    sigdt AS SignupDate,
    lldt AS LastLogin
FROM
    bronze.cust_data;
```

Renaming columns often includes standardizing and conforming data within tables to ensure consistency and reliability. For example, you can adjust data to fit within a specific range or standardizing categorical data by using consistent codes or labels. These type of standardizations in the Silver layer support more seamless transformation and integration of data for the the Gold layer, where data is refined for specific business insights.

Using appropriate data types prevents implicit type conversions, which can slow down queries by consuming extra computational resources. By selecting the smallest data type that can accommodate your data, you can also achieve benefits in terms of data storage efficiency.

Applying specific ranges or standardizing categorical data within Silver tables is an activity that can be closely related to master data management (MDM). MDM focuses on ensuring that an organization's shared data—often called master data—is consistent and accurate. Standardizing data within the Silver tables aligns with these objectives, as it enhances data uniformity and reliability across the organization. We'll revisit MDM in more detail in "Master Data Management" on page 315.

While it's is closely related to the Bronze layer, the practices of renaming columns, establishing uniform data types, and ensuring consistent data that take place in the Silver layer might be particularly effective for later transformation.

We've just seen how the Silver layer follows the structures in the Bronze layer. Sometimes the alignment between the Silver and Bronze layer tables isn't as tight. Deciding how strictly to align these requires considering some trade-offs. In the next section, we'll explore denormalization, which illustrates how the alignment between the Bronze and Silver layers can become less precise.

Denormalization

To optimize query performance in data modeling, you can consolidate data into fewer tables, and, by reducing the need for complex joins, queries can run faster. This process is also referred to as *denormalization*. It sometimes occurs in the Silver layer and is even more common in the Gold layer. If you expect to frequently reload and intensively read data in your Silver layer, it's best to use a more denormalized data model as it generally offers better performance.

With a denormalized model, data is organized around commonly queried subject areas, eliminating the need for extensive joins and aligning well with distributed and column-based storage architectures. This approach simplifies the data structure, making it easier to access the required information quickly and improving query efficiency. Here is an example of how to denormalize data using a SQL statement:

```
INSERT INTO silver.customer_return
SELECT
  cus.CustomerID,
  cus.FullName,
  c.Region,
  c.SignupDate,
  c.LastLogin,
  st.OrderID,
  st.OrderDate,
  st.OrderAmount
FROM
  silver.customers cus
INNER JOIN
  silver.orders st
```

```
      ON cus.OrderID = st.OrderID
    INNER JOIN
      silver.customer_details c
      ON cus.CustomerID = c.CustomerID
```

When applying denormalization, table volumes start to increase because redundant data is intentionally added to improve query performance. This redundancy results in more data being stored in the table, leading to a increased table volumes, which might impact performance depending on the scenario. In light of this, many organizations manage their tables via maintenance and optimization jobs.

Slowly changing dimensions

To build a comprehensive historical record of all changes over time, it's necessary to reprocess data into what are known as slowly changing dimensions type 2 (SCD2). This involves changing tables by adding additional columns such as `start_date`, `end_date`, and `is_current` to track changes more effectively. However, this process is complex and challenging, as defining a "change" can vary significantly between the source and target tables. Using business keys, surrogate keys, or generating hashes is crucial in this process, as they help in making comparisons that determine how to handle the source data.

A business key

> In data modeling and database design, a business key refers to an attribute or set of attributes that can be used to uniquely identify a business concept or entity. Business keys are also often referred to as natural keys. Examples include email address as a primary key in a customer relationship management (CRM) system or a Social Security number.

A surrogate key

> A surrogate key is a system-generated unique identifier used to uniquely identify records within a database table. Unlike business keys, surrogate keys do not have any inherent meaning in the business context and are primarily used for technical purposes. For example, CustomerID can serve as a surrogate key in a customer database, allowing for efficient record identification and management.

A hash

> In data handling, a hash refers to a fixed-size result generated from input data of arbitrary size, using a hashing algorithm. This unique result, or "hash value," serves as a digital fingerprint for data.

Keep in mind that the structure of the target tables impacts this process; any columns not included in the target should not be part of the comparison.

Within the data engineering community, there is a debate about whether building SCDs should take place in the Silver layer or be reserved for the Gold layer. Most engineers argue that the Gold layer is more appropriate for SCD2,[5] as these tables are expensive to create and store and are generally underused. Thus, Silver tables should mainly contain current records.

However, this perspective has its nuances. If your Gold layer involves consolidating and merging various data sources, there might be value in creating a historical perspective in the Silver layer, especially when the authentic context from the source is crucial. This is often the case when building machine learning models that depend on historical data in its original context. Additionally, for operational reporting, maintaining historical data in its original form could eliminate the need for an operational data store close to the source. This is increasingly applicable where organizations have decreasing access to authentic data in operational systems, such as SaaS, outsourced services, and NoSQL solutions, and so on. Ultimately, deciding whether or not to implement SCDs in the Silver layer involves nuances and depends on specific project requirements.

Surrogate keys

The debate about SCDs relates to the one about whether or not to include surrogate keys in the Silver layer. A surrogate key is a unique identifier assigned to records, which has no inherent business meaning but serves to uniquely identify a record within a table. Surrogate keys are typically generated using the auto increment feature, or alternatively, by hashing or concatenating multiple columns to create a unique identifier. Their primary advantage is their stability and permanence—they never change. A surrogate key is helpful for tracking changes in dimension attributes over time because its value doesn't change even if the business key changes.

My perspective is that surrogate keys do not typically belong in the Silver layer. The subsequent stage, where data from different sources is combined and merged to build dimensional and fact tables, is where surrogate keys should first be created. At this stage, tables are joined using natural/business keys to look up and add surrogate keys. Therefore, the Silver layer should focus on cleaning and better representing the dataset, rather than creating surrogate keys.

However, if there is a strong preference for using surrogate keys in all SCDs, it's possible to implement them in both the Silver and Gold layers. In this scenario, the surrogate key generated in the Silver layer could be used as a lookup key to find the corresponding surrogate key in the Gold layer. This approach can work, but it requires careful implementation to ensure data consistency and integrity across layers.

---

5 I discuss the differences between SCD1, SCD2, and SCD3 in "Kimball Methodology" on page 13.

We have approached the end of discussing the Silver's design. In the Medallion architecture, as you learned, the Silver and Bronze layers share a close alignment. However, there are slight differences in how data is presented within these layers. For instance, columns may be renamed, and data may undergo standardization. Additionally, the underlying storage is optimized to enhance performance. Despite these modifications, the data typically maintains its source-oriented nature. At this stage, it is not (yet) integrated with data from other sources. Let's discuss this aspect, as well the need for enrichments.

Harmonization with Other Sources

I often address questions about whether sources within the Silver layer should already be integrated across sources so that an integrated or enterprise view can be created. This type of activity is nuanced.

Generally, my advice is to keep things separate for easier management and clearer isolation of concerns. To facilitate this, I recommend you don't merge or integrate data from different source systems prematurely. Doing so can create unnecessary coupled connections between applications. For example, a user interested in data from a single source might inadvertently be linked to other systems if the data is combined immediately after being loaded into the Bronze layer. As a result, these users could potentially experience impacts from other systems.

Thus, if your goal is to maintain an isolated design, it's better to move the integration or combination of data from different sources to the Gold layer. This strategy aligns with maintaining clear boundaries and minimizing dependencies between different systems. This philosophy also applies to aligning your lakehouses with the source-system side of your architecture. Therefore, if you are building (source system–aligned) data products and are keen on aligning data ownership, I caution engineers against prematurely cross-joining data from applications across different domains.

However, I've also seen organizations that prefer to integrate data from different sources in the Silver layer. In this scenario, the Silver layer acts more as traditional data integration layer, enabling the data to be combined and harmonized across entities before moving it to the Gold layer for final consumption. In this approach, I generally see more traditional data modeling techniques being used, such as the 3NF or data vault. Let's explore these models in more detail.

3NF and Data Vault

The concept of the third normal form (3NF), as mentioned in "Inmon Methodology" on page 11, is a data modeling technique that is often used in operational or transactional database normalization to reduce redundancy and dependency. Some practitioners favor using the 3NF or other normalized forms for lakehouses because of the reduced data redundancy, adaptability, and improved consistency of data it offers.

Expanding on the principles of the 3NF, data vault introduces another normalized data modeling technique. It builds on the concepts of the 3NF by incorporating unique features such as hubs (unique business keys), links (data connections), and satellite tables (detailed descriptive information about the data).

The practical application of data vault modeling concepts generally takes place in the Silver layer of the Medallion architecture. This layer hosts both the raw data vault and the business vault. The raw vault presents structured, normalized representations of raw data, mapped to a conceptual business model. It integrates various sources using business keys, ensuring resilience against schema drift and tracking historical changes. The Silver layer also includes business vault elements like harmonization and intermediate transformations, which enrich the data and align it with enterprise-wide definitions. Point-in-time (PIT) and bridge tables further improve performance and querying, preparing data for use in the Gold layer. The roles of the Bronze and Gold layers, in this setup, remain largely unchanged, with the Bronze layer serving as the raw data staging area and the Gold layer transforming data for business intelligence and analytics.

The data vault structure is known for its adaptability, excelling in environments with frequent changes in data structures and business rules. This makes it particularly suitable for organizations with complex data needs. Several reasons might lead enterprises to prefer to use the 3NF or data vault structure in their Medallion architecture:

High integration needs
Enterprises with multiple, disparate source systems benefit from the 3NF and data vault's ability to create a unified, integrated, and consistent data model.

Complex enterprise environments
Organizations operating across multiple domains or with distributed teams require the flexibility and modularity offered by the 3NF and data vault.

Rapidly changing requirements and schema drift
The data vault's resilience to change and ability to adapt to evolving schemas make it ideal for dynamic environments where business and technical needs evolve frequently. By addressing these challenges, the data vault provides a future-proof framework for managing and delivering high-quality data.

Effective management of complex time dimensions
A data vault model can effectively manage multiple active timelines within the same records, such as creation time, functional processing time, and loading time. This capability enhances the ability to track and understand data evolution, which is crucial for audits, compliance, and detailed historical analysis.

Despite these advantages, using the 3NF or data vault for the Silver layer has drawbacks. While these modeling techniques offer improved flexibility and aim to save on storage costs, they are generally less favored in cloud-based data architectures due to scalability concerns. Practitioners often opt for wide, nested, denormalized tables because this setup maximizes cloud infrastructure efficiency. Denormalized tables avoid computationally expensive joins and data shuffling between Spark compute nodes, which can significantly slow down query performance.

Building a 3NF or data vault model can also be complex and usually requires more time and resources. Both models demand a detailed understanding of data relationships and dependencies, necessitating thorough planning and analysis. They also must adhere to stringent rules and structures in order to maintain their integrity and effectiveness. To address these challenges, organizations might consider frequently reviewing and implementing automation frameworks like VaultSpeed (*https://vault speed.com*).

Furthermore, the flexibility of lakehouse architecture causes practitioners to question the necessity of adopting a heavily normalized model like the data vault, especially if significant schema changes are not a concern. The Medallion architecture simplifies data reloading from the Bronze layer through its queryable raw original tables, and Delta supports the time travel feature, enabling quick rollbacks of Silver-layer data to previous data versions.

For extensive insights on this topic, I highly recommend Simon Whiteley's video on data vault offers (*https://oreil.ly/Pgtc1*).

Given the complexities and demands of models like the 3NF and data vault, organizations often choose larger denormalized tables for practical reasons. These tables offer better performance, ease of use, and simplify overall design, making them particularly appealing in environments where performance and simplicity are prioritized over strict data normalization. I'll come back to this subject when discussing the Gold layer.

In closing, data modeling is a complex topic that requires a strategic and nuanced approach tailored to specific business needs and context. It demands a careful balance of technical, business, and operational considerations. The approach to data modeling isn't simply black or white. Depending on your organization's specific requirements and constraints, you can select different data modeling strategies tailored to various use cases.

Moreover, deciding whether to integrate source systems in the Silver layer doesn't restrict you from applying some level of enterprise standardization to the data. Conforming to defined standards such as data types, centrally managed reference data, and naming conventions is encouraged. Some customers even implement basic business rules, like calculating new values. However, such activities should be kept to a minimum. The Silver layer should focus primarily on ensuring the data is clean and standardized rather than on heavily augmenting data and applying complex business rules. Let's address the need of data enrichments in detail by studying operational querying and machine learning.

Operational Querying and Machine Learning

Machine learning models perform best when the training data is closely aligned with the specific context or domain of the business problem being addressed. Therefore, many organizations utilize the Silver layer immediately for operational querying and machine learning workloads. However, this often leads to a debate on whether to enrich the data further, especially for machine learning applications. For example, transforming categorical data into a numerical format simplifies processing by machine learning algorithms. Many organizations, recognizing the need for an additional (sandbox or machine learning) layer for feature engineering and training models, go beyond the typical three layers in their data architecture.

These considerations play a crucial role in deciding where to position certain enrichment activities. If your goal is to enable operational reporting that necessitates data enrichment, I recommend beginning the enrichment process in the Silver layer. Although this approach may require extra adjustments during the merging process in the Gold stage, the increased flexibility is worth the effort.

Alternatively, if you value maintaining flexibility and prefer to separate concerns for easier management, consider delaying the enrichment of data until the Gold layer. This strategy isolates concerns and simplifies management, making it an effective approach for handling complex data structures.

Managing Overlapping Requirements

Let's continue discussing enrichments. There's an ongoing debate among engineers about where to apply business rules—should it be in the Silver or Gold layer? This discussion often revolves around themes of reusability and standardization. Generally, I suggest keeping transformations minimal in the Silver layer. The Gold layer, which is designed for end use, is where you should place business rules. This allows for customizations that meet specific use case needs and makes it easier to manage updates and maintenance.

However, this approach can lead to complications when the same integration needs to be reused often by other teams. If data in the Gold layer is made specific for one initial business unit, another team needing the same data might find themselves reconstructing the logic. This underscores the need for thoughtful planning in how the Silver and Gold layers are structured and where you choose to enrich and transform data. We'll explore the structuring again when discussing curated and semantic layers for the Gold layer.

Automation Tasks

The key to scalability lies in automating the majority of your tasks. However, it's crucial to recognize that not all processing steps across the various layers of the Medallion architecture can be easily standardized or automated to the same degree.

When it comes to automation, different tools and frameworks present unique considerations. As illustrated in Figure 3-3, transitioning data from the source to the Bronze layer is particularly challenging. This complexity arises from the diversity of technologies and vendor solutions at the source system side. For instance, some vendors may use unique APIs or proprietary services for data extraction, which can result in a variety of data formats. For example, if a vendor supports only a CSV export format, then adapting your processes to accommodate this format becomes necessary.

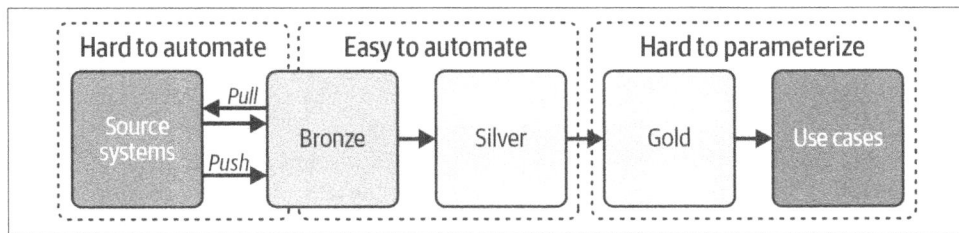

Figure 3-3. Highlighting the easily automated stages versus the complex processing steps within the Medallion architecture

Once you've overcome this initial hurdle and the data is available in a standardized (Delta Lake) format in the Bronze and Silver layers, you can proceed with further standardization and automation. At this stage, tools and metadata-driven frameworks become crucial, facilitating more streamlined and automated processing. This approach helps to maximize scalability and efficiency across the data processing architecture.

Returning to Figure 3-3, the transition from the Bronze to the Silver layer generally appears to be more straightforward compared to the one from the source systems to the Bronze layer. At this stage, transformations are usually predictable and relatively simple, involving tasks such as renaming columns, applying filters, fixing data quality issues, utilizing lookup tables, and defaulting data. Due to its predictable nature, this phase of data engineering is easier to parameterize, making it more efficient and manageable.[6] Consequently, many organizations rely on metadata-driven frameworks with common scripts and/or notebooks.

---

6 *Parameterize* refers to the technique of defining and using parameters to control the processing steps of a data transformation pipeline. In this approach, parameters are variables or settings that can be adjusted externally without altering the underlying code of the scripts or notebooks.

These frameworks enable you to define your data engineering tasks in a declarative manner. Essential elements like schema information, data quality rules, natural and business keys, and mapping rules are all stored within a metadata repository. This repository is then utilized to automatically generate the transformation code. By simply updating the metadata, you can effortlessly modify the transformations, which significantly automates the data engineering process.

Other frameworks to consider include dbt, the open source command-line tool previously mentioned, which excels by allowing transformations to be defined using templates, with a syntax similar to SELECT statements in SQL. Another declarative data engineering framework to consider, especially for those working within the Databricks environment, is Delta Live Tables (DLT). It not only facilitates transformations but also manages task orchestration, cluster management, monitoring, data quality, and error handling.

In Figure 3-3, the final stage involves delivering refined data to consumers based on their unique requirements. This step is challenging to parameterize, primarily due to the complex business logic often required for integration, which isn't easily captured using metadata alone. However, by employing templates and services, you can introduce a level of standardization to your workflows. This approach streamlines the process, enhancing efficiency and manageability.

Understanding and managing the variances in different stages of data engineering is crucial for creating a scalable framework. By effectively leveraging automation tools and frameworks, organizations can optimize their data processing pipelines, ensuring they are both robust and adaptable.

The Silver Layer in Practice

In the Medallion architecture, data's journey began in the Bronze layer, where raw data from diverse sources was ingested and stored without alteration to preserve its original structure and integrity. This ensured a reliable dataset that could be referenced back to its source, which is crucial for both compliance and traceability.

Moving into the Silver layer, you cleanse, standardize, and (slightly) enrich the raw data. The primary focus is on cleaning and enhancing the representation of the dataset. This involves applying minimal transformations and augmentations, conducting data quality checks, and ensuring that the data is clean, usable, and in a standard format. The Silver layer also ensures that data is queryable and primed for further processing in the Gold layer.

Refine and transform source-aligned data in the Silver layer for operational consistency. This approach allows you to maintain a single source of truth, effectively replacing traditional operational data stores with a more dynamic and scalable lakehouse solution.

The structure of the Silver layer itself, whether it constitutes a single physical layer or includes multiple stages, largely depends on specific organizational requirements. For instance, to enhance auditability, you might divide this layer into three distinct stages: one for cleansing, another for conforming to standards, and potentially a third for building SCDs.

If you want to both align data ownership and integrate data, consider setting up separate layers: one for source system-aligned cleaned data and another for harmonized data. Whatever approach you take, keeping each stage clear and consistent is crucial.

Figure 3-4 represents how the Silver layer could look in practice.

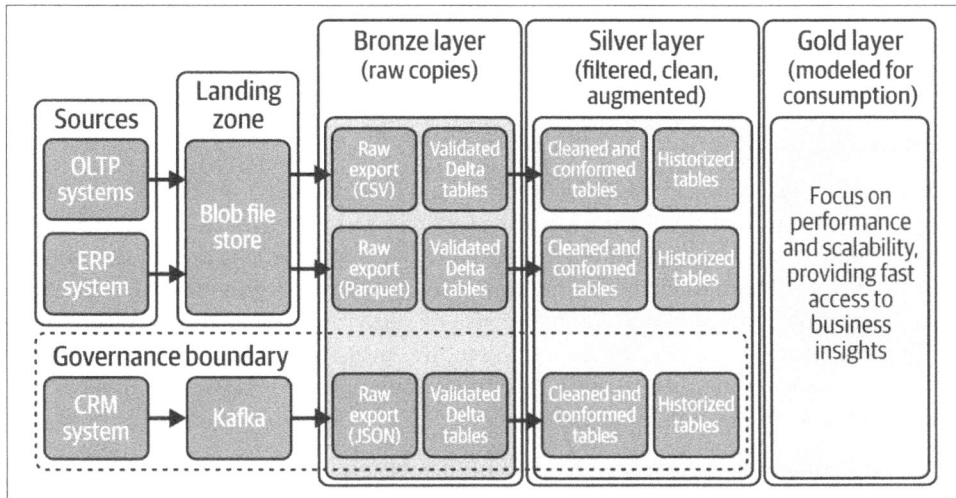

Figure 3-4. How the Silver layer could look in practice

The Silver layer typically mirrors the Bronze layer, presenting an exact representation but with crucial enhancements: tables are cleaned and data is standardized. This simple setup generally suits most organizational needs by ensuring data consistency and usability. However, the architecture of the Silver layer can be adjusted depending on the complexity of your data, the number of source systems involved, and the specific performance and flexibility requirements of your organization. This adaptability allows the Silver layer to not only address current data processing needs but also scale and evolve to meet future demands.

With data now cleaned and organized, the Gold layer takes on the role of refining this information to its most valuable form. This layer is where data is transformed into actionable insights that directly support decision-making processes. The operations in the Gold layer are complex because they involve advanced data modeling techniques, aggregation, and the application of business logic that aligns with strategic goals.

Gold Layer

Reaching the Gold layer, you encounter the most intricate part of your data architecture. This layer is the pinnacle of data refinement, designed specifically for decision making and reporting. As such, the data in the Gold layer is optimized for high-performance querying and analytics, ensuring it supports critical business functions effectively.

The complexity of the Gold layer cannot be overstated. It stems from the variety and intricacies of different source systems and the daunting task of merging all these into a single, harmonized view. This layer incorporates numerous complex business rules and engages in extensive post-processing activities such as calculations, enrichments, application-specific optimizations, corrections, transformations, aggregations, and many more.

Additionally, the work in the Gold layer is heavily influenced by business requirements, which can vary significantly. Some users may need simple flat structures, while others might require a more complex, well-modeled star schema that includes dimensions and facts. There may also be multiple user groups with potentially overlapping and contrasting requirements. This diversity of needs makes the Gold layer a challenging and complex part of the data architecture. Because the Gold layer is multifaceted, it's often broken down into multiple sublayers or stages to manage the complexity effectively.

Given this context, let's focus on the data model design by building a star schema for a straightforward Medallion architecture design. This approach and best practice will help you structure your data effectively, facilitating easier access and analysis. Once you have established a solid foundation with the star schema, you can explore the nuances of this design and further complexities that the Gold layer entails. This step-by-step approach ensures you address both the foundational and advanced aspects of data refinement in the Gold layer.

Star Schema

Star schemas will likely address most of your needs. They excel at conducting complex analyses on historical data and transforming data into entities such as an OLAP cube (a multidimensional data array based on online analytical processing). When you design star schemas, remember that their role extends beyond just boosting performance. They are shaped based on how users interact with data. Think of your data model as a public interface, similar to an API or a function. It's essential to make this interface intuitive and logically structured, just like any tool designed for user interaction. This way, users can navigate and utilize the data more effectively.

Clarity and relevance to business users are paramount. Even if a data model boasts exceptional performance, it will fall short if it doesn't align with how users conceptualize and navigate their domain. If business users find the model unnatural for slicing, dicing, and analyzing data according to their everyday business processes, the model will not be effective.

When designing a data model, prioritize a structure that reflects the end user's intuitive mental model: the star schemas. The star schema gets its name from its shape, a central fact table with dimension tables connecting to it. This approach ensures that the data model is not only efficient but also accessible and valuable to those who rely on it for making informed business decisions.

To develop a star schema, you must first understand the business requirements by engaging with stakeholders to capture their needs and expectations. Following this, you declare the granularity of the schema, which dictates the level of detail in the fact and dimension tables, ensuring they can be properly joined. The level of granularity also determines the aggregations that will be required.

Star Schema

In Kimball methodology, there are two key types of tables used to organize and manage data:

Fact table
> A fact table is the central table in a star schema. A fact table stores quantitative data for analysis and is designed to be compact, fast, and adaptable.

Dimension table
> Dimension tables are used to describe dimensions of the facts; they provide the context for the data. In essence, dimension tables store attributes related to the measurements in the fact tables, which helps in making the data understandable and readable.

In a typical star schema, a single fact table is surrounded by multiple dimension tables. The dimension tables are usually less voluminous than the fact table but have more text fields. This design allows for efficient storage and fast retrieval of data, which is vital for slicing-and-dicing operations in business intelligence and data analysis.

Next, you identify the dimensions that will structure the schema. For example, an air transportation company might need dimensions for time, locations, customers, airplanes, and so on.[7] After establishing the dimensions, pinpoint the facts that will populate the schema, completing the basic framework.

Loading the star schema involves two primary tasks: loading the dimension tables and loading the fact tables. These steps are crucial for operationalizing the schema to support business analysis and decision-making processes. Let's take a closer look at each of these tasks.

Loading the dimension tables

Loading dimension tables in a star schema is complicated by the need to handle SCDs, an incremental process that involves comparing incoming data with the existing data in the dimension table. This comparison helps identify new or changed data, manage surrogate keys, and appropriately insert or update dimension records.

In this step of processing SCDs, the ETL process scans the existing dimension table for the corresponding business key. If it finds a match, the process updates the existing record and inserts a new record with updated information. If it doesn't find a match, the process inserts a new record and assigns a new surrogate key. It's crucial to note that if business keys from different sources overlap, you must make adjustments. Using source system identifiers is one effective way to manage these overlaps.

It's essential to harmonize the data before inserting records into the dimension tables. This process involves transforming data into a common format. Each source system is assessed to identify common attributes and values, a task that often requires significant business knowledge. During harmonization, records may need reorganization, cleaning, and correction. Codes might be decoded, multipart attributes could be split, and null field values might be replaced with mandatory values.

After harmonizing the records, they are ready for insertion into the dimension table. This process might involve several hops or stages. Typically, data is first loaded into a temporary table and then transferred into the dimension table. This multistage approach helps ensure data integrity and consistency in the dimension tables of the star schema.

Loading the fact tables

Loading the fact tables in a star schema, while seemingly simpler than loading dimensional tables, still presents its challenges. The primary task involves replacing the business keys, which describe business transactions, with surrogate keys linked to the

---

7 I'll come back to this in Part III with more concrete examples.

dimension tables. Each row in the fact table includes foreign key references to rows in the dimension tables.

It's crucial to create the dimension tables before the fact tables because fact tables rely on dimension tables for their surrogate keys. Without the presence of business keys in the dimension tables, it becomes impossible to locate and assign the appropriate surrogate keys.

During this loading process, you might encounter situations where certain relationships between the dimensions and facts in the tables cannot be established. This is what practitioners call an *early arriving fact*. In such cases, the creation of placeholder records becomes necessary. These records represent the missing entries and help maintain the integrity of the relationships between the dimension and fact tables, ensuring the star schema functions correctly.

Optimizing loads

When loading a star schema, various bottlenecks can occur, such as excessively long lookup times that force users to endure lengthy waits. To address this issue, you can optimize the data processing by incorporating administrative columns into your tables. For example, adding columns like `type1_hash` and `type2_hash` can streamline the detection of type 1 and type 2 changes during the ETL process.

In a SCD1 model, you overwrite the old value with the new one, keeping no history. The SCD2 model preserves both current and historical records within the same file or table.

Additionally, including columns such as `creation_date` or `update_date` helps in identifying newly added data and modifications to existing data. These columns allow for a more efficient assessment of the data that needs processing, thereby optimizing the loading process and minimizing bottlenecks. This strategic approach not only enhances performance but also improves the overall efficiency of managing and updating the star schema.

Star Schema Design Nuances

Managing the ETL process and building a star schema constitute a deep and complex process; the previous sections have merely introduced a few basic concepts. As you build your own star schema, you'll encounter a variety of nuances and design considerations inherent in this approach to data modeling. You'll likely discover that the process needs to be divided into several substeps, and that what initially appears as a single Gold layer will evolve and increase in complexity over time.

The Kimball approach to developing star schemas is essentially a set of design principles. It provides guidelines and common conventions for you or your developers to follow. However, there is significant diversity in how different organizations manage their models. Let's explore some alternative approaches to give you a broader perspective on the possibilities.

Curated, Semantic, and Platinum Layers

While implementing a star schema with facts and dimensions is a popular strategy for the Gold layer, they can become increasingly complex as dimensional models expand and new data sources are incorporated. This growth often results in overlapping requirements that are similar but distinct enough to require different design approaches, potentially altering the design of the Gold layer and sometimes even the Silver layer.

For example, some organizations might add extra conformed or curation layers, with separate (semantic) layers for data marts that use star schemas. Occasionally, these additional layers are called *Platinum* layers, highlighting their specialized and highly refined nature. In such setups, it's common for organizations to follow some type of enterprise data modeling, like creating standard reference tables and conformed dimensions, which can be used across multiple data marts within a larger lakehouse architecture. Despite being considered complex and time-consuming, this approach remains popular because it ensures data reusability and standardization across different parts of the organization.

The approach of altering the design of the Gold layer comes with various nuances, influenced by factors like the size of the organization, the number of source systems intended for integration, semantic modeling requirements, and specific consumer requirements. Each of these factors can significantly impact how the data modeling strategy is implemented and sustained, making it crucial to tailor the approach to meet specific organizational needs and capacities. Now, let's delve into another design approach that simplifies the data model.

One-Big-Table Design

While designing star schemas can be highly beneficial, the process is also labor-intensive. Consequently, some practitioners prefer to implement a one-big-table (OBT) approach due to its speed and simplicity, which can outweigh considerations of model flexibility and extensibility.

OBT involves storing all relevant data for analysis or operations in a single, large table. This method avoids distributing data across multiple tables or organizing it according to more complex schemas, such as star or snowflake schemas. This approach is favored for several reasons:

Easier to manage

OBT is often simpler to manage and understand, particularly for those who are not specialists in data warehousing. This simplicity can be advantageous for smaller teams or projects where complexity can add significant overhead. Some practitioners point out that maintaining a single big table can reduce the overhead associated with managing multiple tables and relationships in a star schema. This can lead to easier data management and lower costs in terms of both time and resources.

Better performance

For certain types of queries, especially those that do not require aggregating large volumes of data from various dimensions, a single big table can offer better performance. The elimination of joins that would be necessary in a star schema can lead to faster query execution times.

Flexible schema

A single big table provides a flexible schema that can be easier to modify and extend compared to a more rigid star schema. This can be particularly valuable in fast-paced environments where business requirements change frequently, necessitating quick adjustments to the data model.

Preferred by data scientists

Designs featuring one large table can also be preferred by data scientists who work with tools that expect data in one flat format. These OBT designs also offer convenience when transforming data into vector or graph-based datasets for modeling.

Great for long-term analysis

For datasets that inherently track changes over time (like sales or user activity data), a single, large table can make time-series analysis more straightforward. Analysts can observe historical trends and make future predictions based on a continuous stream of data.

Storing all of your data in a single table might seem to simplify the table structure, but it might make it more challenging to compose queries to extract meaningful insights. Let's break this down with a concrete example.

Consider a table called `Orders` where, instead of distributing data across multiple relational tables, all data is stored in a single table using multiple columns such as `OrderID`, `OrderDate`, `CustomerID`, and `Products`. Within this table, the `Products` column stores a nested array of data, allowing the storage of one or multiple products associated with each order. Here's an example:

```
OrderID: 5687
OrderDate: 2024-11-15
CustomerID: 112233
Products: [
  {
    "ProductID": 101,
    "ProductName": "Apple iPhone 15 Pro",
    "Quantity": 2,
    "Price": 1299.99
  },
  {
    "ProductID": 205,
    "ProductName": "Dell XPS 15",
    "Quantity": 1,
    "Price": 1899.99
  }
]
```

Although all data is stored in a single table, the nested structure of the `Products` column can complicate queries that require aggregating or filtering data. For instance, aggregating data based on a specific product can be challenging. This is because the data is stored in a nested format, which requires additional processing to extract the relevant information. Additionally, this strategy often leads to data duplication across multiple rows, which can increase memory demands for systems like Spark and, subsequently, degrade performance.

Managing changes within a single large table can also become complex quickly. For instance, adding a new field that impacts numerous rows can turn update operations into a significant endeavor. Typically, such changes necessitate recreating the entire table, which can be both time-consuming and resource-intensive. This highlights the challenges of maintaining a large, single-table database structure. While it offers simplicity in some areas, it requires careful consideration of potential complexities and performance issues that might arise, especially as data scales and evolves.

Serving Layer

So far, we have discussed the design and data modeling for a lakehouse, including the various layers involved. In the realm of technology architecture, especially concerning the Gold layer, you might still find it necessary to replicate data across other types of databases, in addition to lakehouses, using Delta tables. In this scenario, data is transferred from the curated or presentation layer from the lakehouse to various other services like Azure Data Explorer (*https://oreil.ly/8fqSY*), Azure SQL (*https://oreil.ly/VqC6d*), or a graph database service, to name a few. This transfer makes it easier for end users to access the data and caters to the diverse needs of different business lines.

Take, for example, a business unit proficient in Azure SQL within an organization. This unit has developed applications and utilizes reporting tools that depend on data stored in Azure SQL databases. Rather than having the central team manage data in the lakehouse, this business unit manages the data within their own environment. They transfer data from the lakehouse to an Azure SQL database, essentially creating a "data mart." This approach saves the business unit time in data preparation, enabling them to focus more on extracting deeper insights directly from the data. For more information, visit James Serra's blog post, "Serving Layers with a Data Lake" (*https://oreil.ly/66tgp*).

Something similar is often seen with reporting tools. For instance, Power BI, a widely used reporting tool, can directly connect to Delta tables in a lakehouse. Yet, many organizations opt for Power BI's Import mode to ensure consistent performance and fine-grained security. In Import mode, Power BI replicates data from the lakehouse into its own in-memory engine, called VertiPaq.[8] This approach enhances query performance and data retrieval efficiency, which is particularly beneficial for handling large datasets in a reporting model.

Lakehouse architectures often employ a diverse mix of technology services to satisfy various needs effectively. A typical lakehouse architecture includes serverless compute for ad hoc querying, Spark for big data processing, and Delta tables where the bulk of the data is stored. Relational databases might be used for handling more complex queries, time-series databases that cater to the Internet of Things (IoT) and streaming analysis, and reporting cubes like Power BI for facilitating analytics and visualization. The decision to complement the Gold layer with an additional layer using other database technologies often hinges on usability, compatibility with other services, flexibility, performance, and cost considerations.

This configuration of additional databases is a common setup for many organizations, demonstrating that lakehouse architecture is versatile but also can be tailored and integrated to specific requirements. It's crucial to understand that lakehouse architecture does not offer a one-size-fits-all solution but rather provides a flexible framework that can adapt to the diverse needs of different organizations.

The Gold Layer in Practice

The Gold layer of the Medallion architecture plays a crucial role in optimizing data for decision making and high-performance analytics. To achieve this, aligning closely with data governance is crucial to maintain compliance, integrity, and security. It's important to document and catalog all datasets, maintain transparency about how

---

8 VertiPaq is an in-memory columnar data storage engine used by Microsoft Power BI, as well as other Microsoft products like Analysis Services and Excel's Power Pivot.

data is used, and segment data for specific use cases. Clearly defining roles and responsibilities within this framework also ensures accountability and adherence to best practices. We'll revisit some of these concepts in Chapter 11.

Furthermore, the data stored in the Gold layer needs a structure that is straightforward, self-explanatory, and optimized (see "Managing Delta Tables" on page 43) for reading. This setup must cater to various use cases that interact with this data. To design an effective model in this layer, it's crucial to align technical strategies with business needs. This eventually will result in additional physical (sub-)layers, as depicted in Figure 3-5.

Organizations seeking a competitive edge in a data-driven landscape will benefit from the flexibility offered by the various modeling approaches. While it might be challenging to master the diverse formats on offer, your consumers will benefit from the ability to fully leverage their data assets offered by utilizing the most appropriate model.

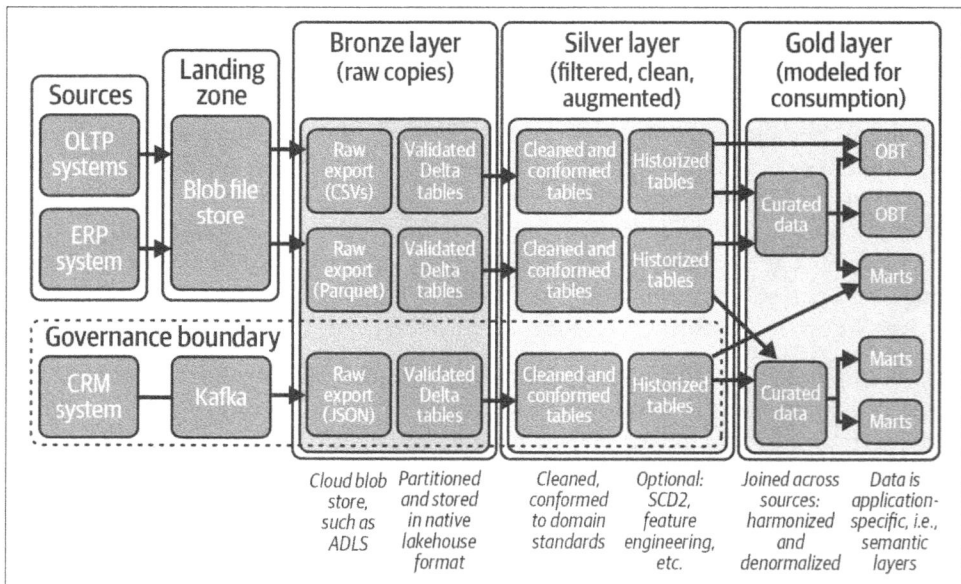

Figure 3-5. How the Gold layer could look in practice

Conclusion

The journey through the Medallion architecture and its layered approach—Bronze, Silver, and Gold—highlights that each layer of this architecture serves a unique purpose, tailored to refine data progressively from its raw form in the Bronze layer to a highly processed and decision-ready format in the Gold layer. Table 3-1 provides a high-level overview of the layers and their key characteristics.

Table 3-1. Medallion layers overview table

Layer	Purpose	Data model	Applied Transformations	File and table format	ETL technology
Landing	Landing zone of raw data from source systems	Raw, as-is from source	None, as-is	Delivery file formats, e.g., CSV, Parquet, and JSON	Azure Data Factory, Kafka, Auto Loader, Azure Event Hubs, Databricks LakeFlow Connect
Bronze	Representation of validated raw data using standardized table formats	Source system schema	Minimal, such as applying filters and adding metadata	Native lakehouse format, e.g., Delta Lake or Iceberg	SQL, Python with frameworks, such as DLT
Silver	Clean, historized, and read-optimized version, although still source-oriented	Varies: mirrors the Bronze layer, subject-oriented, 3NF or data vault	Historized using SCD2, lightweight transformations, aligned with reference data, feature engineering, etc.	Native lakehouse format, e.g., Delta Lake or Iceberg	SQL, Python with frameworks, such as dbt or Great Expectations
Gold	Optimized for value creation	Kimball data modeling or OBT	Harmonized, aggregated and with complex business logic applied	Native lakehouse format, e.g., Delta Lake or Iceberg	SQL, Python with frameworks, such as dbt, semantic models

But what makes the Medallion architecture so crucial for your organization's data strategy? And what compelling conclusions can be drawn from this journey? The answer lies in its flexible, modular approach that allows organizations to tailor their data processes to specific needs. While the concept of three distinct layers offers a structured approach, it's not a one-size-fits-all solution. The key is understanding the strengths and limitations of each layer, which can be adapted to better align with operational realities and strategic goals.

In order to take advantage of this flexible layering, it's essential to recognize the importance of defining organization-wide standards. While flexibility is necessary, clear standards must guide engineering teams to ensure consistency and effectiveness. Given the ambiguity in layer roles and the lack of clear industry definitions, defining what is expected from each layer, how data is validated and signed off at every stage, and the exact roles and responsibilities within the architecture are critical to maintaining a robust data strategy. We'll connect back to these topics in Part IV.

Organizations that initially adopted meticulous models like the data vault sometimes faced performance issues, while those that prioritized performance with simplified models like one big table often encountered inflexibility. These experiences illustrate that effective data architecture requires a dynamic approach, balancing performance and flexibility. It is not just about choosing a model but about allowing for iterative refinements and adjustments to meet both current and future needs. To achieve this balance, organizations should consider setting clear standards for data modeling in relation to what is expected of each layer. By defining these expectations, organizations can ensure that their data is processed efficiently, but also adaptable and usable in relation to evolving business expectations.

Let's continue exploring the Medallion architecture by implementing a practical example, keeping in mind all the best practices and considerations we've learned so far. This hands-on experience will help us gain a deeper understanding of how to apply the Bronze, Silver, and Gold layers in a real-world scenario, providing valuable insights into data modeling and architecture complexities. In the next chapter, we will start by setting up the necessary infrastructure for implementing the Medallion architecture using services such as Microsoft Fabric.

Crafting the Medallion Layers

In Part II, our focus shifts from theoretical foundations to practical application. This part is about making the theory actionable. It is designed as a comprehensive, hands-on tutorial that walks you through the end-to-end process of building a Medallion architecture. Through examples and code snippets, you'll get to apply what you've learned in a real-world context. This approach not only makes the concepts very real but also deepens your understanding of each layer within the architecture. By engaging directly with the tools and techniques, you'll gain invaluable insights into the practical challenges and rewards of implementing a robust data architecture.

In Chapter 4, we set up the necessary infrastructure for implementing the Medallion architecture. You'll learn how to configure Microsoft Fabric to support the architecture. This chapter provides a solid foundation for the subsequent chapters.

In Chapter 5, we begin our practical exploration of the Medallion architecture by implementing the Bronze layer using Microsoft Fabric. This foundational layer is crucial; it involves setting up the initial data ingestion and preliminary processing stages. You'll learn best practices and key considerations for effectively setting up this layer, ensuring a solid foundation for the more structured Silver and Gold layers.

Chapter 6 focuses on constructing the Silver layer. Here, we continue to use Microsoft Fabric to transform data from the Bronze layer into a more structured format optimized for querying and analysis. This chapter covers critical processes such as data validation and cleaning to enhance data quality and reliability, preparing it for advanced analytical tasks. In addition, it touches upon using Apache Airflow for orchestrating data pipelines.

Finally, Chapter 7 guides you through the transition to constructing the Gold layer. You will explore advanced techniques for data aggregation and reporting, enabling you to deliver high-quality insights that can drive business decisions.

## CHAPTER 4

Building a Medallion Foundation with Microsoft Fabric

In Part I, we explored various design aspects of the Medallion architecture layered approach—Bronze, Silver, and Gold. Each layer plays a critical role, transforming data from its raw state in the Bronze layer to a refined, consumption-ready format in the Gold layer. In that part, we also emphasized the importance of robust data models and the need to gather precise business requirements, highlighting the strong interconnection between these elements.

We'll continue to explore these topics, but at the same time shift our focus toward practically applying what we've learned through a hands-on, end-to-end implementation tutorial. A fictional company embarking on a new data adventure will serve as our practical example. This scenario will guide you in building your own Medallion architecture step by step, involving active engagement with code snippets and configuration items.

> Even if you don't plan to implement the tutorial, you'll find value in reading Part II from the explorations of considerations, best practices, and patterns woven throughout the text.

And why will we primarily use vendor-agnostic and portable solutions? There is currently a shortage of practical, public domain examples on implementing end-to-end Medallion architectures. Many materials are either too theoretical, too high-level, or too focused on one single aspect, making it difficult for practitioners to apply these concepts in real-world end-to-end scenarios. I aim to bridge this gap between theory and practice with this comprehensive step-by-step implementation guideline.

Throughout this exercise, you will primarily use Microsoft Fabric as an example. While other services are available, going through the process with Microsoft Fabric will provide you with skills and a foundational understanding that will translate well into other platforms.

Innovation moves quickly, constantly changing services and features. Because of this, I focus on mature services and portable capabilities that are less likely to change. Take Apache Airflow, (Azure) Data Factory, Spark, PySpark, and metadata-driven approaches, for example. These tools are versatile and can be applied in various settings. So, the skills you acquire in this book are transferable to other solution providers. In fact, I've tested all the code snippets in this book on other Spark and Delta Lake-based services, and they work just as well.

> You can also follow the entire learning path by using Azure Databricks. Detailed setup instructions, including insights into using Unity Catalog, are available on my blog (*https://oreil.ly/Z7JS7*), and you might consider skipping ahead to Chapter 5.

Whatever path you choose, the learning approach is largely vendor-agnostic. So, the principles, best practices, and code snippets we discuss will be applicable to other vendors that use Spark and Delta Lake technologies. The connecting thread here is the Medallion architecture, which serves as a common foundation.

We'll kick off this practical exercise in this chapter by setting up the foundational infrastructure, and then we'll sequentially build each layer in Chapters 5, 6, and 7, starting with the Bronze layer, moving through the Silver layer, and concluding with the Gold layer.

However, this guide is way more than a straightforward walkthrough; we will pause after each series of steps for reflection. So, you can expect discussions on various considerations, including how the Medallion architecture fits into the broader context, alternative options, and more, all aimed at enhancing your learning experience.

Our Case Study: Oceanic Airlines

In our exploration of Medallion architectures, we use the example of a fictitious company, Oceanic Airlines. Known for its expansive flight network, Oceanic Airlines has embarked on a mission to revamp its data management system by building a state-of-the-art data lakehouse architecture.

The initiative started with a series of business workshops involving stakeholders from various departments including IT, operations, customer service, and finance. These workshops helped in identifying the specific data-related needs and expectations for the new architecture. After carefully weighting various options, Oceanic Airlines decided to implement Microsoft Fabric in their proposed design, as shown in Figure 4-1.

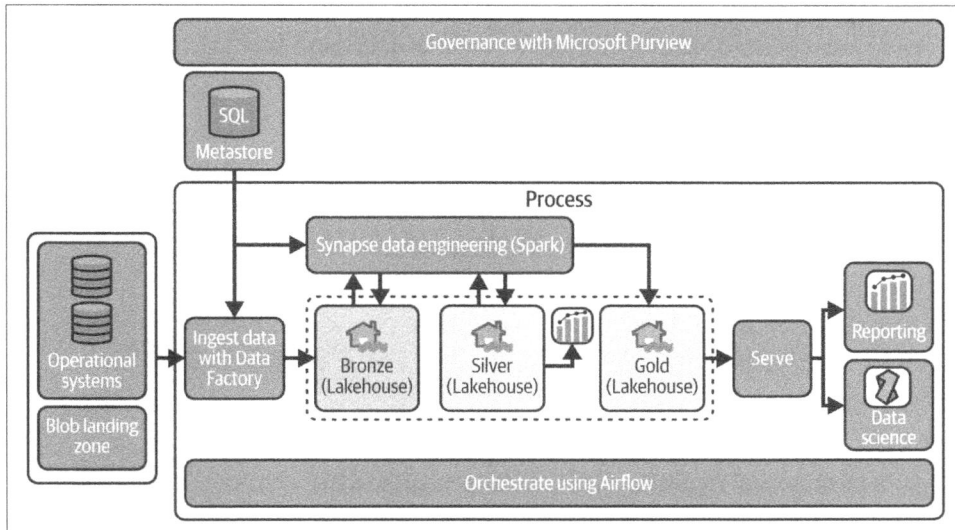

Figure 4-1. High-level architecture design showing proposed architecture

Next, I'll guide you through setting up the foundation. We'll explore the deployment and configuration of Microsoft Fabric and the design considerations and best practices for efficiently ingesting data within the Bronze layer. This step-by-step approach will give you a solid foundation for your data architecture.

Introducing Microsoft Fabric

Microsoft Fabric is a data and analytics platform based on the SaaS model. It provides a collaborative environment for engineers, data scientists, and business analysts. It supports well-known technologies such as Apache Spark and Delta Lake.

Like many other data services, the platform comes with a managed web-based interface and integrates with several other services such as Microsoft Entra ID (*https:// oreil.ly/lZpx-*). For instance, integration with Microsoft Entra ID allows users to sign in to Microsoft Fabric using their personal account. This feature can be configured to require multifactor authentication and other security measures.

Figure 4-2 shows Microsoft Fabric's welcome screen, which bundles all the different experiences into one platform. Let's look at the core components of Microsoft Fabric, beginning with domains, workspaces, and capacities.

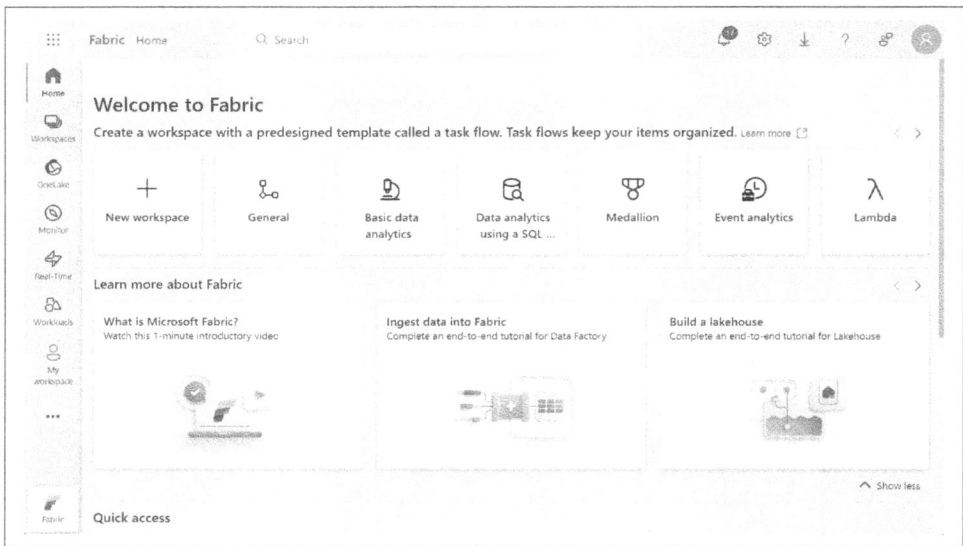

Figure 4-2. Microsoft Fabric's offerings for data transformation, analysis, and insight generation, as well as visualization and reporting capabilities

Domains

With the explosive growth of data, organizations increasingly prioritize organizing and managing data in a way that enhances targeted use and governance. Microsoft Fabric uses domains (*https://oreil.ly/8hiYk*) to facilitate this shift from centralized to decentralized data management.

In Microsoft Fabric, you can group all relevant artifacts and data within a domain, typically aligned with specific organizational units such as departments or business projects. For instance, separate domains might exist for sales, finance, and marketing, each maintaining isolation to ensure data integrity and security.

It's important to know that domains serve as the highest abstraction layer in Microsoft Fabric, operating under a delegation model. This model allows each business unit to set its own rules and restrictions tailored to its needs. Grouping data into domains involves associating them with Workspaces and capacities.

Workspaces and Capacities

Workspaces (*https://oreil.ly/lKfxc*) in Microsoft Fabric are collaborative environments designed for data practitioners to create and share various items, including Lakehouses, Warehouses, notebooks, and reports. Each Workspace connects to a single domain, providing a communal area to make artifacts accessible to end users. Users can experience these through services like Power BI, where they can create and interact with dashboards and reports. This workspace-centric method of collaboration and data sharing is similar to the approach used in other services like Azure Databricks and Synapse Analytics.

On the infrastructure side, each Workspace is linked to a capacity (*https://oreil.ly/SCi_h*), which is a universal bucket, or pool, of compute. In Microsoft Fabric, capacities also serve as licenses that allocate these buckets (or pools) of resources to support computing needs for various activities. In other words, you purchase a certain amount of compute power, measured in Capacity Units.

Capacities come in various sizes and configurations (Fabric Stock Keeping Units, or SKUs), such as F2, F16, and F64, and follow different subscription models like subscribed or *pay-as-you-go* (meaning that you can create a capacity, run a workload, and then pause the capacity). These capacities, hosted within your Azure tenant, are fully managed by Microsoft, meaning the underlying virtual machines are invisible to users. Capacities can be assigned to one or more Workspaces, like you see in Figure 4-3.

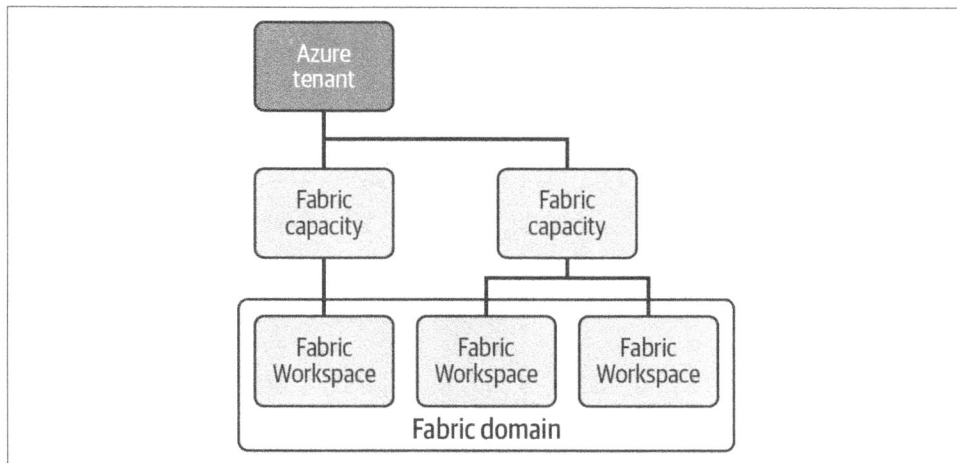

Figure 4-3. Relationships between an Azure tenant, Fabric capacities, and Fabric workspaces

Let's head over to OneLake, a shared storage concept introduced by Microsoft Fabric.

OneLake

OneLake is the primary storage layer within Microsoft Fabric. It utilizes Azure Data Lake Storage (ADLS) Gen2 for data storage and uses the Delta table format by default.

When Fabric is enabled at the tenant level, OneLake is automatically available across all Workspaces, allowing different workloads to access the same data easily. This is particularly useful for compute engines like Lakehouses and Warehouses, which use the Delta format for data storage. The storage layer also integrates with Power BI for analyzing large datasets, ensuring that all tools—from Apache Spark to Power BI—can interact without the need to duplicate data. This means when a data engineer creates a Delta table within a Lakehouse, a Power BI developer can instantly access it for reporting.

OneLake also features a lightweight data virtualization layer, which allows for the creation of shortcuts (*https://oreil.ly/fmE52*) to other storage locations. These locations may be within OneLake or external, like Azure or Amazon Web Services.

Microsoft Fabric has, in addition to shortcuts, a mirroring feature that replicates database snapshots in real time. For example, in Figure 4-4, you can see mirroring to databases like Cosmos DB and Azure SQL Database. Mirroring ensures that replicas are synchronized almost instantly and stored in OneLake in Delta format, ready for immediate use. This approach is similar to the change data capture technology.

Shortcuts facilitate connections to data in formats like Delta Lake and Iceberg, while mirroring is optimal for proprietary formats such as Azure SQL. An illustration of this is seen in how Microsoft Fabric OneLake links to various sources, as detailed in Figure 4-4.

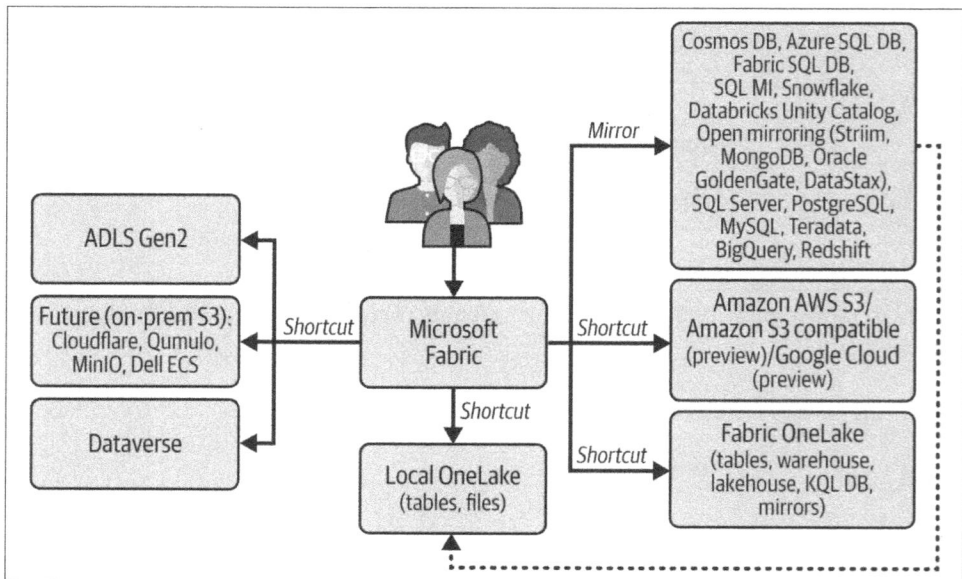

Figure 4-4. Reference diagram from James Serra that demonstrates how Microsoft Fabric OneLake connects to different sources

OneLake acts as a unified storage layer within the Microsoft Fabric ecosystem. It integrates into Workspaces, enabling users access and manipulation of data within different types of workloads. We'll delve deeper into these workload types in subsequent sections.

Data Engineering with Spark

Data Engineering is one of the core workload types of Microsoft Fabric. Within this experience, users have the ability to utilize Apache Spark to process data for their analytics projects, ranging from data integration to data warehousing, data science, and business intelligence. We'll mainly use this workload type for building the Medallion architecture as Spark is a popular choice for data processing and analytics.

Within the Data Engineering experience, which can be seen in Figure 4-5, there is an item or entity type called a Lakehouse, in which users can store and manage their data.

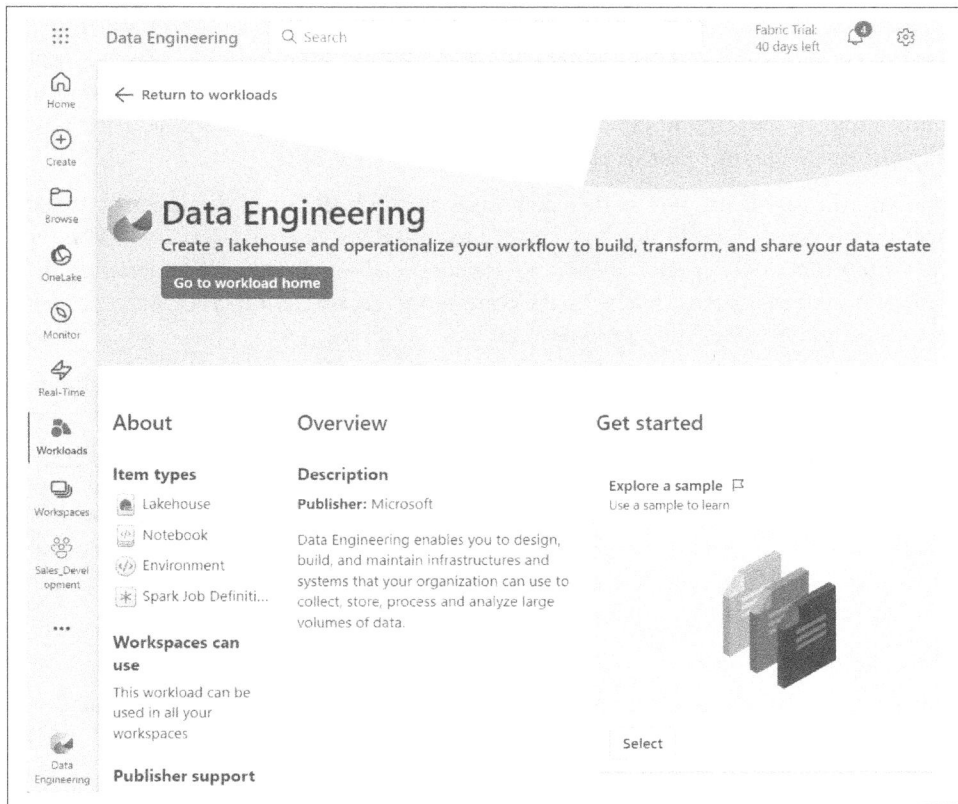

Figure 4-5. Overview of the Data Engineering workload type, which gives immediate access to items, such as Lakehouses, notebooks, environments, and more

With Lakehouses, Microsoft has eliminated the process of setting up storage accounts, containers, and folder structures. To begin data engineering, you create a Lakehouse (or Warehouse) and start working with the data. Behind the scenes, the platform provisions the necessary resources and SQL endpoints and manages the infrastructure for you.

> Microsoft Fabric Lakehouse entities are used to build a lakehouse architecture, but these concepts are not exactly the same! A lakehouse is a modern data architecture that combines elements of data lakes and data warehouses, as discussed in the Chapter 1. In Microsoft Fabric, a Lakehouse entity refers to a specific implementation within Microsoft's ecosystem, including storage, SQL endpoints, and other configuration items. Thus, Lakehouse entities are used to build a lakehouse architecture within Microsoft Fabric.

Within Microsoft Fabric, a Lakehouse entity serves as a shared environment for various types of data, both structured and unstructured data. It supports storing and managing various formats, including CSV, XML, JSON, and Parquet. However, when tables are created through the platform, the default format is set to Delta Lake. Most importantly, all underlying data in a Lakehouse is stored in OneLake, so it is potentially also available for other workloads or users.

You can access and interact with Lakehouses through the Data Engineering experience, which offers a user interface similar to other Spark-based services. Here, you can write notebooks, create tables, and execute Python code. This experience integrates with the managed Apache Spark compute platform, letting you run everything on a serverless Apache Spark pool remotely.

Lakehouse entities also support the creation of schemas. This approach is similar to the concept of managing schemas in other Spark-based services. These schemas facilitate the organization of tables into groups, simplifying data discovery and enhancing access control. Additionally, schemas enable the segregation of onboarded data sources, the isolation of particular activities, or the incorporation of sublayers within a Lakehouse entity. For example, you can create an *oceanic* schema and move all relevant tables into it. This setup simplifies accessing all related tables. Here's an example of how to create a table within a schema in a Lakehouse using Python:

```
df.write.mode("Overwrite").saveAsTable("oceanic.sales")
```

Security at the Lakehouse level is also present. You can grant access to other users or groups specifically for the Lakehouse or Lakehouse objects without exposing the entire Workspace and its components.

Lakehouse entities also integrate with lifecycle management within Microsoft Fabric. They store both metadata and data, which other objects in the Workspace can reference. For instance, you can check a Lakehouse entity into a code repository like Azure DevOps or GitHub. Typically, only metadata is tracked in Git, not the data itself.

A Lakehouse bundles Spark, SQL endpoints, file storage, and schemas using Delta tables into a cohesive entity. Let's turn to another workload type in Microsoft Fabric, data warehousing.

Data Warehousing with T-SQL

Warehouse entities, while similar to Lakehouse entities, offer a distinct workload type called *data warehousing* where you can develop and execute SQL scripts. Like Lakehouses, Warehouses store their data in OneLake and utilize the same Delta format.

The key difference between Lakehouse and Warehouse entities is the processing engines they use.[1] Warehouses operate with a distributed processing engine that supports multitable transactions (*https://oreil.ly/FIj4g*) through T-SQL (*https://oreil.ly/VcBmN*), a proprietary extension to the SQL language. T-SQL is not available in Apache Spark, unlike Spark SQL (*https://spark.apache.org/sql*), which is a Spark module for structured data processing using interactive SQL queries.

This shift from Spark to T-SQL might be relevant when your data processing demands involve intricate transactions or if your engineers are proficient in T-SQL. If so, a Warehouse might be the better choice. However, if your team is more comfortable with Spark or if interoperability and open standards are critical, a Lakehouse would be more suitable.

Microsoft Fabric's Warehouses are designed to manage complex transactions across various tables, although they use a different language and processing engine than Spark lakehouses do. Additionally, their warehouse processing engine boosts performance with V-order-optimized tables. It's crucial to grasp these differences to select the best tool for your needs. Now, let's explore more features within Microsoft Fabric.

Other Fabric Workload Types

The Lakehouse and Warehouse workload types are integrated with other workload types in Microsoft Fabric. For instance, the Data Factory workload type in Microsoft Fabric allows you to orchestrate and automate data movement and data transformation. Furthermore, there is a Real-Time Intelligence workload type that allows you to pull data in real time from Azure Event Hubs or Azure IoT Hub. You can then process and ingest this data into a Lakehouse, Warehouse, or Kusto Query Language

---

[1] Microsoft has posted a decision guide for choosing between a Warehouse and Lakehouse (*https://oreil.ly/W34yL*).

(KQL) database (*https://oreil.ly/PL2Yh*), which is more suitable for handling real-time or time-series data. The integration of workload types extends to tools like Power BI or Fabric Data Science as well. For example, the Notebook experience includes Data Wrangler, a tool that prepares data and generates Python code. You can use this code to further process data for a Lakehouse or Warehouse.

Each workload type is designed for specific data processing needs. They all come equipped with distinct capabilities, yet all the processing engines integrate with the OneLake storage architecture, which uses the Delta table format by default. This integration enables you to use data across different workload types without needing to duplicate it, a method sometimes referred to as the *zero-ETL* approach.

Let's shift gears and dive into the practical setup of the platform. This involves establishing the groundwork or foundation necessary for implementing the Medallion architecture in practice.

Setting Up the Foundation

Let's return to our Oceanic Airlines example. The first step to start using Microsoft Fabric is to deploy it, which requires an Azure subscription (*https://azure.micro soft.com*):

1. Log in to your Power BI tenant at *https://app.powerbi.com*.
2. Click on Settings in the top right corner.
3. Choose "Admin portal" from the "Governance and insights" section.
4. Go to "Tenant settings" and look for Microsoft Fabric at the top of the settings area.
5. Expand the Microsoft Fabric option and enable it.

Once enabled, you can decide whether Microsoft Fabric should be accessible to everyone in your tenant or just a specific security group of users. For more detailed guidance, see the Microsoft documentation (*https://oreil.ly/uAMpW*) and Figure 4-6.

Once you've enabled Microsoft Fabric, you can access it by navigating to *https://app.fabric.microsoft.com*. Here, you'll be greeted with the Microsoft Fabric splash page.

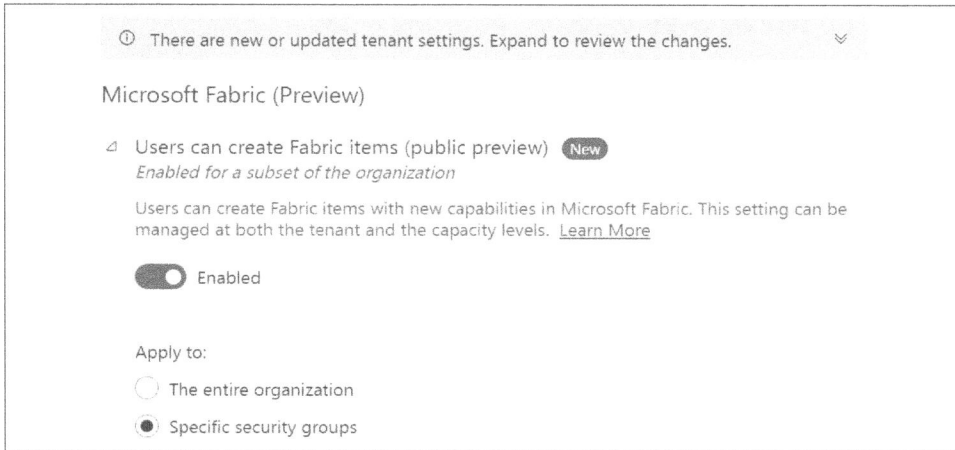

> ⓘ There are new or updated tenant settings. Expand to review the changes.   ⌄
>
> Microsoft Fabric (Preview)
>
> ◁ Users can create Fabric items (public preview) **New**
>   *Enabled for a subset of the organization*
>
>   Users can create Fabric items with new capabilities in Microsoft Fabric. This setting can be
>   managed at both the tenant and the capacity levels. Learn More
>
>   ◖●▭◗ Enabled
>
>
>   Apply to:
>   ○ The entire organization
>   ◉ Specific security groups

Figure 4-6. The Microsoft Fabric admin switch, which lets organizations that use Power BI enable Microsoft Fabric

To fully utilize all the features of Fabric, you'll need to have the necessary capacity.

Setting up Capacities

To explore Microsoft Fabric features, you might have the option to start with a trial period. Check the "Help and support" settings to see if a trial option like "Users can try Microsoft Fabric paid features" is available. This trial could be a great way to test the capabilities of the software without any upfront cost.

To purchase, log in to the at Azure Portal (*https://portal.azure.com*) and set up a new resource group (*https://oreil.ly/iFxZV*). Navigate to the Azure Marketplace and search for Microsoft Fabric. Select the Fabric SKU that best fits your needs—for this exercise, choose F4, a cost-effective option—and deploy it to your newly created resource group. This method allows you to fully and seamlessly integrate Microsoft Fabric into your workflow.

Setting up Domains

Head over to the Admin portal and click on the Domains tab. Here, click the "Create new domain" button. A dialog will pop up where you can enter the new domain name, such as "Sales," assign domain admins, and then click Create.

Once the domain is established, locate the Microsoft Fabric icon in the bottom left corner. By clicking on this icon, you can navigate through different tailored experiences suitable for various workloads. For the purpose of this walkthrough, select Data Engineering.

Setting up Workspaces

Once you select Data Engineering, the page will refresh, and you'll see a new option called Workspaces on the left. Here, create three new Workspaces: one for development, one for testing, and another for production. Make sure to select for each Workspace a licensing mode that includes a Fabric capacity, such as Trial or Premium. Additionally, remember to link all these new workspaces to your Sales domain.

> To promote the exchange of artifacts between environments and implement a CI/CD process, see the Microsoft Fabric documentation on managing deployments (*https://oreil.ly/GEcJh*).

Select the newly created development Workspace. When it opens, it will be empty, ready for you to start your project. Next, navigate to the Workspace settings and enable the "Users can edit data models" feature (*https://oreil.ly/PlcqM*), as shown in Figure 4-7. Repeat this process for the other two Workspaces as well.

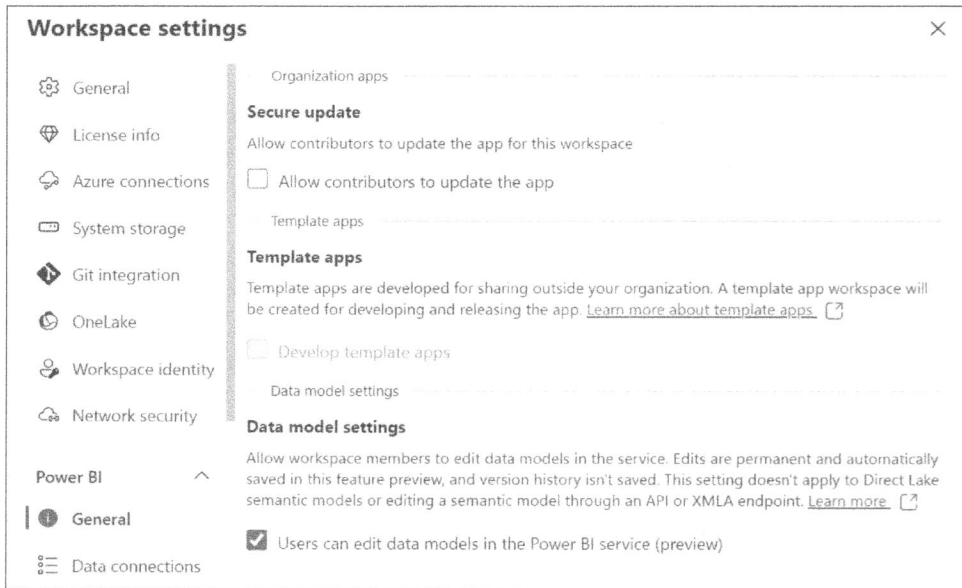

Figure 4-7. The data model editing feature (last checkbox option), which allows you to create relationships between tables in your Lakehouse using a Power BI semantic model

Switching on this feature will enable you to create relationships between tables in your Lakehouse using a Power BI semantic model. You'll use this feature in Chapter 7 when building the semantic model.

Creating Lakehouses

Now that your Workspace is set up, it's time to create a Lakehouse entity within your development Workspace. You'll use it for storing and managing data within your new Medallion architecture.

Start by heading to the Data Engineering home page and create a new Lakehouse named "Bronze." Make sure to check the box next to "Lakehouse schemas" when you create it. In about 20 seconds, your new Lakehouse will be ready, appearing empty initially. Within this Lakehouse, you'll find a default schema named "dbo" under Tables. This schema is a permanent fixture and cannot be altered or removed.

Repeat this last step by creating two more Lakehouses: Silver and Gold. Each Lakehouse will serve as a storage layer for the corresponding Medallion architecture layer. Once you've finished, your screen should resemble Figure 4-8.

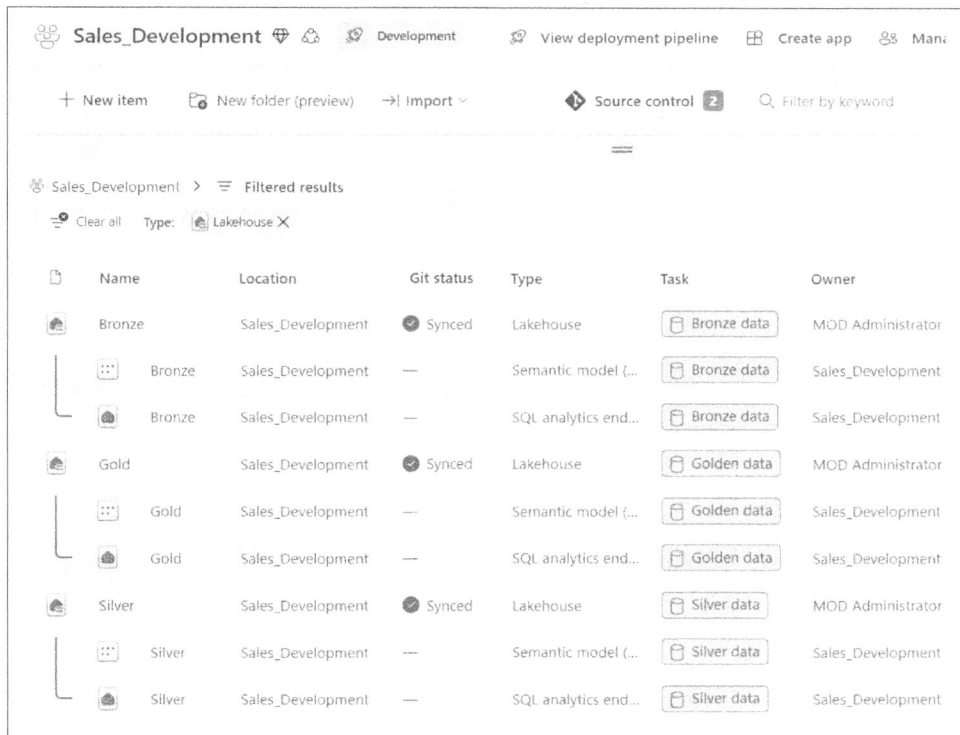

Figure 4-8. Workspace overview page showing the three Lakehouse layers

Creating multiple schemas (*https://oreil.ly/ZKL-8*), or logical groupings of tables within a single Lakehouse entity,[2] is a best practice, mainly for better organization and enhanced security. When you create multiple schemas, you can effectively categorize and manage your data. Moreover, this approach also prevents naming conflicts because you can use the same table name from sources in different layers.

By now, you have successfully set up your foundational services for Oceanic Airlines. We've established essential configurations for a capacity, domains, Workspaces, and Lakehouses. Let's take a moment to review and reflect on the steps we've taken and the design of the setup:

1. *Capacities*

    You kicked things off by creating a capacity for running workloads. Capacities are essential for acquiring the compute resources required for data processing jobs.

2. *Domains*

    You created a new Sales domain for Oceanic Airlines. This domain acts as the main administrative boundary, managing all data-related projects for a specific business segment.

3. *Workspaces*

    You established three Workspaces within Microsoft Fabric for data processing jobs. These Workspaces are designated for development, testing, and production. By linking each Workspace to the Sales domain, you ensure all data and artifacts stay within the same business unit.

4. *Lakehouse resources*

    You deployed three Lakehouse items—Bronze, Silver, and Gold. These layers represent different stages of data processing and refinement, forming the backbone of your data architecture.

In the sections that follow, we'll explore considerations for capacities, domains, and Workspaces, then discuss Lakehouses and Warehouses. Storage accounts also need attention since other Spark-based platforms still rely on them for data storage. Once we grasp these design elements, we'll head over to onboarding the first data source. Note that other services like Azure Databricks and Synapse Analytics also use similar concepts, so the knowledge you gain here is transferable to other data platform-related services.

---

2 I'm using the term "schema" to refer to both a grouping of tables and the schema structure of a database.

Capacity Considerations

When setting up Microsoft Fabric, choosing the right compute resources to run data processing jobs is crucial. In the exercise, you chose the F4 SKU, which is ideal for simple batch ETL jobs that don't require wide transformations and cater to a small set of users.

However, as your requirements expand, consider deploying multiple capacities to handle different types of workloads more efficiently. You might set up a standard reserved capacity for everyday tasks and a smaller, more cost-effective pay-as-you-go (on-demand) capacity for ad hoc or light jobs. This strategy of distributing workloads across various clusters helps optimize both costs and performance. It also makes your architecture more adaptable to evolving demands, keeping your operations smooth and efficient.

Domain Considerations

You created your first domain during the setup of Microsoft Fabric. A domain acts as a logical grouping for all relevant data and artifacts, like notebooks, within a specific area or field of an organization. This feature is especially useful for larger organizations as it allows for data to be grouped by business capabilities, functional areas, or departments. This organization helps users manage their data according to their specific regulations, restrictions, and needs.

Take Oceanic Airlines as an example. This company would likely have many teams across various business units, such as Airport Management, Baggage Handling Management, Sales, Finance, Marketing, and Operations. In this scenario, a domain could represent a department, such as Sales. The responsibility and authority to manage users and Workspaces can be delegated to designated domain administrators or contributors. In addition to this, domains can also have subdomains. For example, the "Sales" domain could have subdomains for "Sales Consumers" and "Sales Businesses."

The number of domains a company needs varies. Some companies have many diverse business domains, while others might be smaller or not as advanced at managing large-scale data. These smaller companies might choose to have fewer domains, but with larger teams handling more datasets. We discuss this at length in Chapter 11 alongside scaling the architecture.

Domains are primarily meant to separate management or administrative concerns. They do not dictate who has access to data or other artifacts. Security and access management are handled on different layers, which we will explore next.

Workspace Considerations

Workspaces are crucial in Microsoft Fabric, acting as collaborative hubs where users engage in a range of activities, including data ingestion, engineering, machine learning, data discovery, and reporting. Managing artifacts in workspaces isn't unique to Microsoft Fabric. Other services, such as Synapse Analytics and Azure Databricks, also use workspaces in a similar manner to streamline their operations and enhance productivity.

Workspaces connect users to specific regions, capacities, and version control systems, which are crucial for managing code and artifacts. Connecting Workspaces to specific regions helps manage all associated storage within that region. This can be done by linking the Workspace to a specific capacity, which is linked to a particular region. In that way, you ensure all data and artifacts are stored in a specific region. This is particularly beneficial for global companies that need to comply with strict geographical data segregation laws. For instance, if a business unit must separate data between Europe and the United States, using multiple Workspaces can effectively fulfill these requirements. As a result, a single business domain with several localized platform instances might operate numerous Workspaces.[3]

Workspaces, as you learned, connect to capacities. Aligning capacities strategically across Workspaces can boost efficiency. For example, a single Capacity Unit might cater to all development Workspaces across various teams, or a high-demand production environment might have its own dedicated capacity. Using additional Workspaces can be an effective way to optimize and segregate compute-intensive workloads within a domain.

Workspaces also integrate with version control systems to manage deployment processes and separate concerns across development, testing, and production stages. Each stage is recommended to have its own dedicated Workspace, which is essential for managing the CI/CD process. For the Medallion architecture, storing all code and artifacts, such as Lakehouses, within a single Workspace is recommended. You can deviate from this approach by creating separate Workspaces for different layers. However, this might complicate the CI/CD process, as you would need to manage multiple Workspaces and their associated artifacts.

Similar to other Spark-based services, Workspaces act as security boundaries for managing permissions. They accommodate different roles such as admin, member, contributor, and viewer, each with specific rights and restrictions. Moreover,

---

3 In this context, a "platform instance" refers to a specific setup of platforms like Synapse Analytics and Azure Databricks within a region, allowing for localized configurations. Microsoft Fabric differs; it operates as a unified SaaS platform, where users manage operations through sets of Workspaces within the same platform architecture, without clear and distinct instances.

Workspaces can segregate activities or distribute data. For example, in a production environment, setting up a new Workspace with read-only shortcuts to other Workspaces can provide certain users with restricted access for exploratory purposes. This method of segregation can facilitate data sharing among teams.

Furthermore, Workspaces also come with a managed identity for secure access to other services. For instance, a newly created Workspace could restrict certain architectural components to connect only with specific parts, like a virtual network connected to an on-premises data source. This feature is particularly useful for organizations that require strict data isolation or have specific data governance requirements.

There are other advantages to using multiple Workspaces. For example, setting up individual Workspaces for different teams can enhance focus and security by providing isolated environments for each team to work on their projects. In scenarios I often see, a single team manages all data onboarding and ingestion due to the complexity involved. Once the data is ingested, cleaned, and curated, it becomes accessible to other teams. These teams typically operate within their own Workspaces, allowing them to concentrate on specific projects. This way of working is visualized in Figure 4-9.

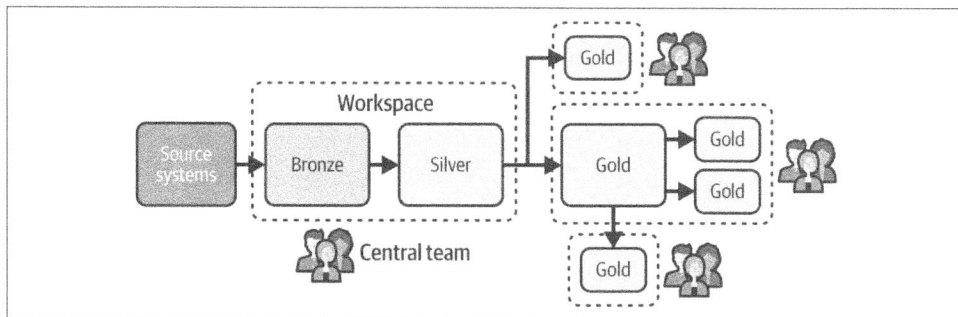

Figure 4-9. All data onboarding and ingestion handled by a single team (common within smaller organizations)

In our example, Oceanic Airlines initially manages all data processing jobs within a single Workspace, which is accessible to engineers for development and collaboration. As the organization grows and the number of projects increases, creating multiple Workspaces might be beneficial, for example to accommodate testing and production. This strategy allows for more effective management of different projects and teams, accommodating growth and evolving needs. We revisit this topic in "Number of Medallion Architectures" on page 303.

Lakehouse Entities Considerations

In the beginning of this chapter, we briefly discussed Lakehouses and Warehouses, which are crucial for structured data storage within Microsoft Fabric. These entities are key components when constructing Medallion architectures. Typically, a Medallion architecture is segmented into three layers or zones, each representing a different level of data quality—the higher the layer, the higher the data quality.

In Microsoft Fabric, it's a best practice to assign each layer to a separate Lakehouse entity. This is better than having a single Lakehouse or Warehouse with multiple schemas for all layers. When you have separate Lakehouses or Warehouses, they come with specific built-in SQL endpoints, which enables you to have more fine-grained control over who can access what endpoint. So, to set up a standard Medallion architecture in Microsoft Fabric, you create a minimum of three entities: a Lakehouse for Bronze, a Lakehouse for Silver, and a Lakehouse or Warehouse for Gold.

The deployment workflow between development, testing, and production (DTP) often involves cloning Workspaces. Each environment typically has at least three Lakehouses or Warehouses. For DTP, this means you would end up with a total of nine Lakehouses across three Workspaces. While that might seem like a lot, this setup can be quite manageable, even if that seems like a large number, since you can allocate different capacities to each layer within each environment's Lakehouse.

Access rights are customizable for each entity. For instance, you might allow additional users read-only access to a layer through a SQL endpoint. This setup is particularly useful if you want to restrict access to only the high-quality data in the Gold layer or for developers who need to troubleshoot in a Bronze production environment but don't need access to other data layers.

Lakehouses also offer an added layer of separation for protection. Consider a scenario where a large domain team manages numerous applications, but not all members should access all raw data. Or, perhaps multiple smaller teams are ingesting data, and you want to prevent them from writing to the same location. In such cases, setting up additional Lakehouses or Warehouses allows each team to manage its own data independently.

For a successful Medallion architecture, standardizing alignment is vital, as it ensures new teams can be onboarded quickly and efficiently. For instance, every Workspace should adhere to a specific layout design of its Lakehouse entities. Adopt descriptive naming conventions reflecting the associated Workspace or project. Another helpful strategy is to script the deployment process in a way that that all essential items, such as a Workspace and Lakehouse entities, are bundled together.

Depending on your specific design needs, a Workspace might house more than the typical three Lakehouses for Bronze, Silver, and Gold. In fact, any of these layers can be designed using multiple Lakehouses to better organize and manage data. For instance, a Bronze or Gold layer might consist of several distinct Lakehouse entities, each labeled with a specific prefix or identifier to clearly delineate their purpose and contents. This approach allows for greater flexibility and control over data management and access within each layer.

For a comprehensive understanding of data management, explore how other Spark- and Delta Lake-based services handle their data lifecycles, particularly those that use Azure Data Lake Storage. By studying these approaches, you can learn how to effectively integrate these services and ensure a robust and efficient data ecosystem.

Storage Account Considerations

When setting up Spark-based services like Azure Databricks, Synapse Analytics, or Azure HDInsight, choosing the right strategy for managing storage accounts is crucial. For example, if you decide to use Azure Databricks, you might opt for a single Azure Data Lake Storage account divided into three containers: Bronze, Silver, and Gold. This setup ensures that all your data is in one place, organized across different containers.

> "The Hitchhiker's Guide to the Data Lake" (*https://oreil.ly/sGrAu*) is a comprehensive guide on key considerations involved in building your enterprise data lake, including ADLS and storage account configurations.

Can you deviate from this setup? Absolutely. For smaller projects with simple data management, a single storage account is often sufficient because it's easy to manage and access. But for larger projects, you might need multiple storage accounts to segregate data for organizational or security purposes. Each data engineering team, then, will have its own storage account with multiple containers for the different layers. This approach can help you manage access control and data governance more effectively.

Another approach is to use a hybrid model that balances locally and centrally aligned data. You can achieve this by implementing both local-domain and central storage accounts. Each domain can use an internal, dedicated storage account for domain-specific processing, which can include activities in the Bronze, Silver, and Gold layers. This account is solely for internal use and is not exposed to other domains. In addition to these local-domain storage accounts, there is a centrally shared storage account. This central account is used for distributing the final versions of data products, which are typically stored in either the Silver layer (source-aligned data products) or the Gold layer (aggregate or consumer-aligned data products), to other domains. This shared storage account is often managed by a central department. This design provides flexibility for domains while maintaining oversight of all data exchanges. I show a pragmatic example of this design in Chapter 11.

Additionally, there are many other reasons to deviate from a default data lake setup. These may include the following:

Organizational structure
    Different departments maintaining ownership of their data

Multi-regional deployments
    Complying with regional data residency requirements

Avoiding Azure limits
    Overcoming subscription or service constraints

Implementing different Azure policies
    Tailoring policies for each data lake

Tracking costs
    Simplifying billing through individual Azure subscriptions for each lake

Separating sensitive data
    Isolating and applying stricter controls to sensitive data

Environment segregation
    Using different lakes for development, testing, and production

Improving latency
    Placing data lakes closer to end users or applications

Limiting privileges
    Restricting elevated privileges to the necessary data assets

Managing governance and compliance
    Meeting diverse regulatory and compliance needs

Departmental needs
    Specific teams requiring dedicated data lakes

Enabling disaster recovery
    Distributing data lakes across regions to ensure data availability

Enabling different service levels
    Using separate lakes to optimize cost and performance for various data types

To learn more about the reasons to implement additional data lakes, read "When to Have Multiple Data Lakes" (*https://oreil.ly/epq6Z*) by James Serra.

Now that we've set up the foundation and discussed key design considerations, let's quickly summarize the deployment steps and what you've learned so far about Microsoft Fabric before continuing with building the Bronze layer in Chapter 5.

Conclusion

This chapter provided valuable insights into setting up Microsoft Fabric, a platform that offers extensive customization to meet various organizational needs. We've looked into aligning domains, Workspaces, and Lakehouse entities.

Here are some key strategies for setting up the foundation of your Medallion architecture:

- Consider organizing Lakehouse entities into Workspaces and further into domains.
- Assess the elasticity of your workloads to enhance the cost-efficiency of your architecture. Explore the option of purchasing reserved compute and strategically aligning your Workspaces with different types of Capacity Units.
- Provide guidelines to your teams regarding the optimal number of Workspaces and Lakehouse entities. Encourage the adoption of standard naming conventions throughout the organization.

Operating a data analytics platform like Microsoft Fabric involves numerous configuration options and considerations, which can make managing workloads both complex and challenging for organizations. Therefore, an experienced data engineering team is essential for effective management and maintenance. This team should adopt a focused approach, starting small and gradually expanding efforts. Regular interactions with other teams through demos, weekly lunches, and monthly social events can foster collaboration and innovation. These activities help build a strong organizational culture and ensure the platform aligns with the organization's broader goals.

In Chapter 5, continuing our use of Microsoft Fabric, we will shift our focus to constructing the Bronze layer.

Construct the Bronze Layer

Having established the foundation of your data platform, whether it is Microsoft Fabric or Azure Databricks, it's time to build the Bronze layer. This is the layer where all the raw data first lands, and the data is maintained in its original form. It serves both as a historical archive and a reliable single source.

As part of the exercise of setting up the first layer, you'll tackle tasks such as setting up connections, building your first data pipeline, and exploring how to handle data ingestion and schema management. You'll come across various code snippets along the way. These snippets are here to help clarify the process—some are just for learning, and some you can actually use in your coding exercises. Keep in mind, though, these examples are streamlined for educational purposes, so you might need to tweak them a bit when you apply them to real-world scenarios.

By the end of this chapter, you will thoroughly understand how to build and implement the Bronze layer of your Medallion architecture, including the nuances that come with ingestion and managing data in the Bronze layer. This solid base will prepare you for the subsequent Silver and Gold stages. Let's start by building the data pipeline.

Building the Data Pipeline

In this section, we will construct a data pipeline using Data Factory,[1] while integrating Spark and Delta Lake into the process. This hands-on journey will equip you with the skills to understand how these tools interconnect in a practical setting.

---

1 A pipeline is a logical grouping of activities that together perform a task.

When using Azure Data Factory, you might notice slight differences in some configuration dialogs compared to Data Factory in Microsoft Fabric. See the initial configuration steps for Azure Databricks (*https://oreil.ly/MjoEK*) if you are using that and run into any discrepancies.

The process begins with the prerequisites of deploying the AdventureWorks sample database, which will serve as the initial data source. From there, you'll onboard this data into the Bronze layer using Data Factory. This will involve tasks such as setting up connection details, creating a new data pipeline, and configuring various pipeline activities. As you progress, you'll receive detailed guidance, complete with instructions, screenshots, and crucial parameters to consider. The intermediate result of this chapter is depicted in Figure 5-1.

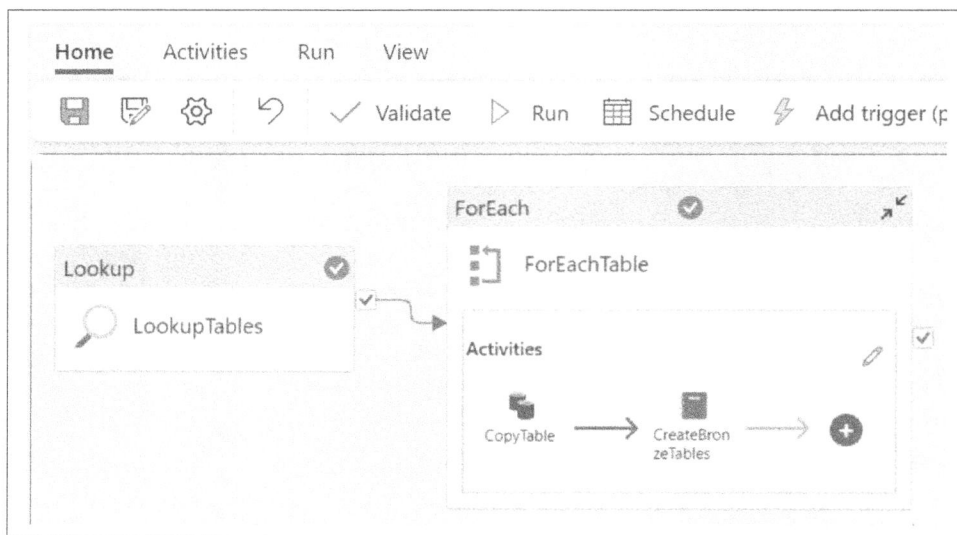

Figure 5-1. Overview of the pipeline in Data Factory

By the end of this section, you will have gained valuable insights and recommendations that will prepare you for implementing Lakehouse tables. After that, we'll explore schema management.

Deploying the AdventureWorks Sample Database

For this exercise, the AdventureWorks sample database will be utilized as a showcase for onboarding a real data source into your new environment. The AdventureWorks sample is a widely used database for demonstration and training purposes, making it an excellent choice for studying data ingestion, fixing data quality, and building data integration activities.

The AdventureWorks sample is included in Azure SQL (*https://oreil.ly/OxKE3*), which is a cloud-based relational database service provided by Microsoft Azure. Azure SQL is a popular choice for organizations looking to create new cloud native applications. It is designed to manage and store structured data, offering high security, scalability, and availability.

To deploy the AdventureWorks sample database in Azure SQL, follow the instructions in "Quickstart: Create a Single Database" (*https://oreil.ly/M_UeH*) and "AdventureWorks Sample Database" (*https://oreil.ly/qQjjm*).

After following the quickstart guides and completing the deployment, you can begin building your first pipeline using Data Factory. In the upcoming sections, you will configure the connection. After that, you'll use Data Factory to load data into the Bronze layer and partition it by loading date. Once the data is loaded, you'll trigger a Spark job to create Bronze tables using the same pipeline.

Set Up an Azure SQL Database Connection

To read data from the AdventureWorks sample database and write it to the Bronze layer, it is necessary to set up the required connection details in Data Factory. These configuration details define the connection properties and credentials required to connect to target sources or destinations.

To set up the database connection, select the Settings gear icon at the top of your screen and choose Manage Connections and Gateways. Next, select New at the top of the ribbon to add a new data source. A new connection pane opens on the right side of the page. Here, you can select the type of connection you want to create.

You'll need to create a connection using SQL Server to use the AdventureWorks sample database. For more detailed guidance, see "Set up Your Azure SQL Database Connection" (*https://oreil.ly/gxLb7*). In addition, I recommend using a service principal account (*https://oreil.ly/84R73*) for authentication, as it provides the most secure and scalable way to authenticate your Data Factory account with Azure services. For an overview screen, see Figure 5-2.

> Each data source comes with its own unique challenges. You may find yourself using different setups and activities than those described here. I discuss this further in "Configuring the CopyTable activity" on page 120. Additionally, the naming convention in this example follows the AdventureWorks sample database. Feel free to adjust it to better match your specific data source.

Once the connection details are configured, you can initiate the project by creating a new pipeline within Data Factory (*https://oreil.ly/4-ZF-*). This data pipeline will form the foundation for future steps, including Lookup, ForEach, Copy Tables, and Notebook activities.

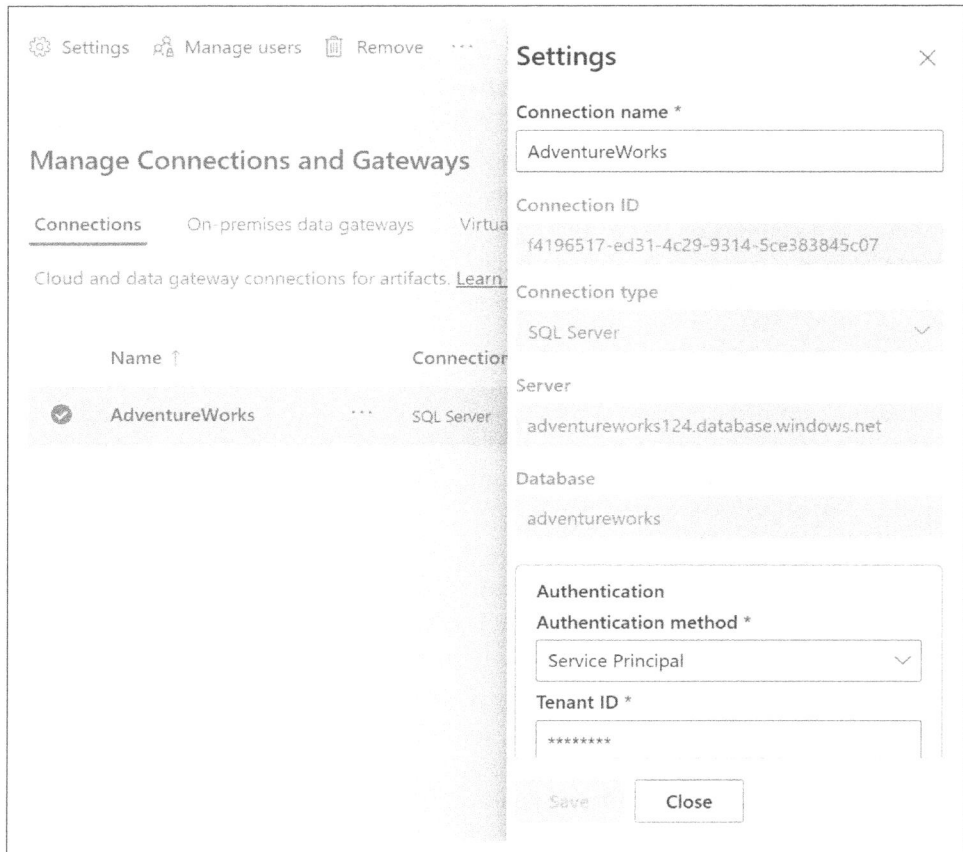

Figure 5-2. Overview of the connection details in Data Factory

Creating a New Data Pipeline

To create a new pipeline, return to the Workspace using the navigation pane on the left side of the screen and open the development Workspace. From there, click on New Item and select "Data pipeline." Then, name the newly created pipeline, for example, "AdventureWorks." The page will refresh, displaying a blank canvas where you can build the pipeline. This canvas is where activities such as Lookup, ForEach, CopyTable, and Notebook will be added to the pipeline. You can find these activities in the Activities pane on the top of the screen.

Begin by incorporating the Lookup activity by dragging it into the pipeline. The Lookup activity will be used to retrieve the schema information from the Adventure-Works sample database. This information will be used in the process of iterating over a list of database tables to perform a copy operation on each one. So each table will be dynamically copied to the Bronze Lakehouse.

Next, click on the activity to configure it. In the settings, select the newly created AdventureWorks Connection for reading information from the database. Then, move to the details section and, in the "Use query" line, select the Query radio button to fetch all relevant table names. Ensure that "First row only" is unchecked to allow the retrieval of all rows from the table. For more details, refer to Figure 5-3.

For the query, the SQL statement that follows is used to retrieve only functional table names from the INFORMATION_SCHEMA view. This view offers an internal, system table-independent perspective on the metadata in the database. It provides a more standardized method for retrieving information about database objects such as tables, columns, domains, check constraints, privileges, and more. Since most modern databases support system tables, this method is commonly used for querying metadata:

```
SELECT * FROM INFORMATION_SCHEMA.TABLES
WHERE TABLE_TYPE = 'BASE TABLE' AND TABLE_SCHEMA = 'SalesLT'
```

To verify everything is functioning correctly, click the "Preview data" button. If the data displays as expected and an overview with tables is shown, you can proceed with developing the pipeline by adding a ForEach activity.

✓ Validate   ▷ Run   ▦ Schedule   ⚡ Add trigger (preview)   ⏱ View run

Lookup ✓

🔍 LookupTables

🗑 </> ▢ ➡

General   **Settings**

Connection *	🗄 AdventureWorks admin	⟳ Refresh ✏ Edit
Connection type	🗄 Azure SQL Database	⌔ Test connection
		✓ Connection successful
Database	sqlbuildingma	⟳ Refresh
Use query	○ Table ● Query ○ Stored procedure	
Query *	SELECT * FROM INFORMATION_SCHEMA.TABLES WHERE TABLE_TYPE = 'BASE TABLE' AND TABLE_SCHEMA = 'SalesLT'	✏ Edit 👓 Prev
First row only	☐	

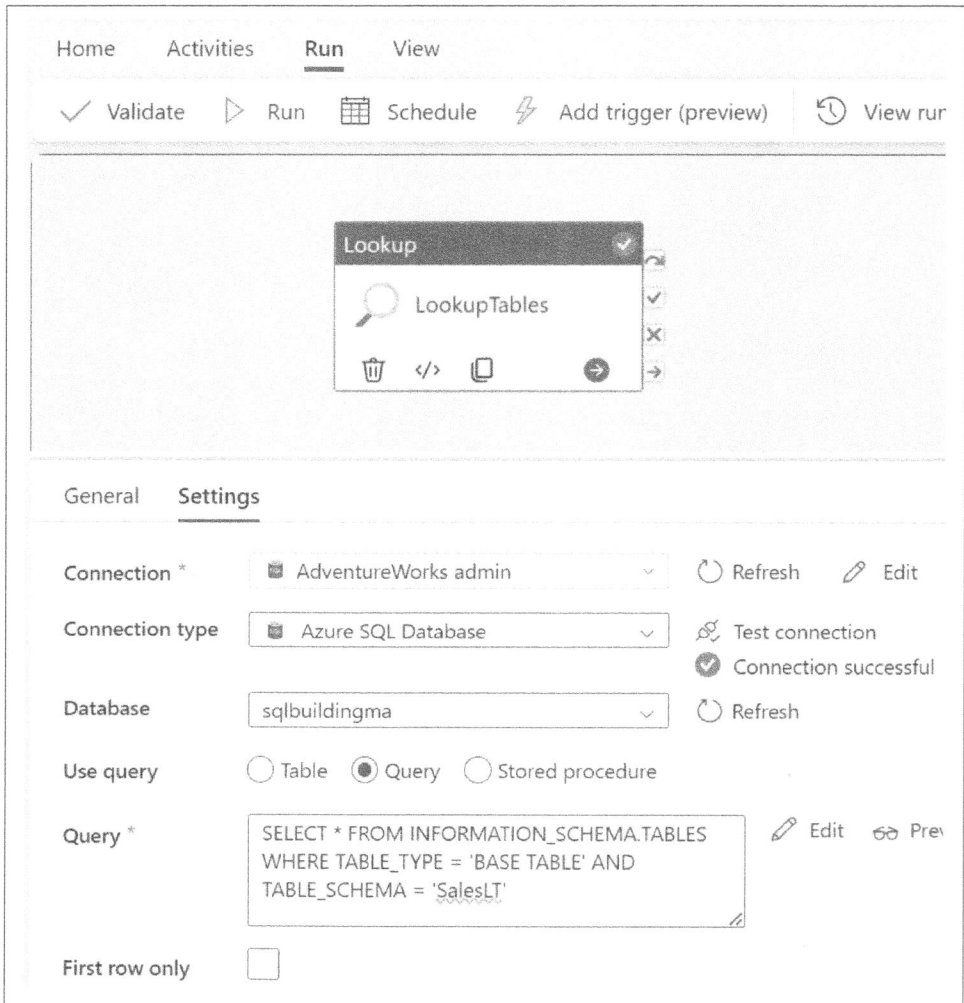

Figure 5-3. Query used for retrieving only the relevant schema information

Building the ForEach loop

A ForEach activity is a control flow activity that iterates over a collection of items and executes an operation for each item in the collection in a specific order. This activity is commonly used in data engineering projects to perform a set of (repetitive) operations on a group of files or tables. In your case, the ForEach activity will be used to iterate over the system object's information returned from the AdventureWorks example database. You will use this information to copy the tables to the Bronze Lakehouse.

To iterate over the system object's information returned from the AdventureWorks example database, add the following information to the Items option within the ForEach activity:[2]

```
@activity('LookupTables').output.value
```

This configuration allows the ForEach activity to extract schema and table names from the query output results from the Lookup activity. The ForEach activity then uses the output as arguments within the loop. When configuring the ForEach activity, ensure that the input name precisely matches the name from the previous activity. For example, if you reference the example from Figure 5-4, the input must link directly to the LookupTables job.

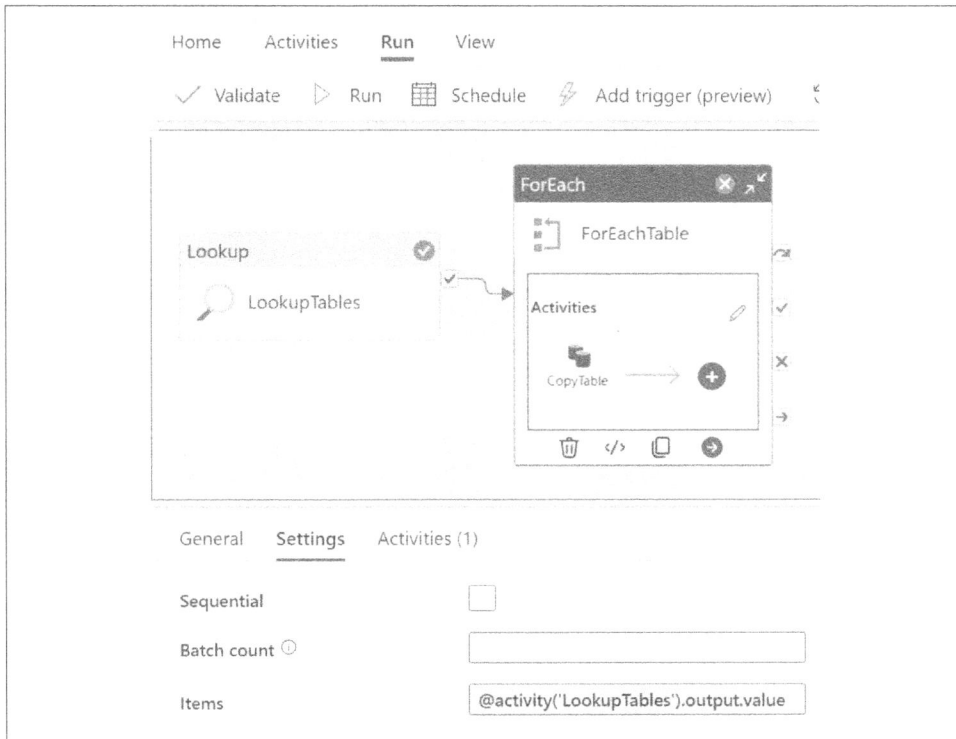

Figure 5-4. Iterating over all tables using a ForEach activity

With the ForEach activity configured, it's time to integrate the CopyTable activity.

---

2 You can also perform looping activities by running Spark notebooks from another notebook. This approach can be more efficient and easier to maintain. For more information, visit "High Concurrency Mode in Apache Spark for Fabric" (https://oreil.ly/uCRIv).

Configuring the CopyTable activity

Open the ForEach loop and drag in a CopyTable activity. This activity facilitates the copying of data from a source to a destination. In this case, it will be used to copy tables from the AdventureWorks sample database to the Bronze Lakehouse. To configure the CopyTable activity, you'll need to configure the Source and Destination properties (see Figure 5-5).

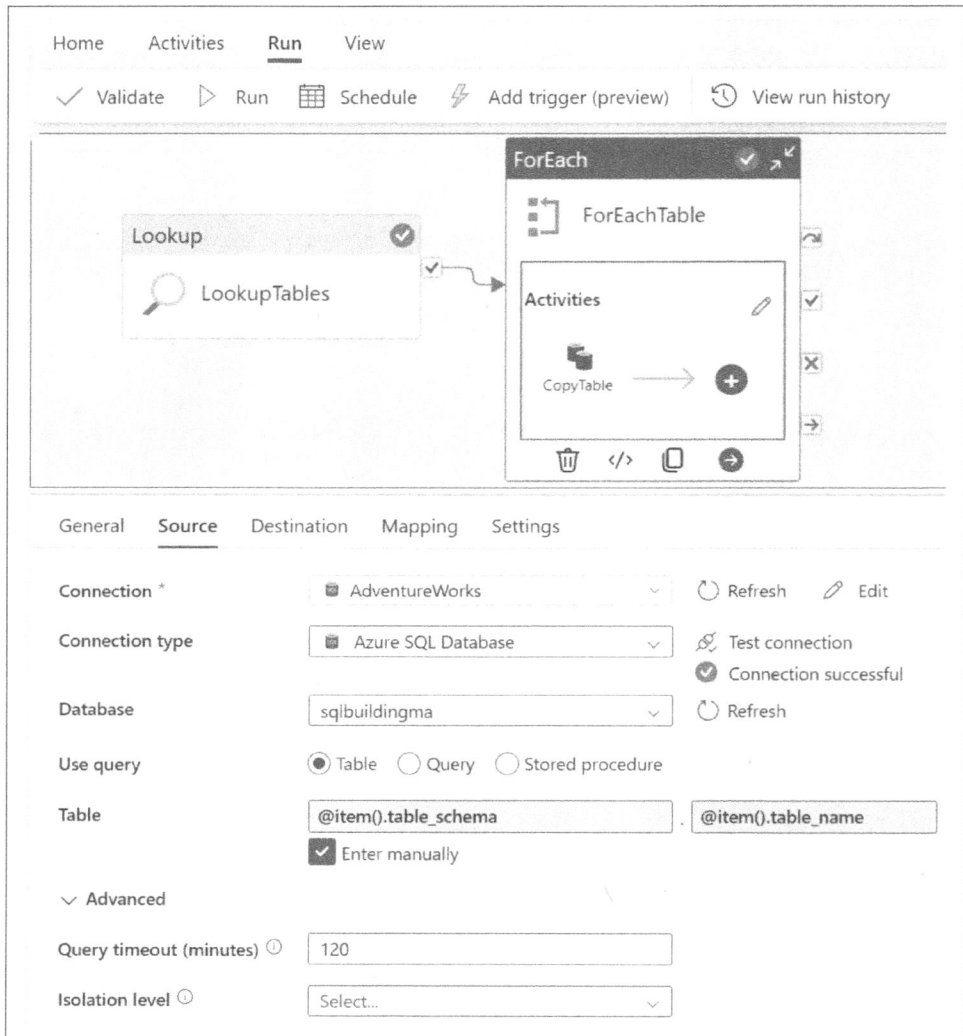

Figure 5-5. Details of the Source properties for the CopyTable activity

For the Source properties, the AdventureWorks Connection must be selected along with the corresponding database. Ensure that both the TableName and SchemaName are specified as input parameters. These item values are connected to the metadata that was retrieved in the Lookup activity.

```
@item().table_name
@item().table_schema
```

Next, head over to the Destination properties. For the Connection, select the Bronze Lakehouse. In the filepath dialog, add the following two properties:

```
@concat('adventureworks/', formatDateTime(utcnow(), 'yyyyMMdd'))
@concat(item().table_name,'.parquet')
```

Figure 5-6 shows the details on configuring this Destination.

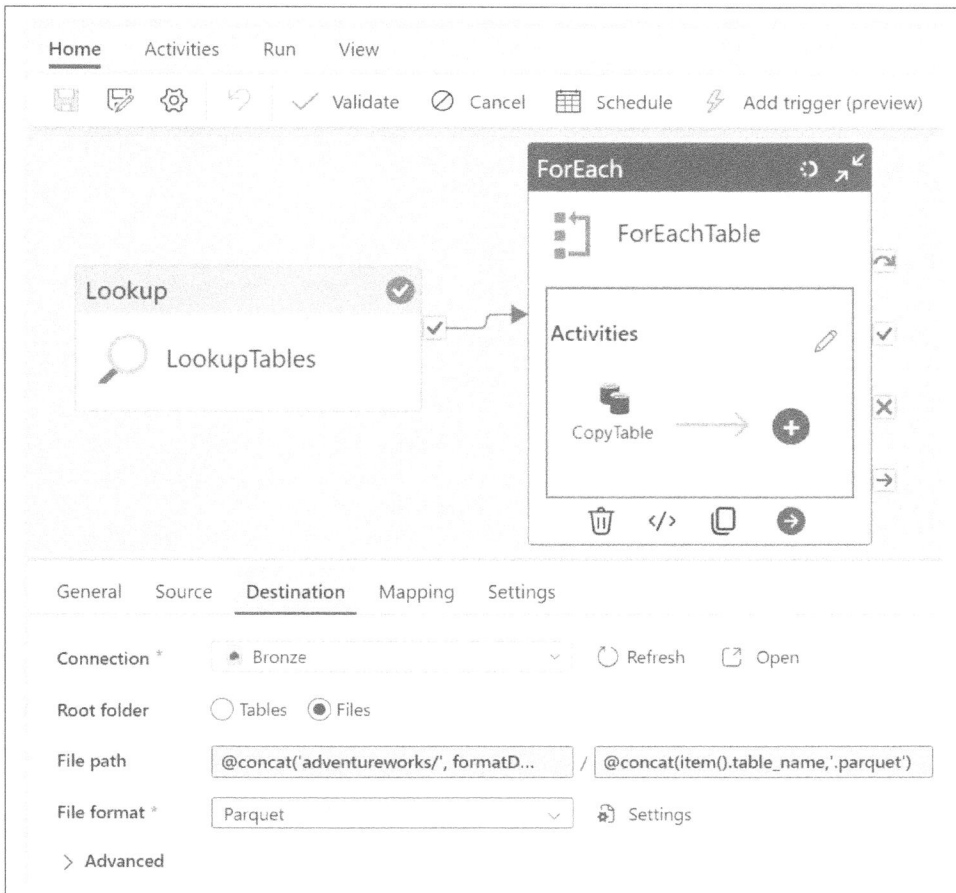

Figure 5-6. Details of the Destination properties for the CopyTable activity

If everything is configured correctly, you should be able to locate the Run button (*https://oreil.ly/SYMjT*) in the toolbar to trigger the pipeline and monitor the process. When things work as expected, a folder should appear within the Bronze container. The folder, illustrated in Figure 5-7, should have today's date.

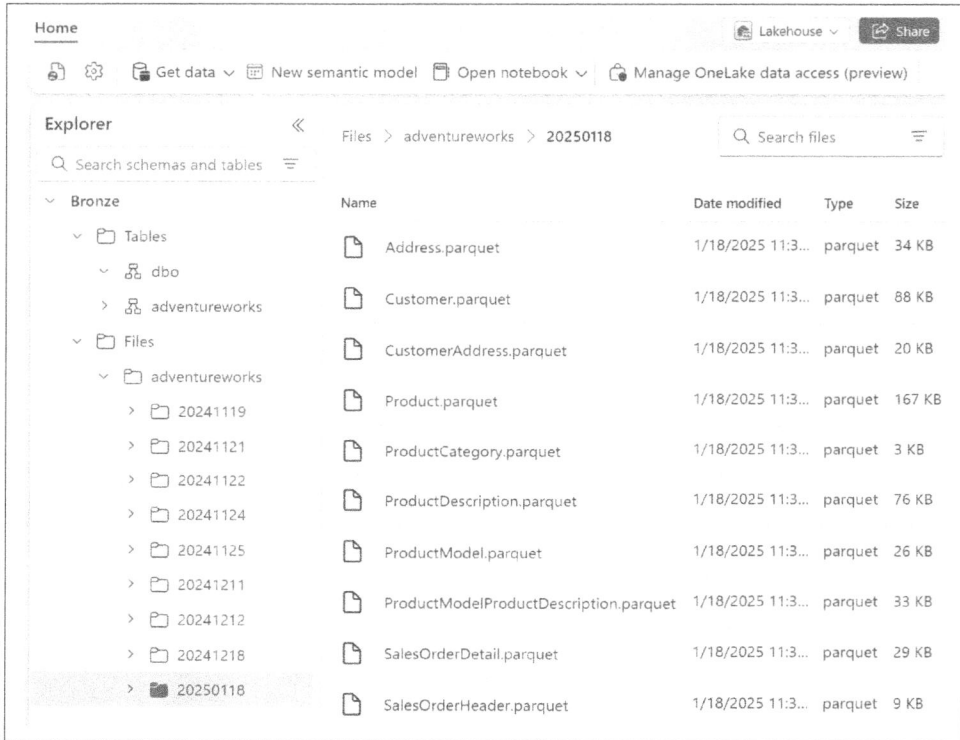

Figure 5-7. Overview of files stored in the Bronze layer

With this configuration, the AdventureWorks data will be stored and partitioned in the Bronze Lakehouse using the following format: *Files/adventureworks/ YYYYMMDD/TableName.parquet*. This method offers the advantage of archiving all data within a daily time window, ensuring a structured and time-based data storage approach. By systematically historizing the data, a well-prepared input is created for Spark processing jobs. This approach also supports auditing requirements and provides a historical record for data recovery in case of errors.

With these last steps completed successfully, you've set up the necessary resources and configuration to create a new data pipeline. You have also onboarded your first data source into your Bronze layer using Data Factory. Before we continue with a discussion of ingestion patterns, let's review the key takeaways from building the data pipeline.

Additional Considerations

Understanding that data extraction and ingestion methods can greatly vary depending on the source system is crucial. In the experience of the tutorial, the process was straightforward as you had direct access to the source without any complex network requirements. However, in other scenarios, data collection approaches can differ significantly.

For instance, data might initially arrive in a temporary storage area, or it could be in a format requiring a technical transformation. Sometimes, accessing the data may involve additional steps like deploying integration runtime services or using a virtual private network (VPN). In other cases, specialized tools such as Azure Functions (*https://oreil.ly/wGFO2*) may be necessary to retrieve data from an API endpoint.

The primary lesson here is that the specifics of the data ingestion process heavily depend on the characteristics of the source system and the nature of the data you need to handle. Understanding these factors is essential for designing an effective data ingestion strategy. There is no silver bullet solution; each scenario requires a tailored and unique approach.

The implementation and management of the Bronze layer vary widely between organizations. This variance depends on flexibility needs, the nature of the data sources, and specific organizational requirements. These factors result in different approaches to the implementation of tables and schema management. These factors will be taken into account moving forward:

Date partitioning scheme structure
> Switching from a flat YYYYMMDD partitioning scheme to a hierarchical YYYY/MM/DD structure offers improvements in data management and query performance. It enables precise partition pruning, reduces the overhead of handling a large number of files in a single directory, and simplifies operations like data deletion and archiving by organizing data into manageable chunks.

Logging and metrics
> When you ingest data, it is crucial to monitor the process for both auditing and troubleshooting purposes. A practical method to achieve this is by logging metrics for each dataset processed in the Bronze layer. For example, with Data Factory, you can access metrics from the `.output.runStatus.metrics` property, recording details such as rows read, rows written, and sink processing time.
>
> Alternatively, when working with streaming or real-time data, the QueryProgress metrics in Apache Spark Structured Streaming provide comprehensive insights into the execution of your streaming queries. These metrics include vital information such as input and processed rows per second, batch duration, and sink commit latency. Utilizing these metrics helps in understanding and optimizing the performance of your streaming pipeline.

Additionally, implementing postprocessing jobs that verify row counts and totals against the source data and across all layers of the Medallion architecture is beneficial. These checks help in identifying any inconsistencies or errors in the data. It is advisable to perform these verification jobs after each incremental update to ensure data integrity.

Implementing a logging framework
The current setup lacks extensive logging, which ties back to the monitoring discussed in the previous item. To scale and enhance your data processing robustness, I recommend implementing a logging framework. This framework should capture essential information for monitoring and troubleshooting. You can develop it using services like Azure Monitor (*https://oreil.ly/ndUub*) or Azure Log Analytics (*https://oreil.ly/CH-c3*), or you can develop a customized solution using, for example, Azure SQL.

Setting up automatic triggers
Orchestration of the data pipelines can be improved with certain functions, for example, those that automatically trigger the data ingestion pipelines when new data arrives. For a practical example, see "Create a Trigger that Runs a Pipeline in Response to a Storage Event" (*https://oreil.ly/ZV-SZ*).

Create shared libraries
Shared libraries with good documentation and tests can greatly improve the efficiency of data teams working across the enterprise. To enhance scalability, I recommend developing repeatable scripts for technical file format transformations, de-nesting complex structures, and append operations. These scripts can be reused across various pipelines, saving time and effort. Additionally, host these scripts in a shared code repository.

Create metadata-informed universal pipelines
Instead of creating separate pipelines for each type of data, you can use a metadata-driven framework to configure universal pipelines that adjust automatically based on the provided metadata. This approach significantly reduces the need for writing and maintaining extensive code. You'll see a concrete example about this in Chapter 6.

Parameterize a linked service to accept dynamic values at runtime
You can parameterize a linked service to accept dynamic values at runtime. For instance, to connect to different databases on the same logical SQL server, you can parameterize the database name in the linked service definition. For more details, see "Metadata-Driven Approach" on page 142 and "Parameterize Linked Services in Azure Data Factory and Azure Synapse Analytics" (*https://oreil.ly/osBjY*).

Take advantage of Data Factory templates

Templates that come with Data Factory provide predefined pipelines that help you quickly start using Data Factory. There is more information on GitHub (*https://oreil.ly/vJjTP*).

Deploy an integration runtime to address specific network requirements

Network requirements may complicate your setup. For instance, if you need to access on-premises data sources or services within other virtual networks, you might need to deploy an integration runtime into a virtual network. For more details, visit "Data Factory Integration Runtime" (*https://oreil.ly/9nYs1*).

Address data security concerns

Data security concerns, especially when handling PII or other sensitive data, can complicate the data ingestion process. You might need to filter out sensitive data or apply encryption or dynamic data masking. For more information, visit "PII Detection and Masking" (*https://oreil.ly/eUIjh*).

Consider redesign to address performance issues

Performance issues may necessitate a redesign of data ingestion strategies. Consider using options like "Parallel Copy" in Data Factory's CopyActivity to increase throughput or adopting incremental loading and delta processing approaches instead of full data extractions.

You've successfully set up the necessary configurations in the data pipeline and have imported raw Parquet files into the Bronze Lakehouse entity. However, the work isn't finished yet. The next important step is to make this data more accessible and ready for broader processing. We'll continue the chapter by setting up real Lakehouse tables. Following that, we'll tackle schema management.

Implementation of Lakehouse Tables

Up to this point, data has been captured using Parquet files. However, the Bronze layer is more than just a storage space for files; it plays a critical role in making data uniform and easily accessible. Therefore, the next steps will involve more data processing to make the data queryable and accessible for further use.

In the sections that follow, we'll explore various patterns for data ingestion, transformation, and table creation. Fully understanding these patterns will aid in designing a data ingestion strategy tailored to your specific needs and goals. Keep in mind that the main function of the Bronze layer is to ingest data in its raw, untransformed state, creating a queryable layer that facilitates exploration and ad hoc analysis, and serves as a foundational source for further data processing.

We'll begin by learning how to read data and directly output it to Delta tables. We then examine the use of external tables for other Spark-based services. Then, we explore real-time data ingestion techniques, such as Spark Structured Streaming and CDC, which facilitate faster updates to the Bronze layer. By the end of this section, you will have gained a solid understanding of the different patterns used to make data queryable and the implications of each approach.

Traverse Parquet Files to Managed Delta Tables

Until now, we've focused on setting up a batch process, which involves processing large volumes of data all at once instead of handling data records individually or continuously. We used Data Factory to transfer tables from the AdventureWorks sample database and saved them in the Parquet file format. This step alone does not make the data ready for querying and analysis. To make the data directly queryable in the new environment, we'll create Delta tables.

Creating Delta tables ensures ACID compliance, which guarantees data integrity and reliability during concurrent read and write operations. Delta tables also support advanced features like time travel and efficient upserts and deletes, making data management more robust and flexible.

To create Delta tables in Microsoft Fabric, and similarly in Azure Databricks, we need to create a script we can call from the data pipeline. Head back to the Workspace using the navigation pane on the left side of your screen and return to the data pipeline you created for the last part of the tutorial. Then, open the ForEach activity and integrate a new Notebook activity by dragging this activity type into the workflow. After this, update the Notebook activity settings by using the following configuration details for the "Base parameters" section:

schemaName
> Set this to adventureworks.

tableName
> Set this to @item().table_name to dynamically pass the table name.

filePath
> Use @formatDateTime(utcnow(), 'yyyyMMdd') to generate a filepath that includes the current date. This helps in organizing or partitioning the data by date.

For more details on configuring the Notebook activity, refer to Figure 5-8.

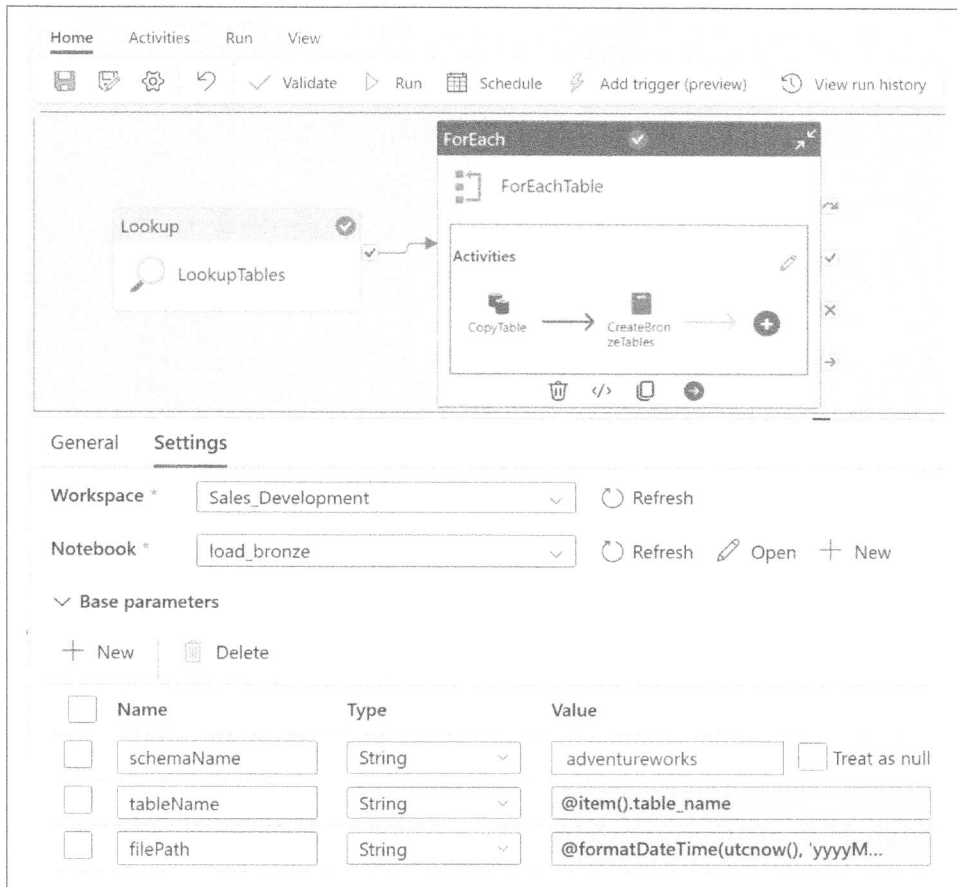

Figure 5-8. Configuration details of the Notebook activity

Next, move to the Workspace and create a new notebook, which will house the script for creating Delta tables. This script will perform the following tasks in the order listed here:

1. Retrieves parameters (`schemaName`, `tableName`, and `filePath`) from Data Factory parameters.

2. Creates a Lakehouse schema, if it does not already exist, using the specified `schemaName`.

3. Drops any existing table.

4. Reads data from the Parquet file and loads it into a DataFrame.

5. Adds a column, `loading_date`, to each dataset in the Bronze layer to record the current date and time when the data is ingested. This timestamp facilitates

change tracking and auditing and is essential for implementing features like SCD2, where precise timekeeping of record changes or additions is crucial for maintaining accurate record versions. For this example, we're adding only one column. In a real-world scenario, you would include additional metadata columns such as `source_system`, `lineage_id`, and others.

6. Finally, this script writes the contents of the DataFrame to a Delta table using the parameters passed in by Data Factory. The `mode("overwrite")` option ensures that if the table already exists, it will be overwritten with the new data.

> In this section, we explore the approach of dropping tables and overwriting them with fresh data, a method particularly suited for handling full data deliveries. While this ensures a clean slate by removing outdated information, it is not applicable for delta deliveries, which involve only incremental updates. See "Create Tables Without Defining Schemas" on page 136 for an alternative method tailored for delta deliveries or accumulating data.

Your new notebook will open a few seconds after you create it, displaying a single cell. Notebooks are made up of one or more cells that can contain code or Markdown (formatted text). When the notebook opens, rename it `load_bronze` (*https://oreil.ly/ CXdAB*) by selecting the Notebook text at the top left of the notebook and entering the new name. Make sure to select the Bronze Lakehouse from the menu on the left to confirm you are in the right environment.

> All the code and scripts are hosted on GitHub (*https://github.com/ pietheinstrengholt/building-medallion-architectures-book*).

Next, paste the following code into the cell:

```
# Infer base parameters from the pipeline context
schemaName = ""
tableName = ""
filePath = ""
```

After the code has been copy-pasted, toggle the "Toggle parameter cell" using the three dots at the top right of the cell. This step is required and allows the parameters (*https://oreil.ly/PZ-BQ*) to be set in the cell. After that, create a new code block by clicking the "+" icon at the bottom of the cell. In this new code block, paste the following code:[3]

```python
# Import functions
from pyspark.sql.functions import current_date

# Create schema
spark.sql(f'CREATE SCHEMA IF NOT EXISTS {schemaName}')

# Drop table
spark.sql(f'DROP TABLE IF EXISTS {schemaName}.{tableName}')

# Read data
df = spark.read.parquet(f"Files/{schemaName}/{filePath}/{tableName}.parquet")

# Add metadata loading_date column using current date
df = df.withColumn("loading_date", current_date().cast("string"))

# Overwrite table
df.write.mode("Overwrite").saveAsTable(f"{schemaName}.{tableName}")
```

Once the notebook has been prepared, return to the Data Factory pipeline and run the pipeline again. If all configurations are correct, the new table names should be listed under the adventureworks database within the Bronze Lakehouse. For an example, see Figure 5-9.

By creating Delta tables in the Bronze layer, you've taken a significant step toward making the data queryable and analysis-ready. For instance, you can now easily query the data using SQL commands or visualize data using services such as Power BI. Furthermore, Delta tables provide a robust and reliable foundation for data processing, ensuring data integrity and enabling advanced features like time travel and efficient upserts and deletes. With the data now stored in the Delta table format, the next tasks of designing the Silver layer can be efficiently approached.

With the Delta tables in place, the tutorial for the Bronze layer is complete. However, other approaches are worth considering. For instance, there are scenarios where it is necessary to work with external tables, particularly when dealing with large datasets that need to be queried without being loaded into a managed environment. We'll explore these approaches in the upcoming sections.

---

3 In this code snippet, tables are being dropped, with the understanding that there is a fallback in the Parquet files. If this is not the case, dropping any existing table can have severe consequences. An alternative approach is to use the createIfNotExists method, which creates a table if it doesn't exist but doesn't overwrite it if it does.

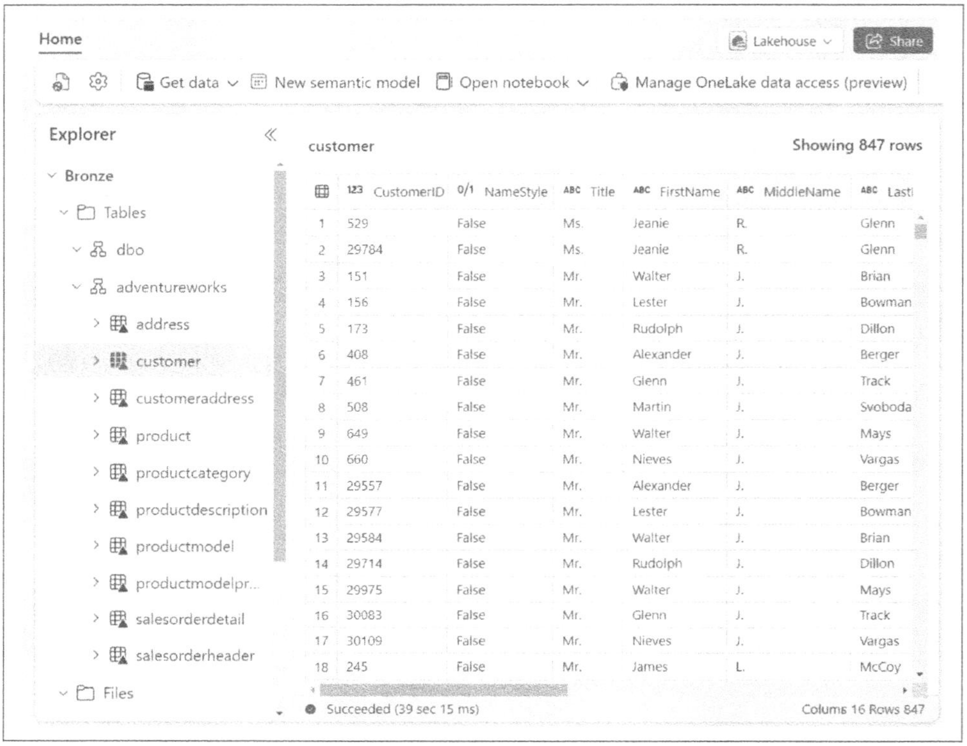

Figure 5-9. Overview of the Delta tables in the Bronze layer

Using External Tables

We touched on external tables earlier in Chapter 1. These tables let you query data stored outside the managed environment, like data that resides in external storage systems like the HDFS or ADLS.

While Microsoft Fabric doesn't support creating external tables on schema-enabled Lakehouse entities at the time of writing,[4] you can do this on many other Spark-based platforms. For instance, in Azure Databricks, you can use the `CREATE TABLE` statement with the `LOCATION` clause to set up an external table. Simply specify the table location as the path to the Parquet files in ADLS. The script will begin by fetching parameters passed from Azure Data Factory using a Databricks Notebook Activity (*https://oreil.ly/iA6s6*). It will proceed to create a new schema, ensuring any pre-existing table with the same name is dropped.

---

4 If you're setting up external tables in Lakehouse entities without an enabled schema, check out Aitor Murguzur's insightful blog (*https://oreil.ly/CVteO*).

Here's how you can create an external table using a Python script (*https://oreil.ly/AZLJ6*):

```
# Fetch parameters from Data Factory
schemaName=dbutils.widgets.get("schemaName")
tableName=dbutils.widgets.get("tableName")
filePath=dbutils.widgets.get("filePath")

# Create database
spark.sql(f'CREATE SCHEMA IF NOT EXISTS bronze_{schemaName}')

# Drop table
spark.sql(f'DROP TABLE IF EXISTS bronze_{schemaName}.{tableName}')

# Create new external table using latest datetime location
ddl_query = f"""
  CREATE TABLE bronze_{schemaName}.{tableName}
  USING PARQUET
  LOCATION '/mnt/bronze/
  {schemaName}/{filePath}/{tableName}.parquet'
"""

# Execute query
spark.sql(ddl_query)
```

Using external tables is simple and straightforward; it does not require data duplication. However, you must keep several considerations in mind:

- Reading from external Parquet tables is generally slower than reading from Delta tables. This performance lag can be attributed to factors like suboptimal partitioning, which affects how data is accessed and processed.

- Unlike managed Delta tables, external Parquet tables lack support for advanced features such as schema enforcement and time travel, which can enhance data management and analytics.

The approach of using external tables is a simple and straightforward way to set up your data pipeline. It isn't wrong and might work well for your specific requirements. However, it is not the most optimized method. In the next section, we explore how to read and output data in a more efficient manner.

Updating Tables with MERGE Operations

In all the previous examples, we examined either using external tables or cloning data. However, processing incremental loads is necessary in scenarios where only changes (updates and new entries) need to be addressed using complex filters. In such cases, merge operations prove to be instrumental.

Delta Lake supports MERGE operations, which enable the merging of new data into existing tables. This feature is particularly beneficial for updating or upserting data in tables. Here is an example script of how to use MERGE in SQL (*https://oreil.ly/mBlLe*):

```
MERGE INTO Bronze_Customer AS t
USING Landing_Customer AS s
ON t.CustomerID = s.CustomerID
WHEN MATCHED THEN
    UPDATE SET
        t.Name = s.Name,
        t.ContactDetails = s.ContactDetails,
        t.PurchaseHistory = s.PurchaseHistory
WHEN NOT MATCHED THEN
    INSERT (CustomerID, Name, ContactDetails, PurchaseHistory)
    VALUES (s.CustomerID, s.Name, s.ContactDetails, s.PurchaseHistory);
```

The merge operation gives you a lot of flexibility; it supports various conditions, such as WHEN MATCHED, WHEN NOT MATCHED, WHEN MATCHED AND, WHEN NOT MATCHED BY TARGET, and WHEN NOT MATCHED BY SOURCE. These conditions allow you to define specific actions based on the matching criteria, providing a powerful tool for managing incremental data loads.

You can execute the same code in a Python script using the DeltaTable API (*https://oreil.ly/kpqCv*), offering the advantage of parameterizing the code with arguments.

```
from delta.tables import *

dTable = DeltaTable.forPath(spark, \
f"abfss://{workspaceId}@onelake.dfs.fabric.microsoft.com/ \
{lakehouseId}/Tables/{schemaName}/{tableName}")

(dTable.alias("original")
 .merge(df.alias("updates"), f"original.{primaryKey} = updates.{primaryKey}")
 .whenMatchedUpdateAll()
 .whenNotMatchedInsertAll()
 .execute()
)
```

Merge operations provide the advantage of handling data more efficiently. However, complexities can arise when the source data is not clean or when the join conditions are not straightforward. In such situations, additional data cleansing or transformation steps might be necessary to ensure the merge operation executes correctly. For example, if the dataset includes duplicate entries, it might be essential to deduplicate the data before performing the merge operation. Because of this, complex merge operations are often performed in the next layers of the Medallion architecture. I connect back to this with concrete examples in Chapters 6 and 7.

Now that we've explored various batch-oriented methods of data processing, let's transition to Spark Structured Streaming: a universal solution for streaming data ingestion.

Spark Structured Streaming

Stream processing is a technique that involves consuming messages from queues or files, performing some processing (such as querying, filtering, and aggregation), and then forwarding the results to a sink (target destination) with minimal latency. It's different from batch or microbatch processing,[5] which typically occurs on a periodic basis.

When considering solutions for real-time stream processing, Spark Structured Streaming is a strong option to take into account, particularly because of its versatility and seamless integration with any Spark-based platform. As explored in Chapter 3, Spark Structured Streaming is particularly useful for scenarios that require low-latency responses, as it can process data in real time. For example, Spark Structured Streaming can be used to process data from IoT devices, edge devices, or other real-time data sources, such as financial transactions or machine logs.

Consider the practical application of building a real-time monitoring system for a fleet of airplanes. In such a scenario, Azure Event Hubs can be used to ingest data from various sensors and devices on each airplane and then process this data in real time using Spark Structured Streaming. This can be accomplished using programming languages such as C#, Java, Python, or Node.js. An example of such an architecture can be seen in Figure 5-10.

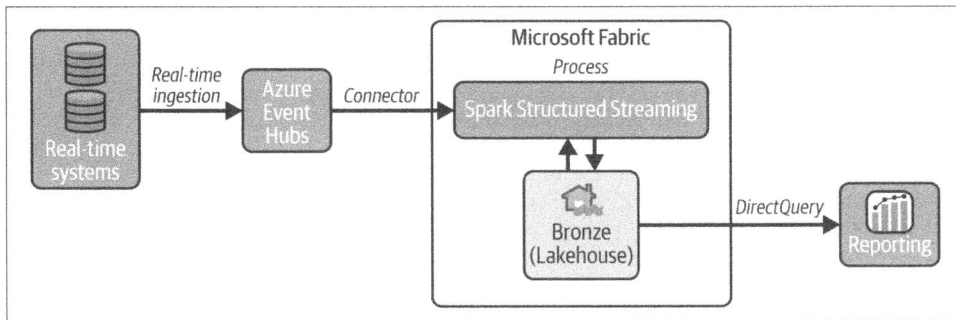

Figure 5-10. Architecture showing Event Hubs ingesting data using Spark Structured Streaming

One of the advantages of Spark Structured Streaming is its support for complex event processing, which enables handling intricate queries and joining streams with static data or other streams. This feature is crucial for applications that require advanced analytics, such as recommendations or user activity tracking. For example, building

---

5 The `foreachBatch` operation (*https://oreil.ly/ttjm3*) in Apache Spark is used primarily with Structured Streaming to apply processing logic on each microbatch of a stream.

on the earlier illustration of a real-time monitoring system for a fleet of airplanes, Spark Structured Streaming could be expertly used by Oceanic Airlines to monitor their aircraft fleet in real time. In the event of an unexpected situation such as severe weather, the event stream can instantly alert the relevant parties. This capability enables quick decision making to reroute the aircraft or implement necessary measures to ensure safety. Spark Structured Streaming can be enhanced by integrating it with Azure Event Hubs, as discussed in the next section.

Example with Azure Event Hubs

To set up Spark Structured Streaming in Spark in combination with Azure Event Hubs (*https://oreil.ly/WUo2f*), use the following code snippet (*https://oreil.ly/eUWVD*):

```
# Library that allows to stream content from Azure Event Hubs
%pip install azure-eventhub

ehConf = {}

# Azure Event Hubs connection configuration
connectionString = "Endpoint=sb://{NAMESPACE}.servicebus.windows.net/ \
{EVENT_HUB_NAME};EntityPath={EVENT_HUB_NAME}; \
SharedAccessKeyName={ACCESS_KEY_NAME}; \
SharedAccessKey={ACCESS_KEY}"

# For 2.3.15 version and above, the configuration dictionary
# requires that connection string be encrypted.
ehConf['eventhubs.connectionString'] = sc._jvm.org.apache.spark.eventhubs \
.EventHubsUtils.encrypt(connectionString)

# Streaming data from Azure Event Hubs
df = spark \
  .readStream \
  .format("eventhubs") \
  .options(**ehConf) \
  .load()

# Writing stream: Persist the streaming data to a Delta table
df.writeStream \
  .option("checkpointLocation","abfss://<abfss_location>") \
  .outputMode("append") \
  .format("delta") \
  .toTable("bronze.weather")
```

The process begins by installing the necessary library for streaming content from Azure Event Hubs. The connection configuration is then set up, including the connection string, which is encrypted for security purposes. Next, the data is streamed from Event Hubs into a DataFrame, which can be written to a Delta table in the Bronze layer. The checkpoint location is specified to store the metadata of the streaming query, ensuring fault tolerance and enabling the query to be restarted in case of a failure.

In addition to writing the streaming data to the Bronze layer, the DataFrame can also be further processed using Spark Structured Streaming. This framework enables the filtering, cleansing, and transformation of data. The refined output can then also immediately be stored in the Silver layer, where it becomes available for more complex analysis and reporting. This step significantly improves the quality and accessibility of the data for downstream processes. We revisit this topic in Chapter 6.

While the focus of this section has been on processing and transforming data using Spark Structured Streaming, it's important to consider how data initially enters the system. This brings us to the concept of using CDC, which plays a crucial role in capturing changes from various data sources before they are processed. While both methods enhance data handling, CDC specifically focuses on the initial capture of data changes, setting the stage for subsequent processing and analysis.

Using Change Data Capture

CDC is used to track changes in a database. It captures changes made to the data, such as inserts, updates, and deletes, and stores them in a separate table. CDC is particularly useful for real-time data replication. It allows you to keep track of changes in your data, enabling you to maintain an accurate and up-to-date view of your data.

For example, Microsoft Fabric supports CDC through the use of *mirroring*. With this feature, databases, such as the AdventureWorks example, can be directly replicated into Fabric's OneLake (see "Tutorial: Configure Microsoft Fabric Mirrored Databases from Azure SQL Database" (*https://oreil.ly/XIxBI*)).

> In addition to the CDC mechanisms discussed, incorporating change data feed, particularly in lakehouse architectures using Delta Lake and Spark, can significantly enhance the efficiency of data replication. This method allows for more granular tracking of data changes—including inserts, updates, and deletes—by offering a streamlined and scalable approach to accessing change records.

CDC is a powerful tool, but it can also be complex to use. It requires careful implementation and primary keys for the mirroring process. Additionally, when there is a schema change, a complete data snapshot is restarted for the changed table, and all data is reseeded. Furthermore, not all column types are always supported, so you need to ensure that the data types are compatible between the source and target tables. Lastly, you are tightly coupled to the real-time source database structures, which often implies an additional layer for archiving and implementing lightweight transformations, such as adding metadata.

Navigating Data Handling Techniques

We have explored a variety of data handling techniques that significantly enhance the way we manage and process information. We began with traversing from Parquet files to managed Delta tables, which offer enhanced performance and the ability to time travel through data versions. We also covered employing external tables for immediate data exposure. We delved into the efficiency of updating tables with MERGE operations, crucial for when you need to process only the necessary changes, such as updates and new entries. Spark Structured Streaming was highlighted for performing real-time data transformations, while CDC exemplifies the zero-ETL pattern by mirroring or capturing database changes in real time.

Each of these patterns plays a pivotal role in modern data architecture. As you consider these techniques, it is important to weigh each pattern based on the specific scenario at hand and the complexities involved in data acquisition. Often, a blend of these approaches will coexist, tailored to meet the unique demands of your architecture.

Having explored various data handling techniques and their considerations, it's crucial to address another foundational aspect: schema management. Understanding and studying schema management strategies is crucial, as they form the foundation for the hands-on activities that follow later in Chapter 6.

Schema Management

As "Schema Evolution and Management" on page 56 highlighted, managing schema evolution is crucial, especially in the Bronze layer, which serves as the initial repository for raw data stored in its original form. Think of schemas as blueprints that detail your data's structure, specifying data types and the relationships among different data elements.

When it comes to managing schemas, you have several approaches to choose from, each with its own pros and cons. We'll start by studying the simplest and most flexible method and then move on to more structured and strict approaches.

Create Tables Without Defining Schemas

One of the simplest methods to generate tables in a lakehouse involves not defining any schemas, thereby allowing Delta Lake to manage the schema evolution. For instance, consider a scenario where the desire is to avoid recreating tables every time a pipeline runs, akin to the prior example. Instead, the objective is to append and accumulate data, enabling Delta Lake's schema evolution features to handle varying data structures as they are ingested over time. Additionally, the decision might be made to partition the data by loading date to enhance performance. In such a case, you can use the following code snippet (*https://oreil.ly/RAgff*):

```
from delta.tables import *
from pyspark.sql.functions import current_date

# Delete any existing data
if (DeltaTable.isDeltaTable(spark, f"{schemaName}.{tableName}")):
    spark.sql(f"DELETE FROM {schemaName}.{tableName} \
    WHERE loading_date = current_date()")

# Read data
df = spark.read.parquet(f"Files/{schemaName}/{filePath}/{tableName}.parquet")

# Add a loading date column to the DataFrame
df = df.withColumn("loading_date", current_date())

# Write the data to the Delta table with schema merge
df.write.format("delta") \
    .mode("append") \
    .partitionBy("loading_date") \
    .option("mergeSchema", "true") \
    .saveAsTable(f"{schemaName}.{tableName}")
```

In this example, Delta Lake will merge the schema of the new data with the existing schema of the Delta table. By including the mergeSchema option in this operation, Delta Lake manages the schema evolution. This means that any columns that are present in the DataFrame but not in the target table are automatically added on to the end of the schema as part of a write transaction. Note that in this example, I've reused the variable names like schemaName, tableName, and filePath to represent the schema, table name, and filepath, respectively. For Microsoft Fabric, and similarly in Azure Databricks, you can replace these with your own values.

This approach of accumulating data is simple and flexible. It allows you to append new data to existing tables without defining schemas. This flexibility is particularly beneficial when you aim to incrementally stack data without concern for schema modifications. For example, this is advantageous in scenarios involving delta deliveries, where only the changes or differences in data are transferred.

This method can also introduce risks, such as compromised data quality and potential unforeseen changes in data formats. These variations can make you lose control over your data structures, making it harder to maintain compatibility with downstream applications. To counter these risks, it's essential to incorporate checks in the subsequent layer.

Let's consider a more structured approach. When data integrity and consistency are paramount, establishing a schema can prove highly advantageous.

Define Schemas with the DataFrame API

Defining schemas through the DataFrame API (*https://oreil.ly/S7Y-0*) is another way to manage schema definitions in a lakehouse. Here's a code example (*https://oreil.ly/jy-vn*) that will accomplish this:

```
from pyspark.sql.types import *

# Define the schema
schema = StructType([
    StructField("CustomerID", IntegerType(), True),
    StructField("NameStyle", BooleanType(), True),
    StructField("Title", StringType(), True),
    StructField("FirstName", StringType(), True)
])

# Read the raw JSON data and apply the schema
df = spark.read.schema(schema).json("/path/to/raw/data")

# Write the DataFrame to a Delta table
df.write.format("delta").saveAsTable("adventureworks.customer")
```

The DataFrame API approach is excellent for managing complex and nested data structures in Spark, especially with unstructured data. It can be used for a schema-on-read approach, where the query specifies the necessary schema, such as column names and data types, from the raw data upon loading into Spark (using Data-Frames). If the schema cannot be applied successfully, you can handle the situation by implementing error-handling logic in your code.

Now, let's shift focus to another method: using SQL data definition language statements, which can streamline the process of creating tables directly within your notebooks. This schema-on-write approach is complementary to the schema-on-read strategy, as it allows for the definition and enforcement of data structures at the point of writing the data.

SQL DDL Statements

The next option is to write data definition language (DDL) statements directly in Spark notebooks. This method is particularly useful when consistency and integrity are important.

The following SQL DDL statement creates a schema named adventureworks:[6]

---

6 The %%sql command in Spark-based environments is a magic command (*https://oreil.ly/O8nKy*) that allows users to run Spark SQL queries against their data stored in various data sources such as tables, views, and external databases. When executing %%sql commands, users can directly write Spark SQL code in the notebook and query their data without the need to create a DataFrame or register a temporary table.

```
CREATE SCHEMA adventureworks
```

And the following SQL DDL statement (*https://oreil.ly/ijBDm*) creates a table named customer within the adventureworks schema:

```
CREATE TABLE customer (
    CustomerID INT COMMENT 'Customer identifier',
    NameStyle BOOLEAN COMMENT 'Style of the name',
    Title STRING COMMENT 'Title of the customer',
    FirstName STRING COMMENT 'First name of the customer'
)
USING delta
```

Using DDL statements in Spark notebooks, as demonstrated, offers an efficient way to create tables, allowing for the rapid setup and management of database structures directly within the notebook environment. Additionally, since many other (relational) databases utilize SQL DDL statements, this approach is ideal for migration or schema replication scenarios or reusing any existing DDLs, ensuring compatibility and ease of integration across different platforms.

> In other Spark-based environments, specifying a location in the CREATE TABLE statement designates the table as an external table.

The DataFrame API and SQL DDL statements are powerful tools for customizing schemas, but their complexity can make managing intricate data structures challenging. You can address this by allowing an application to export its DDL as part of the build process or by using a schema-on-write approach combined with the merge Schema option. This latter method ensures strict data consistency at first while providing flexibility as your data requirements change. Another option is to manage schemas using separate configuration files. Let's explore how this works in the next section.

YAML or JSON Configurations

Using YAML (yet another markup language) or JSON configurations is another effective method for defining schemas. This technique excels when there is a need to store schema definitions in a separate file, which can then be reused across different notebooks or projects. YAML is particularly beneficial due to its human-readable format. Its simplicity and clarity make it ideal for configuration files and data exchanges, where readability is paramount.

Moreover, YAML is quite flexible, allowing the easy addition of extra metadata or comments. For instance, it is possible to include a PII flag for each column to indicate if it contains sensitive data. Another major advantage of using YAML or JSON is that these files can be version-controlled separately from the main codebase. This distinct separation enables teams to efficiently track and manage changes to the data schema over time.

Here's an example of what a schema definition might look like in a YAML format, within a file named *schema.yaml*:

```yaml
columns:
  - name: CustomerID
    type: integer
  - name: NameStyle
    type: boolean
  - name: Title
    type: string
  - name: FirstName
    type: string
    PII: true
```

To integrate YAML files into a notebook, the PyYAML package can be used. Here is a practical example demonstrating how to load a YAML file and use it to generate a PySpark schema from the data within. This code snippet (*https://oreil.ly/cLx7O*) contains two Python functions specifically crafted to work with PySpark and YAML for processing schemas detailed in a YAML file.

> Install the PyYAML package by running the command `pip install PyYAML` to follow along with this example.

The function `load_yaml_file` takes a filepath as input and reads the YAML file. It employs `yaml.safe_load()` to securely parse the YAML content into a Python dictionary. The function `generate_schema_from_yaml` then takes this parsed YAML data as input. It begins by extracting a list of columns from the data. Subsequently, it iterates over each column, verifies the data type, and adds a corresponding `StructField` to a `StructType` object based on the column's type (`integer`, `string`, `boolean`, `datetime`). Here's how these functions are structured:

```python
import yaml
from pyspark.sql.types import *

# Function to Load YAML File
def load_yaml_file(yaml_file_path):
    with open(yaml_file_path, 'r') as file:
        schema_yaml = yaml.safe_load(file)
    return schema_yaml

# Function to Generate PySpark Schema from YAML Data
def generate_schema_from_yaml(yaml_data):
```

```
columns = yaml_data['columns']
schema = StructType()

for column in columns:
    if column['type'] == 'integer':
        schema.add(StructField(column['name'], IntegerType(), True))
    elif column['type'] == 'string':
        schema.add(StructField(column['name'], StringType(), True))
    elif column['type'] == 'boolean':
        schema.add(StructField(column['name'], BooleanType(), True))
    elif column['type'] == 'datetime':
        schema.add(StructField(column['name'], Datetime(), True))

return schema
```

The schema generated from the YAML file can then be used to define the schema of a DataFrame. Here is an example of how to use the functions to load a YAML file and generate a PySpark schema:

```
# Load YAML File
schema_yaml = load_yaml_file('/path/to/schema/schema.yaml')
yaml_data = load_yaml_file(schema_yaml)
schema = generate_schema_from_yaml(yaml_data)

# Define DataFrame with Schema
df = spark.createDataFrame(data, schema=schema)
```

Using JSON or YAML configuration files is particularly beneficial when dealing with a large number of columns or complex schemas. These files allow you to define schemas in a structured and organized way, making them easier to manage and maintain. By specifying an explicit schema, you can ensure data consistency and integrity, giving you greater control over your data by enforcing an expected structure.

In this example, you used a simple schema with only a few columns, but you can easily extend this approach to more complex schemas with nested structures and additional metadata. You can also extend this approach to generate a SQL DDL statement from the YAML data before creating a table in a lakehouse. This can be useful when you want to include more complex data types or constraints in your schema definition.[7]

The only drawback of this approach is that JSON or YAML can become large and unwieldy for complex schemas. For example, if you have a schema with hundreds of columns or complex nested structures, the JSON or YAML file can quickly become

---

7 Apache Spark does not enforce primary key or foreign key constraints. It uses these keys primarily for informational purposes, such as in a data catalog. You need to manually validate and confirm key constraints before adding a primary or foreign key.

difficult to manage. In such cases, it may be more efficient to define the schema using a metadata-driven approach.

Metadata-Driven Approach

A metadata-driven approach is a more advanced method for defining schemas. This approach involves storing schema definitions in a centralized metadata repository, such as a database or data catalog. The metadata repository contains information about the structure of the data, including column names, data types, constraints, and relationships between different data elements. This metadata can be used to generate schema definitions dynamically at runtime, allowing you to adapt the schema to different data sources and destinations. In Chapter 6, I demonstrate how to implement a metadata-driven approach using an Azure SQL database.

> Jaco van Gelder has released a function that skillfully manages the addition of new columns to a database schema, making sure it doesn't duplicate or disrupt the existing column sequence. You can check out the function on his GitHub page: "Jaco's Schema Evolution Function" (*https://oreil.ly/SoWlA*).

Implementing a metadata-driven framework can be complex and time-consuming. As an alternative, let's transition into another powerful tool: Databricks Auto Loader. This technology uses Structured Streaming under the hood and offers features that enhance both batch and real-time data processing and integration. Although this is a Databricks-only feature, it could greatly simplify the process of managing schema evolution.

Databricks Auto Loader

Auto Loader (*https://oreil.ly/BLcPC*) is an exclusive Databricks feature that simplifies the process of ingesting data into existing tables.[8] Essentially, it operates as a Spark streaming mechanism with an added feature for batch-driven ingestion. As it discovers files, Auto Loader stores their metadata in a key-value store (RocksDB) located in the pipeline's checkpoint area. This storage method ensures that each piece of data is processed exactly once. Should a failure occur, Auto Loader can pick up where it left off using the information saved in the checkpoint location. This capability allows it to maintain exactly-once accuracy when writing data into Delta Lake, without requiring you to manage or maintain any state for fault tolerance or accuracy.

---

8 Auto Loader is specifically designed to function within the Databricks environment and does not operate on other platforms.

Auto Loader shines in the way it handles schema evolution. When Auto Loader processes new files, it automatically infers the schema from these files. As your incoming data evolves, Auto Loader seamlessly integrates new schema attributes found in incoming files with your existing schema. This automatic merging means you don't have to worry about mismatches between old and new data formats. Auto Loader keeps everything consistent and up-to-date, providing you with a reliable view of your data.

If you prefer not to have the schema evolve automatically, you can adjust the settings. For example, by setting `cloudFiles.schemaEvolutionMode` to `rescue`, Auto Loader won't automatically update the schema. Instead, it will add a `_rescued_data` column to your schema. The primary benefit of this `_rescue` column is its role in facilitating a flexible and resilient data management strategy. Storing unanticipated data allows data engineers and analysts to review the changes in data structure at their convenience. If the new data elements are deemed to be permanent, the information stored in the `_rescue` column can then be processed retrospectively. This ensures that valuable data isn't discarded and can be integrated into the main dataset, thereby enriching the data resources of the organization. Moreover, this approach minimizes the need for immediate modifications to the data ingestion pipelines, which can be both disruptive and resource-intensive.

Auto Loader is also flexible in terms of data formats. It supports a variety of data formats, including JSON, CSV, Parquet, Avro, ORC, TEXT, and binary. It is designed for incremental data ingestion from cloud object storage, but it can also be used to incrementally copy all data from a specified directory to a target table.

The following code snippet (*https://oreil.ly/WTqLI*) is designed for full data loads as part of the Oceanic Airlines project. If you plan on using Azure Databricks, feel free to use it as is or modify it to meet specific needs.

```
# Fetch parameters from Azure Data Factory
catalogName="prod_sales"
schemaName=dbutils.widgets.get("schemaName")
tableName=dbutils.widgets.get("tableName")
filePath=dbutils.widgets.get("filePath")

# Fetch schema data from landing zone
jsonSchema = spark.read.parquet(f"/Volumes/{catalogName}/sources/landing/\
{schemaName}/{filePath}/{tableName}.parquet").schema.json()
ddl = spark.sparkContext._jvm.org.apache.spark.sql.types.DataType \
  .fromJson(jsonSchema).toDDL()

# Migrate parquet data to delta files
(spark.readStream
  .format("cloudFiles")
  .option("cloudFiles.format", "parquet")
  .option("cloudFiles.includeExistingFiles", "true")
  .option("cloudFiles.backfillInterval", "1 day")
```

```
        .option("cloudFiles.schemaLocation", f"/Volumes/{catalogName}/sources/\
        landing/{schemaName}/_checkpoint/{tableName}_autoload/")
        .schema(ddl)
        .load(f"/Volumes/{catalogName}/sources/landing/\
        {schemaName}/{filePath}/{tableName}.parquet")
        .writeStream
        .format("delta")
        .option("checkpointLocation", f"/Volumes/{catalogName}/sources/landing/\
        {schemaName}/_checkpoint/{tableName}_autoload/")
        .trigger(availableNow=True) # Start immediately
        .toTable(f"bronze_{schemaName}.{tableName}")
    )
```

The process begins by retrieving the schema of the Parquet file from the landing location. This schema is then converted into DDL format, which is used to create a table in the target database. Utilizing Auto Loader, the Parquet data is migrated to this newly created table. The `backfillInterval` option is configured to `1 day`, enabling Auto Loader to backfill data from the previous day.

In the code snippet, you see both `.schema` and `.option("cloudFiles.schemaLocation")` together. This can be beneficial in scenarios where you want to enforce a specific schema while also managing schema evolution. Here's how they work in conjunction:

Schema enforcement

By setting the `.schema` option, you ensure that the data must conform to the specified schema. This can prevent errors during loading if incoming data has unexpected columns or data types that do not match the defined schema.

Schema evolution

This option specifies a location where the schema of the read files is stored and maintained. By setting the `.schema` option `.option("cloudFiles.schemaLocation")`, you allow Azure Databricks to handle changes in the schema over time. For example, if new columns are added to the incoming data, Azure Databricks can update the schema stored at the specified location, and subsequent reads will recognize these new columns. Furthermore, you can set the `cloudFiles.schemaEvolutionMode` option to the type of behavior you want to enforce, such as `addNewColumns`, `merge`, or `failOnNewColumns`.

Now that the capabilities of Databricks Auto Loader have been explored, let's quickly discuss some third-party tools that can simplify and expedite the process, and then move on to the final part of schema management: schema evolution best practices.

Third-Party Tools

Another option for defining schemas is to use third-party tools that provide a graphical interface for designing and managing schemas. These tools allow you to visually create and modify schema definitions, making it easier to work with complex data structures. Some popular tools in this category include SQLAlchemy (*https://sqlalchemy.org*), SqlDBM (*https://sqldbm.com*), erwin Data Modeler (*https://erwin.com*), and Hackolade (*https://hackolade.com*).

Third-party solutions offer a range of features for schema design, data integration, and data quality management, making them ideal for organizations with complex data requirements. However, it's important to consider potential drawbacks, such as extra costs, integration efforts, and the possibility of vendor lock-in, which could limit your flexibility in the future. These factors should be carefully evaluated to ensure that the chosen solution aligns with your organizational needs and long-term strategy.

Let's now move on to the final part of schema management: schema evolution best practices.

Handling Schema Evolution

Predefined tables offer several advantages over creating tables on the fly when writing data to Delta Lake. They provide greater control over the table schema and column types, improving data quality and reducing errors. Additionally, predefined tables enhance query performance by enabling efficient partitioning. For example, partitioning data based on the `Region` column allows for faster queries on large datasets and specific company names.

When managing schema evolution and making your architecture adaptive for change, consider the following best practices:

Plan meticulously
Before making any schema changes, plan carefully and keep detailed records of schema versions. This helps you track and understand the evolution of your data schema over time.

Test in a safe environment
Test schema changes in a development or testing environment before applying them to production. This step allows you to identify and resolve potential issues without disrupting live data.

Maintain backward compatibility
Ensure that schema changes are backward compatible to preserve data integrity. This prevents breaking existing queries and applications that rely on the current schema.

Have a rollback strategy

Develop a rollback strategy to revert to a previous schema if something goes wrong during the migration process. This minimizes disruptions and maintains data integrity.

Use schema migration tools

Consider using database schema migration tools like Atlas (*https://github.com/ariga/atlas*) and Liquibase (*https://liquibase.com*) to automate and manage schema changes effectively. These tools help version control your database schema, apply changes incrementally, and track schema changes over time. Alternatively, you can capture the current DDL statements from your development environment and check them into a code repository. For any breaking changes, write a migration procedure. For example, you could run a GitHub action on a pull request from the development branch, auto-generate migration scripts, and then provision these changes to the production environment.

Use metadata-driven approaches or YAML configurations

By using metadata-driven approaches and/or YAML configurations, you can automate schema changes and ensure consistency across environments. This approach simplifies schema management and reduces the risk of human error.

By following these best practices, you can effectively manage schema evolution in your Medallion architecture, ensuring data consistency, integrity, and reliability.

Conclusion

Creating a queryable Bronze layer within the Medallion architecture has proven to be a multifaceted challenge. This process requires integrating numerous components and services, each presenting unique challenges and demands. Throughout this chapter, you successfully integrated your first data source into the Bronze layer. You developed a pipeline that moves tables from a sample database to the Bronze layer, created a notebook, and loaded the Parquet files as Delta tables in a Lakehouse entity. Additionally, you explored different approaches to the implementation of lakehouse tables and schema management.

Despite the straightforward nature of the process, data collection approaches can vary greatly across scenarios. Data collection remains a fundamental challenge in data engineering due to its complexity and the need for stability and reliability. Consequently, many organizations develop multiple pipelines to manage diverse data sources, each requiring a customized approach, as there is no one-size-fits-all solution. Choosing the right pattern depends on several factors, including data source types, data volume, source system schema fluctuations, and processing needs. Specific project requirements, like real-time processing or batch jobs, and data delivery patterns, such as delta deliveries or full data loads, also need to be considered.

Understanding the details of each pattern and how to apply them in different scenarios is crucial for consistency and success. I also recommended that you provide thorough guidance and training, especially when multiple engineering teams operate different platform instances within the same organization. This ensures that everyone is on the same page and follows the same best practices.

For example, if you're dealing with periodic batch processing of large data volumes, you might guide your teams to use Data Factory for orchestration along with Delta tables for data storage and processing. For real-time data streaming, Spark Structured Streaming could be the go-to. And for scenarios that require a mix of batch and real-time processing or direct data access, combining external tables for direct queries with Structured Streaming for data ingestion and processing might be the best approach. So, it's about understanding the nuances, making careful trade-offs, and being consistent in your approaches. Here are some key takeaways to help you build a robust Bronze layer:

- Acknowledge that each data source may present unique challenges, such as structural or network constraints, during integration. Maintain flexibility in your onboarding strategies.
- Design dedicated pipelines for each data source and use templates for common processing steps to maintain consistency and reusability.
- Develop a strategy to manage schema evolution and conduct technical validations effectively. Implementing a metastore could be beneficial.
- Organize data using distinct schemas or separate Lakehouse entities for each source, ensuring alignment with corresponding data pipelines.
- Issue guidelines on whether Bronze data is already accessible for end users or not.

In the next chapter, the focus shifts to constructing the Silver layer. We will continue to use Microsoft Fabric and discuss transforming data from the Bronze layer into a structured format that is optimized for querying and analysis. This will include activities such as cleaning the data to ensure its quality and reliability. We'll implement technical validation checks, which act as a gate between the Bronze and Silver layers and will be incorporated into the overall design in Chapter 6.

Build the Silver Layer

In Chapter 5, the foundational design and setup of the Bronze layer in the Medallion architecture, based on Oceanic Airlines' reference architecture, was explored. Deployment and configuration were examined, enriching understanding with numerous code snippets and examples. You learned that crafting a queryable Bronze layer presents significant challenges due to the ever-evolving and complex nature of source systems.

Moving forward, this chapter builds on that foundation by advancing to the construction of the Silver layer, the subsequent tier in the Medallion architecture, where the objective is to refine, cleanse, and standardize the data. We'll explore several critical areas in the following order:

- Ensuring data integrity through a metadata-driven approach
- Cleansing data to improve quality
- Transforming data into a denormalized model for ease of access
- Enriching data, potentially by incorporating master data management
- Implementing data historization to keep track of changes over time
- Focusing on optimization jobs
- Orchestrating data pipelines with Airflow to automate end-to-end processing

Like Chapter 5, this chapter guides you through essential configuration steps and coding practices. There will be hands-on activities, including metadata-driven validation, data cleansing, and historization tasks that you can directly implement in your project.

In this chapter, we'll also discusses several data transformation and data quality tools, such as the dbt, DLT, and Great Expectations, among others. Additionally, we'll explore the concept of data products and whether it makes sense for your organization to use them for the Silver layer. By the end of this chapter, you will have a good grasp of the design considerations of the Silver layer and will have learned how to implement it.

It's worth noting that although the example from Oceanic Airlines focuses on batch-oriented processing, the design considerations and best practices also apply to real-time data ingestion. This means the principles you'll learn here are versatile and can be adapted to various data processing scenarios.

Before we dive into the Silver layer, let's quickly recap the progress so far.

Quick Recap

In Chapters 4 and 5, the groundwork of the Medallion architecture was laid. The environment was set up, the AdventureWorks database using Azure SQL was deployed, and a data pipeline was built with Data Factory for ingesting data and storing data in Delta tables. The importance of schema management was also highlighted, setting the stage for deeper exploration later on.

In this chapter, it's time to build on this foundation by creating the Silver layer. The exercise starts with implementing a metadata-driven approach, as illustrated in Figure 6-1 at the top. This metadata store plays a key role in driving technical validation in the Silver layer, making processes more automated and efficient. Following that, you will proceed with all the data transformation-related activities necessary for building the Silver layer.

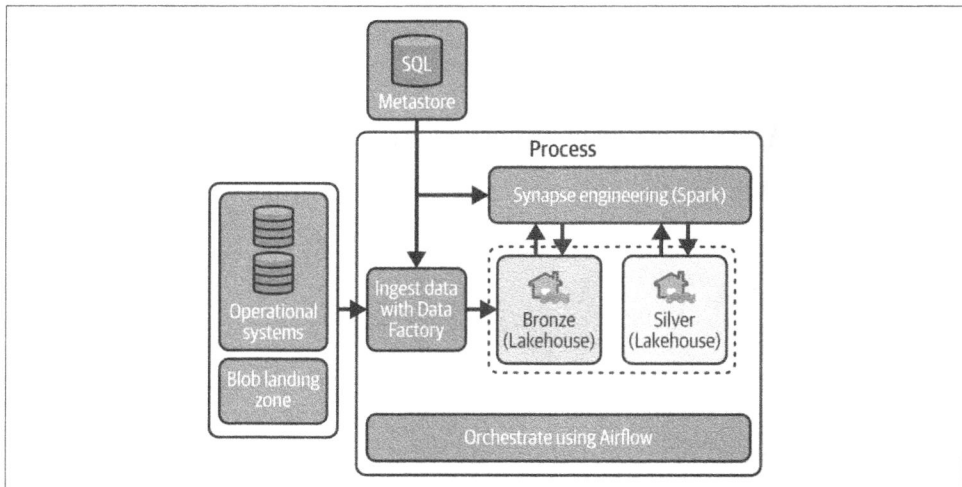

Figure 6-1. The design once the Silver layer has been successfully implemented

Additionally, you'll learn about the orchestration layer, which handles the management of the data pipeline. This component is crucial and is depicted at the bottom of Figure 6-1. Let's actively engage with the Silver layer by rolling up our sleeves and diving into how these pieces come together to enhance the data architecture.

Implementation of a Metadata-Driven Approach

The newly created architecture has entered a dynamic stage. During the ingestion phase, you learned that source systems often necessitate a custom pipeline with specialized scripts to transform data formats. In some cases, additional integration services or extra landing zones may also be needed. The complexity of the Bronze layer can result in a lack of standardization, making it challenging to maintain and scale the data processing pipeline.

However, the Silver layer offers more predictability because data in the Bronze layer has been stored using the standardized Delta table format. This standardization enables you to automate more of the Silver layer activities. Here, metadata-driven approaches become invaluable.

A metadata-driven approach leverages metadata—information about the data—to automate data management and engineering processes. This includes tasks such as data integration, data quality checks, and data governance. By using metadata, organizations can enhance the efficiency and accuracy of their data management efforts. Essentially, this approach reduces the need for custom scripts and minimizes repetition across different parts of your project.

For a metadata-driven approach to work, a metastore is crucial. A metastore is a (centralized) repository that stores metadata such as schema structures, source and target locations, ownership information, and usage details. The metastore also helps enforce data policies and rules, as metadata can be used to define and apply these policies project-wide. Additionally, a metastore facilitates sharing metadata across various tools and systems used in data management and engineering. For instance, you can use metadata to drive identical transformations across different services like Microsoft Fabric and other Spark-based environments, such as Azure Databricks.

> In this example, validation checks serve as gatekeepers, ensuring only technically validated data moves from the Bronze to the Silver layer. However, if ensuring the integrity of the Bronze layer is a critical concern, it might be sensible to move these technical checks up one layer.

In the following sections, I guide you through implementing a metadata-driven approach. You will begin by setting up a new database to store the metadata. Then, you will collect schema metadata from the AdventureWorks example database, which will be used to establish data validation rules. After drawing some initial conclusions, you will proceed to the subsequent tasks. Some of these you will carry out yourself; others are for study purposes only. These tasks include data cleansing, denormalization activities, lightweight enrichments, historization, and managing and optimizing tables.

Implementation of the Metadata Store

Let's create a metadata store by deploying another Azure SQL database.[1] Go back to the Azure portal and create a new database with a name of your choice. For our example, let's call it metadatastore. After deploying the database, open the query editor. Now create a table, which you'll name SchemaMetadata. This table will store all the metadata needed for data processing. Copy and paste the following SQL script (*https://oreil.ly/FKysm*) to create the table:

```
CREATE TABLE SchemaMetadata
(
    Id INT IDENTITY(1,1) PRIMARY KEY,
    SchemaName NVARCHAR(128),
    TableName NVARCHAR(128),
    ColumnName NVARCHAR(128),
    DataType NVARCHAR(128),
    CharacterMaximumLength INT,
    NumericPrecision INT,
    NumericScale INT,
    IsNullable NVARCHAR(3),
    DateTimePrecision INT,
    IsPrimaryKey BIT DEFAULT 0
)
GO
```

The script you just ran creates your new SchemaMetadata table. This table is designed for storing various details about the database schema. This exercise aims to illustrate common concepts rather than provide an exhaustive approach. In real-world scenarios, you'll likely need to expand this with more third-party solutions or scripts to include additional metadata, such as target schema metadata, security labels, row filtering information, and column mappings.

After running the script and creating the table, you need to retrieve the schema metadata from your AdventureWorks example database. To achieve this, I've developed a simple script that reads all the required metadata from the AdventureWorks' system tables. This migration script (*https://oreil.ly/HPw66*) generates the INSERT statements for the metadata store, which you have created using the previous script. In this

---

1 A *metastore* is a specialized type of metadata store that provides a centralized repository for metadata related to data assets, such as tables, partitions, schemas, and database configurations.

example, I demonstrate using a single table: `Address`. In real-world scenarios, you would need to iterate through all the required tables in the database:

```
SELECT
    'AdventureWorks' as 'SchemaName',
    TABLE_NAME as 'TableName',
    COLUMN_NAME as 'ColumnName',
    DATA_TYPE as 'DataType',
    CHARACTER_MAXIMUM_LENGTH as 'CharacterMaximumLength',
    NUMERIC_PRECISION as 'NumericPrecision',
    NUMERIC_SCALE as 'NumericScale',
    IS_NULLABLE as 'IsNullable',
    DATETIME_PRECISION as 'DateTimePrecision',
    COLUMNPROPERTY(OBJECT_ID(TABLE_NAME), COLUMN_NAME, 'IsIdentity')
    as 'IsPrimaryKey'
FROM
    INFORMATION_SCHEMA.COLUMNS
WHERE
    TABLE_NAME = 'Address'
```

After collecting the schema metadata from the AdventureWorks example database, return to the Azure SQL database of the metadata store to insert all records. Here's an example for your reference (*https://oreil.ly/nYKF7*). Head back to the metadata store and execute the following script:

```
INSERT INTO SchemaMetadata
(SchemaName, TableName, ColumnName, DataType, CharacterMaximumLength,
NumericPrecision, NumericScale, IsNullable, DateTimePrecision, IsPrimaryKey)
VALUES
('AdventureWorks', 'Address', 'AddressID', 'int',
NULL, 10, 0, 'NO', NULL, 1),
('AdventureWorks', 'Address', 'AddressLine1', 'nvarchar',
60, NULL, NULL, 'NO', NULL, 0),
('AdventureWorks', 'Address', 'AddressLine2', 'nvarchar',
60, NULL, NULL, 'YES', NULL, 0),
('AdventureWorks', 'Address', 'City', 'nvarchar',
30, NULL, NULL, 'NO', NULL, 0),
('AdventureWorks', 'Address', 'StateProvince', 'int',
NULL, 10, 0, 'NO', NULL, 0),
('AdventureWorks', 'Address', 'PostalCode', 'nvarchar',
15, NULL, NULL, 'NO', NULL, 0),
('AdventureWorks', 'Address', 'CountryRegion', 'geography',
NULL, NULL, NULL, 'YES', NULL, 0),
('AdventureWorks', 'Address', 'rowguid', 'uniqueidentifier',
NULL, NULL, NULL, 'NO', NULL, 0),
('AdventureWorks', 'Address', 'ModifiedDate', 'datetime',
NULL, NULL, NULL, 'NO', 3, 0);
GO
```

In Figure 6-2, you see the final results of the collected metadata. The newly created metastore will enable you to execute the data validation rules in an automated way.

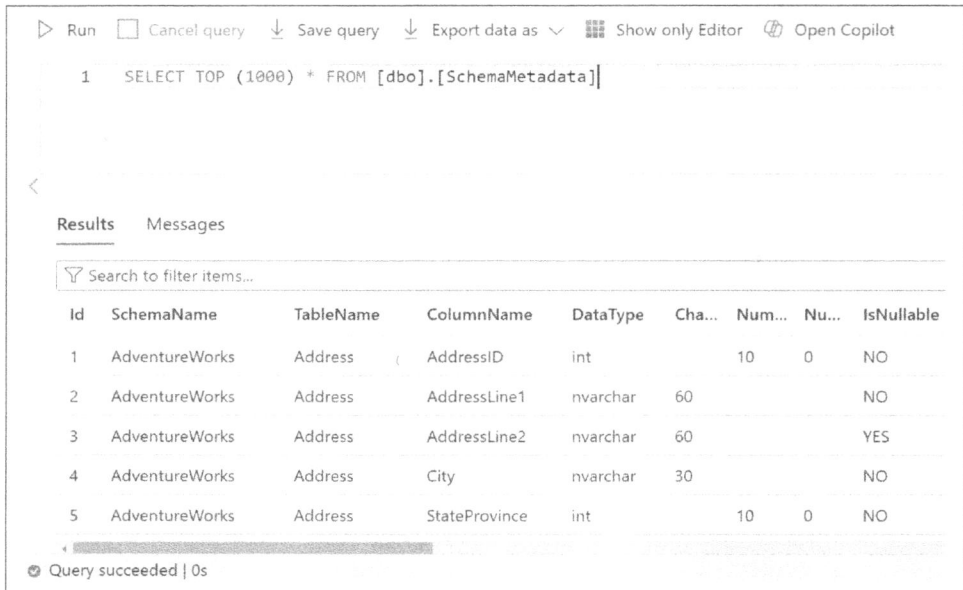

Figure 6-2. This metadata store will be used to drive the data quality validation in the Silver layer

Currently, the collected metadata is basic. It only includes schema information for one database, such as table names, columns, data types, nullable attributes, and primary keys. It is also limited to a single table, `Address`.

As you advance, consider expanding this to include domain-specific information, metadata for multiple sources, and security metadata such as sensitivity labels or row filtering. You might also want to incorporate metadata for more complex processing logic, like renaming source to target columns, executing simple joins or unions, and filtering out irrelevant data. Additionally, to enhance your CI/CD process, you could include metadata related to environment specifics, deployment details, and versioning information. Ultimately, the extent of your metadata framework will depend on your specific requirements.

Next, you'll integrate the metastore using a metadata-driven approach within the data pipeline. There will be a couple of steps to follow. For your reference, Figure 6-3 shows the configuration once you've set up everything.

When you're ready, return to the Microsoft Fabric environment. Then, under Settings, register the new Azure SQL database as a new connection. This experience is similar to the one you had when setting up the AdventureWorks database. Next, navigate to the data pipeline and open the existing ForEach activity. Add a new Lookup activity by dragging it into the workflow. Connect it to the notebook step responsible for creating the Delta tables. Select the Lookup activity, head over to Settings, and configure the Connection to use the new metadata store. For the query, you'll use the table name as input for making calls. Update the Query field with the following code (*https://oreil.ly/UavpD*):

```
@concat('SELECT * FROM [dbo].[SchemaMetadata]
WHERE SchemaName=''AdventureWorks''
AND TableName=''',item().table_name,'''')
```

For more details on configuring this Lookup activity, refer to Figure 6-3.

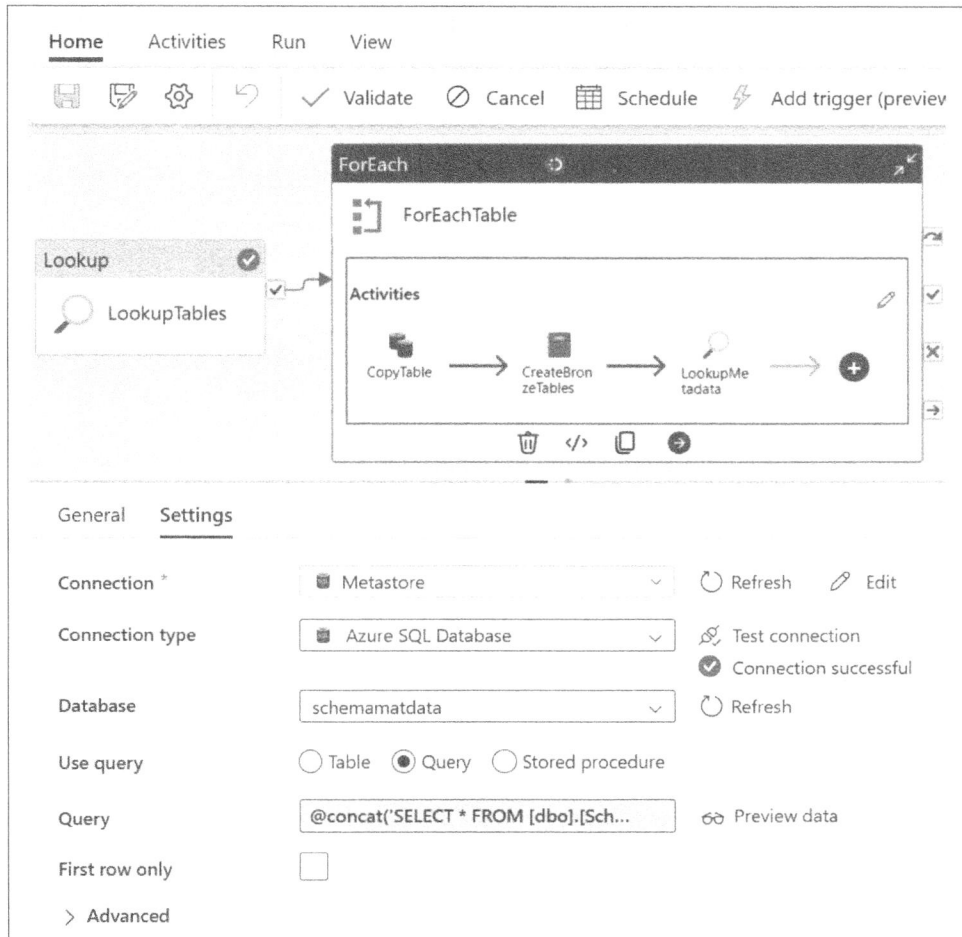

Figure 6-3. Configuration details of the Lookup activity for retrieving metadata

In this setup, only the AdventureWorks database name and dynamic `tableName` arguments are passed in. In a more extensive setup, you might also include additional arguments, such as Workspace configuration parameters, versions, and more. Once you have configured these parameters, save your progress. To summarize, for each table in the ForEach activity, the Lookup activity will retrieve the metadata from the metastore.

Now, proceed to the next step: invoking a technical (data quality) validation script.

Implementation of Dynamic Data Validations

The next task involves extending the empty ForEach activity with additional steps to perform metadata-driven technical validations. Double-click or open the ForEach activity to add new activities.

A metadata-driven approach plays a vital role in the data processing pipeline, ensuring that data remains accurate, consistent, and reliable. It also reduces the reliance on any specific vendor or technology, making it a flexible choice.

When designing how to use metadata within the ForEach activity, you have a couple of options to consider. You can choose a strict approach, where the system requires the metadata from the database for the pipeline to run. This restrictive method guarantees the pipeline won't operate without the metadata. On the other hand, you sometimes might prefer a flexible approach that allows the pipeline to continue running even if the metadata isn't available. For the purposes of our example, let's assume that metadata may not always be on hand.

To implement this flexible approach, drag in a new If Condition activity within the ForEach activity. This new activity can be configured to perform a check or condition depending on whether the result is true or false. In this case, the expression will be configured by counting the input that was received by the LookupMetadata activity. If the count exceeds zero, it indicates that metadata is available for processing. To implement this condition, update the If Condition with the following expression:

```
@greater(activity('LookupMetadata').output.count, 0)
```

After configuring the If Condition activity, proceed by opening the True condition. Here, you'll need to add a new Notebook activity. This activity will be responsible for performing the technical validations based on the metadata retrieved from the LookupMetadata activity.

For more details on configuring this If Condition activity, see Figure 6-4.

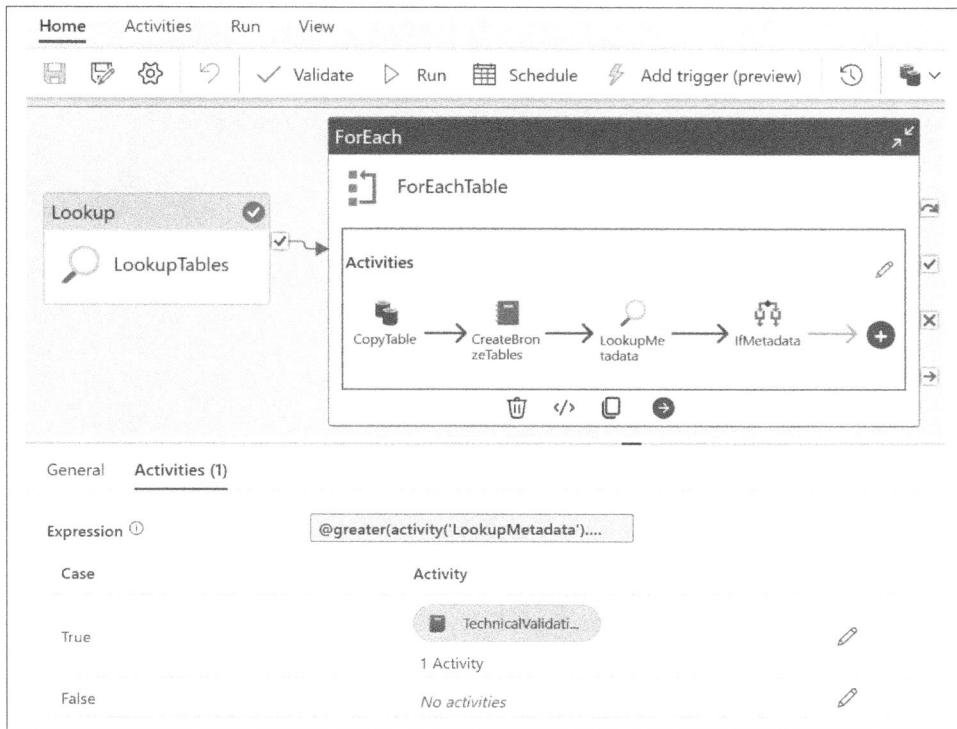

Figure 6-4. Configuration details of the If Condition for starting technical data validations

Next, head over to the "Settings and parameters" section of the newly created Notebook activity. Add three new parameters that you name `schemaName`, `tableName`, and `metadata`. Use the corresponding expression provided for each parameter:

- For `schemaName`, use the following expression: `adventureworks`
- For `tableName`, use `@item().table_name`
- For `metadata`, use `@string(activity('LookupMetadata').output.value)`

For more details on configuring this Notebook activity, see Figure 6-5.

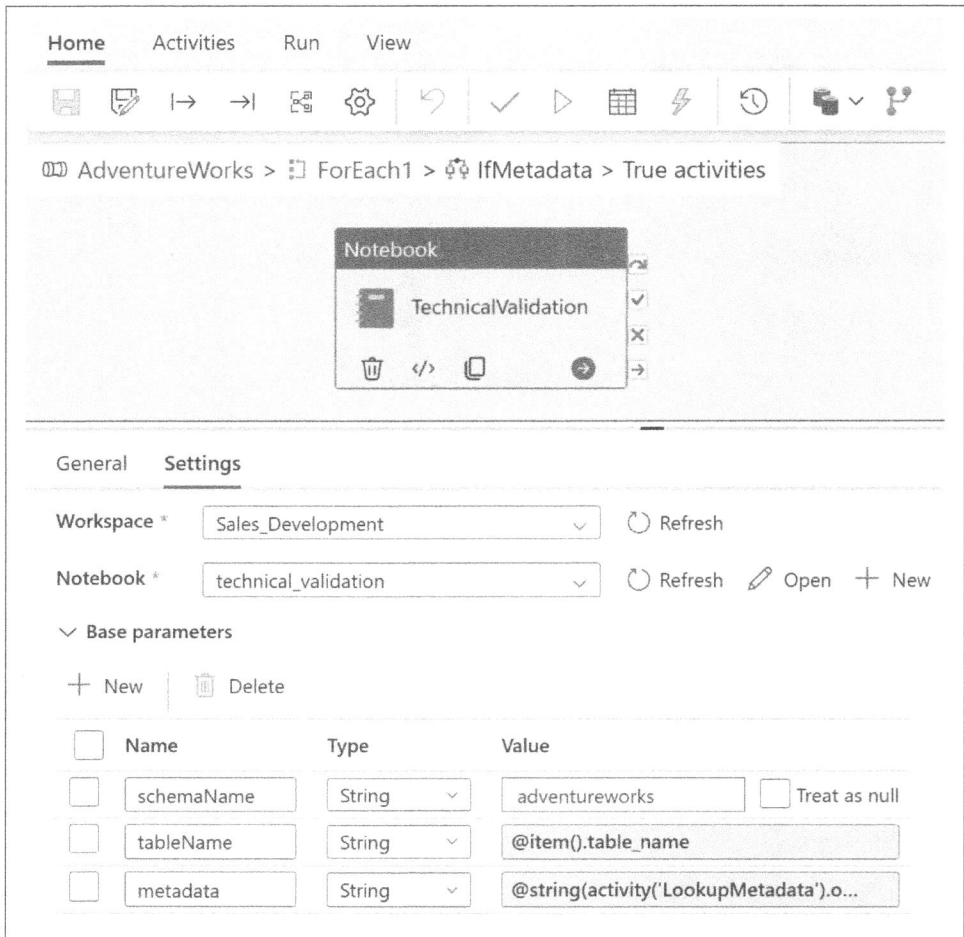

Figure 6-5. Configuration details of the Notebook activity for performing technical validations

Move to the Workspace environment next and open the newly created notebook. The objective is for this new notebook to validate the schema based on the metadata retrieved from the database. Initially, the technical validation script (*https://oreil.ly/ bih7f*) verifies the presence of the `metadata` parameter. Once confirmed, the output metadata is validated and loaded in JSON format. Subsequently, the script iterates through the metadata to dynamically construct data validation rules. If any data is found to be invalid during this process, the execution is halted immediately.

In the newly created notebook, copy and paste the following code:

```
# Infer base parameters from the pipeline context
schemaName = ""
tableName = ""
metadata = ""
```

After, you have copy-pasted the code, toggle the "Toggle parameter cell" using the three dots at the top right of the cell. Next, create a new code block by clicking the "+" icon at the bottom of the cell. In this new code block, paste the following code:

```
# Import the necessary libraries
import json

# Check if the metadata parameter is present
try:
    json.loads(metadata)
except ValueError as e:
    mssparkutils.notebook.exit("Metadata is not a valid JSON object.")

json_metadata = json.loads(metadata)

# Load data and convert DataFrame
df = spark.read.table(f'bronze.{schemaName}.{tableName}')

# Check if columns in metadata exist in the DataFrame
missing_columns = [item["ColumnName"] for item in json_metadata \
if item["ColumnName"] not in df.columns]

# If columns are missing, stop the process
if missing_columns:
    mssparkutils.notebook.exit(f"Technical validations have failed: " \
    + join(missing_columns))
```

Once you complete all the steps, initiate the data pipeline. If everything runs smoothly, the ForEach activity will iterate through all the tables and fetch the corresponding metadata. It will then use the If Condition to check if the metadata is available. If it is, the pipeline will trigger the Notebook activity to perform the necessary technical validations.

Currently, these validations are basic, verifying only column names. However, you can easily expand this script to include rules for primary keys, nullability, uniqueness, field lengths, and more. If any table doesn't meet the required standards, the pipeline will halt. This approach provides a robust gatekeeper for data entering the Silver layer.

You have now completed the hands-on part of this section. After we reflect on the metadata-driven approach and discussing potential improvements in the next section, you will resume practical activities.

Improvement Areas

A metadata-driven framework is built around a simple but powerful concept: using metadata—data about data—to steer the processes of validation, transformation, and loading. At its core, this framework requires a metadata repository where all this data is stored. It also needs an orchestrator, which reads the metadata and dynamically creates jobs, validations, and transformations. This could be managed through a pipeline that triggers a notebook. Moreover, the framework should be equipped to monitor and track the status of various jobs, ensuring everything runs smoothly.

For scaling up further, I encourage you to consider these improvements:

- Externalize the metastore with APIs for a self-service model of managing metadata.

- Enhance the metadata-driven approach to handle various technical file formats. For example, you can use the ForEach condition to transform Parquet to Delta or CSV to Delta, or to parse complex nested XML structures.

- Broaden processing capabilities to include operations such as append, merge, and full overwrite. Consider incorporating complex data transformations, such as SQL templates or user-defined functions. Some companies achieve this by using JSON files that outline all transformation steps, while others use SQL templates.

- Implement schema provisioning in the Silver layer, which ties into the schema management strategies we previously discussed in "Schema Management" on page 136.

- Enhance data security by creating secure views using policy-driven methods such as row- or column-level masking, and implementing user group management through RBAC (role-based access control) or ABAC (attribute-based access control). This approach is particularly beneficial for handling sensitive data.

- Enable the execution of notebooks within other notebooks by using metadata. This approach helps in dynamically managing task execution and dependencies. It simplifies parameter passing between notebooks and adjusts data processing based on metadata, which is also useful for running multiple notebooks concurrently.

- Add an auditing and logging feature to monitor ingested records closely. This will help identify any issues during the process and track performance metrics to highlight areas for improvement.

- Implement a notification system to promptly alert the operations team of both successes and failures, such as using Slack (*https://slack.com*) or Microsoft Teams, to ensure quick communication of important events.

- Develop a reporting or runtime observability component that offers detailed insights on failures, the number of records processed, processing times, source counts, and more. This is vital for disseminating important information and performance analytics.

When it comes to managing data pipelines, a metadata-driven approach has several advantages over traditional code-based strategies. Let's take a closer look at some of the benefits.

Firstly, a metadata-driven approach can enhance the versatility and adaptability of your pipelines. This means you can support various data sources and destinations with different formats, schemas, and frequencies. Additionally, you can adjust the processing technique to accommodate multiple ingestion patterns, such as full loads, incremental loads, or full overwrites.

Another advantage is that a metadata-driven framework significantly reduces the amount of code you need to write and maintain. Instead of creating multiple notebooks, you can maintain only a set of universal pipelines capable of handling diverse data sources and destinations based on the metadata. This can greatly reduce the time and effort needed for code maintenance.

Moreover, a metadata-driven approach simplifies and standardizes the development and deployment process. You can easily add validations and modifications using metadata without altering code or redeploying pipelines. This can make the development and deployment process more efficient.

Lastly, depending on your pipeline design, you can achieve parallelism and concurrency by running multiple copy or notebook activities simultaneously. This can optimize your pipeline's performance and efficiency, making it faster and more effective.

Now that we have established the metadata-driven framework and technically validated the data, you can actively engage in data cleansing. This step is less predictable and often necessitates custom work. Once data cleansing has been actively explored, we'll discuss the possibility of automating this process using metadata.

Data Cleansing

Data cleansing, also known as data cleaning, is the process of identifying and correcting or removing errors, inconsistencies, and inaccuracies in data. Data cleansing is required because data often contains errors or inconsistencies due to various factors, such as human error, system errors, or data entry errors. These errors can have significant impacts on the quality and accuracy of data, leading to incorrect insights, decision making, and business outcomes.

Data cleansing is different from validating data integrity because it involves inspecting and correcting inaccuracies or errors in a dataset to improve its quality. Typically, you first need to query and profile the data to get a better understanding of what data sits inside which tables. During this process, you might detect errors, anomalies, and inconsistencies. Next, you need correct the data. This might include converting data into a consistent format, such as using the same date format across the data. Or, you might need to add missing information to data, such as customers' geo-locations. In addition to correcting anomalies, data cleansing includes the crucial step of remediation, which involves fixing the underlying issues in the original source systems to prevent the recurrence of errors.

Proper data cleansing requires a thorough understanding of both the business context and the processes that generate the data, in addition to knowing the importance of the data within those processes. For instance, consider a scenario in a sales dataset where transaction dates have been recorded incorrectly. The data cleansing process in this case might involve identifying the erroneous entries by comparing them with other sources, such as shipment dates or payment records, and then correcting the dates accordingly.

> Without the relevant business knowledge, it can be difficult to identify the correct data, leading to further errors and inaccuracies in the data. Effective communication is crucial in this process!

The next sections demonstrate the process of performing data cleansing in Spark, exploring the advantages and disadvantages of each approach and drawing conclusions based on the findings.

Implementation of Data Cleansing Tasks

Let's explore the complexity of data cleansing. Return to the Workspace and create a new notebook. This Notebook will handle data cleaning for the AdventureWorks example database. You'll integrate this notebook into the data pipeline in such a way that it comes after the ForEach activity.

Name the notebook clean_data. Ensure you select the Silver Lakehouse from the menu on the left to verify you're in the correct environment. For this demonstration, the data will be loaded from the AdventureWorks example database in the Bronze layer. Open the notebook and start by loading the data from the customer table in the Bronze layer. Here's the code you'll need to execute:

```
customers = spark.read.table("bronze.adventureworks.customer")
display(customers)
```

If you run that query, you'll see that the data is not clean, as illustrated in Figure 6-6.

```
1   df = spark.sql("SELECT CustomerID, FirstName, MiddleName, LastName, Title, SalesPerson, Phone, PasswordHash FR
2   display(df)
```

✓ 8 sec - Command executed in 8 sec 245 ms by System Administrator on 9:18:32 AM. 2/17/25   PySpark (Python) ∨

❯   ▦ Spark jobs (6 of 6 succeeded)   ⅄ Resources   ▤ Log   ⋯

▦ Table   + New chart   ⊞ Data Wrangler   ≡   ⚙ 8 columns, 847 rows ∨   ⋯

Table view   ↓ Download ∨   🔍 Search   ≪

⊞	123 CustomerID	ABC FirstName	ABC MiddleName	ABC LastName	ABC Title	ABC SalesPerson	ABC Phone	ABC PasswordHash	
491	29934	David	O	Lawrence	Mr.	adventure-works...	653-555-01...	HyZexVTTLfKfhx/S...	
492	29954	Paulo	H.	Lisboa	Mr.	adventure-works...	380-555-01...	MO2kc8uiSARHp+...	
493	29959	Todd	R.	Logan	Mr.	adventure-works...	783-555-01...	FV6z03ywMJOumc...	
494	30010	Stephen	A.	Mew	Mr.	adventure-works...	399-555-01...	pBvyGgTiuk2JUwL/...	
495	30016	Thomas	R.	Michaels	Mr.	adventure-works...	162-555-01...	sGgVDtQybwwnAi...	
496	30056	Clarence	R.	Tatman	Mr.	adventure-works...	787-555-01...	266JCMNzG3Y2YO...	
497	30071	Daniel	P.	Thompson	Mr.	adventure-works...	247-555-01...	DgTXKBbRFAv0jGU...	
498	30089	Michael John	R.	Troyer	Mr.	adventure-works...	308-555-01...	Gdklarx2tW1EtZEyr...	
499	30100	Jessie	E.	Valerio	Mr.	adventure-works...	103-555-01...	9EmEkovAOZzHdT...	
500	30111	Ranjit	Rudra	Varkey Chuduk...	Mr.	adventure-works...	810-555-01...	VTpXtJAiSxeJraHh5...	
501	30113	Raja	D.	Venugopal	Mr.	adventure-works...	1 (11) 500 ...	lx5a4+AFGzH6mzjz...	
502	137	Gytis	M	Barzdukas	NULL	adventure-works...	257-555-01...	muiJ85PHJTw5ocO...	
503	202	A.	Francesca	Leonetti	NULL	adventure-works...	645-555-01...	M2iP88O+glF88E9...	
504	29541	Gytis	M	Barzdukas	NULL	adventure-works...	257-555-01...	muiJ85PHJTw5ocO...	
505	29943	A.	Francesca	Leonetti	NULL	adventure-works...	645-555-01...	M2iP88O+glF88E9...	
506	21	Jinghao	NULL	Liu	NULL	adventure-works...	928-555-01...	IaD5AeqK9mRilrJi/...	

Figure 6-6. Inspection of the `customer` *table*[2]

For instance, the `Title` column includes various titles, like *Mr.*, *Ms.*, *Mrs.*, and *Dr.*. Instead of relying on these titles, it's more effective to determine each customer's gender. Additionally, the `adventure-works` prefix should be removed from the `SalesPerson` column. The `ModifiedDate` column needs to be standardized to a consistent date format, and the `PasswordHash` column should be eliminated. Furthermore, all telephone numbers must be formatted consistently because some numbers are prefixed with *1 (XX)*.[3]

These improvements for the customer table represent fundamental data cleansing activities. It's crucial to understand that data cleansing varies across datasets, is often complex, and necessitates a deep comprehension of both the data and the underlying business processes that generate it.

The cleaning script (*https://oreil.ly/-VDuD*) that follows demonstrates how to perform these data cleansing activities using PySpark. The `regexp_replace` function removes the `adventure-works` prefix from the `SalesPerson` column. The *date_for-*

---

2 Due to space limitations, only a subset of the columns that will be cleaned are shown in Figure 6-6.

3 The 1 (XX)-formatted example is located in row 501 of Figure 6-6.

mat function standardizes the `ModifiedDate` column to a consistent date format. The udf function is employed to determine the gender of each customer. Give it a try with the following script:

```
# Import necessary libraries
from pyspark.sql.functions import *
from pyspark.sql.types import StringType

# Load data
customers = spark.read.table("bronze.adventureworks.customer")

# Drop columns that are not needed
customers = customers.drop("PasswordHash", "PasswordSalt", "rowguid")

# Function to determine gender
def determine_gender(title):
    if title == 'Mr.':
        return 'Male'
    elif title in ('Ms.', 'Mrs.', 'Miss'):
        return 'Female'
    else:
        return 'Unknown' # Add a default value for other cases

determine_gender_udf = udf(determine_gender, StringType())

# Adding gender to each dictionary in the list
customers = customers.withColumn("Gender", \
determine_gender_udf(trim(customers["Title"])))

# Define the strip_prefix function
def strip_prefix(value):
    return value.strip("adventure-works\\")

# Define the strip_prefix_udf function
strip_prefix_udf = udf(strip_prefix, StringType())

# Updating SalesPerson in each dictionary in the list
customers = customers.withColumn("SalesPerson", \
strip_prefix_udf(customers["SalesPerson"]))

# Changing ModifiedDate type to YYYY-MM-DD
customers = customers.withColumn("ModifiedDate", \
date_format(customers["ModifiedDate"], "yyyy-MM-dd"))

# Making all telephone numbers consistent
customers = customers.withColumn("Phone", \
regexp_replace(customers["Phone"], r"1 \(\d{2}\) ", ""))

# Write customers data to clean_ table
customers.write.mode("Overwrite") \
.saveAsTable("adventureworks.clean_customer")
```

After you've run the script and examined the newly created clean table, you'll see the results shown in Figure 6-7. The customer data is now clean and consistent. You'll also see some statistics about the data. This information can help you understand the data better and identify any potential issues.

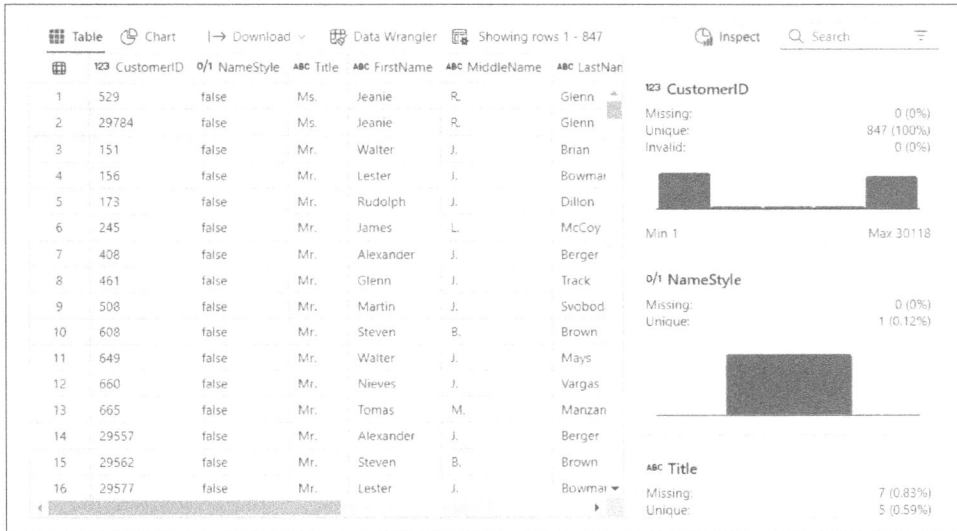

Figure 6-7. The results after cleaning up the customer table

Performing data cleansing with PySpark can sometimes be complex because it requires more code. Another way to perform cleansing tasks is by using a library, such as pandas. Pandas is popular and widely used in data science and machine learning projects for feature engineering, data preprocessing, cleaning, and transformation. This example script (*https://oreil.ly/3xss6*) demonstrates how to perform the same cleansing activities using pandas:

```
# Same code as above but using pandas
import pandas as pd
customers = spark.read.table("bronze.adventureworks.customer")
customers = customers.toPandas().drop(columns=["PasswordHash", \
"PasswordSalt", "rowguid"])
customers['ModifiedDate'] = pd. \
to_datetime(customers['ModifiedDate']).dt.strftime('%Y-%m-%d')
customers['Gender'] = customers['Title'].apply \
(lambda x: "Male" if x == "Mr." else "Female" \
if x in ('Ms.', 'Mrs.', 'Miss') else "Unknown")
customers['SalesPerson'] = customers['SalesPerson']. \
str.replace('adventure-works\\', '', regex=False)
customers['Phone'] = customers['Phone']. \
str.replace(r'.*?(\d{3} \d{3}-\d{4})', r'\1', regex=True)

# Check for shared phone numbers
```

```
customers['SharedPhone'] = customers.duplicated(subset=['Phone'])

# Show results
display(customers)
```

As you can see, the code is more concise and easier to read. Pandas provides a high-level API that simplifies data manipulation tasks, making it easier to clean and transform data.

However, when working with large datasets, pandas does not inherently distribute its operations across all Spark nodes. When used with Spark, operations performed using pandas are usually done on the driver node, not utilizing Spark's distributed processing capabilities. This results in inefficient processing as the capabilities of the worker nodes are underutilized. To address this limitation, Spark offers the *pandas API on Spark* (*https://oreil.ly/L52Vh*), which is designed to bridge the gap between the simplicity of pandas and the scalability of Apache Spark.

> The Silver layer is typically where you handle naming and reformatting to conform to domain or organizational standards. For example, a field named "cust_id" might need to be renamed to "customer_id" to match organizational conventions.

Now that you know how to clean the customer table, I recommend cleaning the remaining tables in the AdventureWorks database. Consider using the same notebook. Create a new block of code for each table. Make sure to also store these tables with the `_clean` prefix to facilitate easy identification. Once you've completed the code, integrate the notebook into the data pipeline to automate the cleansing process. This integration should be positioned after the ForEach activity, which is responsible for the technical validation of all data.

As for storing the intermediate cleansed datasets, it really depends on your organization's needs. Some organizations store these datasets as tables for auditing and debugging, which might lead to them designing an additional sublayer of extra tables in the Silver layer. This was true in our example: you stored the cleaned data using a prefix of `_clean`. Alternatively, you could use another schema or Lakehouse entity. Others prefer processing all DataFrames in one go without writing any intermediate results to Delta tables. Choose the option that suits your organization's needs.

With these practical examples in mind, let's pause the exercise momentarily. In the upcoming sections, we'll explore topics designed to deepen understanding, focusing on the theoretical aspects of data quality instead of hands-on practice. Subsequent discussions will cover data normalization, enrichments, and MDM. The hands-on portion will resume when we address data historization.

Data Cleansing Considerations

When building data quality and cleansing activities using scripts, it's important to consider that all data quality checks or updates can be flagged, logged, and stored in a separate table. This allows the data engineering team to investigate the issues and take corrective actions by fixing data within the source systems. For instance, you can write the errors, such as customers older than 150 years old, into a quarantine table, as shown in the following script (*https://oreil.ly/8gQU1*):

```
customers.filter(age > 150).write.format("delta") \
  .mode("append").saveAsTable("adventureworks.customer_quarantine")
```

You should consider whether the processing should be stopped or not. In Chapter 3, we discussed intrusive data quality processing. If anticipated downstream processes would fail or if data consumers cannot handle these issues, you should halt the pipeline. You can implement such an approach by counting errors and using the `mssparkutils.notebook.exit` function in Fabric Spark.[4] Here, you see an example of how to implement this:

```
customers = spark.read.table("adventureworks.customer")
duplicateIds = customers.toPandas().duplicated(subset=['CustomerID'])
title_not_null = customers.toPandas()['Title'].isnull()

if duplicateIds > 0 or title_not_null > 0:
    mssparkutils.notebook.exit(f"DQ duplicateIds error: \
    {duplicateIds}, DQ title_not_null error: {title_not_null}")
```

These data cleaning examples from the last paragraphs are shown in batch mode, but with a few adjustments, you can also apply data cleansing to real-time data processing. Here's an illustrative example (*https://oreil.ly/9yb2e*) of how you can clean data in real time using Azure Event Hubs with Spark Structured Streaming:[5]

```
# Streaming data from Azure Event Hubs
df = spark \
  .readStream \
  .format("eventhubs") \
  .options(**ehConf) \
  .load()

# Drop rows containing any null or NaN values
output = df.na.drop()

# Write the cleaned data to a Delta table
output.writeStream \
  .format("delta") \
```

---

4 Microsoft Spark Utilities, or MSSparkUtils, is a built-in package designed to help you easily handle common tasks. Similarly, Databricks offers a useful tool called dbutils.

5 See original configuration details on "Example with Azure Event Hubs" on page 134.

```
.outputMode("append") \
.toTable("adventureworks.events")
```

This script pulls data from Azure Event Hubs, removes rows with null or NaN (Not a Number) values and immediately writes the cleaned data to a Delta table, which might be in your Silver layer. This approach allows you to cleanse data in real time as it streams in.

Having discussed the data cleaning activities, let's dive into how you could organize data cleaning activities and how to link these observations to the previous discussions.

You have a couple of options for organizing your data cleaning tasks when using scripts like Jupyter Notebooks. Some engineers prefer to dedicate one notebook to each data source. This method makes it easier to monitor changes and updates since everything is centralized. Others prefer to split their data cleaning activities across notebooks organized by activity. This approach helps keep your workflow tidy, particularly when handling complex datasets or multiple cleaning stages. It also enables different team members to focus on specific areas without stepping on each other's toes.

Achieving complete standardization in data cleaning is challenging due to the diverse and complicated nature of data. Is it possible to simplify the process by making these data cleansing processes metadata-driven? The answer is yes and no. If your data cleaning consists of common quality checks and steps, such as cross-referencing centrally managed datasets with reference data, you might benefit from using metadata-driven generic notebooks where you can pass arguments. However, each dataset as a whole usually requires a unique approach tailored to its specific structure and cleaning needs.

This impracticality often prompts developers to store data quality rules in separate notebooks or scripts, or as metadata in Delta tables, enabling more customized and effective data cleansing strategies. Therefore, it's also crucial to provide clear guidance to your data engineering teams. Encourage them to adhere to best practices for code formatting and readability, such as adding meaningful comments, using consistent indentation, and implementing modularization. Moreover, establishing a standard for the preferred framework or tool is beneficial.

Let's explore more about choosing the right tools and frameworks in the next section.

Data Transformation Frameworks and Data Quality Tools

Several frameworks and tools are available for developing and maintaining data transformations, which also include quality and data cleansing objectives. Each comes with its own set of features, advantages, and disadvantages. Choosing the right framework or tool depends on the specific requirements of your organization. Here are some popular tools and frameworks for data transformation, data quality, and data cleansing:

dbt (data build tool)

One of the most popular ETL tools is dbt (*https://getdbt.com*), which enables data analysts and engineers to transform data using SQL templates for various solutions. By writing these templates in a universal way, dbt offers a way to test data transformations and ensure that they are working as expected.

One of the big benefits is that dbt, as a product, is agnostic as to how you transform your data into your data warehouse or lakehouse. It transpiles your SQL code into the target SQL dialect. This means that you can write your transformations in a single SQL dialect and have them run in any SQL database, for instance Fabric Spark (*https://oreil.ly/wPmSC*), Fabric Warehouse (*https://oreil.ly/bhzI-*), or Databricks Spark (*https://oreil.ly/i_pYO*). On the contrary, as you get more involved with dbt, you might find that straightforward SQL configurations just won't cut it. Here, Jinja templates and Python models help you to dynamically customize and control the generation of your SQL queries. While powerful, this approach does introduce a learning curve and can deviate from dbt's database-agnostic approach.

Furthermore, dbt offers integrated lineage and documentation and a testing framework to ensure your transformations are working as expected. It comes both as an open source version and a SaaS-hosted version with a pay-per-user model.

Delta Live Tables

Delta Live Tables (DLT) (*https://oreil.ly/QlZ7k*) is a declarative ETL framework on the Databricks Data Intelligence Platform that simplifies streaming and batch ETL processes. It integrates with other Databricks services such as MLflow and Unity Catalog to enhance data lineage. DLT also provides methods to establish and assess data quality standards, aiding in the development of data processing pipelines. Furthermore, DLT is particularly well-suited for managing CDC by correctly handling challenges such as out-of-order events, which can be tricky to replicate manually.

DLT doesn't offer a free tier in their pricing model (*https://oreil.ly/gwk5C*) and does increase dependency on Databricks. Since it requires specific coding practices unique to Databricks, it might limit your flexibility to switch providers or integrate with other platforms.

Great Expectations

Great Expectations (*https://greatexpectations.io*) is another tool that is specifically focused on data quality. It is an open source Python library that helps test, document, and profile data. With Great Expectations, data quality expectations can be defined, and data can be tested against those expectations. This tool validates data quality and generates reports that provide deeper insights into whether the data is accurate and reliable.

One key difference is that Great Expectations focuses mainly on validating and documenting data quality rather than transforming data. This approach means that integrating Great Expectations into existing data pipelines can require more setup and configuration. In contrast, dbt and DLT are crafted to blend more seamlessly with a wider array of data ecosystem tools. This makes them potentially more straightforward to implement in such settings.

Furthermore, third-party data quality and observability tools such as Ataccama (*https://oreil.ly/fdfQl*) and Monte Carlo (*https://montecarlodata.com*) offer intelligent profiling using AI services, remediation and follow-up management services, and report generation for in-depth insights into data quality.

When considering tools for data transformation, quality, and cleansing, it's essential to weigh these options against using vanilla PySpark (including libraries, such as pandas and Polars (*https://pola.rs*)). Vanilla PySpark offers maximum flexibility and avoids vendor lock-in, which is a significant advantage. However, it does require more initial effort if you need features such as lineage tracking, automated testing, dependency management, and streaming support. You'll likely need to create custom libraries to handle these aspects, adding to the initial workload.

Some developers prefer using plain SQL statements for data transformations, appreciating their simplicity and portability across various database systems. Storing these SQL statements in notebooks or as database views allows for easy access and management. This method leverages a universally understood language, avoiding the complexity of specialized tools and providing direct database interaction for precise control over data operations. However, SQL is less flexible than Python, limiting the complexity of transformations you can perform.

In summary, selecting the appropriate framework or tool for data transformation, quality, and cleansing hinges on specific needs. It is essential to evaluate various tools and frameworks to identify the best fit for your situation. This process ensures data accuracy and reliability, which are critical for informed decision making. Once the ideal approach and toolset are chosen, establish an organization-wide standard for data transformation and quality tools. This step guarantees consistency and efficiency across all data engineering teams.

Let's shift to another critical concept: data denormalization. While data cleansing helps ensure the quality of data, data denormalization optimizes how you access and query that data, particularly in complex data structures.

Optimization of Query Performance with Denormalization

Chapter 3 discussed the importance of robust query performance. One strategy for enhancing query performance is *denormalization*, which facilitates data retrieval by reducing the number of required computationally intensive joins. Why should you consider this approach for the Silver layer?

Denormalization is recommended when dealing with highly complex raw data, such as scenarios involving hundreds of small system tables that can impede efficient data access. Using a denormalized format proves advantageous for columnar file formats like Parquet, provided that data is partitioned correctly to prevent data skew—an uneven distribution of data across nodes in a distributed system. This approach is also valuable when data scientists and analysts require rapid access to Silver data for machine learning and operational reporting. For more on this topic, revisit "Denormalization" on page 68 and "One-Big-Table Design" on page 82.

> Apache Spark 2.3 and later versions allow you to join two streaming DataFrames in real time. This feature is useful for combining data from multiple streams and can be used to denormalize data in real time. More information can be found in the Apache Spark documentation on join operations (*https://oreil.ly/XParg*).

Before you start denormalizing, it's crucial to validate and clean the data to prevent issues like duplicates or missing values. Always make sure your data is clean before moving forward! When it's time to join tables, use subselects and filters to boost efficiency. Be clear about your join conditions and specify whether, for example, you're using INNER or LEFT joins to ensure the data combines correctly. This approach helps maintain the integrity and usability of your data.

In summary, when implementing denormalization in the Silver layer, careful consideration is necessary. For the AdventureWorks example, it's advisable to maintain the existing data structures in Silver as they are already in a workable format. Now, let's move on to explore how to enhance the value of data through enrichments.

Lightweight Enrichments

Enriching data means adding extra details to existing data to make it more useful and contextual. In the Silver layer, this typically includes simple enhancements that boost the data's value without needing complex processes. Some examples are appending new attributes, geocoding, adding timestamps, converting units from imperial to metric, aggregating data, or incorporating reference data. These enrichments ensure the data is not only clean but also improved in ways that are directly beneficial for deeper analysis.

Data enrichment can take on more advanced dimensions depending on the specific context. For instance, large language models (LLMs) unlock new possibilities for enriching data with contextual insights or generating synthetic features. In feature engineering, enrichments are carefully designed to transform raw data into meaningful inputs for machine learning models. Meanwhile, in the realm of MDM, enrichments play a pivotal role in ensuring consistency, accuracy, and reliability across datasets.

> In a Medallion architecture, complex business rules typically belong to the Gold layer. This layer is designed to handle complex logic and advanced calculations. These are the processes that transform clean data into valuable insights tailored to specific business needs.

Enrichments can also be complex, demanding advanced processing logic and use of LLMs. For instance, incorporating AI services like Azure OpenAI (*https://oreil.ly/vSiXx*), Fabric AI Services (*https://oreil.ly/EBJA-*), or Databricks AI functions (*https://oreil.ly/uahpt*) can enhance data in sophisticated ways. These enrichments typically require more sophisticated processing techniques.

In the following code snippet, which is passive and for study purposes, you see an example (*https://oreil.ly/_fT3P*) of performing an enrichment using the Azure OpenAI service.[6] This service allows you to generate human-like text responses to prompts. In this example, you can use the Azure OpenAI service to classify companies based on their names. You can use the company names from the `CompanyName` column in the `customer` table as prompts. You then generate a response using the Azure OpenAI service and print the response for each prompt:

```
# Configure Azure OpenAI
AZURE_OPENAI_API_KEY="<your API Key>"
AZURE_OPENAI_ENDPOINT="<your_OpenAI_Endpoint>"

# Load openai library
from openai import AzureOpenAI

# Initialize Azure OpenAI client
client = AzureOpenAI(
  api_key = AZURE_OPENAI_API_KEY,
  api_version = "2024-10-01",
  azure_endpoint = AZURE_OPENAI_ENDPOINT
)

# Load data
```

---

6 The example comes from the OpenAI Python API library (*https://oreil.ly/QZiC6*).

```
df = spark.read.table("adventureworks.customer")

# Extract CompanyName from DataFrame
prompts = df.select('CompanyName').map(f=>f.getString(0)) \
.collect.toList.distinct

# Iterate over prompts
for prompt in prompts:
    response = client.chat.completions.create(
        model="<your_model_name>",
        messages=[
            {"role": "user", "content": \
            "Classify this company by returning the NAICS: " \
            + prompt}
        ],
        max_tokens=100
    )

    # Print response for each prompt
    print(f"Prompt: {prompt}")
    print("Response:", response.choices[0].message.content)
    print()
```

AI simplifies and automates data engineering workloads, promising a significant future impact. It automates code production, eliminates labor-intensive tasks, and enhances data quality by generating synthetic data, profiling, cleansing, and enriching existing datasets. As of 2025, AI is expected to be a game-changer in data engineering, especially when merging technical and semantic data, such as information from your data catalog. This integration will lead to more accurate and robust data enrichments.

> LLMs are inherently nondeterministic, which means their responses can vary slightly even when you use well-crafted prompts. For instance, when you use LLMs to retrieve NAICS codes (*https://census.gov/naics*), it's essential to carry out consistency checks. These checks help verify the format and accuracy of the responses. To maintain data integrity and consistency, I recommend implementing data cleansing best practices after using each AI-enhanced feature. This approach ensures the data you work with remains reliable and accurate. We revisit this in Chapter 13.

Data enrichments are closely connected with feature engineering in data science. Feature engineering involves creating and selecting relevant variables from raw data to boost machine learning model performance. Additionally, data enrichment helps validate or refine these features. For example, in a dataset containing customer information like birth date and gender, one could enrich the data by calculating and adding a new *age* attribute. This attribute could then be used in a machine learning model to predict customer churn, possibly by grouping customers into different age brackets, such as *u35* and *o35*.

MDM is another pivotal approach to enhancing data. MDM takes the principles of data enrichment a step further by creating a unified source of truth for all critical business data. In the Silver layer, integrating MDM processes significantly enhance the data. MDM is vital here for improving data consistency, accuracy, and value. Consider the AdventureWorks example: MDM could standardize reference data in the `CountryRegion` and `StateProvince` columns in a way that ensures consistency across data that comes from different source systems. Introducing a default reference value for `CurrencyCode` can eliminate confusion for those unfamiliar with the data. Moreover, consolidating customer data from various sources and adding a `MasterCustomer` identifier establishes a reliable single source of truth for customer information across the organization.

> MDM often involves complex processes that require managing vast amounts of data across different systems. Solutions like Profisee (*https://profisee.com*) and CluedIn (*https://cluedin.com*) are essential because they streamline these processes.

Within the Silver layer, it's common to find additional sublayers catering to various focus areas, such as a data cleansing layer, a stable machine learning layer for feature engineering, an experimental machine learning layer, and an MDM layer. When these sublayers are present, it's crucial for different engineering teams to understand the dependencies between them. Here, metadata and lineage become invaluable for providing insights into how data flows between these layers.

Let's move beyond theoretical aspects and actively dive into the concept of data historization, which you will undertake by incorporating a new notebook into the data pipeline. This process uses the cleaned data we've created as input and enhances it by adding a time-based dimension to track and display changes within the table over time.

Data Historization

Historizing data involves tracking changes over time, which is essential for recording data alterations, monitoring its lifecycle, and supporting analysis. This process helps identify trends, patterns, and anomalies, aiding in informed decision making, forecasting, and building predictive models. Historization occurs through various methods and layers, each offering unique advantages. Let's explore these methods:

Bronze layer partitioning

Historization in the Bronze layer uses data partitioning to organize and store historical data, making it readily accessible when needed. This method structures historical data at the point of delivery, which facilitates easy access but may lead to isolated datasets that are challenging to integrate.

Delta time travel

This feature of Delta Lake captures snapshots of data at different moments, allowing users to restore and query previous versions of data. Users can access a table as it existed at a specific point in time by leveraging metadata that retains all versions of the data. Although the default retention period is seven days, it can be extended indefinitely. However, Delta time travel requires additional manual effort to compare changes between two versions as it does not automatically list these changes.

Slowly changing dimensions (SCD2)

Unlike the isolated historization in datasets and the manual effort required in Delta Time Travel, implementing SCD2 provides a more straightforward method to track and retrieve changes over time in dimensions. This method automatically tracks historical data changes, making it easier to see how data evolves.

Each method has its strengths and, depending on the specific requirements of a project, a combination of these historization techniques may offer the most comprehensive approach to managing historical data.

When transitioning to the Silver layer, the SCD2 approach is considered a best practice. It consolidates all historical data into a single, centralized table. This simplification enhances both access and analysis. The consolidation process involves appending columns that record the data load date to the table. These columns facilitate the filtering and retrieval of historical data based on specific dates, streamlining the management of historical records. Figure 6-8 shows how an SCD processed in Spark would appear.

Notice that `CustomerID` 1, which is the first column in Figure 6-8, was updated on January 22, 2025, following the closure of the previous record on January 21, 2025. Also, the current field has been updated to *false* for the previous record. Current values are represented by a 1, indicating current data, while 0 represents historical data.

Within the data engineering community, debates persist regarding whether to implement SCDs in the Silver layer or postpone and implement them in the Gold layer. This decision hinges on an organization's specific needs.

	123 Customer...	ABC Title	ABC FirstName	ABC MiddleNa...	ABC LastName	0/1 current	⊞ effectiveD...	⊞ endDat
1	1	Mr.	Joan	N.	Gee	1	2025-01-22	9999-12-31
2	1	Mr.	Orlanda	N.	Gee	0	2025-01-21	2025-01-21
3	2	Mr.	Keith	F.	Harris	1	2025-01-21	9999-12-31
4	3	Ms.	Catherine	F.	Carreras	1	2025-01-21	9999-12-31
5	4	Ms.	Janet	M.	Gates	1	2025-01-21	9999-12-31
6	5	Mr.	Lucy	NULL	Harrington	1	2025-01-21	9999-12-31
7	6	Ms.	Rosmarie	J.	Carroll	1	2025-01-21	9999-12-31
8	7	Mr.	Dominic	P.	Gash	1	2025-01-21	9999-12-31
9	10	Ms.	Kathleen	M.	Garza	1	2025-01-21	9999-12-31
10	11	Ms.	Katherine	NULL	Harding	1	2025-01-21	9999-12-31
11	12	Mr.	Johnny	A.	Caprio	1	2025-01-21	9999-12-31
12	16	Mr.	Christopher	R.	Beck	1	2025-01-21	9999-12-31
13	18	Mr.	David	J.	Liu	1	2025-01-21	9999-12-31
14	19	Mr.	John	A.	Beaver	1	2025-01-21	9999-12-31
15	20	Ms.	Jean	P.	Handley	1	2025-01-21	9999-12-31
16	21	NULL	Jinghao	NULL	Liu	1	2025-01-21	9999-12-31

Succeeded (2 sec 527 ms)   Columns: 8 Rows: 848

Figure 6-8. How data would look in an SCD2 table—you see current, effective, and end dates for each record, showing which records are active at a specific point in time

If historical data is needed for analysis and reporting in its original context, incorporating SCDs into the Silver layer is advantageous. This strategy keeps the Bronze layer dedicated to ingestion and the Gold layer optimized for quick, efficient querying without complex transformation logic overhead.

Conversely, if an organization needs historical data transformed into a cohesive and unified view, placing SCDs in the Gold layer might be more fitting. This approach is especially beneficial when historical dimensional data is frequently accessed for querying and reporting, as it helps optimize performance. Therefore, while there are compelling reasons to situate SCDs in the Silver and/or Gold layers, it is crucial to weigh these advantages against the potential increase in complexity when setting up and maintaining SCDs in each layer.

Enhancing SCDs with Delta Lake Deletion Vectors

Delta Lake deletion vectors are designed to manage and track deletions efficiently in Delta tables. This capability is particularly useful in environments where deletions are frequent. For instance, in scenarios involving high data turnover or regular updates and deletions, such as managing SCDs, deletion vectors enhance the efficiency of these operations.

To activate deletion vectors, you need to modify your Delta Lake table's properties. Start by executing the following command:

```
ALTER TABLE tblName SET TBLPROPERTIES ('delta.enableDeletionVectors' = true);
```

With this setting enabled, Delta Lake marks the positions of deleted rows separately from the actual data files, a method known as a "soft delete." This technique does not alter existing data files during deletions. Instead, it merges changes only when the data is read (a.k.a. merge-on-read), preserving the integrity and performance of your data operations.

Let's implement SCD2 using a script. The approach begins by selecting a cleaned table from the Silver layer. It then compares the data to identify changes. Next, it establishes a new table within the Silver layer to track these changes over time, providing a comprehensive view of the data's evolution.

To implement this pattern, navigate to the development Workspace using the navigation pane on the left side of the screen. Next, create a new notebook. Integrate this notebook into the data pipeline, ensuring it follows the data quality steps. A suitable name for this notebook might be historize_data_scd2. Ensure you select the Silver Lakehouse from the menu on the left to confirm you're in the correct environment.

You can model your SCDs using different timelines. If the source operational system includes its own functional timeline, such as effective or validity dates, you can use these to understand changes in the data based on their functional timeline, regardless of the order they arrived in your data solution. If a functional timeline isn't available, you'll have to depend on the technical timeline. This timeline uses the load date or timestamp, which your Bronze layer provides.

Before you copy and paste the code, let me provide a high-level overview of the SCD2 script (*https://oreil.ly/YcLFU*). It is divided into three main parts:

1. The first part of the Notebook activity involves loading the necessary functions.

2. The second part contains a function that begins by reading tables with a `clean_` prefix. It then proceeds to set timestamps, checks for the presence of a primary key, and merges data by invoking another function. Following this, the snippet compares the previous dataset with the new one. For data comparison, it utilizes the business key,[7] originally assigned in the source system, which is crucial as it uniquely identifies each record. In cases where the primary key is absent, the script generates a hash key to ensure each record has a unique identifier. Then, by comparing these keys, the script efficiently determines whether a record is new, modified, or should be deleted.

3. The third and final part involves calling the function for each table, using arguments such as schema name, table name, and primary key.

Now, let's move forward with the exercise by pasting the following code into your designated code cell. This first part of the script imports the necessary functions and libraries to perform the historization process:

```
# Import functions
from pyspark import *
from pyspark.sql import functions as F
from pyspark.sql.functions import *
```

Next, click on the "+" icon to add a new code cell and paste the following code. The next part of the script contains the main function that reads the data from the cleaned table, generates a hash key if the primary key is missing, and sets the current date.[8]

The function also contains the logic that merges the original and new data, creates dynamic columns, and generates target selections based on action codes. It then separates the records that need no action, need to be inserted, need to be deleted, and need to be updated. Lastly, the function overwrites the existing table using the data from the final DataFrame.[9]

```
# SCD2 function
def fn_SCD2(schemaName, tableName, primaryKey):
```

---

7 Business keys can and do serve as primary keys in many systems. Therefore, the primary key can also be seen as the business key.

8 The script provided is set up to handle data that's been organized using a YYYYMMDD datetime partitioning scheme. If you're working with a different partitioning system or plan to read from a intermediate layer using a snapshot date, you'll need to tweak the script to fit those requirements.

9 Delta Lake's time travel feature remains fully functional even when overwrite operations are performed on the data.

```
# Fetch data from Bronze or intermediate Silver layer
dataChanged = spark.read.table(f"{schemaName}.clean_{tableName}")

# Remove loading_date column from dataset
dataChanged = dataChanged.drop('loading_date')

# Generate a hash key if the primary key is missing
if not primaryKey or primaryKey == "":
    dataChanged = dataChanged.withColumn("hash", \
    sha2(concat_ws("||", *dataChanged.columns), 256))
    primaryKey = 'hash'

# Create list with all columns
columnNames = dataChanged.schema.names

# Set date
current_date = datetime.date.today()

# Try and read existing dataset
try:
    # Read original data - this is your SCD2 table holding all data
    dataOriginal = spark.read.table(f"{schemaName}.hist_{tableName}")
except:
    # Use first load when no data exists yet
    newOriginalData = dataChanged.withColumn('current', lit(True)) \
    .withColumn('effectiveDate', lit(current_date)) \
    .withColumn('endDate', lit(datetime.date(9999, 12, 31)))
    newOriginalData.write.format("delta").mode("overwrite") \
    .saveAsTable(f"{schemaName}.hist_{tableName}")

# Read original data - this is your SCD2 table holding all data
dataOriginal = spark.read.table(f"{schemaName}.hist_{tableName}")

# Rename all columns in dataChanged, prepend src_ to column names
df_new = dataChanged.select([F.col(c).alias("src_"+c) \
for c in dataChanged.columns])
src_columnNames = df_new.schema.names
df_new2 = df_new.withColumn('src_current', lit(True)) \
.withColumn('src_effectiveDate', lit(current_date)) \
.withColumn('src_endDate', lit(datetime.date(9999, 12, 31)))

# Create dynamic columns
src_primaryKey = 'src_' + primaryKey

# FULL Merge, join on key column and also
# date column to make only join to the latest records
df_merge = dataOriginal.join(df_new2, (df_new2[src_primaryKey] \
== dataOriginal[primaryKey]), how='fullouter')

# Derive new column to indicate the action
df_merge = df_merge.withColumn('action',
```

```
        when(concat_ws('+', *columnNames) == \
        concat_ws('+', *src_columnNames), 'NOACTION')
        .when(df_merge.current == False, 'NOACTION')
        .when(df_merge[src_primaryKey].isNull() & df_merge.current, 'DELETE')
        .when(df_merge[src_primaryKey].isNull(), 'INSERT')
        .otherwise('UPDATE')
)

# Generate target selections based on action codes
column_names = columnNames + ['current', 'effectiveDate', 'endDate']
src_column_names = src_columnNames + ['src_current', \
'src_effectiveDate', 'src_endDate']

# For records that needs no action
df_merge_p1 = df_merge.filter(df_merge.action == \
'NOACTION').select(column_names)

# For records that needs insert only
df_merge_p2 = df_merge.filter(df_merge.action == \
'INSERT').select(src_column_names)
df_merge_p2_1 = df_merge_p2.select([F.col(c) \
.alias(c.replace(c[0:4], "")) for c in df_merge_p2.columns])

# For records that needs to be deleted
df_merge_p3 = df_merge.filter(df_merge.action == \
'DELETE').select(column_names).withColumn('current', lit(False)) \
.withColumn('endDate', lit(current_date))

# For records that needs to be expired and then inserted
df_merge_p4_1 = df_merge.filter(df_merge.action == \
'UPDATE').select(src_column_names)
df_merge_p4_2 = df_merge_p4_1.select([F.col(c) \
.alias(c.replace(c[0:4], "")) for c in df_merge_p2.columns])

# Replace src_ alias in all columns
df_merge_p4_3 = df_merge.filter(df_merge.action == \
'UPDATE').withColumn('endDate', date_sub(df_merge.src_effectiveDate, 1)) \
.withColumn('current', lit(False)).select(column_names)

# Union all records together
df_merge_final = df_merge_p1.unionAll(df_merge_p2) \
.unionAll(df_merge_p3).unionAll(df_merge_p4_2).unionAll(df_merge_p4_3)

# At last, you can overwrite existing data using this new DataFrame
df_merge_final.write.format("delta").mode("overwrite") \
.saveAsTable(schemaName + ".hist_" + tableName)
```

Finally, create another code cell and paste the following code. This part of the script calls the SCD2 function for each table in the AdventureWorks dataset. It specifies the schema name, table name, and, when present, the primary key for each table:

```
fn_SCD2("adventureworks","address","AddressID")
fn_SCD2("adventureworks","customer","CustomerID")
fn_SCD2("adventureworks","customeraddress","")
fn_SCD2("adventureworks","product","ProductID")
fn_SCD2("adventureworks","productcategory","ProductCategoryID")
fn_SCD2("adventureworks","productdescription","ProductDescriptionID")
fn_SCD2("adventureworks","productmodel","ProductModelID")
fn_SCD2("adventureworks","productmodelproductdescription","")
fn_SCD2("adventureworks","salesorderdetail","")
fn_SCD2("adventureworks","salesorderheader","SalesOrderID")
```

After pasting the code, click on the Run button to execute the script. If everything works well, you should see the historical data stored in the hist_-prefixed tables in the Silver layer. With this, the hands-on exercise for the Silver layer is complete. You've successfully historized the data, enabling you to track changes over time and gain deeper insights. In the last part of this section, you'll learn more about handling historical data.

> In the metadata-driven approach discussed in this chapter, a field is identified as a primary key by marking it with IsPrimaryKey in the metadata. You could use this attribute for automating the process of data historization.

In the script, I've opted to use PySpark to demonstrate the process of comparing and filtering identical records. Each step is clearly outlined, including identifying records that require no action, isolating records for insertion, selecting those for deletion, and pinpointing expired records.

PySpark is particularly effective due to its versatility, which allows for seamless integration and manipulation of data across various storage formats, such as Parquet, Delta Lake, or Iceberg tables. For example, switching from Delta Lake to Iceberg involves a simple change in the code: modifying write.format("delta") to write.format("iceberg"). However, as you've seen, a lot of code is needed to implement this process in PySpark.

Alternatively, you can use SQL or the native merge function from Delta Lake to achieve similar results in a single operation, specifically and only for Delta tables. The merge function is particularly useful for upserts. It allows you to insert new records, update existing ones, and delete outdated records efficiently, thereby managing historical data and ensuring data integrity. Chapter 7 provides practical demonstration of using the merge function with Delta Lake.

To review, you learned that constructing a data pipeline for the Silver layer typically involves a series of sequential activities. You should begin by technically validating the data followed by cleansing it. Next, you may optionally join and enrich the data. Historization marks the end of the pipeline. It's crucial to maintain this order to build an effective pipeline. In some instances, splitting the pipeline into multiple segments, such as a separate one for data cleansing and another for data enrichment, is beneficial. This strategy enhances manageability and maintenance, and allows for parallel processing without overlapping activities. However, it's vital to coordinate these pipelines to ensure that the data processes in the correct sequence.

Let's move on to discussing optimization and orchestration. The following sections are passive, not part of the Oceanic Airlines tutorial, and intended for study purposes only.

Optimization Jobs

As your data estate expands, effective table maintenance becomes essential for managing Delta Lake tables in the lakehouse. The OPTIMIZE command is crucial in this process.

The OPTIMIZE command (*https://oreil.ly/s2f_I*) compacts small files into larger ones and organizes data for faster query performance. Regular use of this command not only enhances query speed but also ensures cost efficiency. For optimal results, schedule this command to run daily or weekly, depending on your data processing needs. Alternatively, you could automate this command as part of your data pipeline. For instance, at the end of the data pipeline, you could include an extra notebook that runs the OPTIMIZE command to maintain and optimize your Delta Lake tables.

Let's see how you can stitch together the different tasks within the entire data pipeline using Apache Airflow.

Orchestration with Apache AirFlow

Throughout this exercise, you've explored many data processing steps and the importance of sequencing them correctly. (Azure) Data Factory, with its robust orchestration capabilities, can sometimes become visually overwhelming due to its complex interface of boxes and arrows. This complexity often leads to the need for a more streamlined approach to managing workflows.

Apache Airflow (*https://airflow.apache.org*) is an open source tool that simplifies management of data engineering workflows. It's widely used because it's versatile and compatible with various data processing engines, like Microsoft Fabric, Azure Databricks, Synapse Analytics, and many more.

Apache Airflow allows data engineers to create workflows as directed acyclic graphs (DAGs). These DAGs are collections of tasks, arranged to reflect their relationships and dependencies, providing a clear structure for task execution and conditions. Creating a DAG in Airflow involves writing a Python script. This script, which acts as the workflow configuration, defines the tasks and their dependencies. Each task generally represents an Airflow operator, and the dependencies set the execution order. One major advantage of this method is the ability to commit these DAGs to version control systems like Git. Using Python also means you can incorporate complex logic and control structures into your workflows.

In the rest of this section, we'll explore a practical demonstration of Airflow. There are two main paths you can take to set it up:

Manual installation with integration into Spark-based environments locally
This option offers great control and doesn't rely on any other service. Installation instructions can be found here: "Installation of Airflow" (*https://oreil.ly/H2cj_*). For connecting to Microsoft Fabric, make sure to include the `apache-airflow-microsoft-fabric-plugin` package (*https://oreil.ly/DF9ht*) in your Airflow environment.

A managed Airflow service
You can opt for a managed Airflow service, for example, through Data Workflows in Data Factory. This choice demands less upkeep and automatically integrates with other Azure services. More information is available in "Tutorial: Run a Microsoft Fabric Item Job in Apache Airflow DAGs" (*https://oreil.ly/TiVIs*).

After deciding whether to go for a self-hosted or a managed option, and once you're logged into the Airflow web interface, you can start creating your DAGs. For Microsoft Fabric, I recommend using the managed service because it's simpler and doesn't require extra steps. For this, just make sure you follow the prerequisites (*https://oreil.ly/7-YEJ*) and enable the "Users can create and use Apache Airflow jobs" option in the Microsoft Fabric settings. After that, you can choose "Apache Airflow job" when creating a new entity within the Workspace. Next, give it a suitable name, click Create, and you're done. The page will automatically redirect you to the Apache Airflow web interface.

To create a new DAG, simply click the "New DAG file" card. Give your file a name, such as `Adventureworks`, and then click Create to proceed. Here's an example of how you can create a DAG in Apache Airflow:

```
from airflow import DAG
from apache_airflow_microsoft_fabric_plugin.operators.fabric \
import FabricRunItemOperator
from airflow.utils.dates import days_ago
from airflow.operators.python import PythonOperator

# Define default arguments
default_args = {
    'owner': 'airflow',
    'depends_on_past': False,
    'email_on_failure': False
}
```

```
def my_python_callable():
    pass

with DAG('fabric_dag',
    description="An ELT workflow with medallion architecture",
    start_date = days_ago(2),
    schedule_interval = None,
    default_args = default_args
) as dag:

    clean_data = FabricRunItemOperator(
        task_id="clean_data",
        workspace_id="92187CE0-B7EB-4FDF-80CE-EFF76639EED8",
        item_id="27DE4FE9-666D-40BB-8C71-CFF017976D7",
        fabric_conn_id="fabric_conn_id",
        job_type="RunNotebook",
        wait_for_termination=True,
        deferrable=True,
    )

    clean_data_failure = PythonOperator(
        task_id="clean_data_failure",
        python_callable=my_python_callable,
        trigger_rule="all_failed",
    )

    # Set the task dependencies
    clean_data >> clean_data_failure
```

This code snippet (*https://oreil.ly/YsVjd*) shows how to orchestrate tasks for cleaning and joining data using an example DAG for Microsoft Fabric named `fabric_dag`. You can add as many tasks as needed to your DAG, each representing a specific data processing step. This example DAG highlights the following method for running tasks:

FabricRunItemOperator

This operator is designed to trigger an existing item in Microsoft Fabric. You must provide the `item_id` of the item you wish to run. It's designed for running any artifact, such as notebooks and data pipelines. This operator can be more flexible and maintainable if you replace hardcoded `workspace_ids` and `item_ids` with dynamic identifiers using the sempy package (*https://oreil.ly/6hpFA*).

After saving your DAG, you can view and manage it through the Apache Airflow web interface. In Figures 6-9 and 6-10, you'll find two screenshots that show how the DAGs appear in Airflow. Figure 6-9 displays the tasks' order and their dependencies within your newly created DAG.

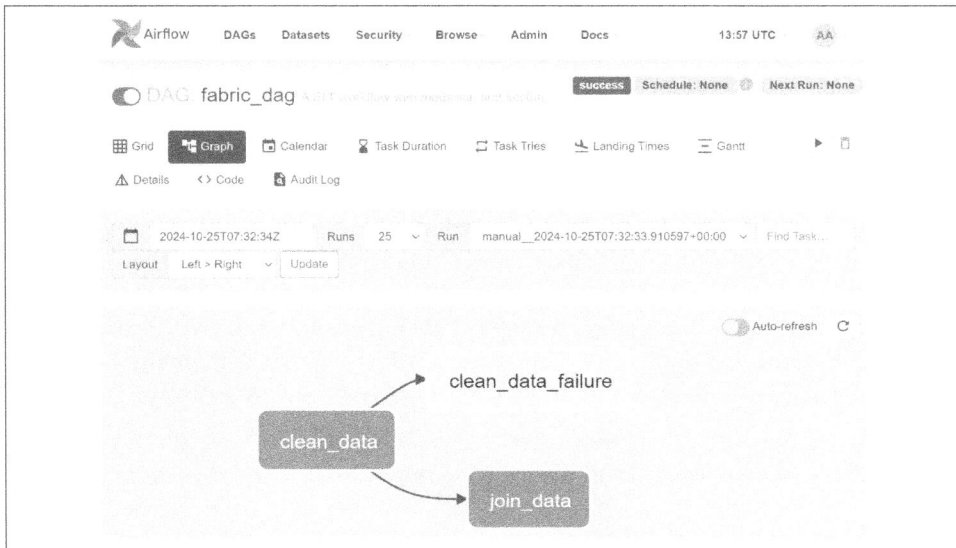

Figure 6-9. The Apache Airflow UI's DAGs view for a DAG named `fabric_dag`

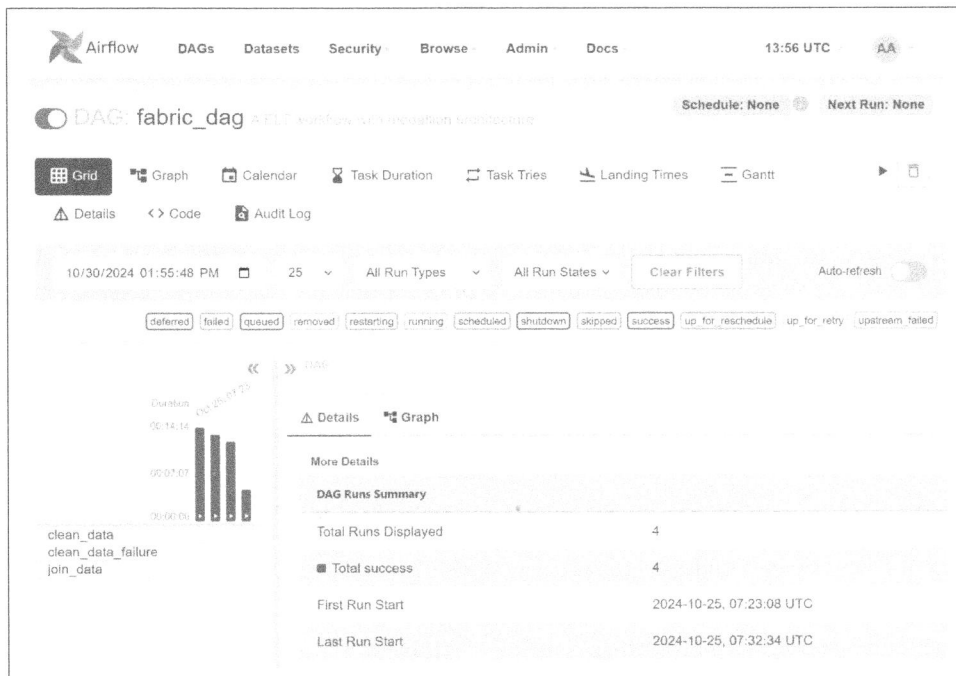

Figure 6-10. Airflow's bar chart and grid of the DAG that spans across time

Figure 6-10 provides a monitoring overview within the Apache Airflow web interface. Here, you can see all the executed tasks along with their current statuses. This feature is incredibly useful for tracking the progress and performance of your DAGs, allowing you to quickly identify and address any issues that arise during execution. The top row is a chart of DAG runs by duration, and below, you can see task instances.

In summary, Apache Airflow excels as a highly effective platform for orchestrating complex data workflows. It has robust integration capabilities with Microsoft Fabric as well as other services, such as Azure Databricks. Additionally, Airflow's distinctive method of defining orchestration through code allows for increased flexibility and precision in managing data tasks. Therefore, Airflow is favored by many data engineers for its ability to streamline and automate data workflows effectively.

Let's wrap up our discussion about the practical aspects of of the Silver layer with some final recommendations, and then we'll move on to discuss data products.

Final Recommendations

Now that you've covered the different aspects of processing data for the Silver layer, let's recap assembling the entire data pipeline for Oceanic Airlines, and I'll offer some final recommendations. Picture yourself as an engineer at Oceanic Airlines, tasked with developing a robust data pipeline.

The pipeline process, as you learned in Chapter 5, starts with data ingestion from multiple sources into the Bronze layer. After ingestion, the system retrieves metadata that describes the data's structure, which is essential for validating the data. The next steps in the pipeline include data cleansing and historization. Optionally, you may also choose to join and enrich the data. It is crucial to execute these activities in the proper order. When executed correctly, the pipeline delivers data to the Silver layer as outlined in Figure 6-11.

While this approach as outlined in this exercise might seem straightforward, in practical applications, complications often arise. Data quality, for instance, is a vast and complex area. It's unlikely that a single notebook can address all potential issues and checks needed. You may need to validate accuracy, completeness, consistency, and reliability, with each of these tasks potentially requiring its own set of rules and processes. As your data grows and evolves, so does the complexity of ensuring its quality, often necessitating multiple notebooks, each tailored to specific types of data or checks.

The same increasing complexity applies to other activities, like data enrichments, denormalization, and historization. Different users might need different slices of data or have unique performance needs, leading to various strategies and, consequently, multiple notebooks. Historization also adds complexity, as you might need to manage different versions of data, ensure efficient archival, or provide easy access to historical data. This often requires diverse techniques, each with its own set of notebooks.

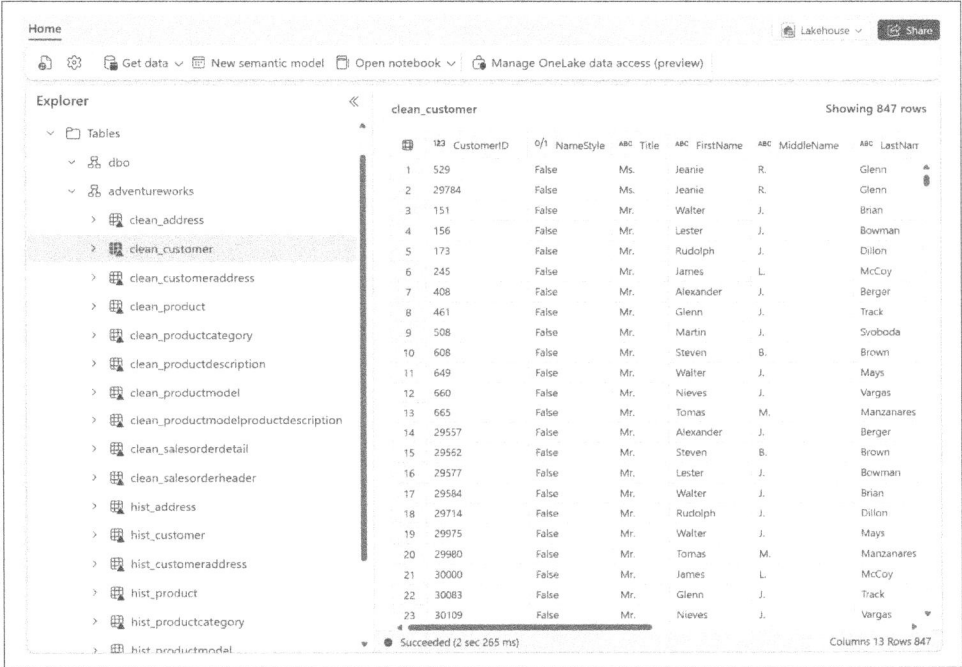

Figure 6-11. In this example, the Silver layer contains data that has undergone validation, cleansing, enrichment, and historization

In essence, a realistic data pipeline often needs to be more dynamic and adaptable than just a few static notebooks can provide. So, when it comes to improving the development practices for engineers at Oceanic Airlines, here are some practical recommendations to ensure projects are well-structured and maintainable:

Develop a mature data engineering culture
   Adopt a DevOps mindset, implement CI/CD pipelines, and foster a culture of collaboration and knowledge sharing. Embracing these practices can improve the quality, reliability, and efficiency of your data projects.

Use Azure Data Factory for data movements and Airflow for orchestration
   Start by using ADF to handle the extraction and initial movement of your data. ADF is excellent for these tasks, allowing you to orchestrate data flow seamlessly from various sources. Apache Airflow, on the other hand, is perfect for orchestrating complex workflows, managing dependencies, and scheduling tasks. By combining these two tools, you can create a robust data pipeline that efficiently moves and processes data.

Leverage metadata

Once your data is in place, retrieve the necessary metadata. This metadata can be crucial for informing how data is processed downstream in the pipeline.

Improve query speed with high concurrency

Consider using high concurrency or session sharing modes. This allows for the sharing of Spark compute resources across multiple notebooks, speeding up query execution significantly when jobs run in parallel. Note that Fabric's high concurrency mode, which facilitates this efficiency, should not be confused with Databricks' High Concurrency cluster mode.

Switch from print statements to logging

Instead of using print statements for debugging, implement a logging module. This will help keep the output clean and professional, and it's crucial for tracking errors in production. Additionally, it's a great practice to implement a unified logging approach across both ADF and your notebooks. This makes it easier to monitor, debug, and analyze the system's behavior from end to end.

Secure sensitive information

Never store passwords or credentials directly in your Python files or notebooks. Use a secure vault like Azure Key Vault (*https://oreil.ly/wz6Rn*) to keep sensitive data safe.

Organize code logically

Group related lines of code together. This enhances readability and context, making your code easier to follow and maintain. Furthermore, organize your notebooks logically. Group them by their purpose: data cleaning, transformation, enrichment, and so on. This makes it easier to manage and understand the workflow. Use clear, descriptive names for each notebook so you can quickly identify its function.

Version control with Git

Store each team artifacts, such as notebooks, in a Git repository. This practice helps you track changes, collaborate with others, and maintain a historical record of your work. Organize your repository with folders like *notebooks/*, *src/*, and *tests/*.

Replace hard-coded values with function arguments

To increase the reusability and maintainability of your code, convert any hard-coded data in your notebook into function arguments.

Keep your code concise

Aim to keep notebooks under 300 lines and functions under 100 lines. If a function starts to grow too large, consider breaking it down into smaller, more manageable pieces.

Enforce code styles

To ensure your code adheres to industry standards, enable Pylint (*https://pylint.org*). This tool performs static code analysis to catch errors and enforce a consistent coding style. Furthermore, consider adopting a style guide, such as PEP 8 for writing Python code more consistently.

Optimize storage with views

If you're creating intermediate tables, use views instead of physical tables to minimize storage usage and reduce costs.

Clean up after execution

Always clean up temporary tables and Spark compute resources after running your notebook to avoid incurring unnecessary costs.

Test your code

Utilize testing frameworks such as pytest (*https://docs.pytest.org*) to ensure your code works as expected and to prevent future bugs.

Use IDEs for writing production code

For better efficiency in production, it is recommended to switch from Jupyter Notebooks (.ipynb) to Python scripts (.py files). This transition enhances code management with version control systems like Git and improves execution speed. Adopting a local integrated development environment (IDE) like Visual Studio Code further boosts this process. These IDEs offer advanced editing features and direct Git integration, simplifying complex code management and enhancing collaboration.

By implementing these guidelines, engineers at Oceanic Airlines can enhance the structure, efficiency, and security of their coding projects, leading to more reliable and maintainable outcomes. Once these improvements are achieved, the refined data from the Bronze layer offers trustworthy data, suitable for a variety of purposes. Silver-layer data is an ideal candidate for operational reporting, as the context of the source system often remain as is, despite the refinements that have been introduced. Silver-layer data is also great for (operational) machine learning, especially when creating digital feedback loops with the operational application domains. Beyond these uses, Silver-layer data can sometimes be considered for direct application as a data product.

Silver-Layer Data as a Product

Data as a product is a concept that has gained significant traction in recent years. It was first described by Zhamak Dehghani in "How to Move Beyond a Monolithic Data Lake to a Distributed Data Mesh" (*https://oreil.ly/23m-B*). The data-as-a-product approach seeks to ensure that users are committed to managing data the same way they manage real-world products. This approach emphasizes treating data as a valuable asset that requires careful ownership, management, maintenance, and optimization.

In the context of Medallion architectures, data products have evolved into logical representations within a data catalog, comprising various data assets such as tables, files, and reports. These data products essentially package data for business value creation, along with the necessary metadata to describe their structure, lineage, and relationships to physical data.

You can categorize data products into types: for example, operational and analytical. Operational data products are typically stored and utilized in the Silver layer. They are usually source system-aligned, which makes them a candidate for operational reporting and machine learning. In contrast, analytical data products are usually sourced from the Gold layer and are used for broader data analysis and reporting.

The design of data products and usage carries several nuances. Firstly, data products should be consumer-centered, meaning they must be accessible, understandable, and usable. This consumer and reusability focus imposes design constraints to ensure stability and backward compatibility. This can limit the flexibility of restructuring the Silver layer frequently. As a best practice, if you are directly providing data products from your Silver layer, consider the impact of schema changes on these datasets. Another solution could be to create a (virtual) sublayer that houses stable copies of your data specifically for these products.

Secondly, data in Silver layer is often grouped according to the source system, which makes it less suitable for cross-functional analysis with other data sources. When this is true, you should establish principles stating that operational data products or those from the Silver layer should only be used within their specific domain. This strategy ensures that data products are applied appropriately and maintains data quality. We'll revisit this subject again in Chapter 7.

Conclusion

As we conclude this chapter on building and streamlining the Silver layer, it's crucial to acknowledge that the actual design of the Silver layer will vary based on specific organizational requirements. The architecture might be composed of several sublayers, each tailored to meet different processing needs or to handle various types of data transformations and validations. This flexibility in design allows for a customized approach, ensuring the data management strategies align closely with the unique objectives and challenges of each organization. However, all of the processing steps within Silver should occur in the right sequence!

One of the key questions is how to organize these different processing steps. For instance, do you store everything in one Lakehouse entity by using table name prefixes, such as `clean_`, `quarantine_`, or `hist_`, or do you create separate Lakehouse entities for each processing step? The answer to this question will depend on the complexity of your data processing and separation of concerns. It's essential to consider the trade-offs between manageability and security when making this decision.

Adopting a metadata-driven approach has been shown to be beneficial. It not only will streamline your processes but also bring a significant reduction in manual scripting and errors. This approach ensures that as you move data through your pipeline—from validating its integrity to enriching and historizing it—you maintain a high standard of data quality and reliability.

Envisioning data as a product opens up exciting opportunities. When you treat data with the same level of care as a tangible product, you ensure it's effectively managed, maintained, and optimized. This approach not only improves operational efficiency but also enhances an organization's ability to analyze information and make swift, informed decisions.

Here are some other key considerations from this chapter:

- Concentrate on performing essential transformations to refine the raw data acquired in the Bronze layer. This involves addressing missing values, rectifying errors, and standardizing formats to guarantee data quality and uniformity.

- Provide recommendations for effective data modeling to support clear structure and analysis.

- Decide whether to integrate data from various sources to form a consolidated view. If integration is not currently suitable, establish guidelines to maintain alignment between the data and its original source systems.

- Incorporate a strategy for managing reference data to ensure consistency and conformity of reference values across different sources. This involves defining a centralized approach for reference data governance to maintain accuracy and integrity in data comparisons and analytics.

- Implement idempotence in your design. For instance, ensure that every operation in the data pipeline (like `merge` or `append overwrite`) can be repeated without changing the result beyond the initial application. Avoid using `append` without prior truncation to prevent duplicates and ensure consistency.

- Enhance data storage and processing capabilities to efficiently manage increased data volumes. Include optimization and housekeeping tasks at the conclusion of your data pipeline to ensure optimal performance.

- Establish procedures for managing incremental updates to keep the Silver layer current without the need to reprocess the entire dataset.

- Create standard functions for automated data processing tasks, including routine checks and maintenance operations.

- Issue guidelines on whether Silver-layer data should be accessible for end users and other domains or not. If not, consider creating a sublayer within the Silver layer to provide stable copies of data for user access.

- Explore the adoption of data transformation frameworks, such as dbt, to simplify the management of complex data processing tasks traditionally handled in notebooks. Additionally, consider using Airflow for robust orchestration of these tasks, ensuring efficient workflow management and scheduling across your data pipeline.

In Chapter 7, we will delve into what it means to build the Gold layer. We will explore how to optimize data for analytics, create a unified view of data, and design a layer that supports business decision making. In addition, we will discuss how to set up the data catalog for robust data governance and management. This will be the final chapter in the journey to building an end-to-end Medallion architecture.

CHAPTER 7
Streamline the Gold Layer

In Chapter 5, we constructed the Bronze layer, addressing the challenge of creating a queryable structure despite the diversity and complexity of source systems. I emphasized the importance of stability and reliability in this foundational layer. Moving on to Chapter 6, our attention shifted toward the Silver layer for enhancing data quality and establishing a robust data processing framework. You learned how to adapt the design of the Silver layer to meet specific organizational needs, tailored for different processing requirements. We wrapped up our discussion with datasets that were thoroughly refined and validated, setting the stage for the next steps.

In this chapter, we'll continue the exercise by diving into the specifics of designing the Gold layer—the final and most detailed stage of our Medallion architecture. This layer is pivotal for decision making and reporting. It is the crown of data refinement, designed to optimize data for high-performance querying and analytics. It plays a crucial role in supporting critical business functions.

You'll be using a similar approach to what we used for the previous layers, and you'll find that the skills you've acquired will translate into the context of the Gold layer. This allows you to apply all the learnings to other Delta Lake- and Spark-based environments too. Part of the tutorial also includes constructing the semantic layer, another refinement or abstraction layer that provides a more business-oriented view of the data. After you've completed the exercises and studied many examples, we'll discuss the usage of data and how data products can be created from the Gold layer. We'll conclude the chapter with a detailed discussion on data governance and Microsoft Purview.

Design of the Gold Layer

Reaching the Gold layer, you encounter the most intricate part of the Medallion architecture. This layer stands as the ultimate stage for data refinement, tailored for decision making and reporting. Here, we typically merge data from various sources, harmonize it, and present it in a unified way. In this exercise, though, you'll concentrate on refining data from just one source. This approach not only simplifies the process but also highlights the main objective of this layer, which is enhancing business decision making and reporting.

Transform Data Using a Star Schema

The Gold layer is best utilized when using a star schema. This type of data model is particularly effective for data warehousing and business intelligence tasks. As explored in "Star Schema" on page 78, a star schema structures data around a central fact table, with dimension tables branching off like the points of a star. This structure simplifies complex data relationships, making it easier for business users to retrieve information for reporting and analysis. Moreover, star schemas optimize query performance, making them perfect for data analysis and reporting environments.

To start building a star schema, you first have to identify the relevant business entities and business events, as they will represent the dimensions and facts in your star schema model. Identifying this information is usually done in close collaboration with the business users as they know the context around the business objectives and processes. During this conversation, you also need to discuss the grain of the data, which is the level of detail in the data. For example the business might like to see individual products and individual sales orders within their reports, but not the underlying transactions that make up each sales order.

Considering the exercise and AdventureWorks database example, relevant subjects might include products, product categories, customers, addresses, and dates. Once you've defined the subject area you're focusing on, determine the central fact table(s). This table should contain key measurements or metrics for analysis, such as sales, revenue, or customer counts. Next, you should design the dimension tables to provide context for the facts, with attributes like time, geography, product, or customer. Finally, you should establish relationships between the fact and dimension tables using foreign keys to complete the schema. It is important to note that when loading data into the star schema, you must always start with the dimension tables, followed by the fact table(s). This sequence is crucial to maintain the integrity of the key relationships.

For the AdventureWorks example, the star schema will include the following tables:

Address dimension
> Contains details about each address, including fields like address line 1, city, state, and country, to categorize and identify addresses uniquely.

Customer dimension
> Includes information about customers such as customer name, company name, and salesperson, helping in identifying and analyzing customer demographics and behavior.

Date dimension
> Provides a time dimension, which encompasses fields like date, day, month, and year, essential for time-based analysis and reporting.

Product dimension
> Contains details about each product, including fields like product name, category, and model name, to categorize and identify products uniquely.

Sales fact
> Central to the schema, this table logs transactional data with fields including product key, customer key, and sales amount, crucial for tracking and analyzing sales performance.

In the context of a Gold layer in a Medallion architecture, where decision making and historical accuracy are crucial, you regularly use SCDs (especially type 2)[1] to ensure that the data accurately represents both current and historical states. This approach supports deep analytical capabilities and strategic insights. For the tutorial, you'll continue to use this method, even though the Silver layer already contains historized data. This is mainly for improving your learning experience and understanding of the process.

> Applying SCD2 in the Silver layer is highly beneficial as it stores all historical changes to data using the authentic context. The applicability of SCD2 in the Gold layer should be driven by specific business requirements. If your end users need to access historical states of data directly for reporting or analytical purposes, implementing SCD2 can be valuable. For demonstration purposes, we are using them in the Gold layer, although this may vary depending on specific circumstances.

---

1 Type 2 involves creating a new record in the data warehouse for each change that occurs, while still retaining the original record.

In the upcoming sections, you'll discover how to build the Gold layer by designing tables using a star schema approach and loading the data into the Gold layer as Delta tables. As shown in Figure 7-1, the construction of the Gold layer involves three key steps: 1) creating tables, 2) processing dimensional tables, and 3) and processing the fact table.

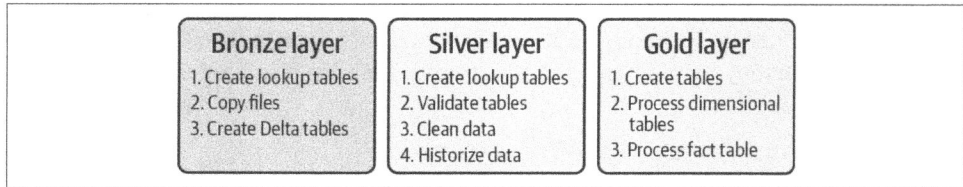

Bronze layer	Silver layer	Gold layer
1. Create lookup tables	1. Create lookup tables	1. Create tables
2. Copy files	2. Validate tables	2. Process dimensional tables
3. Create Delta tables	3. Clean data	3. Process fact table
	4. Historize data	

Figure 7-1. The tutorial's overall objectives

After building the star schema design, we will also draw some intermediate conclusions before delving into the semantic model to establish relationships between tables. Finally, you'll learn how to create a Power BI report and document the overall design of your end-to-end project using task flows, providing a comprehensive and clear overview.

Creation of the Gold-layer tables

Let's return to Microsoft Fabric and open the development Workspace. From the "Open notebook" menu, select "New notebook." In a few seconds, a new notebook with a single cell will appear. Once the notebook is open, rename it `create_gold_tables`. This renaming process is similar to what you experienced in Chapters 5 and 6. Select the Gold Lakehouse on the left side of the screen to ensure you're working in the correct environment.

On to the coding: paste the following code into a cell in your notebook. This script starts by creating dimensional tables for address, customer, date, and product, and the fact table for sales in the Gold layer of your Lakehouse. The code snippet (*https://oreil.ly/SkPU5*) follows the best practices, as discussed in "Schema Evolution and Management" on page 56. It includes the necessary steps for defining the schemas and saving the tables as Delta tables. For better manageability, consider breaking up the code into separate cells for each table:

```
from pyspark.sql.types import *

# Create the schema
spark.sql(f'CREATE SCHEMA IF NOT EXISTS adventureworks')

# Define the schema for address
schemaAddress = StructType([
    StructField("ID", StringType()),
    StructField("AddressID", IntegerType()),
```

```
        StructField("AddressLine1", StringType()),
        StructField("AddressLine2", StringType()),
        StructField("City", StringType()),
        StructField("StateProvince", StringType()),
        StructField("CountryRegion", StringType()),
        StructField("current_flag", BooleanType()),
        StructField("current_date", DateType()),
        StructField("end_date", DateType())
])

# Create the DataFrame
dfAddress = spark.createDataFrame([], schemaAddress)

# Create the table
dfAddress.write.mode("append").saveAsTable("adventureworks.dimension_address")

# Define the schema for customer
schemaCustomer = StructType([
        StructField("ID", StringType()),
        StructField("CustomerID", IntegerType()),
        StructField("Title", StringType()),
        StructField("FirstName", StringType()),
        StructField("MiddleName", StringType()),
        StructField("LastName", StringType()),
        StructField("CompanyName", StringType()),
        StructField("EmailAddress", StringType()),
        StructField("Phone", StringType()),
        StructField("current_flag", BooleanType()),
        StructField("current_date", DateType()),
        StructField("end_date", DateType())
])

# Create the DataFrame
dfCustomer = spark.createDataFrame([], schemaCustomer)

# Create the table
dfCustomer.write.mode("append").saveAsTable("adventureworks.dimension_customer")

# Define the schema for date
schemaDate = StructType([
        StructField("ID", StringType()),
        StructField("OrderDate", DateType()),
        StructField("Day", IntegerType()),
        StructField("Month", IntegerType()),
        StructField("Year", IntegerType())
])

# Create the DataFrame
dfDate = spark.createDataFrame([], schemaDate)

# Create the table
dfDate.write.mode("append").saveAsTable("adventureworks.dimension_date")
```

```
# Define the schema for product
schemaProduct = StructType([
    StructField("ID", StringType()),
    StructField("ProductID", IntegerType()),
    StructField("ProductNumber", StringType()),
    StructField("Color", StringType()),
    StructField("Size", StringType()),
    StructField("Weight", StringType()),
    StructField("CategoryName", StringType()),
    StructField("ProductModelName", StringType()),
    StructField("current_flag", BooleanType()),
    StructField("current_date", DateType()),
    StructField("end_date", DateType())
])

# Create the DataFrame
dfProduct = spark.createDataFrame([], schemaProduct)

# Create the table
dfProduct.write.mode("append").saveAsTable("adventureworks.dimension_product")

# Define the schema for sales
schemaSales = StructType([
    StructField("SalesKey", StringType()),
    StructField("AddressKey", StringType()),
    StructField("CustomerKey", StringType()),
    StructField("ProductKey", StringType()),
    StructField("DateKey", StringType()),
    StructField("Revenue", DoubleType()),
    StructField("OrderQty", IntegerType()),
    StructField("UnitPrice", DoubleType()),
    StructField("current_flag", BooleanType()),
    StructField("current_date", DateType()),
    StructField("end_date", DateType())
])

# Create the DataFrame
dfSales = spark.createDataFrame([], schemaSales)

# Create the table
dfSales.write.mode("append").saveAsTable("adventureworks.fact_sales")
```

After you've entered all the necessary code into your notebook, go ahead and run the cells. Take a moment to validate the results to ensure everything is set up correctly. You should now have five empty tables in the Gold layer of your Lakehouse. By managing DDLs in this way, you can version your schemas and evolve them as needed while maintaining backward compatibility. Let's move on to the next step, populating the tables with data, starting with the dimensional tables.

Creation of the dimensional table for address

The next steps are about building the dimensional tables. Let's start with the address dimension. For this step, create another notebook and name it `dimension_address` (*https://oreil.ly/4yRg8*). For writing to the Gold layer, it is recommended to use a V-order-optimized write. Hence, you should include the following configuration settings at the beginning of your notebook for all the Gold layer tables:

```
# Set up the session for V-Order writing
"spark.sql.parquet.vorder.enabled", "true"
"spark.microsoft.delta.optimizeWrite.enabled", "true"
"spark.microsoft.delta.optimizeWrite.binSize", "1073741824"
```

These settings set up the session for V-order-enabled writing. The `optimizeWrite` option reduces the number of files created and aims to increase the size of each individual file. The default value for `optimizeWrite` is set to 1 GB,[2] or 1,073,741,824 bytes.

After configuring your settings, add a new code block to the notebook and paste the following code into it:

```
from pyspark.sql.functions import *

# Load data to the DataFrame
address = spark.read.table("silver.adventureworks.hist_address") \
.where(col("current") == True)
address = address.dropDuplicates(["AddressID"])
address = address[["AddressID", "AddressLine1", "AddressLine2", \
"City", "StateProvince", "CountryRegion"]]

# Add hash code using all selected columns
dimension_address = address.withColumn("ID", \
sha2(concat_ws("||", *address.columns), 256))
```

The code starts by loading and filtering data. It then hashes each row using all fields, producing one hash per row. These hashes act as surrogate keys, offering unique identifiers for all records in the dimension table.[3] Surrogate keys are crucial for ensuring consistency and accuracy in the overall design. They provide a stable reference, accommodating potential changes in business identifiers or data over time, and maintain the integrity of historical data.

---

2 Based on years of customer insights, Delta Lake recommends a default file size of 1 GB, as this size performs efficiently on typical computational instances. More information can be found here: "Delta Lake Small File Compaction with OPTIMIZE" (*https://oreil.ly/IVggo*).

3 In these dimensions, the surrogate keys serve as the primary keys.

After you have entered the code into your notebook, run the cells. You can run the `display(df)` command at any time to check the progress of your work. In this case, you'd run `display(dimension_address)` to see the contents of the DataFrame.

Next, add another code block. This part of the script manages updates to the `dimension_address` table using the Delta Lake merge operation. This feature allows you to update, insert, and delete data in a Delta table using a single operation. The provided code snippet achieves this by merging the previously created DataFrame with the target Delta table in the Gold layer. The snippet is designed for a SCD2. Here's how it functions:

- If a record in the DataFrame matches an existing record in the Delta table (based on the surrogate identifier), the code will update the existing record with the current date.

- If no match is found, it inserts a new record into the Delta table.

- If a record in the Delta table doesn't have a corresponding record in the Data-Frame, the code will update the old record in the Delta table to reflect that it is no longer current.

Continue by copying the following snippet into your notebook to implement these update and insert operations:

```
from delta.tables import *

deltaTable = DeltaTable.forPath(spark, \
'Tables/adventureworks/dimension_address')

deltaTable.alias('gold') \
```

---

4 An alternative to SHA-2 would be to use the `monotonically_increasing_id` function. See "How to Overcome the Identity Column Limitation in Microsoft Fabric" (*https://oreil.ly/EF-xW*) for more information.

```
.merge(
  dimension_address.alias('updates'),
  'gold.ID = updates.ID'
).whenMatchedUpdate(set =
  {
    "current_flag": lit("1"),
    "current_date": current_date(),
    "end_date": """to_date('9999-12-31', 'yyyy-MM-dd')"""
  }
).whenNotMatchedInsert(values =
  {
    "ID": "updates.ID",
    "AddressID": "updates.AddressID",
    "AddressLine1": "updates.AddressLine1",
    "AddressLine2": "updates.AddressLine2",
    "City": "updates.City",
    "StateProvince": "updates.StateProvince",
    "CountryRegion": "updates.CountryRegion",
    "current_flag": lit("1"),
    "current_date": current_date(),
    "end_date": """to_date('9999-12-31', 'yyyy-MM-dd')"""
  }
).whenNotMatchedBySourceUpdate(set =
  {
    "current_flag": lit("0"),
    "end_date": current_date()
  }
).execute()
```

Once you've entered all the necessary code into your notebook, go ahead and run the cells. This action will populate the dimensional table for products in the Gold layer of your Lakehouse with data. After running the cells, take a moment and perform additional consistency checks to validate the results to ensure everything is set up correctly.

> At the time of writing, Lakehouse schemas (*https://oreil.ly/jZvpI*) is still in the preview phase, and the `DeltaTable.forName` method isn't fully supported yet. This means that you need to use the `DeltaTable.forPath` method to access the Delta tables. This is expected to change in the future.

Once you've confirmed the table looks good and the data is accurate, you can proceed with the next step: building the dimensional table for customers.

Creation of the dimensional table for customer

Next, create a new notebook and name it `dimension_customer` (*https://oreil.ly/NvgeJ*). Simply repeat the previous steps for the address dimensional table, but this time, apply them to customer data. Use the code snippets provided:

```
from pyspark.sql.functions import *

# Load data to the dataframe as a starting point to create the gold layer
customer = spark.read.table("silver.adventureworks.hist_customer") \
.where(col("current") == True)
customer = customer.dropDuplicates(["CustomerID"])
dimension_customer = customer[["CustomerID", "Title", "FirstName", \
"MiddleName", "LastName", "CompanyName", "EmailAddress", "Phone"]]

# Add hash code using all selected columns
dimension_customer = dimension_customer.withColumn("ID", \
sha2(concat_ws("||", *dimension_customer.columns), 256))
```

Finally, copy the code snippet to handle the updates to the `dimension_customer` table into a new cell:

```
from delta.tables import *

deltaTable = DeltaTable.forPath(spark, \
'Tables/adventureworks/dimension_customer')

deltaTable.alias('gold') \
  .merge(
    dimension_customer.alias('updates'),
    'gold.ID = updates.ID'
  ).whenMatchedUpdate(set =
    {
      "current_flag": lit("1"),
      "current_date": current_date(),
      "end_date": """to_date('9999-12-31', 'yyyy-MM-dd')"""
    }
  ).whenNotMatchedInsert(values =
    {
      "ID": "updates.ID",
      "CustomerID": "updates.CustomerID",
      "Title": "updates.Title",
      "FirstName": "updates.FirstName",
      "MiddleName": "updates.MiddleName",
      "LastName": "updates.LastName",
      "CompanyName": "updates.CompanyName",
      "EmailAddress": "updates.EmailAddress",
      "Phone": "updates.Phone",
      "current_flag": lit("1"),
      "current_date": current_date(),
      "end_date": """to_date('9999-12-31', 'yyyy-MM-dd')"""
    }
  ).whenNotMatchedBySourceUpdate(set =
    {
      "current_flag": lit("0"),
      "end_date": current_date()
    }
  ).execute()
```

Run the cells in your notebook again to validate your results.

Creation of the dimensional table for date

Let's create a dimensional table for dates. This table will be used to provide context for the sales data in the fact table. It contains fields like day, month, and year. Note that for this table, you won't historize the data because the attributes of dates are fixed and do not change over time.

Create a new notebook and name it dimension_date (*https://oreil.ly/OuN18*). Copy-paste the following code into a cell in your notebook to set up the date dimension table:

```
from pyspark.sql.functions import *

# Load data to the dataframe
dim_date = spark.read.table("silver.adventureworks.hist_salesorderheader") \
.where(col("current") == True)

dim_date = dim_date.dropDuplicates(["OrderDate"]).select(col("OrderDate"), \
        dayofmonth("OrderDate").alias("Day"), \
        month("OrderDate").alias("Month"), \
        year("OrderDate").alias("Year") \
    ).orderBy("OrderDate")

# Add hash code using all selected columns
dim_date = dim_date.withColumn("ID", \
sha2(concat_ws("||", *dim_date.columns), 256))
```

This code snippet extracts the day, month, and year from the OrderDate column and sorts the DataFrame by OrderDate. To maintain consistency with other tables, it will ultimately generate a unique hash code for each row in the dimension table. This hash code will act as the surrogate key for the date dimension table.

The next step is to merge the DataFrame with the target Delta table in the Gold layer. Use the following code snippet to handle updates to the dimension_date table:

```
from delta.tables import *

deltaTable = DeltaTable.forPath(spark, \
'Tables/adventureworks/dimension_date')

deltaTable.alias('gold') \
  .merge(
    dim_date.alias('updates'),
    'gold.ID = updates.ID'
  ).whenNotMatchedInsert(values =
    {
      "ID": "updates.ID",
      "OrderDate": "updates.OrderDate",
      "Day": "updates.Day",
```

```
    "Month": "updates.Month",
    "Year": "updates.Year",
  }
).execute()
```

Run the cells in your notebook again to validate your results.

Creation of the dimensional table for product

Now, create a new notebook named `dimension_product` (*https://oreil.ly/MkzXF*). This notebook initiates by loading and filtering data from the product, product category, and product model tables, ensuring only the latest and unique entries based on specific identifiers are retained. It then trims these tables to maintain only essential columns and executes joins among them. Simply repeat the steps you previously undertook by using the following code snippet:

```
from pyspark.sql.functions import *

# Load data to the dataframes
product = spark.read.table("silver.adventureworks.hist_product") \
.where(col("current") == True)
product = product.dropDuplicates(["ProductID"])
product = product[["ProductID", "Name", "ProductNumber", \
"Color", "Size", "Weight", "ProductCategoryID", "ProductModelID"]]
category = spark.read.table("silver.adventureworks.hist_productcategory") \
.where(col("current") == True)
category = category.dropDuplicates(["ProductCategoryID"])
category = category[["ProductCategoryID", "Name"]]
category = category.withColumnRenamed("Name", "CategoryName")
model = spark.read.table("silver.adventureworks.hist_productmodel") \
.where(col("current") == True)
model = model.dropDuplicates(["ProductModelID"])
model = model[["ProductModelID", "Name", "CatalogDescription"]]
model = model.withColumnRenamed("Name", "ProductModelName")

# Perform the joins
dimension_product = product.join(category, on="ProductCategoryID", how="left")
dimension_product = dimension_product.join(model, \
on="ProductModelID", how="left")

# Select only the relevant columns
dimension_product = dimension_product[["ProductID", "Name", "ProductNumber", \
"Color", "Size", "Weight" , "CategoryName" , "ProductModelName"]]

# Add hash code using all selected columns
dimension_product = dimension_product.withColumn("ID", \
sha2(concat_ws("||", *dimension_product.columns), 256))
```

Next, copy the code snippet that handles updates to the `dimension_product` table into a new cell:

```
from delta.tables import *

deltaTable = DeltaTable.forPath(spark, \
'Tables/adventureworks/dimension_product')

deltaTable.alias('gold') \
  .merge(
    dimension_product.alias('updates'),
    'gold.ID = updates.ID'
  ).whenMatchedUpdate(set =
    {
      "current_flag": lit("1"),
      "current_date": current_date(),
      "end_date": """to_date('9999-12-31', 'yyyy-MM-dd')"""
    }
  ).whenNotMatchedInsert(values =
    {
      "ID": "updates.ID",
      "ProductID": "updates.ProductID",
      "ProductNumber": "updates.ProductNumber",
      "Color": "updates.Color",
      "Size": "updates.Size",
      "Weight": "updates.Weight",
      "CategoryName": "updates.CategoryName",
      "ProductModelName": "updates.ProductModelName",
      "current_flag": lit("1"),
      "current_date": current_date(),
      "end_date": """to_date('9999-12-31', 'yyyy-MM-dd')"""
    }
  ).whenNotMatchedBySourceUpdate(set =
    {
      "current_flag": lit("0"),
      "end_date": current_date()
    }
  ).execute()
```

Once you've entered all the necessary code for the product updates, it's time to run the cells in your notebook again. This action will create the dimensional table for products in the Gold layer of your Lakehouse. After running the cells, take a moment to validate the results to ensure all dimensional tables are set up correctly. Now, you're ready to move on to the final step of your data project: creation of the fact table.

Creation of the fact table for sales

Let's build the scripts for populating the fact table: the center of your star schema. The fact table stores quantitative data for analysis and is surrounded by dimension tables, which contain descriptive attributes related to the facts. For the purposes of the exercise, the fact table will include sales-related data and keys for linking to dimension tables. These keys are essential as they enable us to join the fact table with dimension tables, facilitating multidimensional analysis.

In your Lakehouse environment, create a new notebook named fact_sales (*https://oreil.ly/YKmYC*). You'll follow a similar process to what you did with the products and customers. This involves copying the information into the cell for selecting, joining, and filtering the data. For demonstration purposes, there is a tiny bit of business logic involved in this step, as you need to calculate the revenue for each sales order detail.

When ready, use the provided code snippets to set up and populate the sales DataFrame:

```python
from pyspark.sql.functions import *

# Load data to the dataframes
orderdetail = spark.read.table("silver.adventureworks.hist_salesorderdetail") \
.where(col("current") == True)
orderdetail = orderdetail.dropDuplicates(["SalesOrderID"])
orderdetail = orderdetail[["SalesOrderID", "SalesOrderDetailID", \
"ProductID", "OrderQty", "UnitPrice"]]
orderdetail = orderdetail \
.withColumn("Revenue",orderdetail["OrderQty"] \
* orderdetail["UnitPrice"] )

orderheader = spark.read.table("silver.adventureworks.hist_salesorderheader") \
.where(col("current") == True)
orderheader = orderheader.dropDuplicates(["SalesOrderID"])
orderheader = orderheader[["SalesOrderID", "CustomerID", \
"BillToAddressID", "OrderDate"]]
orderheader = orderheader \
.withColumnRenamed("SalesOrderID", "SalesOrderID2")

# Perform the joins
sales = orderdetail.join(orderheader, \
orderdetail['SalesOrderID'] == orderheader['SalesOrderID2'], "left")

sales = sales.withColumn('SalesKey', concat(sales['SalesOrderID'], \
sales['SalesOrderDetailID']))

# Select only the relevant columns
sales = sales[["SalesKey", "ProductID", "CustomerID", \
"BillToAddressID", "Revenue", "OrderDate", "OrderQty", "UnitPrice"]]
```

Now, let's prepare the DataFrame for the fact table by incorporating the surrogate keys from the dimensional tables. To expedite this process, you will join the fact table with the dimension tables using the business keys and only current data. The business keys are the original keys from the source system, such as CustomerID, ProductID, and OrderDate. The script will select the surrogate keys from the dimension tables and rename them to align with the fact table's schema.

The use of surrogate keys is crucial for maintaining data integrity and consistency. They serve as unique, database-assigned identifiers that reduce reliance on business keys, which may vary over time for business or operational reasons. Even if attributes of business keys change, the surrogate keys remain constant, preserving the consistency of historical data. Moreover, surrogate keys effectively handle different versions by assigning a unique identifier to each, ensuring that fact tables accurately connect to the appropriate version of dimension records.

Continue by copying and pasting the content provided into the cell in your notebook:

```
# Load the current data from the dimension tables
dimension_address = spark.read.table("adventureworks.dimension_address") \
.where(col("current_flag") == True)
dimension_customer = spark.read.table("adventureworks.dimension_customer") \
.where(col("current_flag") == True)
dimension_product = spark.read.table("adventureworks.dimension_product") \
.where(col("current_flag") == True)
dimension_date = spark.read.table("adventureworks.dimension_date")

# Join the fact table with the dimension tables using the business keys
fact_sales = sales.join(dimension_address,(sales.BillToAddressID \
    == dimension_address.AddressID), "left") \
    .join(dimension_customer,(sales.CustomerID \
    == dimension_customer.CustomerID), "left") \
    .join(dimension_product,(sales.ProductID \
    == dimension_product.ProductID), "left") \
    .join(dimension_date,(sales.OrderDate \
    == dimension_date.OrderDate), "left") \
    .select(col("dimension_address.ID").alias("AddressKey"), \
    col("dimension_customer.ID").alias("CustomerKey"), \
    col("dimension_product.ID").alias("ProductKey"), \
    col("dimension_date.ID").alias("DateKey"), \
    col("SalesKey"), col("Revenue"), col("OrderQty"), col("UnitPrice"))
```

Finally, the last code snippet handles the updates to the fact_sales table. Copy-paste the following content into the cell:

```
from delta.tables import *

deltaTable = DeltaTable.forPath(spark, \
'Tables/adventureworks/fact_sales')

deltaTable.alias('gold') \
  .merge(
    fact_sales.alias('updates'),
    'gold.SalesKey = updates.SalesKey \
    AND gold.AddressKey = updates.AddressKey \
    AND gold.CustomerKey = updates.CustomerKey \
    AND gold.ProductKey = updates.ProductKey \
    AND gold.DateKey = updates.DateKey' \
  ).whenMatchedUpdate(set =
    {
```

```
      "current_flag": lit("1"),
      "current_date": current_date(),
      "end_date": """to_date('9999-12-31', 'yyyy-MM-dd')"""
  }
).whenNotMatchedInsert(values =
  {
      "SalesKey": "updates.SalesKey",
      "AddressKey": "updates.AddressKey",
      "CustomerKey": "updates.CustomerKey",
      "ProductKey": "updates.ProductKey",
      "DateKey": "updates.DateKey",
      "Revenue": "updates.Revenue",
      "OrderQty": "updates.OrderQty",
      "UnitPrice": "updates.UnitPrice",
      "current_flag": lit("1"),
      "current_date": current_date(),
      "end_date": """to_date('9999-12-31', 'yyyy-MM-dd')"""
  }
).whenNotMatchedBySourceUpdate(set =
  {
      "current_flag": lit("0"),
      "end_date": current_date()
  }
).execute()
```

After you've entered the code, run the cells in your notebook once more. This time, the fact table will be created in the Gold layer of your Lakehouse. Once the table is set up, take a moment to validate the results. They should match the example shown in Figure 7-2.

With the fact table in place, you've successfully completed the setup of the Gold layer for Oceanic Airlines. This layer is now ready to support high-performance querying and analytics, enabling you to derive valuable insights from your data. However, one step remains: the inclusion of the notebooks in the data pipeline. I recommend connecting the creation of the Gold-layer tables step to the data historization step, which is the last activity of the Silver layer. Following this, you should add the dimensions notebooks; you might consider running these in parallel, as there are no dependencies between them. Finally, incorporate the fact notebook responsible for processing the fact table to complete the setup. Figure 7-3 illustrates the final stages of the data pipeline.

After you've revised the data pipeline, the Gold layer is now ready to support high-performance querying and analytics, enabling you to derive valuable insights from your data.

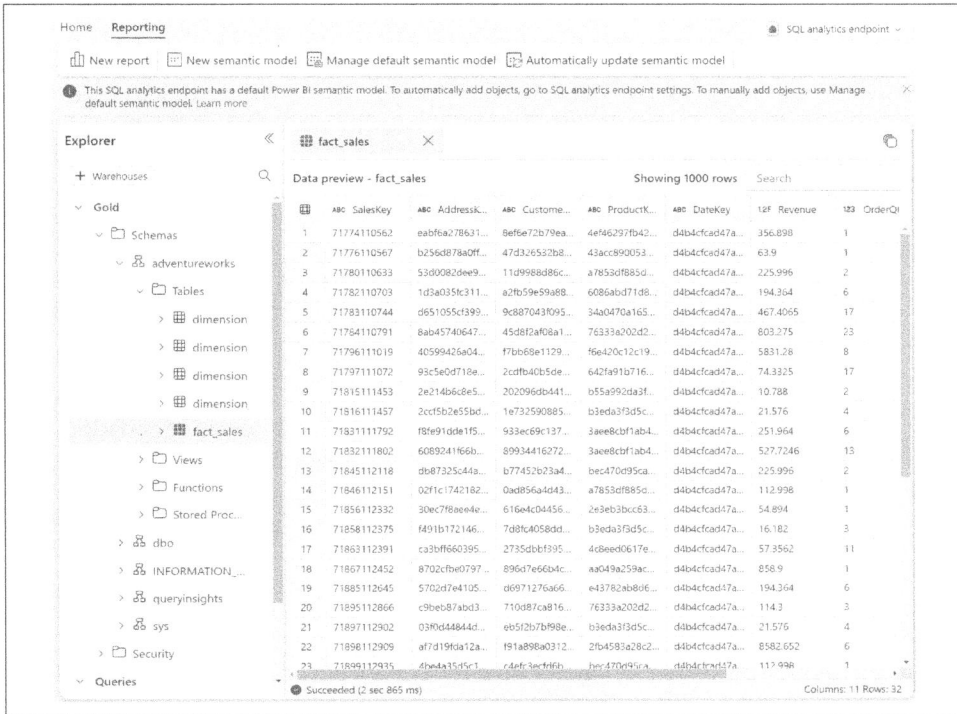

Figure 7-2. Using a SQL endpoint to show the final results: highly curated data that has been transformed and optimized for analytics

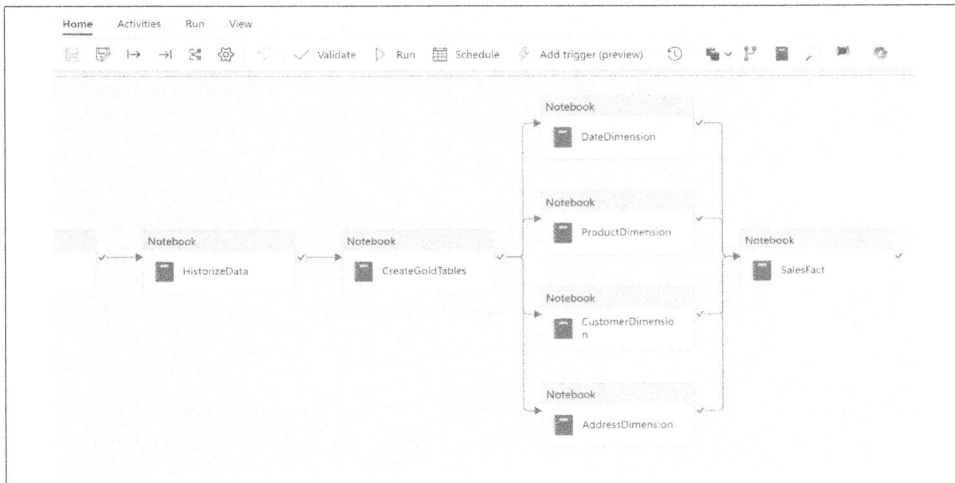

Figure 7-3. The final steps of the data pipeline, showing historization, parallel dimension processing, and fact table completion

Now, let's dive into constructing the semantic model and creating relationships between the tables. This step is key to ensuring your data model is well-structured and that the tables interact efficiently. With this, you'll enhance the integrity and usability of your data, paving the way for insightful and reliable analysis. Let's proceed to the final phase.

Creation of the Semantic Model

Now that your Gold layer is set up, it's time to leverage this data to create reports and analyze your findings. To do this, I recommend creating a semantic model in your workspace. A semantic model is essentially a way to represent and organize data so it's easier to understand and analyze. Think of it as translating a complex data model with technical column names into a more user-friendly design. This is a powerful feature that greatly enhances self-service capabilities for business users as they can interact with data without needing deep technical expertise in data handling or query languages. Furthermore, semantic models can be used in conjunction with other tools, like Power BI, Excel, mobile applications, and components of the Microsoft Power Platform.

Attention is crucial when constructing the semantic model due to its significant implications regarding the overall design and functionality of the Gold layer. Missteps in this process can lead to inefficiencies, increased costs, and potential errors in data handling and reporting.

In the Gold layer, you have created tables using SCD2. This means you have the complete history of data changes. In the design of your tables, you have `current_flag`, `current_date`, and `end_date` columns so that you can access both the current and past versions of the data.

However, you have a dilemma. Direct Lake (*https://oreil.ly/EVRga*),[5] a query mode for directly querying Delta tables, comes with a limitation: it queries data as it exists and does not support the use of SELECT or WHERE statements within queries. This constraint requires us to explore alternative solutions. Each of these options has its own advantages and drawbacks.

The first viable option is to create views in the Gold layer, which can then be integrated into the semantic model. This view can be used to filter out historical data and only include the most current data. Here is an example (*https://oreil.ly/4le1q*) of how to set up such a view using a SQL statement:

```
IF OBJECT_ID('adventureworks.v_dimension_customer', 'V') IS NOT NULL
    DROP VIEW adventureworks.v_dimension_customer
GO

CREATE VIEW adventureworks.v_dimension_customer
AS SELECT * FROM adventureworks.dimension_customer WHERE current_flag = 1;
```

This setup ensures that only the most current data is included in your reports. However, it's important to note that when connecting a semantic model to a Lakehouse view, the Direct Lake mode switches to DirectQuery mode (*https://oreil.ly/NgKTq*) by default, which might slow down performance.

The second option is to use the Import mode (*https://oreil.ly/tzFy8*) in Power BI, which allows for the selection, filtering, or manipulation of data before importing it into the model. While this method involves data duplication and necessitates initial data loading, thereby compromising real-time data access and potentially increasing complexity and costs, it offers customizations and fast access to the data. Additionally, it can serve many users simultaneously without the need to fetch data repeatedly from the source.

The third option involves applying filters directly in the reports after all data is loaded from the Delta tables. This approach is less efficient as it requires additional processing in Power BI to filter out historical data. This can lead to slower performance. Furthermore, this approach raises questions about the readiness of the Gold layer for consumption if further filtering is required in reports.

The fourth option involves changing the Gold layer design to enhance data consumption more efficiency. This can be achieved in several ways. For this exercise, you could argue that you already have historized data in the Silver layer. You could consider keeping only current data in the Gold layer by rewriting the transformation logic. This change would reduce the complexity of the data model and improve

---

5 Direct Lake mode makes Power BI connect directly to the Delta tables and query them in real time, eliminating the need to import data into Power BI with scheduled refreshes. Alternatively, Import mode is available, where data is imported into Power BI.

performance. At the same time, this approach might set constraints on future use cases that may require historical data within their designs. Another method is to maintain the existing data model while adding extra tables that are optimized for specific use cases. This maintains a curated layer for generic use and semantic layers for specific use cases. This latter strategy requires writing extra code to manage the data, potentially increasing the complexity of the pipeline. However, it can also boost efficient reuse of data and allows for more tailored data models for different use cases. So, there are considerations to keep in mind for this option.

Understanding the considerations and applicability of each option is essential for making informed decisions. For enterprises, best practices are about focusing on the trade-off between using Import mode and optimizing the Gold layer's design to enhance data consumption with Direct Lake mode. Combining strategies, such as using both views and data duplication in the Gold layer, can create a more adaptable and efficient data model, improving performance and facilitating easier data access.

With these trade-offs and best practices in mind, let's create a semantic model that incorporates the Gold tables developed during this exercise. This model will require users to apply filters directly within their reports, allowing for dynamic data exploration and analysis.

Here's how to get started:

1. Navigate to your Gold Lakehouse in your Workspace.

2. Click on "New semantic model" from the ribbon at the top of the Lakehouse explorer view.

3. Name your new semantic model, for example, "Sales."

4. Select the transformed Gold tables to be included in your semantic model: `dimension_address`, `dimension_customer`, `dimension_date`, `dimension_prod uct`, and `fact_sales`. As shown in Figure 7-4, you can select the tables for the semantic model.

5. Connect the tables by creating relationships between them. For example, you can create a relationship between the CustomerKey field in the `fact_sales` table and the ID field in the `dimension_customer` table. Repeat this process for all the tables to establish the necessary relationships.

6. After that, define the cardinality of the relationships. For instance, the relationships between dimension IDs and fact Keys are one-to-many relationships.

7. Next, rename the tables and hide any unnecessary columns to make the model more user-friendly. For instance, you could rename the `dimension_customer` table to `customer` and hide the columns ID and CustomerID.

8. Next, create measures for the sales table. For example, you can create a measure for Revenue to calculate the total revenue from sales. You can do this by right-clicking on the TotalRevenue column and selecting New measure. At the top of the screen, you can define the measure using the DAX language:

```
TotalRevenue = SUM(sales[Revenue])
```

9. Click Confirm to finalize your work.

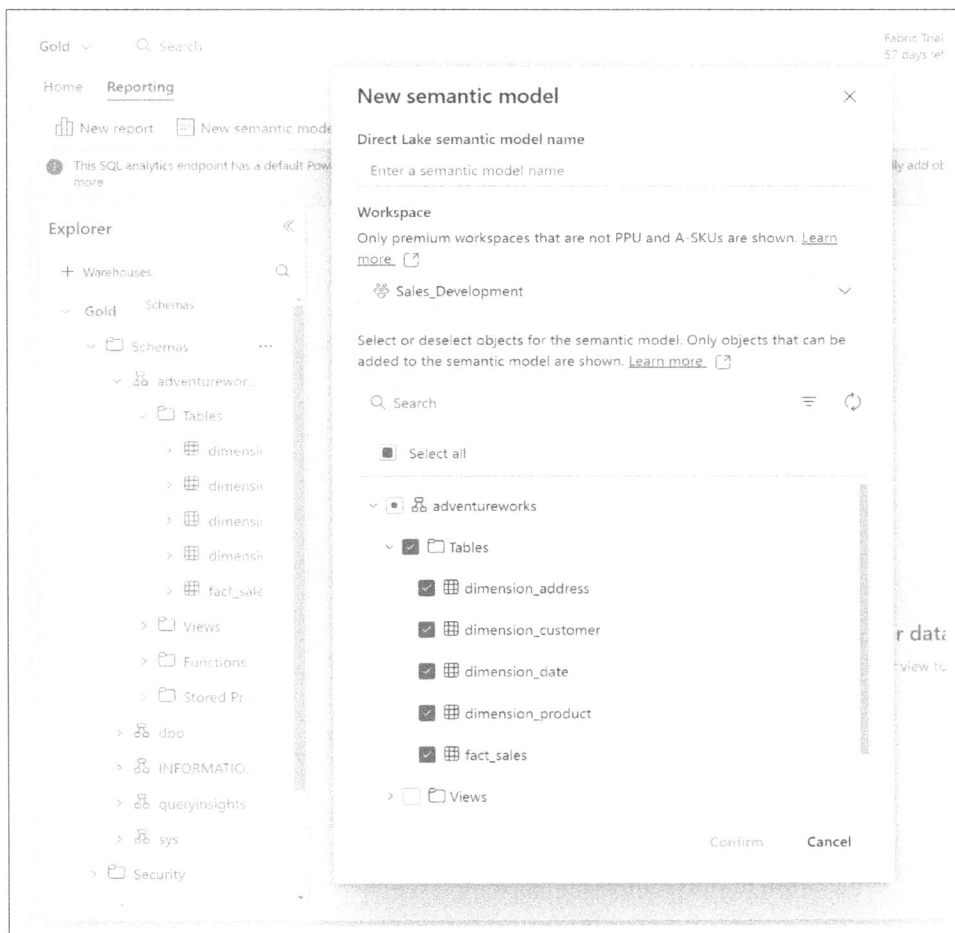

Figure 7-4. Create a new semantic model for the dimensional and fact tables

After you've set up your new semantic model, the setup should look like Figure 7-5.

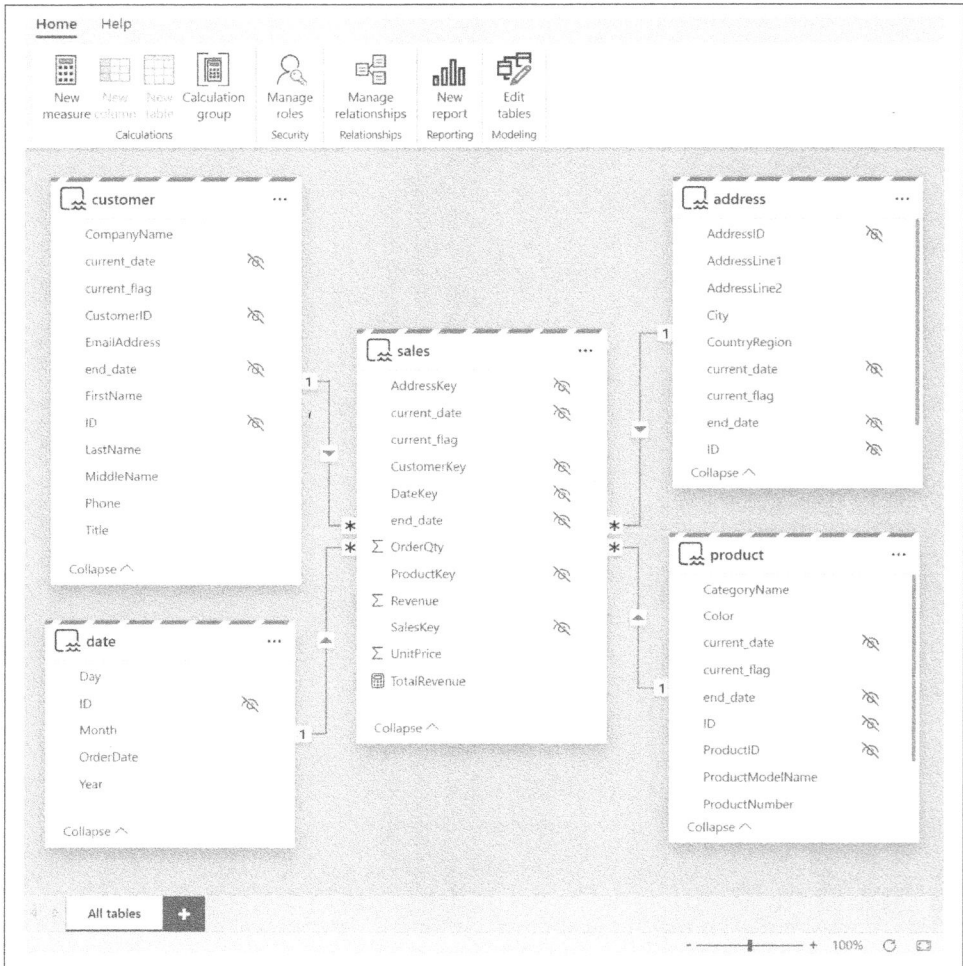

Figure 7-5. Overview of the semantic model for address, customer, date, product, and sales

Power BI DAX, short for Data Analysis Expressions, is a formula language used in Power BI to perform calculations and generate new information from existing data in your model. However, it can also make the calculations computationally intensive. Therefore, it is recommended to pre-calculate as much data as possible in the data source before importing it into Power BI. Additionally, optimizing DAX formulas by minimizing context transitions and using efficient functions can significantly enhance performance. Properly designing your data model, particularly using a star schema, and managing relationships with correct cardinality will further ensure that your Power BI reports and other consuming applications will be both fast and scalable.

Once you've established the relationships and measures in your semantic model, you're all set to create reports and dashboards in Power BI. This marks the final development step in the exercise.

Creation of the First Power BI Report

Power BI is a collection of software services that enables users to visualize data, share insights across an organization, or embed them in an app or website. It allows users to connect to a wide array of data sources, transform data into a model, and create visually appealing reports. For instance, you can create interactive reports on top of your Lakehouse data and share them with colleagues.

In this exercise, you'll use the semantic model as your data source. To start creating your report in Power BI, click on New Report and wait for it to load. Once the report canvas is open, begin by dragging and dropping fields from your tables onto the canvas. For example, pull in the TotalRevenue field from the `sales` table and the State-Province field from the `customer` table.

Next, create your visualizations. You can do this by selecting a clustered column chart from the visualization options and dragging it into your report. Arrange and format your visualizations to make the data clear and engaging.

After setting up your visualizations, your final report should resemble the example shown in Figure 7-6.

Once you are satisfied with the layout and content of your report, save it, for example, as RevenuePerState and publish it to your Workspace. This report will be directly connected to the Gold layer of your Lakehouse, ensuring it always reflects the most current data.

You now have the option to share this report with members of your organization or incorporate it into a PowerPoint presentation. Linking it to PowerPoint has the advantage of keeping the information connected to the Gold layer in the Lakehouse. This connection ensures your presentation data stays up-to-date effortlessly, while also adhering to the security practices and policies defined in the Lakehouse.

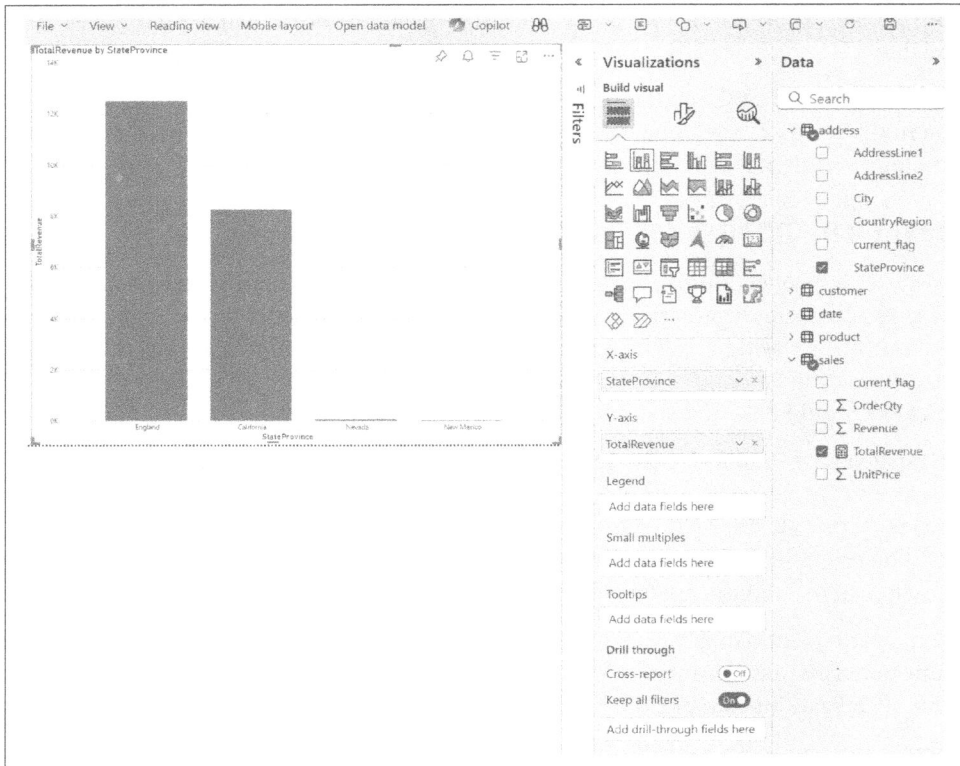

Figure 7-6. Example report in Power BI showing the total revenue per state/province

Before wrapping up and considering your next steps, let's document the process using task flows to ensure clarity and ease of replication in future projects.

Creation of Task Flows

Microsoft Fabric offers a feature called task flows (*https://oreil.ly/U3Xo5*), which helps visualize the workflow within your Workspace. This tool is helpful for understanding how different items relate to each other and work together, making it easier to navigate your Workspace as it grows in complexity.

To create a task flow, adjust the slider to the middle position, like in Figure 7-7. Then, start dragging tasks into the flow. Each task you add can represent a different type of work, such as processing, storing, or visualizing data. This visual tool is useful for documenting the steps you've taken in this exercise.

Once you've set up your task flow, it will automatically appear within your Workspace. Figure 7-7 is an example of how you could document the entire process flow.

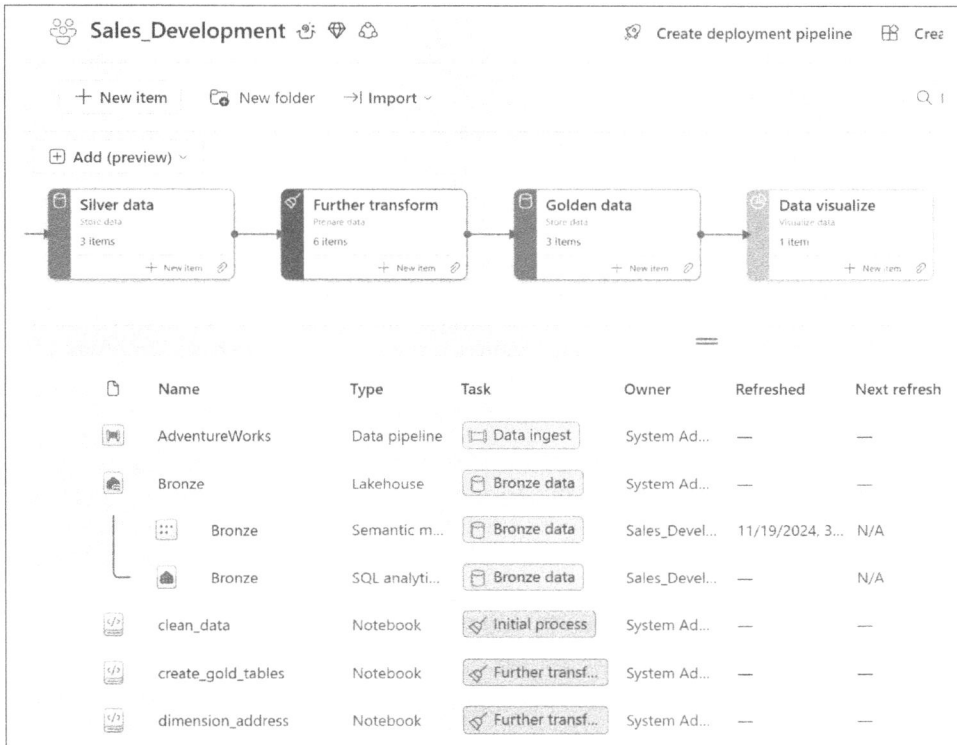

Figure 7-7. Canvas presentation of the different activities within the Workspace

Now that we've completed the exercise and all the hands-on activities are done, let's reflect on the steps we've taken and consider the overall design. This reflection will help you understand your achievements and plan future improvements.

Enhancements for Gold-Layer Design

You have approached the end of the tutorial. You've seen that the design of a star schema is both simple and effective. It provides a clear and concise view of the data, which speeds up analysis and decision making. Originally, the data was in a complex 3NF structure within the AdventureWorks source database, which was challenging for non-developers to work with. By transforming it into a more user-friendly structure, you've enhanced both readability and performance. This breakdown into clearly defined entities makes it easier for users to understand the data, its usage, and how to enhance it with additional data. Dimensional modeling in this exercise also assisted in creating layers of models for use in business intelligence tools.

However, there are several enhancements you could consider for the design:

Simplify for non-SQL users

For end users or data scientists who are not well-versed in SQL, a single, large table may be easier to understand than a star schema, even though it may not be as efficient for queries and maintenance. Additionally, creating a semantic model that features tables and columns with user-friendly names can also help those unfamiliar with SQL. Therefore, your Gold layer might include additional sublayers designed to be more accessible and user-friendly.

Improve data quality

Incorporating an additional data quality step in the Gold layer is strongly recommended, following the cleaning and joining of data in the Silver layer, to ensure the successful construction of the integrated dataset.

Furthermore, to ensure records can be accurately joined, you could ingest a placeholder record into each dimension in the Silver layer. This record would have a value of 0 for each column, making it easier to identify and address any missing data in the Gold layer. This is for situations where there is not a dimension record for an ID in the fact table. This placeholder record would help to identify the missing data and ensure the join is still successful.

Enhance performance

Adding partitioning to the schema could improve query performance by reducing the data volume scanned during queries. Another performance improvement could be implemented by using smaller lookup tables for retrieving the hashes of the dimension tables. This would reduce the amount of data scanned during joins.

Include auditing and processing columns

Adding columns like `created_at`, `updated_at`, and `source_system` to both fact and dimension tables helps track data lineage and facilitate troubleshooting.

Implement data security measures

You can introduce columns for row-level security to restrict data access based on user roles or permissions. For example, for the AdventureWorks database, you could introduce an additional `HumanResources.Employee` table to restrict data access based on the department each employee belongs to. You could then use the system function `USER_NAME()` to match the `LoginID` in the `Employee` table, determining which data the user can access. See Microsoft Fabric (*https://oreil.ly/ kk_MQ*) and Power BI (*https://oreil.ly/F7fJN*) for more information on row-level security.

Consider additional layers

Depending on the complexity of the data and the needs of the users, you might need to introduce additional layers (with fit-for-purpose tables) within the Gold layer. These layers could be for different use cases or business units; different applications might have varying requirements regarding data structure, granularity, or aggregation levels. These sublayers can be optimized individually, for instance by partitioning based on the usage characteristics. You could do something similar for overlapping requirements. You could create a common integration layer with conformed dimensions and data that is often input for different use cases. Then, you could add sublayers for specific use cases that require additional data or different aggregations.

Consider a physical serving layer

Depending on the complexity of the data and the needs of the users, you might need to introduce a physical serving layer. This is where data is copied from the Gold layer into one or more services as a way to make it easier for end users to access—products such as Azure Cosmos DB, Azure SQL Database, or a database for real-time intelligence (*https://oreil.ly/YqaJi*).

When it comes to technology architecture, particularly for the serving layer, it's crucial to understand that choosing a database or service is a complex procedure. It requires considering various factors and making numerous compromises. Beyond data structure, you'll need to assess your requirements in terms of consistency, availability, caching, timeliness, and indexing for enhanced performance. There are a variety of methods for storing and retrieving data, such as using small or large chunks, sorted chunks, etc. Contrary to what some enthusiasts may suggest, no single service can perfectly cater to all aspects simultaneously. A typical lakehouse architecture, therefore, usually comprises a blend of diverse technology services, such as a serverless SQL service for ad hoc queries, a columnar store for fast reporting, a relational database for more complicated queries, and a time-series store for IoT and stream analysis, among others.

Consider no-code or low-code tooling

Depending on the user base, it might be beneficial to introduce a no-code or low-code tooling layer on top of the Gold layer. This would allow users to (self-service) transform data without needing to write notebooks or SQL queries.

For example, in Microsoft Fabric, this could be achieved by using Dataflow Gen2 (*https://oreil.ly/qp-7B*).[6] See Figure 7-8 for an illustration of how the Gold layer could be transformed using a visual and low-code experience.

---

6 Mapping Data Flow to Microsoft Fabric (*https://oreil.ly/x2uE3*) is a converting solution for Azure Data Factory that allows you to translate your ADF data flows to Spark code.

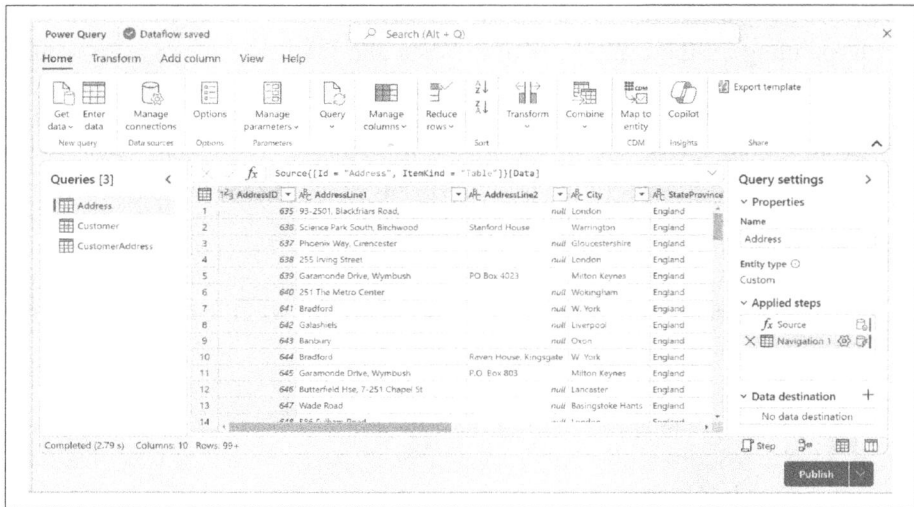

Figure 7-8. Dataflow Gen2 is a self-service and low-code data transformation service

Alternatively, Microsoft Fabric offers a tool called Data Wrangler (*https://oreil.ly/ RyAk8*) to speed up data exploration and preparation. This tool integrates with the pandas library and includes built-in visualizations to simplify the process. Check out Figure 7-9 to see how it prepares the Gold layer.

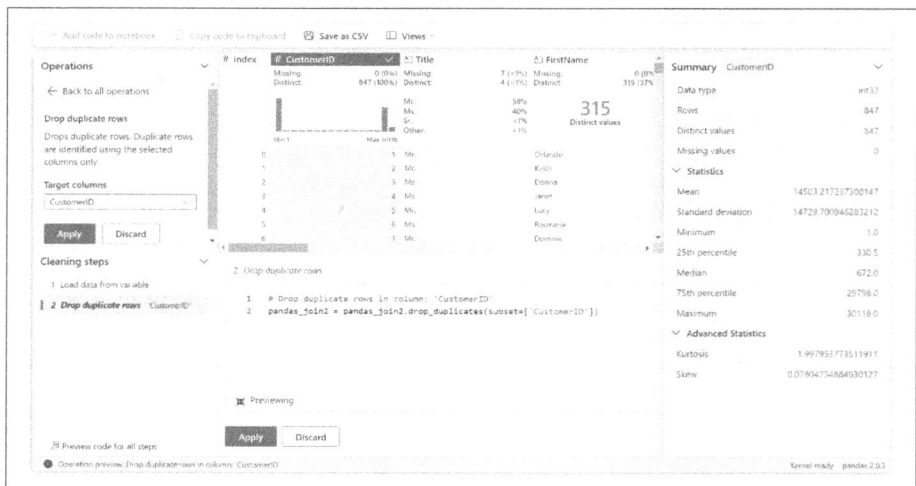

Figure 7-9. The Data Wrangler tool (a notebook-based resource that provides an immersive interface for exploratory data analysis)

Add Apache Airflow for orchestration
> Depending on your organization's requirements, you should consider adding Apache Airflow to orchestrate the data pipelines. You saw this in "Orchestration with Apache AirFlow" on page 182. This service can help automate the data pipeline, schedule jobs, and monitor the data processing.

Feature engineering and machine learning
> Design your Silver and Gold layers to enhance feature engineering and experimentation for machine learning. This might involve adapting the design to include additional Lakehouse and Spark environments to support these activities.

By considering these changes and incorporating semantic models into your design, you can further refine your Gold layer to better meet the needs of your users and handle the complexities of your data more effectively. Ultimately, the choice of this layer's design depends on the organization's maturity and data strategy, the specific areas of focus, and how data is utilized.

Let's conclude the exercise by summarizing the key takeaways and reflecting on the usage of Microsoft Fabric. After that, we'll explore the concept of data products and the management of those products using a data governance solution called Microsoft Purview.

Microsoft Fabric in Practice

As we conclude the tutorial on using Microsoft Fabric to develop the Medallion layers for Oceanic Airlines, we've highlighted its capabilities for managing large-scale data operations. In this context, it's worth noting that Microsoft Fabric offers more than just domains, Workspaces, and Lakehouses. It includes Copilot, AI tools, time-series KQL databases (*https://oreil.ly/qXzEs*), SQL databases (*https://oreil.ly/z1tFd*), real-time analytics, event streaming, machine learning, and integration with Microsoft Purview, all combined within a unified SaaS experience.

This integrated approach, with a more straightforward experience, lowers the entry barrier for newcomers. However, it offers less customization. Organizations with highly specific requirements or those that need granular control over their data operations might find Microsoft Fabric's all-in-one model somewhat restrictive. Additionally, as a relatively new platform, Microsoft Fabric may occasionally lack certain features. Understanding the differences between platforms is crucial for recognizing how they support different scenarios, and why there is room in the market for both individual and hybrid solutions.

Transitioning from the capabilities of Microsoft Fabric in creating data architectures, it is essential to delve into the concept of the data products that can be used within these architectures. Data products are essentially reusable building blocks that are designed to be easily consumable, scalable, and valuable in various contexts across an organization. They are pivotal in delivering actionable insights that drive business decisions and operations.

In Medallion architectures, data products represent a core component. Data products are often situated in the Gold layer, where they are refined and optimized for consumption by end users or downstream applications. Let's dive a bit deeper into the concept of data products and explore best practices for designing and managing them within the Gold layer.

Data Products

In "Silver-Layer Data as a Product" on page 189, the concept of data products was introduced, highlighting their importance as valuable assets that require careful management and attention. In the Medallion architecture, the Gold layer is vital for defining and creating data products. This layer focuses on making data directly usable for end users and applications, ensuring it is ready for business.

> There is no one-size-fits-all standard for data products in the industry, so there is no universal taxonomy, metadata standard, or interoperability standard to follow. Adding to the confusion, many viewpoints are overly conceptual and theoretical. For example, there is an ongoing debate about whether data products must include the data, metadata, processing code, and supporting infrastructure.
>
> My advice: develop your own standards with guidelines. Don't wait for others; take the initiative to create a standard that works for your organization. This will ensure consistency and clarity throughout your teams.

Organizations approach qualifying and designing data products in the Gold layer differently. Smaller organizations usually focus on offering insights into available data for consumption. This data often integrates into a broader data lakehouse architecture without clearly separating use case-specific data from data-product data. Then, the data catalog simply lists everything available that has been marked as ready for consumption.

Larger organizations typically adopt a different strategy. They set standards to separate use case-specific data from data meant for broader consumption. They might create distinct layers within the Gold layer, tag data products clearly in the catalog, or store them in a separate lakehouse entity. Data virtualization is another tactic, allowing the creation of virtual layers using views or shortcuts without needing physical copies. We'll explore these practices in "Separate Data Product Layers" on page 306.

No matter which approach you choose, having clear guidelines is essential for developing and managing data products effectively. When data teams work independently without guidance, they often end up creating data with slightly different and incompatible models. Sometimes, they produce data that's too narrowly focused on specific use cases. This makes data difficult to (re)use and leads to point-to-point interface problems. To tackle these challenges, it's essential to design data products with reusability in mind. Effective data modeling is crucial for achieving this versatility, yet it often gets overlooked.

Moreover, there's confusion about what a data product actually is and what reusability entails. In Table 7-1, I share some common physical examples I've encountered and explain the reasoning behind them.

Table 7-1. Example representations of data products

Scenario	Suitability	Best practice or design considerations
Raw system data in Bronze layer	Inadequate	Creates tight coupling; process data in Silver layer to reduce dependencies.
Delta table in Gold layer	Optimal	Design as a reusable dataset, such as "one big table," for efficient and versatile data access.
Several Delta tables in a dimensional model within the Gold layer	Exemplary	Optimize for easy consumption with minimal joins to enhance performance and usability. Ensure the model is well-documented and easy to understand. Also, ensure the model is decoupled from domain-specific workloads.
Report	Marginal	Reports are highly context-specific; consider them for local sharing only.
AI Model	Marginal	Models are hard to generalize. Instead, share underlying data.
Semantic model	Optimal	Develop for broad application and reusability.
Kafka or Event Hub topic	Adequate	Use state-carrying events and ensure reusability and compatibility.
Folder with PDF files	Inadequate	Unstructured data, such as a folder containing PDF files, requires additional processing and is not easily reused. Instead, provide a refined, processed version in a markup language that includes metadata for better usability and integration. More on this in Chapter 13.

To prevent issues and misunderstandings, it's crucial to set clear standards and guidelines for creating data products across different teams. These guidelines should focus on important aspects of data product design, including interoperability, data quality, data modeling, metadata, and governance. Here are some key areas that these guidelines should cover:

Introduction to data product guidelines

When it comes to data products, you'll notice there is no set industry standardization. This lack of uniformity underscores the importance of establishing an internal company standard. Therefore, clearly describe the definition of a data product, the purpose of the guidelines, and how they should be used in practice. In the context of Medallion architectures, consider defining a data product as a reusable logical entity, referenced by denormalized Delta tables or semantic models, that can be easily consumed.

It's vital to articulate the business rationale behind data product management. This includes the importance of robust data product design, as well as emphasizing data ownership and quality.

Types of data products

Creating various types of data products, each with its own maturity level and set of guiding principles, is an effective way to manage and utilize data strategically. For instance, you could differentiate between operational data products (in a Silver layer) and analytical data products (in a Gold layer).

Data modeling guidance

To ensure consistency, reliability, and usability of data across the organization, establishing strong data modeling standards is vital. Consider the following:

- Adopt best practices for granularity, reference data, data types, schema details, keys, and classification.
- Require atomic data that enables correctly linking data elements to business terms within a catalog.
- Handle data concatenation effectively. For example, you could construct the SKU (e.g., "ELC-00123") in sales system fields by concatenating the `Category_Code` (e.g., "ELC" for electronics) and `Product_ID` (e.g., "00123") from inventory system fields.
- Provide guidelines on managing keys within and across systems to simplify integration between domains.
- Develop strategies for addressing incomplete data entries and managing scenarios where essential fields are missing.
- Offer guidance on local-to-local and enterprise-wide reference mappings.
- Encapsulate or provide metadata for security purposes.
- Use reserved column names wisely and manage historical data with clear strategies for appending, overwriting, merging, and structural changes.

Governance guidance

Data governance is essential for ensuring data quality, compliance, and security. Here are some key governance guidelines to consider:

- Provide guidance for correct data cataloging.
- Provide detailed guidance on the organizational roles involved, along with development, onboarding, and registration processes.
- Recommend strategies for identifying unique and external data sources.
- Outline guidelines to ensure data quality, including remediation processes for addressing data quality issues within source systems.
- Set guidelines for managing data products used by multiple business teams.
- Provide guidance on managing snapshots from legacy systems like outdated data warehouses.
- Develop strategies for effective master data management, including the inclusion of master identifiers within data products.
- Address the handling of data redeliveries and overwrites.
- Detail the escalation process and the use of discussion boards for issue resolution.
- Describe the lifecycle of data products from creation to retirement, including version management.
- Detail the process of consuming data products, including the process for requesting access and the approval workflow.

Understanding the nuances between data products and use case-specific data is pivotal for effective data management. In Chapter 12, we explore the critical role of data products in scaling operations and delve into the importance of robust data governance within the Medallion architecture. This discussion will equip you with the knowledge to enhance organizational efficiency and data utility.

Having explored the concept and implementation of data products within the Medallion architecture, it's crucial to address the governance of these data assets. Effective data management is not complete without a robust data governance framework to ensure data quality, compliance, and security across the board. This is where a data governance solution, such as Microsoft Purview, comes into play.

Data Governance with Microsoft Purview

Microsoft Purview (*https://oreil.ly/jMSvv*) offers a suite of features designed to manage and monitor data effectively. It serves as a data governance and security solution that simplifies management and enhances visibility and control throughout the entire data lifecycle. For data governance, the platform provides Microsoft Purview Unified Catalog (*https://oreil.ly/WMBZ_*), which comes with features such as lineage tracing, data products, critical data elements, objectives and key results (OKRs), and data quality measures, which assist organizations in overseeing their data assets from multiple perspectives.

Clarifying the Ambiguity of Domains

The concept of "domain" gained prominence through domain-driven design (DDD), a methodology tailored for complex systems within large organizations. This approach has significantly influenced contemporary software and application development strategies, including microservices and data mesh.

In the realm of DDD, domains are defined as specific problem spaces that an organization aims to address. These domains encapsulate knowledge, behavior, laws, and activities, and are characterized by semantic coupling—this includes organizational or behavioral dependencies among teams, systems, or services. To simplify management and enhance clarity, domains are often segmented into subdomains, each aligning with different organizational facets.

However, the use of the term *domain* can lead to ambiguity due to varying interpretations. For instance, a "business domain" might refer to a company's core activities, priorities, applications, and data. In contrast, a "governance domain" could encompass aspects like common governance, ownership, and the cataloging of data products and crucial business concepts, such as glossary terms. Similarly, a "data domain" may be concerned with the boundaries within which data is collected, processed, harmonized, and distributed, while a "technical domain" or "application domain" might focus on the technology and applications that support specific business functions.

Despite the popularity of domain-driven design in defining these boundaries, I have reservations about its application within data mesh environments, particularly due to its heavy reliance on software-centric methodologies. Instead, I propose defining boundaries based on business capabilities, which can provide a more practical and effective framework for delineating responsibilities and roles within an organization. An alternative approach could involve employing principles from the International Society for Knowledge Organization (*https://oreil.ly/THcAp*), which offers another robust method for clearly defining these areas.

It is crucial to address that domains can overlap or merge, adding layers of complexity to their management. For example, a single business domain might rely on multiple data domains, which in turn could depend on various technical domains. Conversely, multiple business domains might be grouped under a larger governance domain. Therefore, it is imperative to precisely define each domain's boundaries to avoid overlaps and prevent unintended mergers. This clarity is essential for maintaining organizational efficiency and coherence.

In Microsoft Purview, the term *domain* refers to data management organization at both the technology and business levels. It's used in different settings as a boundary for grouping metadata together and facilitating governance tasks, such as data ownership and discovery of data. In the following sections, we will explore how domains relate to Medallion architectures by focusing on the concept of domains within Microsoft Purview.

Microsoft Purview Design Considerations

Let's kick things off with Microsoft Purview. To get started, create a Microsoft Purview account.[7] Next, it's essential to focus on setting up governance domains and collections. These are your first steps for Microsoft Purview, and they are crucial for managing data products and business concepts effectively.

You can find excellent resources to guide you through these initial setups. I suggest checking out "Get Started with the New Data Governance Experience in Microsoft Purview" (*https://oreil.ly/i_kLY*) and "Set Up Your Governance Domains" (*https://oreil.ly/nH-jU*) for a solid foundation on how to organize and govern your data.

> Sarath Sasidharan and I have a YouTube channel called Data Pancakes (*https://oreil.ly/JM2Hf*), where we discuss various data topics, including data governance with Microsoft Purview.

For Microsoft Purview, two types of domains are essential: governance domains and collections. Governance domains are all about managing your data products and business concepts. Collections, on the other hand, are used to group metadata during technical scans. In the next sections, we'll explore each of these concepts in more detail.

Governance domains

In a flat data catalog, every data asset appears as a separate piece of information, making it challenging for data owners and stewards to govern each one effectively. Since data is dynamic and grows with the organization, these stewards need scalable tools to manage the increasing number of data assets.

This is where governance domains come into action. At its core, a governance domain acts as a boundary that facilitates common governance across the organization. These domains are designed to be flexible, allowing your organization to establish boundaries that best suit your data needs. For example, you might set up a

---

7 For guidance, see the quickstart documentation (*https://oreil.ly/V5RT6*).

governance domain specifically for a business unit like finance, or focus on a particular subject area, such as customer data or product information.

To get a clearer picture, take a look at the example of governance domains in Microsoft Purview shown in Figure 7-10. This screenshot shows information about data ownership, data products and business concepts like glossary terms, OKRs, and critical data elements.

Governance domains set clear boundaries and provide a wide view of your contextual information and technical data assets. These domains connect to data products, and from there, to data assets, all of which are organized within collections.

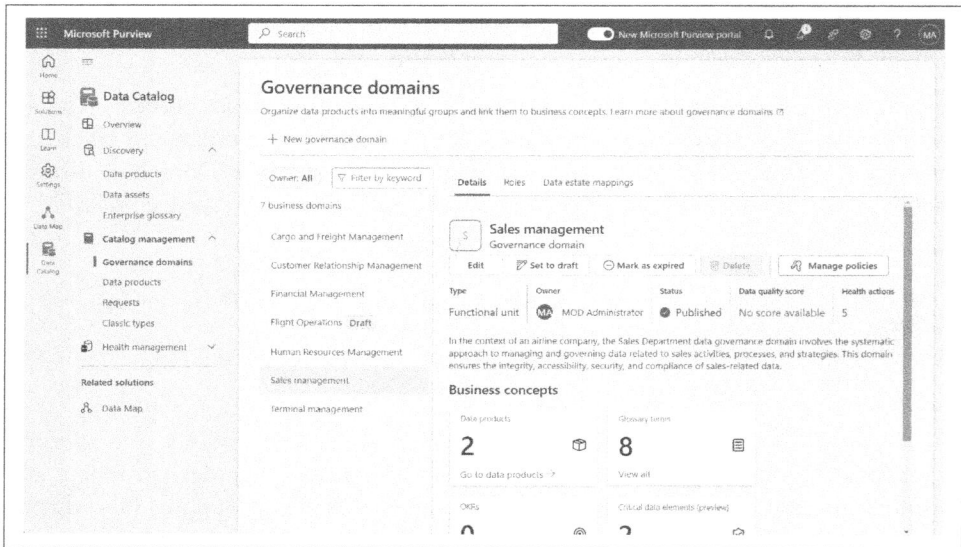

Figure 7-10. Microsoft Purview's Governance Domain overview page

Collections

Collections manage and organize information (metadata) about your technical domains. At this stage, you can also assign specific roles, including data source administrators and collection administrators, to oversee the management of these data assets. This configuration is crucial for scanning and managing metadata about source systems and applications.

In Figure 7-11, you can see how a collection structure is organized in Microsoft Purview. Within the collection overview, you have the ability to register and manage data sources, scans, and assets.

Figure 7-11 showcases the Oceanic Airlines project as an example. It features a root collection named Oceanic Airlines, which includes shared services like Microsoft

Fabric and Azure Databricks. Positioning these shared services higher in the hierarchy is essential for two main reasons. First, you can't register data sources multiple times in a single Microsoft Purview account. So each unique service can only be registered in a collection once. Second, Microsoft Purview only allows metadata to be distributed across its children collections, not siblings. So, placing a shared service, such as Microsoft Fabric, higher in the hierarchy ensures that metadata can be distributed effectively within the catalog.

You see a collection named "Operational systems." This collection groups metadata from operational systems like the Azure SQL database from AdventureWorks. This arrangement helps to keep all the related services together. In a larger organization, you might have multiple operational systems, each with its own collection.

Lastly, the "Lines of Business" collection groups metadata from the different lines of business within the organization, such as the Sales business domain. It seems empty in the screenshot, but it is a placeholder for aligning with the metadata that will be scanned when collecting metadata from the platform, such as Microsoft Fabric.

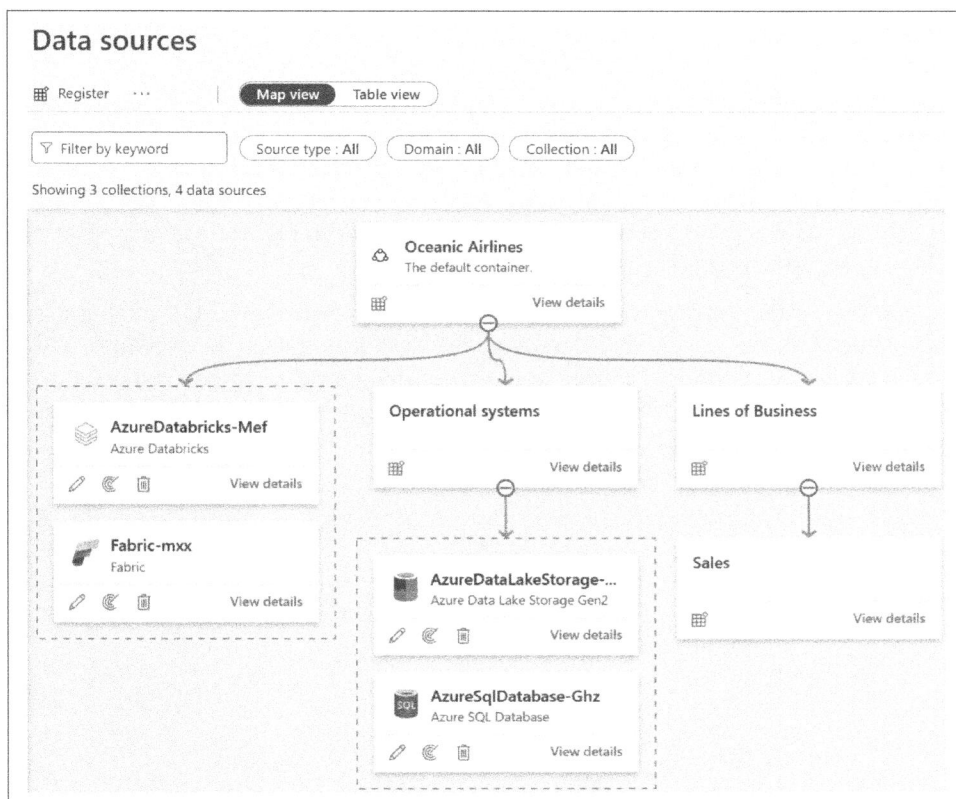

Figure 7-11. Microsoft Purview's Data Sources overview page

Integrating Unity Catalog with Microsoft Purview

Unity Catalog (*https://oreil.ly/lkixC*) is a data governance tool for managing and securing data in Azure Databricks, which is explored in greater detail in Chapter 12. It primarily focuses on the operational aspects of data governance within Azure Databricks, whereas Microsoft Purview offers a wider strategic perspective on data governance across your entire data landscape. If your data governance needs to extend across various technologies and platforms, Microsoft Purview might be the more suitable choice.

However, you can integrate the two catalogs to enhance your data management capabilities. This integration allows you to discover data and visualize lineage from your Azure Databricks Workspaces and organize it into collections within Microsoft Purview. The process for scanning is quite straightforward and similar to scanning of Microsoft Fabric. You start by registering Unity Catalog, then choose the Azure Databricks Workspaces you want to scan, and finally, categorize the data into a specific collection. You can find more information about connecting and scanning in the documentation (*https://oreil.ly/s2htd*).

When it comes to scanning Microsoft Fabric as a technical source for metadata, you can use a feature called *scoped scanning*. This feature not only allows you to choose specific Workspaces to scan for metadata but also lets you decide which collection the metadata should fall into. For instance, metadata from Fabric Workspaces related to the Sales domain will be inserted into the Sales collection. Figure 7-12 is an example of how to set up a scoped scan in Microsoft Purview.

Once you scan the Workspace, the metadata becomes available to the catalog users. This metadata covers technical details about data assets such as pipelines, Lakehouses, tables, columns, and more. You can use this metadata to effectively describe your data products. Let's delve deeper into the concept of data products and explore how they relate to data assets in Microsoft Fabric.

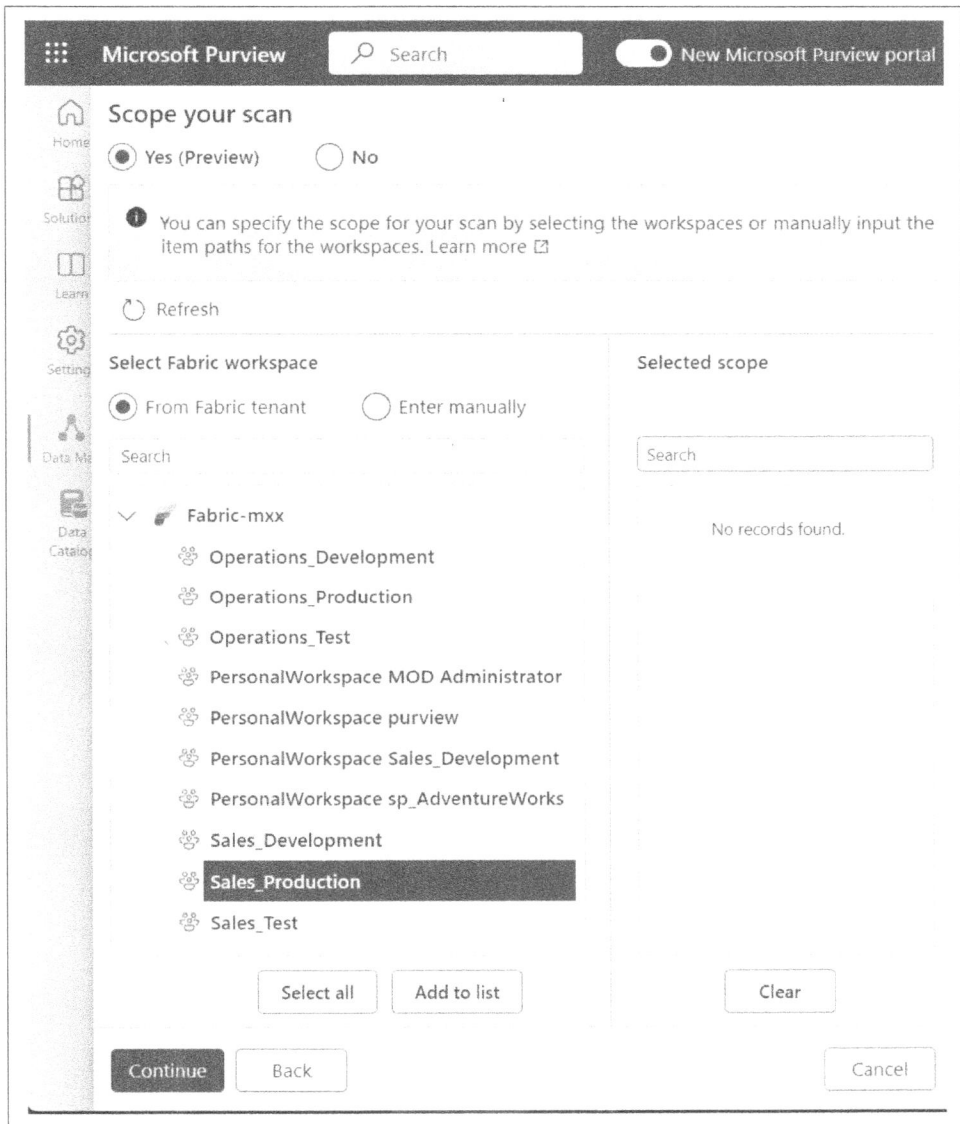

Figure 7-12. Microsoft Purview's scoped scanning feature in action

Microsoft Purview data products

After you've set up your collection structure and scanned for metadata about your technical domains, you should start creating data products (*https://oreil.ly/bSlpm*). In essence, this means drawing lines between your technical metadata (collection structure) and your business concepts (governance domains). This is where data products come into play.

In Microsoft Purview, data products are logical entities that group one or more data assets together for a particular business purpose. They are the linking pin between governance domains and collections. They help organizations manage, govern, and promote data effectively, ensuring data quality, lineage, and compliance. For an example screenshot of a data product in Microsoft Purview, see Figure 7-13.

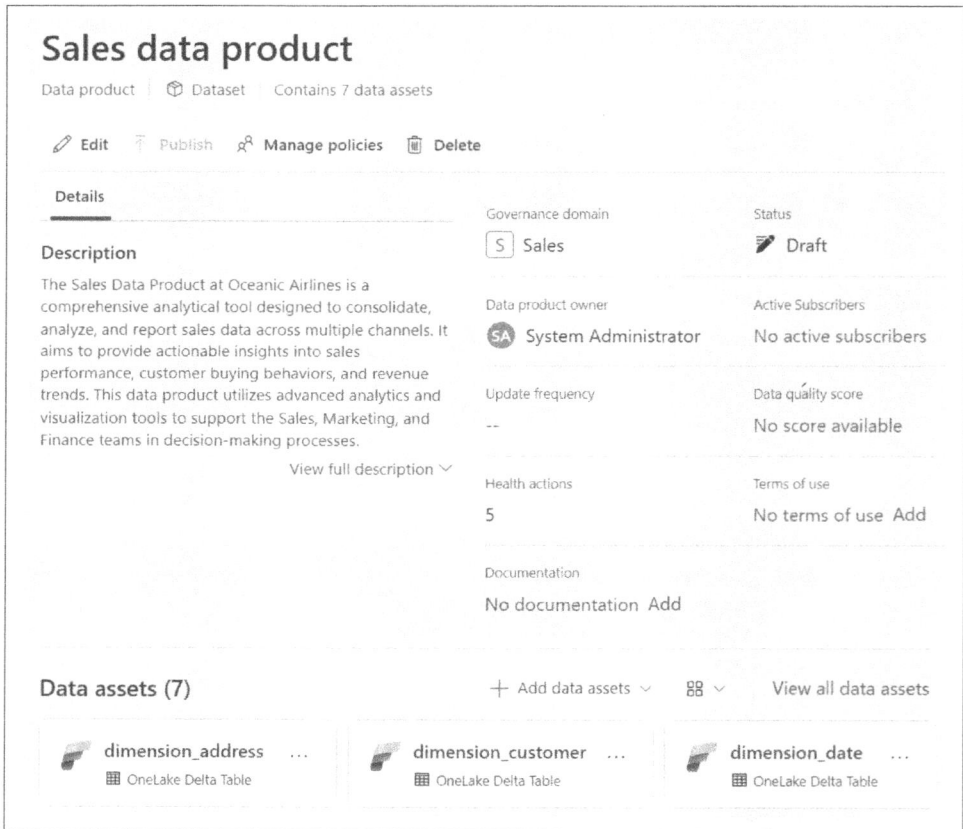

Figure 7-13. A data product in Microsoft Purview

In Figure 7-13, you see a data product belonging to a specific domain, owned by an employee within the organization. You'll also notice health actions, update frequency, and the data assets used for the data product. Furthermore, and depending on the access rights, you could also see a button, "Request access," which allows users to request access to the data product. This feature is particularly useful for ensuring data security and compliance. What you don't see in the screenshot is the lineage of the data product, which is crucial for understanding the data's origin and how it's been transformed. The data product might contain business terms, critical data elements, and OKRs, which are essential for understanding the data's context and usage.

Microsoft Purview's data products are designed with flexibility in mind. They can store a variety of items, including tables, files, Power BI reports, and machine learning models. This means they're not limited to just Delta tables from your lakehouse. You can also categorize these data products into types like dataset, operational, business system/application, and more. Additionally, you can share data assets across multiple data products, which enhances the flexibility in managing them.

While this flexibility is beneficial, it's critically important to establish clear standards for defining data products. Like we discussed before, you need to define guidelines on what data products encompass, how they connect to other elements, and their overall definitions to ensure consistency and effectiveness. If not, you might end up with a catalog full of data products containing technical system tables or different data product owners for the same data asset. This highlights how crucial it is to have clear guidelines to avoid these pitfalls.

To review, data products in Microsoft Purview are logical entities that can group one or more data assets together for a particular business purpose. They are the linking pin for governance domains and help organizations manage and govern data effectively, ensuring data quality, lineage, and compliance.

Now that we've covered the basic concepts of data governance and Microsoft Purview, let's explore how it can effectively manage the Medallion architecture.

Guidance for Medallion Architectures

Let's explore how Microsoft Fabric and Microsoft Purview connect within the Medallion architecture in terms of data management. We'll begin with Microsoft Fabric. Here, as you explored in Chapter 5, a domain is a way of logically grouping together all the data in an organization that is relevant to a particular area or field. To group data into domains, Workspaces are associated with domains. In this setting, a domain is considered either a technical domain or a data domain. Using consistent domain terms is crucial when employing services like Microsoft Fabric and Microsoft Purview, as their meanings can vary.

In the context of Microsoft Purview, a *governance domain* is used to define a boundary that encapsulates specific business concepts and data assets under a unified ownership structure. Microsoft Purview also introduces the concept of *collection*.

The term *domain* also appears within the collection interface, but it carries a different meaning in this context. Here, *domain* refers to a method for organizing technical metadata when scanning source systems and applications. This usage aligns closely with the concept of a domain in Microsoft Fabric, but it should not be confused with a governance domain.

The key question now is: how do these different types of domains in Microsoft Purview and Microsoft Fabric interact together with the business domains within the overall architecture?

Figure 7-14 illustrates the interaction between different types of business domains. For example, you have the Sales business domain that was part of the hands-on exercise. There's another business domain called "Airflight Operations Management." This business domain handles its own source systems using another Medallion architecture. Last, but not least, there's the Consumer Services business domain. Unlike the others, it doesn't have its own source systems but relies on data from both the Sales and Airflight Operations domains, integrating this data into its own Medallion architecture. Thus, in total, there are three Medallion architectures.

To ensure effective data governance, each business domain will align with its own governance domain in Microsoft Purview. These governance domains are at the top of Figure 7-14. Each governance domain oversees the governance of data products and business concepts. From a governance perspective, a governance domain manages data throughout its entire lifecycle, from operational systems to data products.

One level lower, you'll encounter collections, which organize metadata about data assets. It's crucial to maintain clear relationships between collections and governance domains to prevent any overlap or merging. In this design, there is a split between operational systems and analytical services. This separation ensures that metadata about operational systems is kept separate from metadata about data products, making it easier to manage and govern data effectively.

Moving closer to the middle and bottom, you'll notice how the collections are connected to source systems and Microsoft Fabric Workspaces. This setup ensures metadata is accurately linked to data from specific parts of the architecture. These source systems and Workspaces together form what is often referred to as a *business domain*. This is the domain where data is actively used and managed by the business, such as in the Sales business domain.

However, there is an exception in the Consumer Services business domain. Unlike others, it doesn't collect data from its own source systems. Instead, it relies on data from the Sales and Airflight Operations Management business domains. Consequently, it only possesses a data domain without an application domain.

The main takeaway from this governance structure is that, in this example, governance domains oversee the entire data lifecycle. They manage data in both operational systems, which you call application domains, and data used for analytics, known as data domains. This involves horizontal teams that handle everything from operational systems to data products. The only exception is the Consumer Services domain, which doesn't have its own source systems but uses data from other domains.

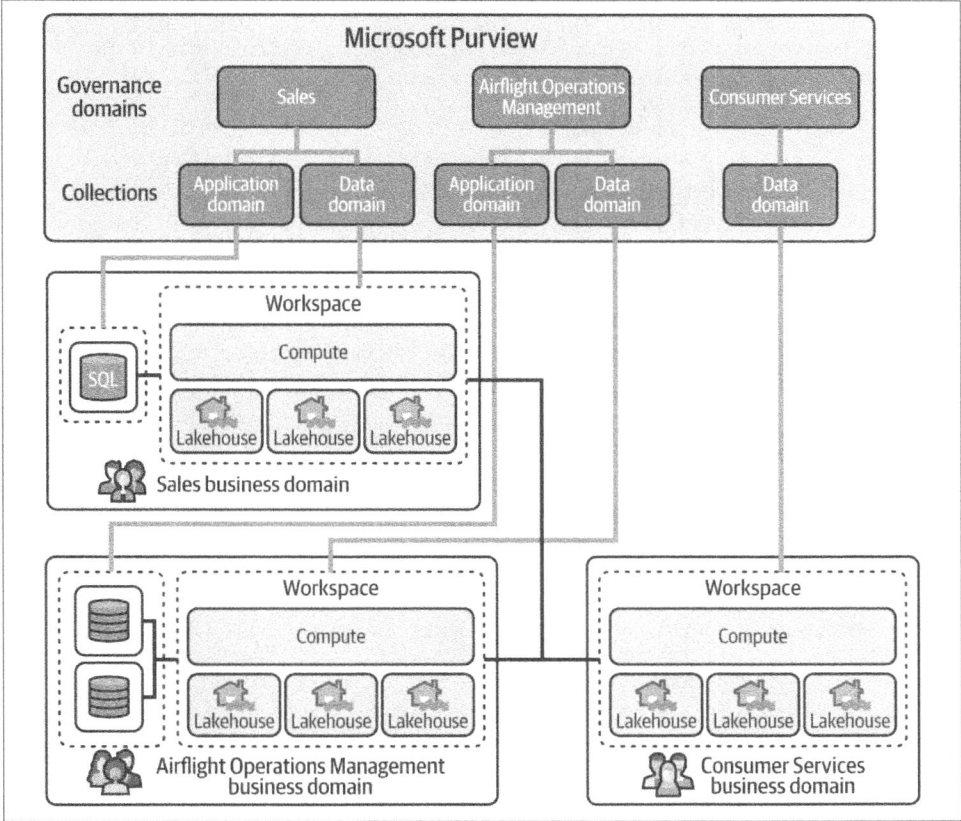

Figure 7-14. The connections between business domains, governance domains, and collections of Microsoft Purview, and the data domains and Workspaces of Microsoft's Fabric (the Sales business domain, which manages both an application domain and a data domain, is highlighted)

Could you approach this differently? Absolutely. For example, you might choose to create separate governance domains for operational systems and analytical services. This strategy allows you to independently manage data from operational systems and data products. This setup could be particularly useful in organizations where different teams handle the source systems and the data products. Imagine a scenario where an application team handles the source systems, while a different data engineering team takes care of the data products.

Alternatively, you could group all collections related to application domains and connect them to a single or larger governance domains. This arrangement would work well if a centralized IT or larger team oversees all the source systems and applications.

What implications do these insights have for the Medallion architecture? To ensure effective data governance, it is essential to align the architecture's different layers with the roles and responsibilities of your teams or team members.

Begin by defining your objectives for the catalog and devising a detailed plan for implementing data architecture. This initial step will help organize and manage domains effectively while setting clear criteria for granularity to avoid confusion and overlap. Next, evaluate the structure of the workspaces, layers, and data products within your Medallion architecture. Consider crucial questions such as the following: should the Bronze, Silver, and Gold layers always be managed within a single workspace? Do these workspaces align with specific collections and governance domains? Is there a need for additional layers or separate workspaces tailored to particular use cases or business units? Also, explore whether these adjustments might require new governance domains. Reflecting on these questions will aid in establishing a robust governance framework. Consider the following scenarios:

Decentralized management

Each business domain manages its own source systems and maintains a separate Medallion architecture, which includes multiple workspaces for development, testing, and production. It might be beneficial to establish distinct governance domains for each business unit or department to ensure proper alignment.

Centralized engineering with distributed usage

A single Medallion architecture comprises multiple workspaces housing various lakehouse entities. For example, all ingestion and cleaning tasks are handled by a single engineering team, while additional workspaces are dedicated to different teams that perform data harmonization for various business use cases. In this scenario, multiple governance domains may be linked to the same collection structure(s).

Central management

A central IT team manages all source systems, applications, and data integration. Here, you could organize all collections related to application domains and connect them to various governance domains.

Hybrid approach

This scenario combines elements of decentralized and centralized management. For instance, certain critical data domains might be managed centrally to maintain control over key data assets and ensure compliance with regulatory requirements, while other less critical data domains are managed by individual business units for improved agility and responsiveness.

By considering these scenarios, you can select a structure that best suits the needs and operations of your organization, ensuring a smooth and effective implementation of the architecture. In all cases, clear guidance is essential to maintain consistency and prevent confusion.

It is crucial to develop a clear governance framework that aligns with your organization's data strategy. First, determine who owns the data. Understanding the internal roles involved in data management is vital. Consider whether you are moving toward decentralized data management, or if there is potential for a central data governance team to oversee critical data. Answering these questions will help you refine your governance framework and may introduce new requirements for your architecture.

> If you want to strictly define how data products relate to specific data assets in Microsoft Fabric, consider using my Purview-Bulk-Collection-Mover application (*https://oreil.ly/lZArX*). This small web app lets you move metadata in bulk between collections, ensuring metadata in a collection only relates to data from one specific layer of your Medallion architecture.

Finally, consider the processes and access control policies you need to establish to ensure that only authorized users can access the data. For example, you might provision empty workspaces with shortcuts to data, allowing users to access data only through read-only interfaces. This approach ensures that users cannot access data directly but only through the shortcuts, governed by access control policies. For more insights into managing and scaling strategies effectively, refer to Chapter 11. This chapter guides you in making informed decisions that enhance your architecture's functionality, efficiency, and security.

Conclusion

On your journey through the Medallion architecture, you began with ingesting data into the Bronze layer, moved on to the more refined Silver layer, and finally delved into the complex Gold layer. The primary objectives are to improve data quality, enhance performance, and align the data architecture with business goals.

The Gold layer plays a pivotal role in effective decision making and generating insightful reports. By developing this layer, you made sure the data is accurate, readily accessible, and optimized for high-performance querying and analytics. You also explored creating reports using Power BI and examined Microsoft Purview for data governance. Here are some key insights from this chapter:

- The Gold layer requires the implementation of complex business logic to accurately reflect business needs. It must ensure that the data models are both meaningful and accessible. In this context, prioritize use cases based on business impact, feasibility, and resource availability, and conduct regular reviews to identify and manage overlapping business logic centrally.

- When constructing reports and semantic models, it's crucial to balance data retrieval from the lakehouse. Use Import mode for optimal performance and handling complex calculations, while employing DirectLake or DirectQuery for accessing real-time data. For direct querying, you have the option to either use predefined views or to apply filters directly within the reports themselves. As you learned, there are implications for each mode, so choose wisely.

- For data governance, evaluate the appropriate number of governance domains, collections, and their levels of granularity carefully. This requires a data governance framework that aligns with your organization's data strategy. It should describe roles, processes for onboarding and consuming data, and responsibilities for managing data products and business concepts.

- Create your own set of standards for data products since there's no one-size-fits-all rule in the industry. Start by setting clear guidelines for designing data products. This will help maintain consistency and clarity throughout your company. Your guidelines should cover how to structure data and make data products easily accessible for business users. You might also consider including specific instructions, such as using `optimizeWrite` to enable V-ordering when creating Delta tables.

- Consider segregating use case-specific data and data-product data by using separate workspaces and lakehouse entities. Alternatively, use the data catalog to differentiate between them.

- Define clear access control policies to ensure that only authorized users can access sensitive data, for example by provisioning empty workspaces with shortcuts to data. We will revisit these topics in Part IV.

Finally, building the Gold layer is more than just a technical task; it's about strategically aligning technology with your business vision and data strategy.

That wraps up Part II, as the Gold layer marks the end of the journey of building a Medallion architecture. We've covered a lot of ground! You started with the Bronze layer by exploring how to ingest and set up data using Data Factory. Then, you moved on to the Silver layer, refining data and managing processes with Airflow, while sharpening your SQL and PySpark skills. Finally, you rounded out your skills with the Gold layer by building a dimensional model and enabling reporting with Power BI.

This tutorial is just one way of designing a Medallion architecture. There can and will be many variations depending on your specific requirements and the nuances you wish to incorporate, which is explored in Chapter 11.

As a closing remark, in this exercise, you built a basic lakehouse architecture from scratch, by taking some shortcuts and using a simplified process. While it's not ready for production yet, it serves as a solid starting point. Hopefully, this has helped you gain a better understanding of the key activities that must be performed and how they relate to each other. Moving forward, knowing which recommendations to follow could further enhance your understanding and implementation of this architecture.

For this project, I opted for Microsoft Fabric but also made sure to focus on patterns and technologies you can take anywhere. Spark, Delta Lake, and Airflow, for instance, are flexible enough to fit into various environments. Data Factory and Power BI are well-known for their robustness and extensive integration capabilities with other platforms. This means the strategies and best practices we've embraced can also be applied to other platforms, like Azure Databricks. Essentially, you can build a Medallion architecture on any platform that supports Spark and Delta Lake using the guidance from this book.

Interestingly, I had to revise the exercise for the Bronze and Silver layers before finalizing this book. Since I couldn't use certain services anymore, I quickly switched gears and replaced the guidance in just a few days. This experience highlighted the importance of being adaptable, embracing portability, and using an open architecture in the fast-changing tech world.

Let's carry the lessons learned from this part into practical insights from the field. In Part III, we'll learn from real enterprises to see how they've implemented their Medallion architectures. This will give you valuable insights that you can apply to our own initiatives.

Real-World Case Studies

In this part, we delve into real-world applications of the Medallion architecture through detailed case studies from leading companies. This part not only showcases the adaptability and effectiveness of the Medallion model across different industries but also provides practical insights into scaling these architectures. By examining these case studies, you will gain a deeper understanding of how to tailor the Medallion architecture to meet specific business needs and objectives. The final chapter focuses on strategies for managing and scaling multiple Medallion architectures within the same organization and looks forward to the future developments in this field.

Chapter 8 explores how AP Pension, a prominent pension fund, implemented the Medallion architecture to enhance their data handling and analytics capabilities. This case study provides insights into the challenges faced by AP Pension and how they overcame them by adopting a layered approach.

In Chapter 9, we look at Amadeus, a leader in providing technology solutions for the travel industry. This case study demonstrates how they adopted the Medallion architecture to handle vast amounts of data and streamline their operations. We focus on their strategies for integrating disparate data sources and leveraging real-time data processing to enhance customer experiences and operational efficiency.

In Chapter 10, we examine how ZEISS, a global leader in the optics industry, utilized the Medallion architecture to improve their data management and analytics processes. This case study not only sheds light on the technicalities of managing large-scale data systems but also reflects on the broader implications for data governance, integration, and sharing within a global operation.

Case Study: Data, Analytics and Business Strategy at AP Pension

In this chapter, we delve into the Medallion design employed by AP Pension (*https:// appension.dk/en*), a venerable Danish pension fund. Head of Data Platform Jacob Rønnow Jensen shares his vision of the integration of AP Pension's business and data strategy. He highlights the company's journey toward adopting a modern data platform using Microsoft Fabric. We will explore how AP Pension addresses technical challenges, aligns data protection with data democratization principles, and optimizes the operation and overall efficiency of their analytical platform.

Jacob offers a transparent look at the evolution of data platforms, the role of lakehouses, and AP Pension's management of a complex data landscape to maintain a competitive edge in the financial sector. We begin with an introduction to the company and its data strategy before delving into a detailed examination of the Bronze, Silver, and Gold layers of their Medallion architecture.

During this exploration, we will uncover how AP Pension manages data ingestion, metadata, and real-time data, along with their approach for deserializing JSON, and handling sensitive personal information. Jacob will share insights on CI/CD processes, workspace design, and the integration with Microsoft Purview.

We conclude with Jacob's recommendations and insights on workload isolation, security, and logical data separation, as well as workspace and capacity management. This chapter offers a comprehensive look at how AP Pension leverages data to drive business success in the era of data and AI with Microsoft Fabric.

Piethein Strengholt: Jacob, thanks for joining me today. Let's start by getting to know you. Could you share a bit about yourself, your role, and the company you work for?

Jacob Rønnow Jensen: Thank you for having me, Piethein. My name is Jacob Rønnow Jensen, and I head the data platform team at AP Pension. Our company is a customer-owned Danish pension fund with a history spanning 105 years. Originally, we were founded by some of Denmark's largest cooperatives. Today, we serve approximately 400,000 customers across many industries and employ over 700 people. We remain independent and are dedicated to the democratic principles established at our founding. Our customer-focused strategy centers on delivering high yields while maintaining low costs, sharing profits, and investing sustainably.

Piethein Strengholt: You briefly touched on your business strategy. Can you explain how it connects to your data strategy?

Jacob Rønnow Jensen: In 2023, AP Pension launched a new business strategy that includes a comprehensive digital strategy set to unfold through 2029. The initial phase, spanning 2023 and 2024, was dedicated to reducing technical debt and establishing foundational elements for future activities. Key initiatives included a new cloud-based administrative platform for handling customer and policy data, as well as a modern analytical platform—the latter being my team's responsibility. In the "Acceleration Phase" running from 2025 to 2027, we begin rolling out the new foundation and capabilities to the users and customers.

As part of this digital strategy, we've outlined several guiding principles focused on customer-centricity, automation, modularity, cloud adoption, digital responsibility, documentation, and enhancing collaboration.

To supplement the digital strategy, we have a separate data strategy. In this strategy, we describe the concept of data products and our vision for data quality and governance in a setup where we differentiate strictly between operational and analytical data, since they serve different purposes, each tailored to support our overarching goals. To integrate this relatively comprehensive and extensive data strategy effectively into our day-to-day decision-making processes in the data platform team, we have encapsulated the essence of the strategy for analytical data into four key statements—the first being strategic and the latter three being more operational:

1. Data should be well-protected, documented, user-friendly, and aligned with AP Pension's information model.
2. We should move data around as little as possible—but not less.
3. We should employ as few technologies as possible—but not fewer.
4. Total cost of ownership should be as low as possible—but not lower.

These four statements all have focus on streamlining the operations of the analytical data platform and enhancing our service delivery, as well as aligning with AP Pension's long-term business and digital objectives.

Piethein Strengholt: Can you share how AP Pension's data platforms have evolved, given AP Pension's long history?

Jacob Rønnow Jensen: Absolutely. AP Pension, like many companies in the financial sector, has a long-running history of data management and analysis. Over time, as data demands have increased and we've gone through several mergers, our data and IT landscape has become quite complex. Our analytical data spans from customer transaction and policy information to investment, environmental, social, and governance (ESG) data, to a broad variety of other operational and market data. This data supports internal analysis as well as internal and external reporting.

When I joined in 2023, I inherited a dedicated and highly skilled team, but also a fragmented data landscape, with data warehouses both on-premises and on Azure VMs, alongside a data vault model on Synapse dedicated pools in Azure. Unfortunately, the former setups did not align well with the digital strategy, and the latter did not deliver the necessary value to the analytical teams in AP Pension. Thankfully, initiatives had already been launched to re-engineer some of the core processes, such as the anonymization and archiving of data using Databricks.

Since 2022, I had been involved with Microsoft Fabric's private preview, and it wasn't difficult to show management at AP Pension how Fabric's features and Microsoft's development roadmap aligned well with the digital strategy, existing initiatives, and the goal to simplify both architecture and operations. This alignment also promised to support AP Pension's analytical teams more efficiently with timely and relevant data.

Furthermore, AP Pension had already invested in Power BI, and the shared capacity model of Fabric and Power BI allows us to better utilize that investment. Given the company size, the amount of data handled, and the highly regulated nature of the sector it operates in, AP Pension needed an enterprise data platform that could handle automated data management and centralized governance, security, and data curation. However, we are also small enough to make agile decisions at the enterprise level, as we operate in only one region and maintain close connections with our users, decision makers, and system owners. In that way, you can say that we were right in the sweet spot for being early adopters of Fabric.

We have now transitioned many of our cloud-based workloads to this modern data platform with a full migration of data planned for 2025. We've implemented a metadata-driven framework, centralized governance, streamlined data ingestion, and created a platform for continuous deployment. Even at this relatively early stage of using Fabric, we are already seeing significant benefits from transitioning to a fully managed SaaS data platform and integrating it with our new cloud-based policy and administration system.

Piethein Strengholt: Thank you very much for sharing these insights! Could you provide a broad overview of your platform's design?

Jacob Rønnow Jensen: Absolutely. Our data platform, which we refer to as "AP Data," is structured around a Medallion architecture. You can see the detailed layout of the architecture in Figure 8-1.

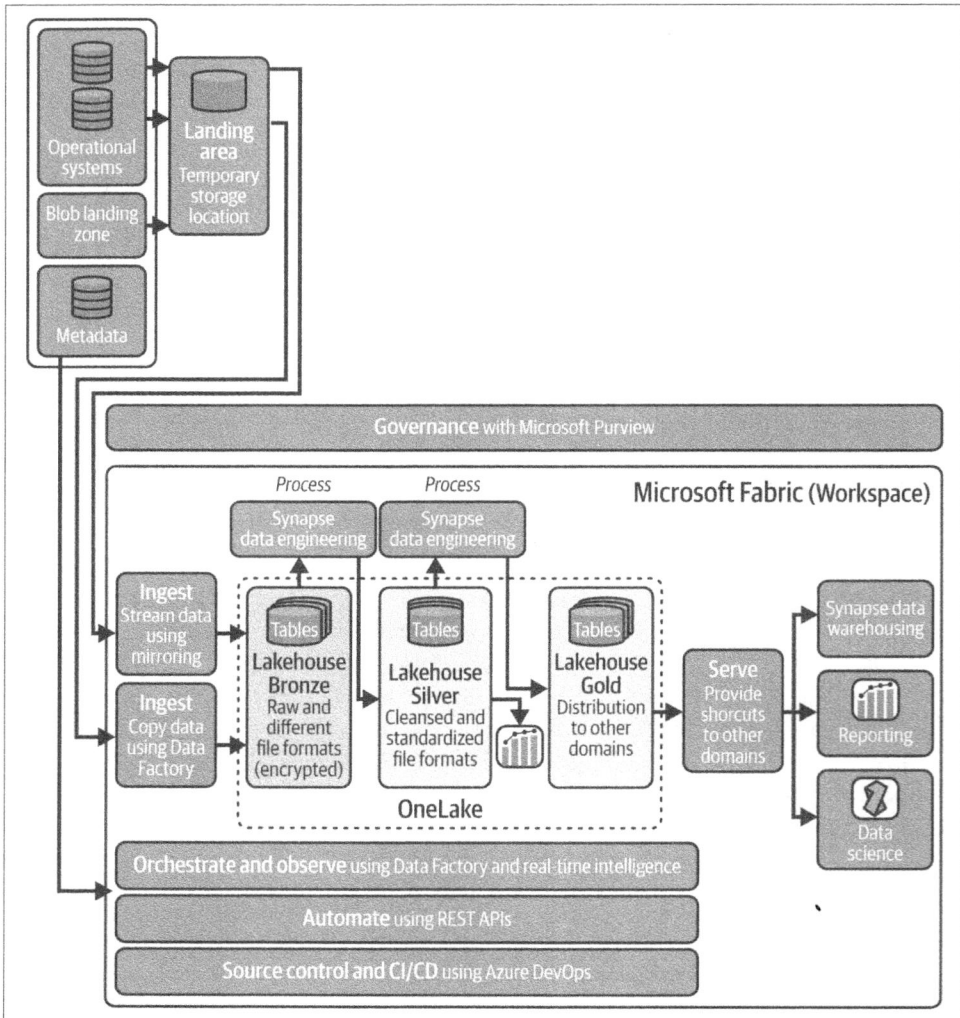

Figure 8-1. High-level overview of AP Pension's data platform, which is based on Microsoft Fabric

At the core of our design is the Lakehouse model. We utilize the REST APIs provided by Microsoft Fabric to automate our processes based on a robust metadata layer seamlessly integrated with Microsoft Purview for data governance. For data ingestion, we use the mirroring and Data Factory features in Fabric. Data Factory also handles the orchestration of the processes in the data platform, but looking ahead, we plan to also implement event-based orchestration with event streams and/or Microsoft Fabric Activator (*https://oreil.ly/dn8rI*). This comprehensive design supports our goal to streamline operations and enhance the effectiveness of our data management.

Piethein Strengholt: Why do you mainly focus on designing Lakehouses in your architecture instead of considering, for instance, Warehouses?

Jacob Rønnow Jensen: Since Microsoft Fabric offers SQL endpoints for data access for all data in OneLake, our preference for the Spark-based Lakehouses over the SQL-based Warehouses in the Medallion layers of AP Data is influenced by several key factors.

Firstly, our data includes multiple file formats and frequent row-by-row operations in the Bronze and Silver layers. The Lakehouse model, coupled with the distributed compute capabilities of Spark, is ideally suited for handling these complexities. This suitability is enhanced by the introduction of a new native Spark engine in Fabric, which further increases performance for certain types of workloads, and which Microsoft is offering at no additional cost.

Secondly, Python and Spark offer more versatility than SQL for developing frameworks. Tasks that would typically require dynamic SQL in stored procedures can instead be deployed using functions and classes and packaged in wheels. Moreover, we can utilize the `%%sql` magic command in PySpark to write SQL directly in notebooks, allowing us to write our transformations in SQL and combine it with traditional Python code as needed.

Thirdly, adopting a Spark-based approach for data ingestion and curation has allowed us to run processes in parallel in Databricks and Fabric during the public preview and early generally available phases of Fabric. This has been extremely helpful for benchmarking and fallback purposes.

Lastly, we can serve data from Lakehouses directly to our users through shortcuts in Warehouses in their own workspaces, eliminating the need to physically move data.

These advantages make the Lakehouse model a central component of our data strategy, enhancing our processing capabilities, data distribution, and operational flexibility.

Piethein Strengholt: Are there any circumstances under which you would consider a Warehouse artifact in your Medallion layer?

Jacob Rønnow Jensen: Both the Warehouse and the Lakehouse artifacts write data to OneLake, and since the SQL endpoints on Lakehouses and SQL Warehouses run on the same engine, there should—in theory—not be much difference between them from a downstream consumption perspective. However, the Warehouse experience in Fabric currently supports case-insensitive SQL queries as well as multitable transactions, which Spark does not. In scenarios where these particular features are critical, I would consider including a Warehouse artifact in the Medallion layer. However, as you can see in the high-level architecture, today we view the Warehouse as being more relevant in the serving layer, where many of our use cases involve users being able to join data and create new tables with T-SQL.

Medallion Architecture

Piethein Strengholt: Let's explore the specific layers of the Medallion architecture, starting with the Bronze layer. How do you manage data there, and could you describe the components involved?

Jacob Rønnow Jensen: Sure, let's dive into the layers of our Medallion architecture. While the traditional Medallion model typically features three layers, we've subdivided these into multiple physical layers to create a physical and logical separation of tasks and configuration in AP Data. We have named the sublayers in Bronze: Landing, PreArchive, and Archive.

In the Bronze layer, our primary goal is to decouple data from the source systems and manage PII. We store the data as we receive it from the source systems. Managing PII effectively is crucial at this early stage of ingestion. Initially, PII can be present in the Landing layer, which is why we keep it completely isolated from the rest of AP Data and truncate tables once the data is moved to the PreArchive layer, which is mainly a housekeeping layer. In the Archive layer, all PII data is encrypted with individual—but symmetrical—keys for each customer, making it possible to have a process for decrypting data when there is a valid business reason for doing so. The encryption keys are stored in a keystore outside of Fabric and have their own governance and lifecycle processes, as illustrated in Figure 8-2.

This meticulous staging and encryption process ensures that we handle PII responsibly while preserving historical data and the critical information that our company needs for reporting and analysis. Note that if the relationship between a person and the encryption key is deleted in the keystore, it does not affect the analytical data itself. We still know that there was an individual customer in the historical data, but we have removed the ability to decrypt the PII data, and in doing so, anonymized the data and respected the customer's right to be forgotten.[1]

---

[1] While the processes described by AP Pension are intended to ensure responsible handling of PII in accordance with internal data protection standards, adherence to legal compliance is the direct responsibility of the designated compliance officer or the legal department within the organization.

In terms of data formats, in the Landing layer, we collect data from databases and in formats such as CSV, JSON, Parquet, Delta, and XML. This data is then moved to the PreArchive layer and converted to Delta. The Archive layer serves as a resilient base, from where we can reload data into the preceding layers of AP Data independently of the source systems. This structure not only secures sensitive information but also maintains the integrity and accessibility of our data.

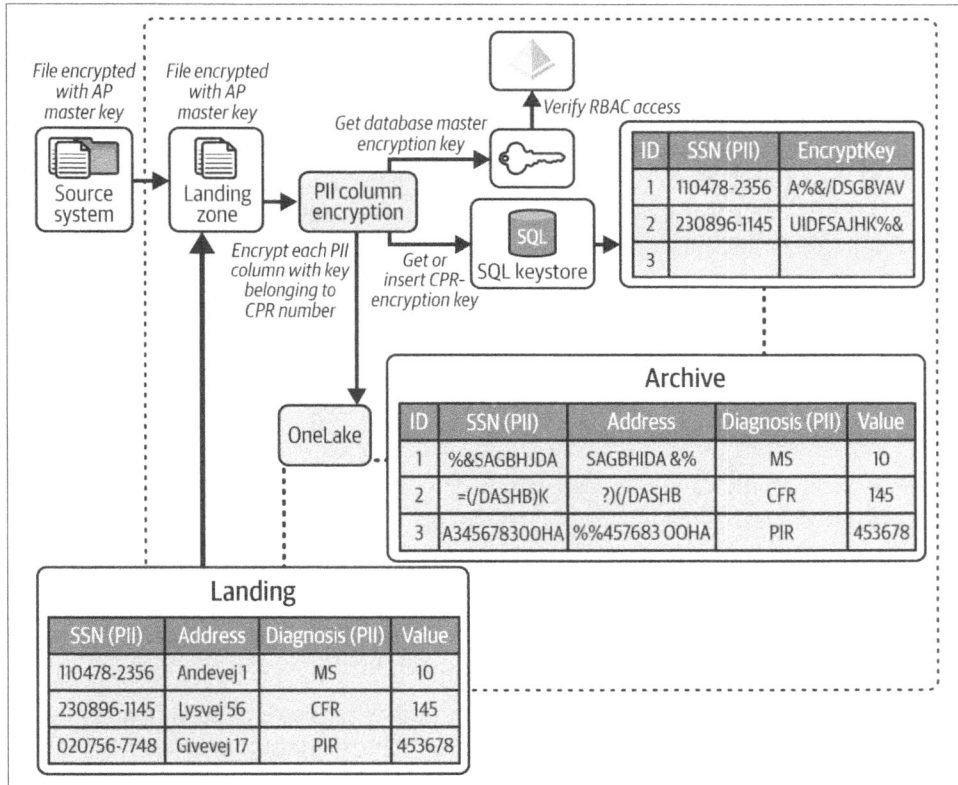

Figure 8-2. High-level overview of AP Pension's encryption process in the Bronze layer

Piethein Strengholt: Do you use data partitioning or Delta tables with versioning for time travel features?

Jacob Rønnow Jensen: Initially, we explored using unrestricted time travel with Delta tables in the Archive. However, our tests indicated that this approach was too demanding in terms of storage and negatively impacted query performance. Instead, we chose to build history by physically partitioning data in the Archive. This strategy allows us to efficiently save data with full history without the drawbacks of high costs and poor performance.

Piethein Strengholt: Does this approach resemble a SCD?

Jacob Rønnow Jensen: It does resemble a SCD in some of our load patterns. However, our primary method for handling updates and changes involves UPSERT operations to Delta tables. This ensures that we maintain a complete historical record, allowing us to trace any piece of data back to its origin effectively. This method balances efficiency with the ability to preserve and access historical data as needed.

Piethein Strengholt: How do you manage data ingestion from various sources? Do you have a standard method, or do you tailor the process for each source?

Jacob Rønnow Jensen: We have developed a versatile ingestion framework to handle the variety of data types we encounter, such as APIs, databases, flat files, Delta tables, and semi-structured files. The approach varies depending on the source type. For instance, SQL databases typically allow for more straightforward and automated metadata registration and ingestion. In contrast, flat files often require manual intervention, especially to correctly flag PII. No matter the source, all data first enters our landing area and is then securely processed and passed on to the Archive layer. Even though this might seem like a lot of unnecessary data movement, this method ensures that we maintain consistency in data handling and securely decouple our analytical platform from the operational systems—all while adapting to the specific characteristics of different data formats.

Piethein Strengholt: Could you explain how you manage metadata? Do you use a catalog for this?

Jacob Rønnow Jensen: Metadata plays a crucial role in our operations. We use a metastore to manage it, identifying source formats and columns containing sensitive data. This metadata is vital for several processes, including depersonalizing data, validating schemas, and managing input that doesn't fit into OneLake.

Piethein Strengholt: So, once a column is flagged as sensitive or incompatible, does your system automatically know how to handle it in downstream processes?

Jacob Rønnow Jensen: Exactly. We have automated this process and have also implemented what we call "hard rules" for managing specific table names or formats from the source systems that Delta can't hold. These rules are embedded in our metadata, enabling automated management in subsequent steps. This automation streamlines our data handling and ensures consistency and compliance throughout our processes.

Piethein Strengholt: During any of these stages, do you technically validate the data? If so, how do you manage disruptive schema changes?

Jacob Rønnow Jensen: Yes, we do perform data validation. However, we allow for schema drift in the archive for certain types of loads. This support for schema drift in

OneLake enables us to adapt to evolving data structures without disrupting existing processes.

Piethein Strengholt: Do these schema changes trigger notifications for your teams?

Jacob Rønnow Jensen: Changes in schemas generate alerts, prompting us to review and address the changes. While the Delta format in OneLake can absorb adding new columns, we need to ensure they are handled correctly in the downstream layers. A proactive notification system helps us maintain control and ensure data integrity.

Piethein Strengholt: Do you also handle real-time data ingestion in the Bronze layer?

Jacob Rønnow Jensen: Currently, our primary method for ingesting (near) real-time data is through Microsoft Fabric's mirroring capability, which we'll refer to as mirroring from here on. For Azure SQL, this functionality mirrors changes from the transaction logs of the source system, similar to traditional CDC on SQL databases. However, unlike CDC, which writes to a set of tables on the source database, mirroring writes directly to OneLake. This gives us the best of both worlds by minimizing the impact on the source database and reducing maintenance requirements on the target to a minimum. The same applies when mirroring data from CosmosDB and Snowflake databases.

Additionally, the mirrored data can serve as a new, immediate source, which is particularly useful in test scenarios and for our AI and machine learning teams. Users can access near-real-time data from these mirrors to simulate interactions with the production environment.

Piethein Strengholt: Do you plan to implement operational reporting on the mirrored data?

Jacob Rønnow Jensen: We supply data from test environments in this way, but we have not yet created shortcuts to mirrored data in the Silver and Gold layers of our data platform in production. Here, the mirrored data remains in the Bronze layer and is treated like any other source. We suspect that the business case for near-real-time reporting and analysis might arise in the not-so-distant future, but as mirroring is a relatively new addition to our enterprise data fabric, we are primarily exploring its capabilities in relation to our new administrative platform, where it has a near-perfect fit. However, we've also realized that in scenarios where direct database access isn't feasible, mirroring provides an excellent alternative. This setup could enable users to query and monitor data in real time without the risk of impacting performance on the source systems.

Piethein Strengholt: Can you elaborate on how data is structured and managed in the Silver layer?

Jacob Rønnow Jensen: The Silver layer is divided into two subdivisions: the Base layer and the Enriched layer. The Base layer is the first point within AP Data where we allow for user access. Populating this layer involves processes like deduplication, renaming, and deserialization of JSON.

Piethein Strengholt: So, the structure in the Silver layer aligns closely with the original source systems, despite occasional differences?

Jacob Rønnow Jensen: Exactly. We sometimes need to tweak the technical names from the source system to make them more usable, but we maintain the basic structure in sync with the source, ensuring that the data representation remains intuitive for those familiar with the source systems. One significant exception is how we handle unstructured data like JSON. Instead of storing the individual documents, we store the JSON as rows in Delta tables in the Bronze layer. The SQL endpoint in Fabric has already deserialized the root elements of the JSON into columnar data, but nested arrays within the JSON remain as JSON. To handle this, we have developed a framework to automatically deserialize the "residual JSON" data from the nested arrays. Figure 8-3 illustrates how this process can be integrated with a mirror of a Cosmos DB.

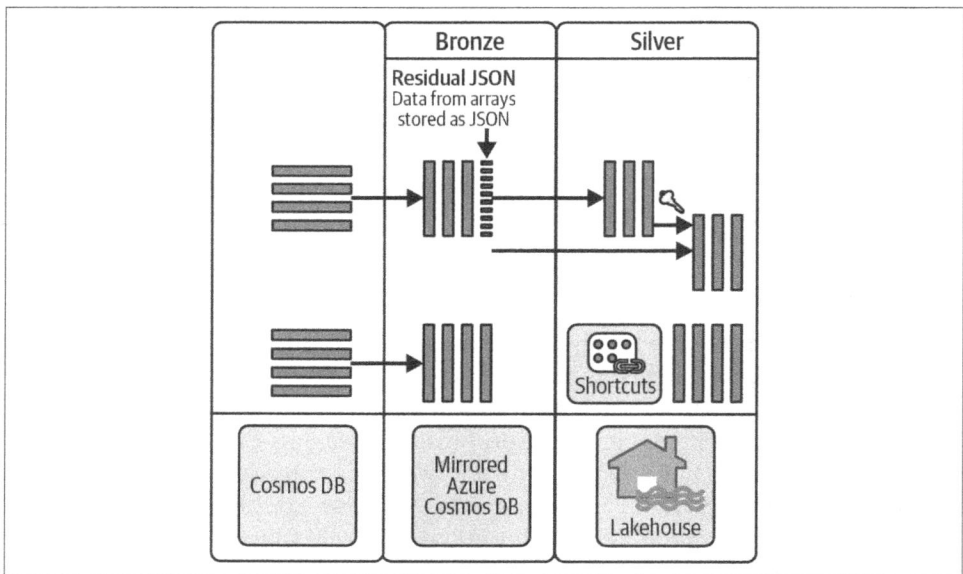

Figure 8-3. High-level overview of AP Pension's deserialization process from a Cosmos DB mirror in Fabric

This data-driven process involves identifying nested arrays within the JSON columns of the Delta tables and creating new tables and columns for each level of nesting, linking them with keys based on the ordinal position within the original JSON document. This iterative deserialization transforms all the data into a structured, columnar format, making it more accessible, readable, and queryable from a SQL perspective.

Piethein Strengholt: This sounds like a comprehensive approach, right?

Jacob Rønnow Jensen: Yes, but it adds significant value for the business users, and handling only new rows at the time of ingestion with Spark seems to us to be the most efficient way—from a usability, performance, and capacity perspective. The method allows us to maintain a flexible yet robust data structure that supports a wide range of analytical and operational needs. By automating the deserialization and structuring process, we ensure data consistency and reliability across different systems and use cases, which is crucial in our dynamic environment.

Piethein Strengholt: Do you also use the Base layer for preserving historical data from old legacy systems?

Jacob Rønnow Jensen: Absolutely. We store historical data and ensure compliance with the General Data Protection Regulation (GDPR) by implementing policies like the right to be forgotten, ensuring that we can recreate past reports and maintain long historical series essential for predictions and analyses, such as longevity studies.

Piethein Strengholt: How do you manage data history in the Silver layer? Do you, for example, build SCDs?

Jacob Rønnow Jensen: In the Base layer, where the data is still organized according to the source system, we primarily rely on the history we built in the Bronze layer. However, in the Enriched part of the Silver layer, we do begin the process of implementing SCDs.

Piethein Strengholt: Let's discuss the Enriched layer. What is its purpose?

Jacob Rønnow Jensen: The Enriched layer is where we begin some lightweight dimensional modeling. For the Gold layer, we use pre-built dimension and fact loaders that require data in a specific format. In the Enriched layer, we focus on preparing data for our framework and staging data that will be used for multiple purposes in subsequent processes—again focusing on minimizing the need for redundant computation and data management.

Piethein Strengholt: Can you explain how these loader functions work?

Jacob Rønnow Jensen: Certainly. Firstly, the loaders perform essential housekeeping tasks such as computing hash keys for identifying changes in the source data. Since we can't enforce primary keys directly in Delta tables, these loaders also ensure data integrity by checking for duplicate values. Surrogate keys are calculated by hashing the relevant business keys—a method that allows us to load data efficiently and simultaneously for both facts and dimensions. This approach also simplifies the handling of late-arriving master data, ensuring that data is rapidly available and consistent across all parts of the data model.

Piethein Strengholt: At the Enriched stage, is the data still source-oriented?

Jacob Rønnow Jensen: In the Enriched layer, we merge data from various source systems. This involves tackling challenges such as aligning mismatched timelines from different sources, which often leads to issues like "gap islands"—problems where we need to find and fix holes in sequences (the gaps) or find and collapse ranges of consecutive, identical values (the islands).

Piethein Strengholt: That makes a lot of sense. Let's talk about the Gold layer. How does it differ from the previous layers?

Jacob Rønnow Jensen: The Gold layer is divided into three sublayers: Curated, Modeled, and Modeled PII. In the Curated layer, we implement the general enterprise dimensional model. This is our main processing stage, where a framework handles the creation of surrogate keys mentioned before and ensures full integration between different elements of the dimensional model. It's heavily metadata-driven, focusing on transforming the system-oriented data from the Silver layer into a single version of the truth.

Piethein Strengholt: Does that make you responsible for the information model and MDM?

Jacob Rønnow Jensen: My team is not directly responsible for AP Pension's information model or MDM. However, we engage in extensive dialogues to align our efforts with the work done in this area. AP Pension's business intelligence and architectural teams play a crucial role in these discussions, ensuring that our implementations effectively meet organizational needs. As part of our data strategy, we have named a master system for every data domain going forward, and the master system will be responsible for master data. But since we are only in the very beginning of the second strategy period, where we begin rolling out the new foundation and still have many legacy systems and data, some form of MDM on the analytical platform is necessary to ensure a common understanding and a solid foundation for analysis and reporting.

Piethein Strengholt: You are essentially talking about conformed dimensions—so, may I conclude that the Curated layer primarily uses a star schema?

Jacob Rønnow Jensen: Yes, the Curated layer exclusively uses a star schema design, incorporating dimensions with SCDs. Before we transitioned to Fabric, we used a data vault model with PIT tables to manage multiple timelines, which is particularly useful for pension data. For example, a payment received that refers to a past date can affect a person's historical status. This requires some of our more advanced users to be able to report on multiple timelines, such as the creation date, value date, or the transaction receipt date. The PIT tables were implemented to manage these timelines, but the data vault model itself was too complex to work with for most business users.

In our new framework, we have incorporated the concept of PIT tables into our design in order to manage multiple SCD2 dimensions within the Curated layer. Some might argue that our method is an SCD type 7 hybrid, where we save type 1 keys on the fact and allow for multiple type 2 keys in the PIT tables. This allows us to follow different timelines separately in the Modeled layer, ensuring that our data handling remains manageable, intuitive, and effective. Figures 8-4 and 8-5 show examples of the processing of data in the Curated layer.

```
 1    dim_loader.run(df)
 ✓  1 min 37 sec - Command executed in 1 min 37 sec 655 ms by Mia Hang Knudsen on 4:08:41 PM, 1/21/25      PySpark (Python) ∨

 >  ▤ Spark jobs (20 of 20 succeeded)   ⓘ Resources   ▤ Log                                          ...

Start loading dimension Dimensions_Agent to curated
Computing the hashed entity key for business key..
Creating dimension table if it does not exist..
Filtering for new records..
max date: 1900-01-01 00:00:00
Upserting the new records to the source dimension table..
Successfully executed merge on table Dimensions_Agent
Creating the PIT table if it does not exist..
Upserting the new records to the source pit table..
Successfully executed merge on table Pit_Agent
Dimension successfully loaded in.
```

Figure 8-4. How dimensional tables are processed in the Modeled layer

```
 1    fact_loader.run(df,'append')
 ✓  5 sec - Command executed in 5 sec 248 ms by Mia Hang Knudsen on 4:00:33 PM, 1/21/25                  PySpark (Python) ∨

 >    Spark jobs (11 of 11 succeeded)   ⓘ Resources                                                  ...

Start loading fact Facts_AgentEvent to curated using load type append
Renaming the sequence key column 'apdata_sourcesnapshottimestamp' to the default timestamp column name 'DW_TS'.
Filtering for new records..
max date: 2024-12-16 09:57:41.242508
Computing the hashed entity keys for all business keys..
Validating input for duplicate primary keys in the same period.
Validation passed.
Creating the table
Executing the fact table loading process.
Fact successfully loaded in.
```

Figure 8-5. How a fact table is processed in the Modeled layer

Piethein Strengholt: And what happens in the Modeled layer that follows the Curated layer?

Jacob Rønnow Jensen: The Modeled layer is where we prepare data specifically for our data consumers. Here, we establish singular dimensional relationships between the facts and dimensions using the appropriate history keys from the PIT tables. This approach helps us create clear join paths and simplifies the data model for the users. We also prepare data for semantic models and for consumption by applications that, like Power BI, require a single key for joining tables.

Additionally, we distribute some data in denormalized tables when that better meets the user's needs. Often, these pre-joined tables are preferred for further data wrangling and experiments by data scientists, whose tools are usually optimized for this type of input. This format can also be achieved using views or semantic models, so we make a case-by-case evaluation based on performance and practicality to decide the best approach.

Piethein Strengholt: So, the Modeled layer will have various tables for different use cases and timelines depending on the specific needs?

Jacob Rønnow Jensen: Exactly. We are more likely to let users work with data from the Modeled layer rather than from the Curated layer because the Modeled layer presents a "single version of the truth" from the user's perspective and for query needs.

Piethein Strengholt: So, are there multiple versions of the truth based on different queries?

Jacob Rønnow Jensen: I would rather say that the same question should always result in the same answer. However, different use cases and questions might require viewing the data from various perspectives. We accommodate these different perspectives in the Modeled layer.

Piethein Strengholt: So, essentially, these are views or semantic models built on top of the data?

Jacob Rønnow Jensen: Yes, the Modeled layer can include both physical and semantic models, or it can be a conglomerate view that combines shortcuts with persistent data. These are preferably built on top of the dimensional model in the Curated layer. However, for very simple, self-contained use cases, it could also be a view directly on shortcuts to data in the Base layer. This approach might be used in mirroring scenarios like the ones we discussed earlier, where near-real-time data is a requirement.

Piethein Strengholt: So, may I conclude again that the Model layer primarily uses a star schema, unless there is a special request for a single large table?

Jacob Rønnow Jensen: That is correct. The star schema is our standard structure because it efficiently supports a wide range of analytical needs. However, for specific scenarios, such as data science, quick delivery, or unique data that isn't used elsewhere, we might opt for a simpler, possibly temporary solution like more denormalized tables.

Piethein Strengholt: Lastly, can you explain the purpose of the Modeled PII layer?

Jacob Rønnow Jensen: The Modeled PII layer is crucial for handling sensitive personal information responsibly. As we went through earlier, all data in AP Data is pseudonymized or anonymized, and unique integration keys are assigned to each customer. This ensures that no personal information is stored in AP Data. This setup not only secures the data but also supports compliance with GDPR. However, there might be legitimate business needs where personal information must be made available, and for that, we have stringent processes to decrypt data safely and provide it in a controlled environment. This ensures minimal exposure and maximum security.

At AP Pension, we tag this data in Microsoft Purview so data loss protection can be managed through data policies and so that we are able to log and report on access to decrypted data. This method is, at its core, based on the principle of data minimization, and is an infinitely better solution than giving business users access to all decrypted data before they do their selections. As a company, we focus on identifying which data individual users or groups have a legitimate reason for decrypting and only then proceed down this path. Control and documentation are key in this process.

Piethein Strengholt: My colleague James Serra often mentions a Serving layer, which is a physical layer utilizing different technologies than the typical Lakehouse or Warehouse. Do you have something similar at AP Pension?

Jacob Rønnow Jensen: Definitely. At AP Pension, our Serving layer consists of individual workspaces for each logical group of consumers. Figure 8-6 provides a conceptual overview of how we serve our internal customers with data for consumption from the Base and Curated/Modeled layers.

The APData Function Workspace always includes at least one Fabric Lakehouse and one Fabric Warehouse. In this setup, users are viewers of the Workspace and owners of the Warehouse. The shortcuts to data within the Medallion layers are housed in the Lakehouse. The Warehouse is initially empty, but from it, users can seamlessly query data made available in shortcuts in the Lakehouse in the same Workspace and save data to the Warehouse. This setup grants the data platform team full control over data distribution, while also allowing the users of the Workspace to read and write tables in OneLake with SQL—either in the Fabric GUI or in tools like SQL Server Management Studio.

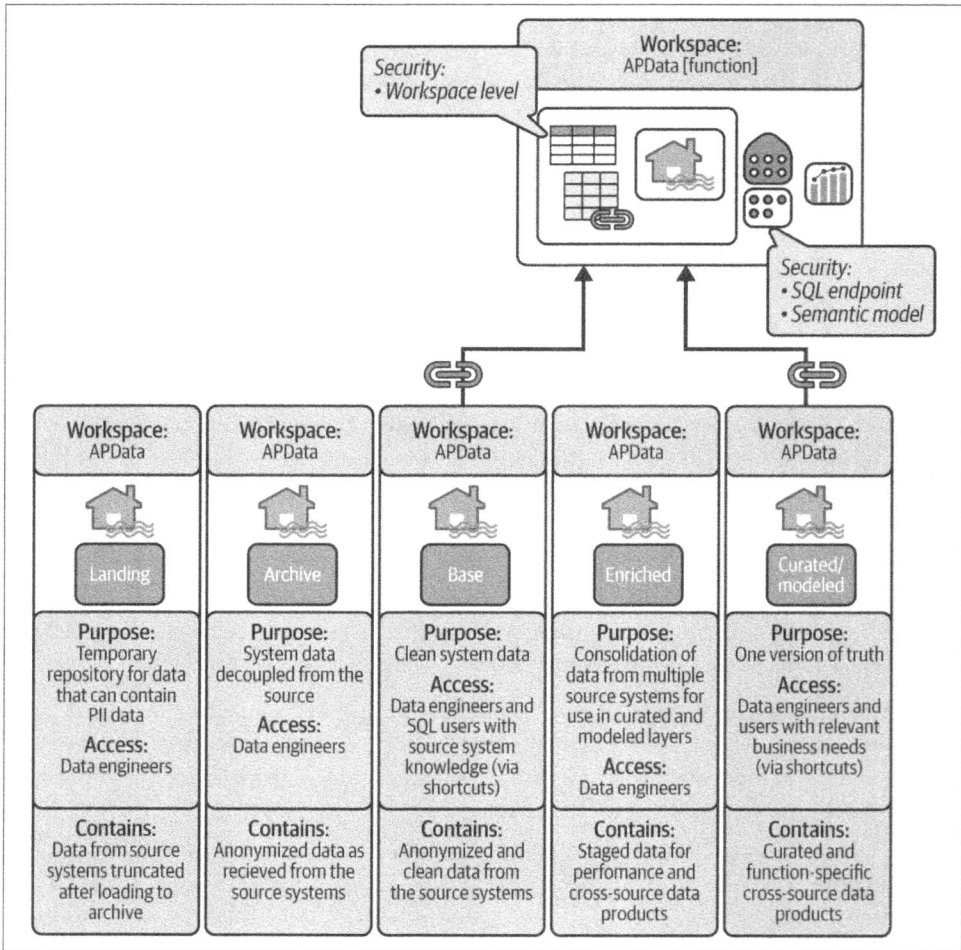

Figure 8-6. AP Pension delivers workspaces on the fly for specific domains

Piethein Strengholt: Regarding workspace design, how do you decide when to create different Workspaces?

Jacob Rønnow Jensen: The decision to create new and separate Workspaces is based on several key factors: functional roles, security, logical data grouping, and workload isolation. We maintain the Workspaces, artifacts, and shortcuts through an automated and well-documented process. Since data is not physically moved into the serving layer, we achieve low latency and quick time to market for the distribution of existing data products at no extra storage cost. This approach ensures high data integrity and security while providing users with maximum flexibility.

Piethein Strengholt: Can you elaborate on the need for workload isolation?

Jacob Rønnow Jensen: Certainly. In Fabric, resources are shared across various types of compute within a Fabric capacity. Capacities are assigned at the workspace level, so a comprehensive workspace strategy is needed to ensure that every process and every user has access to adequate compute without the risk of blocking other users of the same capacity.

For example, some Workspaces might be designed for heavy loads that occur monthly and thus require different capacity management than one that is used daily for ad hoc queries. The former may be more time-critical than the latter, and for this reason, we manage the capacities differently. To manage them efficiently, we have decided on the described model, monitor capacity usage closely, implement surge protection, and set up Workspaces based on metadata and templates, which helps maintain order and efficiency.

Piethein Strengholt: So, it seems there's an AP Data domain managing everything up to the Curated and Modeled layers, with additional workspaces on the edges for specific business-oriented workloads and users?

Jacob Rønnow Jensen: Exactly.

Other Considerations

Piethein Strengholt: Some large customers are considering pushing ingestion and data management towards other domains as part of a data mesh approach. Is that something you're considering too?

Jacob Rønnow Jensen: Definitely—but at the same time, I am grateful that Microsoft named their product "Fabric" rather than "Mesh," which likely has been considered at some point or other. A data fabric focuses on automating processes, whereas a data mesh often implies a more decentralized approach with governance and compliance responsibilities shifted towards the edge.

We categorize users into cocreators, advanced users, and report users, each with different needs for data interaction. Cocreators are domain experts who can develop data products as working prototypes. To this end, Microsoft Fabric offers a wide range of development experiences, ranging from the Spark notebooks and SQL experiences we have discussed so far, to both low- and no-code experiences like Data Wrangler, Data Factory, and Dataflow.

The available low- and no-code tools in Fabric can be very useful for citizen developers and can really help organizations like AP Pension in the decentralized creation of new data products. From a performance and capacity perspective, however, these tools often have a substantial overhead compared to well-authored Spark running on an appropriately scaled cluster.

Since a capacity is something we share, it makes a lot of sense that these prototypes are subsequently refined and integrated into the data platform by the data engineers in the data platform team. This approach helps maintain a balance between autonomy and control, ensuring data integrity, performance, and security across the platform.

Piethein Strengholt: It sounds like working prototypes of data products is a key goal for your setup. Is that essentially your data mesh approach?

Jacob Rønnow Jensen: You could see it as a data mesh approach, but it's not quite that strict. Our focus is on creating working prototypes that can evolve into solid data products. This approach lets us simultaneously leverage the unique expertise of the domain experts, data platform team, and co-creators respectively—and together.

Piethein Strengholt: Given the high regulation in the financial sector, maintaining a certain level of maturity and adhering to standards and best practices is crucial, isn't it?

Jacob Rønnow Jensen: Absolutely, and that's why we have implemented privacy by design and default in AP Data and centrally create, manage, and govern our most central data products. We want to free the users from concerns about GDPR, dimensional modeling, CI/CD, common naming conventions, or code standards. By eliminating these complexities, we reduce risk and let our users focus on what they excel at: driving business value through data.

Piethein Strengholt: I'm glad you mention CI/CD. With Microsoft Fabric, there are different methods. Currently, you either use deployment pipelines to promote artifacts across workspaces or implement CI/CD yourself using Git and the Fabric REST APIs. What's your approach?

Jacob Rønnow Jensen: We have adopted a metadata-driven approach for managing data in AP Data as well as artifacts and shortcuts at the edge. This involves a pipeline that generates a script based on the registered metadata for each environment, which then calls the Fabric administrative APIs. We use Azure DevOps to create these pipelines. Azure DevOps is, at this point, a more mature product than pipelines in Fabric, and it allows us to manage both Fabric and non-Fabric items. The implemented method provides the control we need and effectively bridges the gap between traditional infrastructure as code and newer, more flexible SaaS solutions like Microsoft Fabric.

Piethein Strengholt: This is almost like configuration as code!

Jacob Rønnow Jensen: Yes—and having full control over our deployment process is crucial. Our current setup serves as our minimum viable product (MVP) for a sensible deployment process. It includes source control and automated movement between environments. While it's not fully continuous yet, it allows for as many deploys as needed. As Microsoft now also has a Terraform Provider for Microsoft Fabric (*https://oreil.ly/OGtxB*), we expect to use this functionality to further professionalize and automate our process.

Piethein Strengholt: Do you have something like data contracts, given that your automatic deployment of workspaces is backed by metadata or a template?

Jacob Rønnow Jensen: We have some internal standards for when we approve the quality of data, but not actual data contracts. One of the main reasons for having one data platform is to govern data and processes in one tool—that tool being Microsoft Purview, as illustrated in Figure 8-1. According to this aspiration, data quality measures should reside in Purview along with the data catalog. Data contracts seem to fit in a gray area between the data catalog and data quality. We aim for users to know if the data they're accessing is up-to-date and valid, but defining those rules varies by each data object. This is something we are working on in Purview, starting with our most central and critical data products.

Piethein Strengholt: Could you elaborate more on how you're implementing or using Microsoft Purview?

Jacob Rønnow Jensen: At AP Pension, we use Microsoft Purview to manage and maintain data classifications for both structured and unstructured data, and here we benefit greatly from the automatic integration between Microsoft Fabric and Microsoft Purview.

Initially, we are working on a data catalog that enables users to see descriptions of available data and its lineage without needing direct help from the engineering team or access to data or code. Next, we focus on classifying data, particularly PII, and setting up data loss protection through data policies and permissions at the Entra ID level. These policies and permissions ensure that only authorized users can access sensitive data in the Modeled PII layer.

Moving forward, our goal is also to document and enhance data quality beyond the basic metrics we have today. If we want to make data quality operational and relevant for the business users, traditional metrics such as ranges and the count of nulls are not enough. We are also interested in identifying significant changes or anomalies in data patterns. We have started with a rule-based approach and are considering incorporating AI to detect anomalies or risks as Purview scans our data. This proactive approach to identifying potential issues is where I see significant advancements happening as Purview and Fabric evolve.

Piethein Strengholt: Have you adopted the concept of data products, and how do you decide which layer of the Medallion architecture to connect these data products to?

Jacob Rønnow Jensen: Yes, we integrate the concept of data products directly into our metadata management, addressing it early in the process rather than retrofitting later. This approach is aligned with concept of data products that Purview offers. For us, it seems redundant to manage this information in both our own metadata and in Purview, and, therefore, the two worlds need to be integrated, so that when users access the data catalog, they are met with a logical representation of data that makes sense to both them and us.

Final Recommendations

Piethein Strengholt: Lastly, do you have any recommendations for readers of this book?

Jacob Rønnow Jensen: Absolutely. My main recommendations for any new data platform project are that you need to have a data strategy that aligns with the business strategy and you need to focus on establishing executive, IT, and user buy-in very early in the process.

Piethein Strengholt: Based on this interview, it makes total sense that you would focus on that.

Jacob Rønnow Jensen: Yes. If you recall how I summarized our data strategy using four principles, it might have seemed trivial at the time. However, you can see that many of the topics and decisions I've described tie back to these. In fact, I would go so far as to say that choosing Fabric in AP Pension is deeply rooted in these principles as well as our business strategy, and the principles and timelines in the digital strategy.

Piethein Strengholt: So, is Fabric not necessarily for everyone?

Jacob Rønnow Jensen: I believe that the SaaS implementation, and the separation of compute and storage in Fabric, along with features like Shortcuts, Direct Lake, and automatic SQL endpoints on OneLake, are truly transformative and definitely worth exploring.

I also believe that it's important to be aware of the service model differences—SaaS versus PaaS—and choose what best fits your control, business, and operational needs.

Additionally, keep an eye on Microsoft's roadmap and release plans for Fabric. In this discussion, we haven't even touched on the Copilot and AI capabilities of the Microsoft Analytical stack. The landscape evolves rapidly, and staying informed can help manage expectations and planning for the future. The possibilities are endless, but to truly be data-driven and reap all the benefits of generative AI and cloud computing, it is important to consider the order and structure of how you implement and use these technologies. They must align with your strategic goals and operational capacities. Needless to say, for me, it all starts with data quality, governance, and security.

Piethein Strengholt: Thank you for sharing all your insights. This discussion has been incredibly informative. I'm sure our readers will appreciate your detailed explanations and recommendations.

## CHAPTER 9

Case Study: Amadeus, a Tech Leader in the Travel Industry

In this comprehensive chapter, we explore the intricate data architecture of Amadeus (*https://amadeus.com*), a global leader in travel technology solutions. We delve into insightful discussions with Joel Singer, the head of data engineering at Amadeus, who brings over two decades of experience steering the company's data initiatives.

Joel outlines the three main pillars of Amadeus's data strategy: data mesh, open data, and Data 360, which collectively aim to harness data to build knowledge and continuously improve products. We explore the nuanced implementation of the data mesh concept at Amadeus, which spans both operational and analytical data to meet diverse customer demands effectively.

As we navigate through the interview, Joel elaborates on the sophisticated Medallion design of Amadeus's data architecture, detailing each layer from data ingestion to data exposure. He discusses the challenges and solutions in managing the Bronze, Silver, and Gold layers, emphasizing the importance of data quality, security, and accessibility.

This chapter also touches on the broader implications of data management at Amadeus, including data governance and the innovative approaches to data integration and sharing across various domains within the company.

Piethein Strengholt: Can you introduce yourself and tell us about your role and the company you work for?

Joel Singer: Certainly! My name is Joel Singer, and I am the Head of Data Engineering at Amadeus, which is a leading technology provider for the global travel and tourism industry. We operate in over 190 countries and offer advanced technology solutions to various sectors within the industry, including airlines, travel agencies, and hotels. We have a workforce of 19,000 employees globally, with 10,000 dedicated to research and development. This team size highlights our strong commitment to technological innovation.

I have been with Amadeus for 23 years, leading various engineering groups. My experience includes managing the development of data-intensive products such as airline revenue management systems and loyalty programs. These systems require analyzing vast amounts of historical data to forecast flight demand and understand passenger behavior. The quality and accessibility of this data are crucial for delivering top-notch products to our customers. Over the past five years, I have transitioned to a more cross-functional role, overseeing the design and delivery of data platforms used by all Amadeus teams to develop our solutions.

Piethein Strengholt: Can you describe the evolution of your data architecture?

Joel Singer: Initially, our data architecture was quite fragmented. We had multiple data platforms utilizing various technologies, such as different Hadoop distributions and hosting solutions. Some applications were hosted on-premises in our data center in Germany, while others were already cloud-based. This heterogeneity was largely due to acquisitions over the years, where acquired companies brought their own data stacks.

This situation resulted in a landscape of diverse data platforms with limited data sharing capabilities. Most of the shared data was raw, leading to multiple copies and different processing interpretations, which increased costs and caused inconsistent data understandings.

A significant shift occurred with our strategic partnership with Microsoft, announced in February 2021. This partnership included a plan to migrate our on-premises data center to the cloud. We saw this not just as a migration but as an opportunity to revamp our entire data architecture. We chose to integrate Azure Databricks and other cloud technologies, moving on-premises data platforms to the cloud, which represent about two-thirds of all our data platforms—a process that is progressing well.

Interestingly, the remaining one-third of our data platforms, initially not included in the cloud migration project, also saw the benefits and decided independently to migrate. They built their cases and eventually moved to the cloud, becoming part of the Amadeus data mesh.

This move created a kind of *data gravity*, as applications outside the initial project recognized the advantages of being in the cloud, such as enhanced data exchange and access. Ultimately, this led to the central management of our entire data architecture in the cloud, overseen by my group. This evolution is a testament to the power of strategic partnerships and the benefits of a unified cloud-based approach.

Piethein Strengholt: Does Amadeus have a data strategy in place? Could you elaborate on that?

Joel Singer: Yes, we have a well-defined data strategy at Amadeus, endorsed at the highest level of the company. Our strategy is built around three main pillars:

Data mesh

We aim to create a data mesh at the company level. Since Amadeus serves the entire travel ecosystem, each sector, such as airlines, airports, travel agencies, and hotels has its unique requirements and expertise. The data mesh architecture allows each domain to manage its data, leveraging specific knowledge and skills.

Open data

Our focus is on making our data open and accessible. We ensure our data is valuable by monitoring its quality and tracking its lineage. We make it discoverable through data catalogs and accessible via tools that allow users to integrate this data into their products. We emphasize security with an approval workflow and clear audit trails to monitor data access and usage. Our data is also protected against loss and designed to be interoperable to enhance reusability through analytics, APIs, or other methods.

Data 360

This pillar involves using data to build knowledge, which in turn helps improve our products. For example, in revenue management, understanding traveler needs helps us refine our offerings. These improved products generate more data, creating a continuous loop of insight and enhancement. One practical application of this is in shopping—when you search for flights on an online travel agency. We handle billions of such transactions daily, using data and machine learning to optimize the process and ensure we find the most cost-effective travel options efficiently.

These pillars support our goal of leveraging data to enhance our services and offerings in the travel industry.

Piethein Strengholt: Have you expanded the data mesh concept at Amadeus to include both operational and analytical data?

Joel Singer: Absolutely, our implementation of the data mesh concept at Amadeus is comprehensive and encompasses all types of data usage. While many people initially associate data mesh primarily with analytics, our vision extends beyond that. We recognize the increasing demand from our customers to become event-driven and to be able to react to events in real time. Therefore, our data mesh architecture also supports operational data needs. It facilitates access to data through various interfaces, including APIs and events, ensuring that all forms of data are reachable for our customers. This holistic approach allows us to meet diverse customer requirements more effectively.

Piethein Strengholt: Have you set standards for the different types of interoperability within your architecture?

Joel Singer: Yes, we prioritize using existing standards rather than creating proprietary ones. For instance, for events, we utilize AsyncAPI (*https://asyncapi.com*), for APIs we use OpenAPI (*https://swagger.io/specification*), and for analytics and big data, we implement a sharing agreement. These are established industry standards that ensure our specifications are clear and universally understood. While we would like to see more convergence among these standards, adopting them helps us maintain clarity and consistency in how data is handled across our systems.

Piethein Strengholt: You mentioned that within your data mesh architecture, you apply machine learning for deriving insights and optimizing travel options. Is this activity for aggregated or pre-integrated data? Or does it align with MDM?

Joel Singer: Our approach leans more towards aggregating data to extract value rather than traditional MDM. We focus on using the data functionally to enhance the capabilities of our products. Essentially, we're replacing older heuristics with more sophisticated machine learning algorithms. These algorithms can identify patterns and insights that are not easily discernible by humans, leveraging historical data to improve accuracy and effectiveness. This method allows us to continually refine our processes and offer more advanced solutions.

Piethein Strengholt: Could you describe the high-level architecture of your data platform at Amadeus?

Joel Singer: Certainly! From a high-level perspective, our data platform architecture incorporates a mix of open source tools and Microsoft technologies.

Piethein Strengholt: How many data domains and workspaces do you manage, and do they all follow the same architectural blueprint?

Joel Singer: Currently, we manage 10 data domains at Amadeus, each corresponding to specific areas of expertise. These domains are mapped to landing zones,[1] which are not tied to organizational structures because we anticipate that organizational needs may change over time.

Within these 10 domains, we've created a total of 130 workspaces in our current environment. Each workspace is designed to support specific types of workloads and is not linked directly to any particular team to accommodate team changes. Figure 9-1 provides a high-level overview of our data platform architecture.

---

1 An Azure (data) landing zone (*https://oreil.ly/IaBVH*) is a foundational element within Microsoft Azure's Cloud Adoption Framework, specifically tailored for streamlining the process of building and managing a secure, scalable, and efficient environment for handling data and analytics workloads.

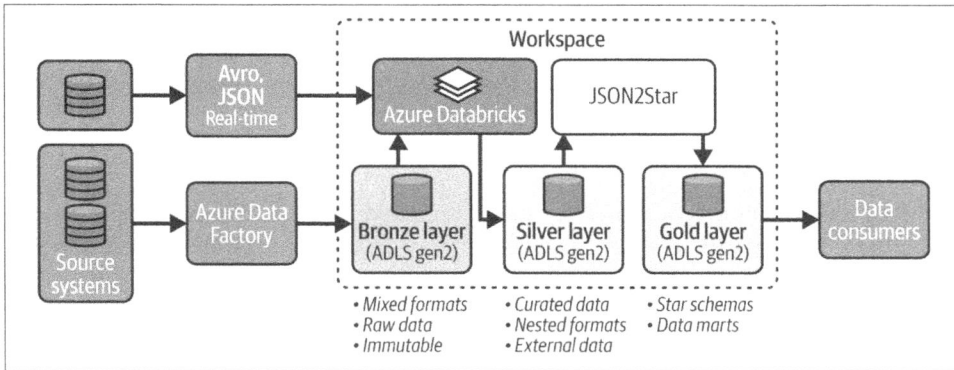

Figure 9-1. High-level architecture of what teams can deploy within their designated environments

The blueprint for each workspace depends on the needs of the product utilizing it. For instance, a product that requires advanced AI capabilities will have Azure AI services deployed within its designated workspace. This tailored approach allows us to meet the diverse and evolving needs of our various products effectively.

Piethein Strengholt: Do you customize the services based on the specific needs of each domain?

Joel Singer: Exactly. We maintain a catalog of all approved and secured services that are part of our data platform blueprint. Teams can then select from this catalog, choosing the services that meet their specific needs. They can create a workspace and deploy the selected services within it. This approach allows each team to tailor the data platform to their unique requirements while ensuring security and compliance with our overall architecture standards.

Piethein Strengholt: Are you referring to a catalog that functions as a self-service portal for establishing infrastructure?

Joel Singer: Indeed, that's the direction we're heading. Currently, the system isn't fully automated yet, but we are working towards that goal. The plan is to have a comprehensive catalog of all available services, enabling fully automated deployments. This will allow teams to access and utilize these services in a self-service manner. Automating these processes is crucial for us, especially given the size of our organization, as it helps our central teams operate more efficiently and at scale.

Piethein Strengholt: For setting up these workspaces, do you use a single infrastructure template for all domains, or are there options to customize?

Joel Singer: We provide two options to accommodate various needs within the domains. There are standard templates available that can be reused across different domains if they share similar patterns. Additionally, there is flexibility for teams to select specific services tailored to their unique requirements. This dual approach allows for both efficiency and customization, enabling teams to either quickly deploy using existing templates or to fine-tune their setup by choosing specific services.

Piethein Strengholt: Can you explain how workspaces are structured within a landing zone for a specific domain?

Joel Singer: Yes, within each landing zone designated for a specific domain, there can be multiple workspaces. These workspaces are set up to support the entire data workflow. This includes the initial data ingestion, followed by the core data processing, then data transformation, and finally, the exposure of the data for business use. Each workspace is structured to facilitate these stages effectively, ensuring a smooth flow and management of data throughout the process.

Medallion Architecture

Piethein Strengholt: Do all teams follow the same setup in terms of the layering in the Medallion architecture, and how many layers are there?

Joel Singer: Yes, all teams adhere to a consistent setup based on the Medallion architecture, which includes three main layers. These layers correspond to the stages of the data lifecycle: data ingestion, data processing, and data exposure. This uniform approach ensures that regardless of the team, the method for managing data remains consistent across the organization.

Piethein Strengholt: How does Amadeus handle the Bronze (ingestion) layer of the Medallion architecture, especially given the variety of applications and data formats you deal with?

Joel Singer: At Amadeus, we treat the Bronze layer primarily as an archive. Our approach is to take the data in its original form, whether it's in EDIFACT (*https://oreil.ly/FNpfv*), XML, JSON, or other formats commonly used in the travel industry. We archive the data exactly as it is received to avoid any corruption and make it immutable, which helps protect against data loss. Some sensitive information like credit card details is concealed at the source at this stage.

The Bronze layer serves two main purposes. First, it acts as an archive to comply with regulations that might require us to keep data for legal reasons. Second, it's valuable for data scientists who might find useful insights in the some of raw, *noisy* data. So, while the primary goal is to maintain a reliable archive and a single source of truth for incoming data, this layer also supports deeper data exploration and analysis when needed.

Piethein Strengholt: Is the Bronze layer in your architecture designed to be a queryable layer using the Delta format, similar to some organizations?

Joel Singer: No, that's not the case for us. The primary users of our Bronze layer prefer to work with the raw data using their own tools rather than needing the data to be processed for querying. We focus on keeping it simple by preserving the data in the format it arrives in.

Piethein Strengholt: How do you make this Bronze data accessible for these purposes?

Joel Singer: We utilize external tables in Azure Databricks to make the data accessible from the platform.

Piethein Strengholt: What transformations occur when moving data to the Silver layer?

Joel Singer: The Silver layer is where significant data transformation occurs. The main tasks involve normalizing the data into a consistent format, typically using JSON. We clean and enrich the data, ensuring that elements like dates are standardized across datasets to simplify later use. The goal in the Silver layer is to prepare the data in a unified format that's ready for business applications. Notably, we've moved away from using raw vault from this stage because it was proving to be costly and impacting performance. Instead, we've adopted a programmatic approach to transform the normalized JSON of the Silver into star schema in the Gold layer.

Piethein Strengholt: So, for the Silver layer, is the data modeling approach focused on making data more denormalized?

Joel Singer: Yes, exactly. One of the key processes in the Silver layer involves denormalizing the data. Some data records are highly unstructured, with a complex hierarchy, and can contain up to 2,000 data elements. In the Silver layer, we denormalize this data, simplifying its structure to make it easier for subsequent use. This step is crucial for preparing the data for more efficient analysis and processing in later stages.

Piethein Strengholt: Do you maintain alignment with the source systems in the data or integrate data across different systems?

Joel Singer: We generally strive to keep the data aligned with its original source systems. However, there are exceptions, particularly with reference data, where integrating it directly in the Silver layer can make querying the data easier later on. The main goal is to preserve a clear data lineage, allowing for clean separation. This approach ensures that if additional aggregations or transformations are needed, the original data source remains accessible and minimally altered. Integration at this stage is primarily limited to reference data for practical reasons.

Piethein Strengholt: Regarding reference data, do you have an enterprise data model that outlines which reference data is critical for your operations?

Joel Singer: Yes, we do have a master data management system where our reference data is stored according to a clear data model. This model is shared across all teams, which is particularly important in the travel industry. For example, data like the mapping between airports and cities is commonly and widely used throughout the company. This ensures consistency and accuracy in our data handling across various applications and processes.

Piethein Strengholt: Can you confirm if the data format in the Silver layer is Delta?

Joel Singer: Yes, that's correct. Currently, we use the Delta format in the Silver layer, leveraging Azure Databricks for this purpose. We're also keeping an eye on industry developments, such as the Iceberg format. It's interesting to note that there's a convergence happening with the Delta Lake 3.0 version, which is compatible with the Iceberg format.[2] We are pleased to see this kind of convergence, as it allows us to stay updated with the latest technologies and potentially integrate them into our systems.

Piethein Strengholt: Could you explain how the Gold layer is organized in your architecture?

Joel Singer: In the Gold layer, we've developed an in-house library called JSON2Star, which facilitates the transformation from the Silver to the Gold layer. This library processes JSON datasets from the Silver layer and, using a configuration file that defines our desired final data model or star schema, generates all the necessary scripts. These scripts are used to create tables and include Databricks commands needed to build the final star schemas. You see a high-level overview of this process in Figure 9-2.

This process is automated and runs hourly, taking data from the Silver layer to construct the star schemas. This automation has not only increased our efficiency but also integrated a CI/CD approach into our data pipeline. It relies on a single source of truth, which is the configuration file defined in an open format. This setup greatly simplifies the structuring of our documentation and scripts related to the star schemas.

---

2 In 2024, Databricks made a strategic decision by acquiring Tabular, a company that supports the Apache Iceberg initiative, one of the leading open source lakehouse table formats. More information about the different table formats can be found in "Apache Hudi, Apache Iceberg, and Delta Lake" on page 26.

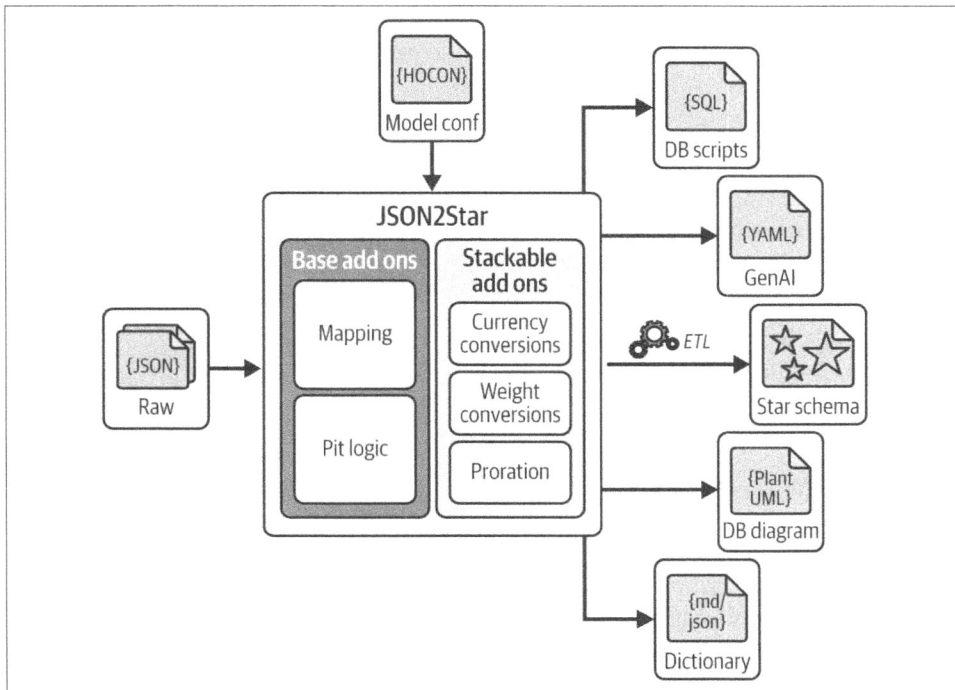

Figure 9-2. High-level overview of JSON2Star, which facilitates the transformation from the Silver to the Gold layer

Piethein Strengholt: Are the structures in the Gold layer based on dimensional modeling, such as star schemas with a fact table and surrounding dimensional tables?

Joel Singer: Yes, that's correct. Our Gold layer consists of fact and dimension tables. However, it's a bit more complex than traditional star schemas because we have multiple fact tables and multiple dimensions that are interconnected. Due to this complexity, we refer to our structure not just as a star schema but as a constellation of star schemas, which we call a Galaxy schema. This intricate setup with multiple dimensions and facts all linked together allows us to deliver substantial value to our customers.

Piethein Strengholt: How is data integration managed within a domain, and how is it shared across other domains?

Joel Singer: The process begins with a workflow where a team that needs data from another domain must request access.

Once a team requests access to a dataset, we collaborate with the data owner and legal teams to ensure sharing that data is permissible. After gaining approval, we grant access via Microsoft Entra ID to the data container where the data resides.

Additionally, because some of our data is complex, we use Unity Catalog for more granular access control. For example, some records might include information from multiple entities, like travel agencies and airlines, each requiring a different view of the data. Unity Catalog helps us manage these intricate data access needs based on specific use cases or user identities.

All data access requests and uses are meticulously tracked. We maintain an audit trail to monitor who requests and accesses each dataset, ensuring that data usage is both transparent and secure. This structured approach allows us to manage data sharing effectively across different domains while maintaining strict compliance and data security standards.

Piethein Strengholt: Can the data access system also be used for production use cases, where it's not just individual users querying data but also service principles or managed identities requesting data?

Joel Singer: Absolutely. In our system, we accommodate both personal users with individual accounts and service principles, which you can think of as robotic users that represent products. For instance, one of our products, called Amadeus Dynamic Pricing, utilizes data from multiple sources. It leverages data from our reservation system to understand current shopping requests, incorporates third-party data, and uses reference data. By integrating all these data sources, dynamic pricing can fine-tune prices based on market conditions. This demonstrates how our data access system supports complex production use cases by facilitating the integration of diverse data sources.

Piethein Strengholt: How does your enterprise team maintain oversight of all the different data distributions and datasets being produced?

Joel Singer: To manage and oversee our diverse data distributions and datasets, we rely on a data catalog. This tool not only helps in requesting access to data but also tracks and monitors these access requests. Additionally, we've implemented a control plane that provides an overarching view of who is accessing which type of data.

In our data mesh, we have a dedicated node that specifically monitors data exchanges, whether they occur through big data processes, APIs, or events. This comprehensive monitoring allows us to maintain an audit trail of all data exchanges, ensuring transparency and accountability in how data is accessed and used across the enterprise.

Piethein Strengholt: So, from your data catalog you can oversee all data movements?

Joel Singer: Yes, everything is meticulously cataloged in a data catalog. From this catalog, you can oversee all requests, available API endpoints, data products, data movements, and more. We ensure that the actual usage of data aligns with what has been declared. This means we not only monitor declared data usage but also verify that the ongoing data activities match those declarations. This system helps maintain data integrity and compliance across all our data operations.

Piethein Strengholt: What is Amadeus's definition of a data product?

Joel Singer: At Amadeus, a data product is central to our strategy of becoming a more data-driven company. A data product must encompass several key features: it should be valuable, discoverable, accessible, secure, trustworthy, and interoperable, aligning with open data standards. We aim for our data to be accessible in various forms, whether for analytical needs, through APIs, or via events. Ownership of the data product resides with the data domain responsible for producing the data, as they hold the expertise on that specific data. This comprehensive approach ensures that our data products are effective and meet the high standards we set for our data operations.

Piethein Strengholt: Are there specific principles regarding which data layers can be used as input for data products, particularly for serving data to others? For instance, is the Bronze layer allowed to be used for this purpose?

Joel Singer: We permit the use of any layer. However, employing the Bronze layer to serve data is generally not advantageous, as previously mentioned. Typically, the Gold layer is more commonly utilized. This layer is refined and dependable, making it suitable for extensive data distribution and application across various services and platforms.

Piethein Strengholt: So, while there is flexibility in using any data layer, the data products do come with specific terms and conditions?

Joel Singer: Exactly. While we offer the flexibility to use any layer, each data product comes with its own set of conditions to ensure the integrity and reliability of the data being used. This approach helps maintain standards across all layers and uses.

FinOps

Piethein Strengholt: Could you explain your perspective on FinOps and how it relates to the data mesh at Amadeus?

Joel Singer: FinOps has become a significant focus for us at Amadeus, especially as we look to optimize the data mesh. Initially, the basic implementation of our data mesh placed the financial burden, including storage and processing costs, primarily on the data producers. However, this setup doesn't incentivize producers to share more or improve the usability of their data.

> FinOps, short for financial operations, is a business practice aimed at maximizing the financial value of cloud spending. It brings together technology, business, and finance professionals with the goal of collaboratively managing cloud costs and investments more effectively. As cloud adoption has increased, organizations have recognized the necessity to control and optimize their cloud expenditures, and FinOps has emerged as a strategic approach to achieve this.

To address this, we've shifted towards a more consumer-centric approach, where the costs are allocated to the end products that use the data. This sounds straightforward, but it can be complex. For example, if shopping data is used by 20 different products, we need to distribute the costs among these products using a specific key. This first step ensures a fairer distribution of costs, focusing more on the consumers rather than just the producers.

Currently, we are exploring further innovations where we might even incentivize data producers by creating a virtual profit and loss (P&L) model. This model would not only cover costs but also generate virtual revenue for producers, encouraging them to create more and higher-quality data. This requires additional work, including mapping the data from producers to the final products that consume it.

This evolution in our FinOps strategy is exciting because it fosters greater enthusiasm among data domains to share their data. Ultimately, as data sharing increases, so does consumer engagement, product innovation, and overall success within our data mesh.

Piethein Strengholt: Did implementing this virtual P&L require changes to the financial processes within IT, especially considering IT is usually seen as a cost center?

Joel Singer: Yes, that's correct. We refer to it as a virtual P&L because it represents a shift in how financial responsibilities are perceived—from viewing IT merely as a cost center to potentially recognizing it as a profit center. This change is a significant step forward, and while we're not at the stage of having a true P&L yet, the concept of a virtual P&L helps us reimagine and realign our financial processes to better support our data-driven initiatives.

Piethein Strengholt: Is transitioning to a more efficient profit and loss model the next step for your financial processes in IT?

Joel Singer: Yes, that's the direction we're heading. Currently, the virtual P&L allows data producers to see which products are consuming their data and how costs are distributed among these consumers. It also enables producers to understand the revenue generated from their data, at least virtually. This visibility acts as a strong incentive for producers to share more data because they can see the impact of their data—how popular it is and how it's being successfully utilized by various teams to build products. This knowledge motivates them to increase their data contributions.

Data Models

Piethein Strengholt: Can you provide insights into the underlying data model you use for APIs, events, and building data products?

Joel Singer: Absolutely. At Amadeus, our approach involves establishing a common data model, which we refer to as the logical model. This model is designed to be polyglot, meaning it isn't tied to any specific implementation. From this logical foundation, we create more specialized physical models tailored to the type of interface being used, whether it's for events using AsyncAPI specifications, APIs using open API specifications, or big data contracts. A schematic representation of this process is shown in Figure 9-3.

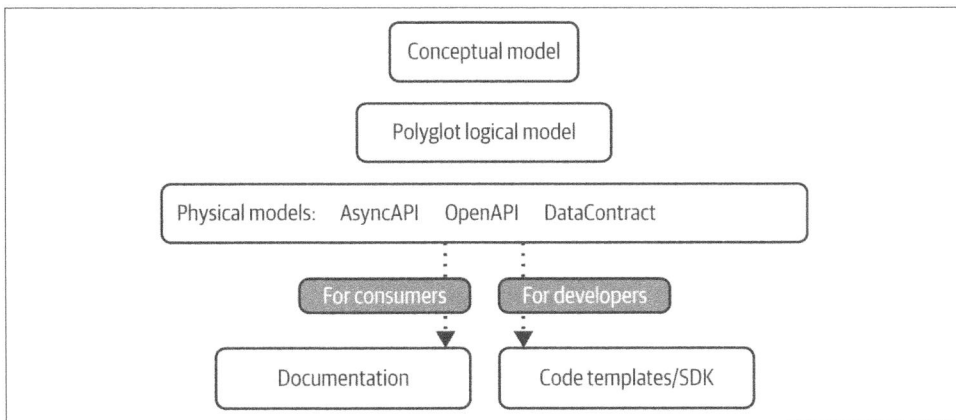

Figure 9-3. Governance is implemented as code by automating the creation of all new interfaces

Once we have these physical models, we generate related resources, such as consumer documentation and code templates or software development kits (SDKs) for developers. Our goal is to maintain the same logical model across different implementations, and manage everything through a CI/CD pipeline. This allows us to ensure a single source of truth, efficient delivery, and consistently aligned documentation regardless of the interface our customers use.

It's an ambitious vision, and currently, we haven't found existing tooling on the market that fully meets our needs. To overcome this, we are leveraging tools, including open source tools like the OpenAPI Generator to implement the physical models and generate the necessary documentation. However, there's still significant work to be done to fully realize our vision, especially concerning the availability of appropriate tooling.

Piethein Strengholt: Could you be more specific about how these logical data models are stored?

Joel Singer: Yes, we've organized the code repository to mirror our data domain hierarchy. From there, we use a combination of CI/CD pipelines and various tools to derive the physical models, documentation, and SDKs. This setup aligns with our vision of a more programmatic approach to data modeling.

We primarily use visualization tools to view the models at any stage, but not for editing, as these tools aren't designed for modifications. This programmatic approach allows us to manage changes more effectively and offers several advantages, such as the ability to validate models and ensure they comply with our data standards and guidelines. This system helps us maintain consistency and accuracy across our data models.

Piethein Strengholt: Does each team have its own repository, and is there also a central repository for shared common models?

Joel Singer: Yes, within our global company repository, we organize the different data domains of the data mesh, including subdomains. Each team is responsible for their specific subdomain. While we push responsibility to the team level, the overall hierarchy is centrally managed to ensure sustainability and alignment with our broader data vision. This central management is crucial because it helps maintain consistency even as organizational structures might change over time. We aim to ensure that our data management practices are adaptable yet consistently aligned with our long-term goals.

Piethein Strengholt: Do teams have the ability to view each other's work to potentially reuse logic or resources?

Joel Singer: Indeed, we actively encourage this kind of collaboration through our data governance practices. In the travel industry, where data elements for flights, travelers, and pricing are common across different services like airlines and hotels, it's essential to have standardized and shared data models. To facilitate this, we centrally manage what we call *data families*—these are data models that are common to most areas of the company. By doing so, we ensure our systems are not only standardized but also easier for our customers to use. This setup promotes efficiency and consistency across different teams and projects.

Piethein Strengholt: Does your approach suggest a hybrid model where central management of crucial data models is combined with local extensions and customizations?

Joel Singer: Exactly, that's our strategy. We recognize that each business line has its unique requirements. To address this, we provide standard data families, or common data models, centrally. Each domain can then adapt these models by removing unnecessary elements or adding specific features relevant to their area. This method ensures there is a common foundation, yet it's flexible enough to meet specific needs. We also regularly discuss how to refine these common data models to accommodate new trends, preventing the need for each team to customize independently. This approach aims to maximize commonalities across the company while allowing for necessary variations.

Piethein Strengholt: This approach requires a high level of standardization in provisioning, CI/CD, and orchestration processes, right? Could you elaborate on that?

Joel Singer: Yes, standardization is crucial in our approach. We primarily utilize a single tool for our CI/CD processes. This setup has become the standard we advocate to ensure all our workflows are automated using common tools. Our aim is to maintain a single source of truth for our data to prevent duplication and the need to manage data in multiple places, which we recognize as impractical.

By starting from this single source of truth, we use our tooling to derive all other necessary models, including documentation, code templates, SDKs, and schemas. This method helps streamline our operations and maintain consistency across our data management practices.

Data Contracts

Piethein Strengholt: You mentioned *data contracts*. Could you explain more about this concept?

Joel Singer: Certainly. In the context of APIs, there's a well-known standard called open API, which outlines how to exchange information or communicate through APIs between two parties. For events, there's an emerging standard gaining popularity known as AsyncAPI, which facilitates event exchange between two parties. However, we noticed a gap for big data, which led to the development of a new standard called a data contract.

We are closely monitoring and starting to implement this emerging standard because we see the need for a structured way to share big data, similar to how we manage APIs and events. This standard appears to align well with existing protocols for APIs and events, suggesting a potential for these standards to converge in the future. We are optimistic about the development and integration of this standard into our systems, as it represents a significant step towards standardizing big data exchanges.

Piethein Strengholt: Regarding the standardization of data contracts, have you adopted an existing standard, or have you developed your own?

Joel Singer: We decided to adopt existing standards rather than creating our own. Currently, we are evaluating these standards to ensure they meet our needs. So far, we are quite satisfied with the standards we are using. Our hope is that these standards will be adopted by more teams and companies, potentially becoming as popular and widely accepted as open API. This widespread adoption would greatly benefit the consistency and efficiency of data exchanges across different platforms and industries.

Data Governance

Piethein Strengholt: Data contracts are closely related to data governance. How does the evolution of your data architecture facilitate easier data sharing, standardization, and governance?

Joel Singer: The transformation of our data architecture not only streamlines data sharing but also enhances standardization and governance. Initially, our approach to data governance was quite centralized, which we refer to as Governance 1.0. About 15 years ago, when there was only one R&D group in the company, it was relatively straightforward to impose standards because everyone reported to the same line.

As the company expanded, our structure evolved into what I call Governance 2.0. Our engineering groups were divided according to business lines, and there wasn't a single head of engineering overseeing the entire company. This change made it challenging to enforce top-down standards and decisions. Consequently, we shifted to a community-based governance model. In this setup, while we still had a central body issuing guidelines, the implementation of changes was managed by community members who were part of this governance framework.

With our recent move to the cloud and our ongoing efforts to integrate our various business verticals more closely, we recognized the need for a new governance model—Governance 3.0. This model is a federated approach to governance. We established a central governance body that sets global policies, processes, and rules, provides the data families to be used, and manages a catalog of data that can be consumed by internal users, and shared with customers. Each domain within our company has its local governance body responsible for implementing these rules and managing day-to-day changes to their APIs and other data-related functions. These domain-specific bodies are empowered to publish their data externally in compliance with the rules set by the centrally federated governance body.

We believe this federated governance structure is the most effective way for a company like Amadeus to operate today. It balances centralized oversight with local empowerment, facilitating compliance and agile responses to changing needs. This structure significantly supports our goal of easier data sharing, standardization, and robust governance across the company.

Piethein Strengholt: We are approaching the end of the interview. Do you have any recommendations for the readers of the book?

Joel Singer: Absolutely. My primary advice would be to recognize that there is no one-size-fits-all data platform; every company is unique. Start by evaluating how critical data is to your company, assess your current position, and determine where you want to be. It's crucial to develop a company-wide data strategy that aligns with these ambitions and to ensure it has strong endorsement from the highest level of the company.

For implementation, I firmly believe in the importance of having a central body for both data governance and architecture. This ensures consistency across the company in how the strategy is applied. Additionally, as much as possible, empower individual data domains to execute this strategy and make their data accessible to users in an easily usable format. Essentially, govern centrally but empower locally to achieve the best results.

Piethein Strengholt: I couldn't agree more! Thank you for your openness. These insights are truly inspiring. Readers will be excited to learn more!

## CHAPTER 10

Case Study: Strategic Data Transformation at ZEISS

In this chapter, we explore the data strategies and infrastructure at ZEISS (*https://zeiss.com*), a leader in the optics industry. We engage with Markus Morgner, head of the Enterprise Data Foundation; Sascha Saumer, a senior data engineer; and Gert Christen, who manages the Microsoft BI platform. These members of the ZEISS data team offer insights into the evolution of their data systems, strategic shifts, and the implementation of innovative technologies.

The discussion begins with an examination of the significant shift towards a centralized data strategy initiated in 2021. This strategic pivot aimed to consolidate scattered data practices into a streamlined, cohesive model, enhancing efficiency across the company's various segments. Markus Morgner details the transition from a decentralized setup to a federated model that not only strengthens core control but also empowers individual segments with greater autonomy.

Further, Sascha Saumer and Gert Christen delve into the technical aspects of ZEISS's data platforms, highlighting the transition to cloud technologies and the adoption of the data mesh concept. They explain how the company tailors its data handling to meet diverse business needs through a combination of centralized and decentralized approaches.

This chapter not only sheds light on the technicalities of managing large-scale data systems but also reflects on the broader implications for data governance, integration, and sharing within ZEISS's global operations. The insights provided by the ZEISS data team illuminate the complex world of data management and offer rich insights into the future of enterprise data strategy.

Piethein Strengholt: Thanks for having me here. Before we get started, could each of you introduce yourselves, describing your role and responsibilities within ZEISS?

Markus Morgner: Sure, I'll start. My name is Markus Morgner. I am the head of the Enterprise Data Foundation at ZEISS. Our department oversees the major enterprise data platforms, which includes data management and data governance activities.

Sascha Saumer: I'm Sascha Saumer, next in line. I'm a senior data engineer in Markus's department. My role involves onboarding new use cases onto our platform and ensuring they run smoothly.

Gert Christen: Lastly, it's me, Gert Christen. I manage the Microsoft BI platform in the data foundation team, which includes a large deployment of Power BI services. I'm also involved in the upcoming implementation of the Fabric Data Platform at our company. Together with Sascha, we're working to create a cohesive platform that provides optimal solutions based on different use cases.

Piethein Strengholt: Thank you for the introductions. Let's dive into the first question. Could you share some details about ZEISS, such as the industry you operate in, and talk about your data strategy and how it supports the organization?

Markus Morgner: Certainly. ZEISS is a pioneer in the optics industry, founded in 1846, making us a company with a rich heritage. We employ around 45,000 people and generated about 10 billion in revenue last fiscal year. We established a data strategy in 2021. Before this strategy, our data initiatives and teams were decentralized and operated in silos across the organization.

The first step in our strategy was to harmonize these competencies and capabilities by bringing them together under one team, the data and analytics team, also formed in 2021. This team includes roles from master data governance, the business intelligence team, and management reporting. We also added new roles such as data scientists, more data engineers, and architects. Additionally, we introduced data governance and data management capabilities, focusing on data catalogs, policies, and compliance.

We are now more than halfway through implementing this strategy. We have a central organization but also federate many topics into our segments. These segments now use our platforms and adhere to our governance processes. We actively share our knowledge and resources with these segments to help them grow. Our model is becoming a fully federated one with a strong core that maintains central control over essential functions while also empowering highly capable segment units.

Data Platform Evolution

Piethein Strengholt: Thanks for that detailed explanation. Can you delve a bit deeper into the evolution of your data platform? Where did you start, and what direction are you heading towards now?

Markus Morgner: The evolution of our data platform began around 2017–2018 when we started exploring the capabilities of Azure cloud. Initially, the platform functioned more like a sandbox—a place to experiment without many concrete use cases. By 2018–2019, we started integrating real use cases and significantly expanded our user base, continuing until 2022. However, the architecture wasn't optimally designed—it grew organically with use cases, which led to issues with repeatability and reusability. We had a single analytics stack with a data lake underneath, which caused shared resource problems.

Realizing this, we took a step back at the end of 2022, consulted with Microsoft, and decided to adopt their Cloud Adoption Framework (*https://oreil.ly/N7eya*). This helped us establish a new platform incorporating best practices from the start, including built-in data governance and high security standards. The eVA platform is based on the Cloud Adoption Framework. It uses data landing zones (DLZs) for domains, which consist of one or more Azure subscriptions. The platform includes central hub for data management, security, monitoring, and metadata extraction for the data catalog. Figure 10-1 shows a high-level overview of our data platform.

We also began implementing ideas similar to the data mesh concept, though we hadn't formally labeled it as such initially. We structured the platform into domains or areas, which later we realized aligned closely with what Zhamak Dehghani describes in her book called *Data Mesh: Delivering Data-Driven Value at Scale* (O'Reilly).

Now in our third iteration, we've launched the eVA Enterprise Big Data Analytics Platform 3.0. We have 30 instances, each with three to four subscriptions, all built on the same Terraform module stacks and infrastructure. We've included areas for data management, security, monitoring, and metadata extraction for our data catalog. We're scaling up and have developed different patterns for data handling:

Central instances
   These provide data products used company-wide, such as in finance, where it doesn't make sense for everyone to reinvent the wheel.

Decentralized data landing zones
   These are unique to specific business domains or processes where data is very restrictive and needs to be kept separate with minimal communication to other zones.

Hybrid instances

These are collaborative spaces with business units where we provide the infrastructure and security monitoring as a minimum. The additional development can be handled by the business unit, if they have the capability, or in collaboration with us depending on their maturity level.

This approach allows us to cater to different needs across the organization while maintaining robust data management and governance.

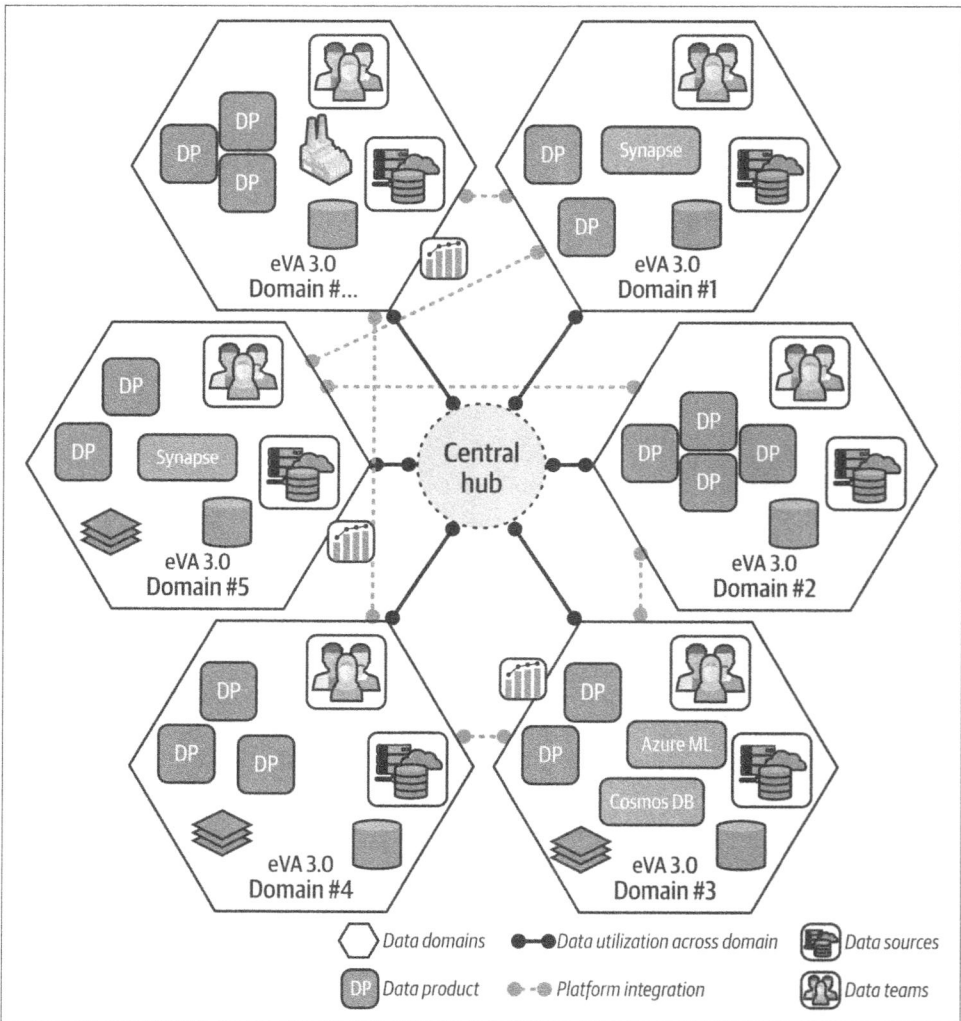

Figure 10-1. High-level overview of the eVa platform

Piethein Strengholt: Just to clarify what you mentioned earlier, when you refer to a "landing zone," are you using it in the same context as described in the cloud adoption framework? That is, a subscription with a set of resources, and you have many of these?

Markus Morgner: Yes, that's correct. However, "landing zone" might not be the best term to use now. I prefer referring to them as "instances" of our platform because it encompasses the entire setup. Each instance is a self-sustained platform that includes all the capabilities needed to build end-to-end data products.

Piethein Strengholt: Considering the variety of different services you use, such as Azure Synapse Analytics, Azure Databricks, and Microsoft Fabric, do you prescribe what domains have to use? And do you have a future state strategy? Is there a long-term plan or need to rationalize these services?

Sascha Saumer: Regarding your first question, there is no prescribed strategy for the technology platform domain teams must use. Teams should choose what best suits their needs. We offer guidance and support, but the choice is ultimately theirs. We do not enforce a specific technology stack.

Regarding your second question, we do have a migration strategy that primarily focuses on transitioning projects from older platforms like eVA 2.0 to the newer eVA 3.0 environment, rather than specific technologies. This strategy aims to standardize workflows and ensure everyone adheres to the same standards. Thus, we continue to support the use of Synapse, Databricks, and Fabric as needed. Currently, there are no plans to phase out any of these technologies. The migration is driven organically, influenced by the increasing use and community support for certain services within our company, which naturally encourages more people to adopt those platforms. We do not enforce the discontinuation of any technology.

Looking ahead, we have developed a high-level strategy to integrate eVA 3.0 and Fabric into our new eVA 4.0 data platform. In this integration, Fabric will be used in the consumer-aligned layer to utilize the data products created on the eVA 3.0 data mesh.

Gert Christen: To add to that, our approach isn't so much a deliberate strategy as it is a natural evolution. Initially, we heavily utilized Synapse in our data lakehouses, but we've noticed a shift towards Azure Databricks, especially for more complex scenarios that require additional flexibility and advanced features. However, we still use SQL serverless pools from Synapse due to their ease of use.

This migration towards Azure Databricks for more demanding workloads has occurred organically, not through a planned strategy. The introduction of Unity Catalog has also simplified this transition.

One outstanding issue is the cost of infrastructure. Additionally, many users, especially those in consumer-aligned domains, seek true self-service with no dependencies on other teams. They prefer to manage their operations independently, minimizing coordination with other teams when deploying new resources or views. Although not initially recommended, there is growing interest in using Fabric, as it offers greater independence in project management. For consumer-aligned domains, Fabric is becoming the recommended solution. However, for source-aligned and aggregate domains, we plan to continue using the established eVA3.0 DLZs for the time being.

Medallion Architecture

Piethein Strengholt: Transitioning to the topic of Medallion architecture, is that considered a best practice within these platform instances?

Sascha Saumer: Yes, definitely. Within each platform instance, we base our approach on the specific business requirements and needs. We usually recommend implementing the Medallion architecture. This could involve setting up different storage accounts and layers of code within the instance. The exact technical structure can vary depending on the services used, but we generally advise using this architecture, and in most cases, it is adopted.

Piethein Strengholt: Just to confirm, when you set up a platform instance or what you previously referred to as a landing zone, you customize it to meet specific needs. So, even though the infrastructure blueprint may be the same, you tailor the components according to the unique situation, correct?

Sascha Saumer: Exactly. While some components are standard—like a raw and an enriched storage account, which are usually included—the specific provisioning of components is tailored to meet the distinct needs of each instance. But then, depending on the requirements, if a NoSQL database is needed, we might provision a Mongo DB or another appropriate instance. If something SQL Server-based is required, we tailor that to their specific needs as well.

Piethein Strengholt: Are foundational data services like Azure Synapse Analytics or Azure Databricks always in each instance?

Sascha Saumer: No, we differentiate primarily between batch processing and real-time processing scenarios. Each scenario has a standard set of resources, but there's flexibility depending on the organizational needs. For example, one business unit might choose Azure Databricks over another setup, and we provide guidance on which service would best fit their requirements. The same variability applies to real-time processing; clients might use Synapse, Databricks, or even Azure Functions. While some resources are standard, like the two storage accounts and networking components, the specific data services are not fixed and can vary by instance.

Piethein Strengholt: Regarding the layering of data architecture, does that also depend on the specific scenario or situation? Could there be fewer or more layers?

Sascha Saumer: Yes, the layering definitely varies depending on the situation. As Markus mentioned earlier, we have around 30 of these platform instances across the company. They are harmonized but not identical because of the variety of use cases. Typically, you see architectures with three layers, like Bronze, Silver, and Gold, which could be divided into different schemas or processes within a storage account. Some instances might work with just one or two layers, often referred to as a staging and a presentation layer. So, it really depends on the specific needs and setup of each instance.

Piethein Strengholt: Could we delve deeper into those platform instances? Starting with the first layer, how does data ingestion work?

Sascha Saumer: Data is ingested directly into services like storage accounts through various means. One example is using Azure API Management. Typically, data is produced in an event stage or, in real-time scenarios, it might involve other methods. Additionally, there's the classical batch approach where a nightly run connects to source systems to pull data. So essentially, both push and pull methods are utilized for data ingestion.

Markus Morgner: To add, there is an area for improvement. Handling the ingestion of SAP data has always been challenging. We are considering introducing a layer before the Bronze layer to consolidate SAP data within the SAP systems before transferring it to our data platform in Azure. This would involve streamlining data from multiple SAP systems, such as S4 and older versions, during our transformation process. By consolidating and processing the data in SAP—where it's easier and faster due to the available meta models and SAP technology—we can then extract refined views for analytics on our Azure platform. This approach should significantly simplify the integration and ingestion process.

Piethein Strengholt: In the first layer of ingestion, do you preserve the data as it is, using the original file format, or do you apply any transformations to the data, such as transforming to Delta?

Sascha Saumer: In the first layer, we usually preserve the data as it comes in, without applying any transformations. There might be some minor technical adjustments necessary, for example, if a column name contains special characters that can't be stored as is. But really, those are exceptions. Ideally, we keep the data as close to its original form as possible to maintain independence from the source, which is helpful for things like reloading data. Typically, the data might be in a format like JSON files. Transformations, such as enforcing data types, changing data structures, or denesting, are applied in subsequent layers.

Piethein Strengholt: Transitioning to the Silver layer, what kind of activities are typically done there?

Sascha Saumer: In the Silver layer, we usually handle tasks like changing data types or converting the format from many small JSON files to larger, more compact files. We also perform data cleansing and schema modifications. For example, we might encounter a column storing measurement values, where each cell contains an XML with varying numbers of measurement values and structures. In the Silver layer, we standardize this by creating a proper structured format.

Piethein Strengholt: Do you join data from different sources in the Silver layer?

Sascha Saumer: That's a good question. Keeping in mind all our 30 landing zones, I'd say joining data across sources mostly happens in the Gold layer. There might be cases where it's necessary to map data in the Silver layer, but typically, such integrations occur at a later stage.

Piethein Strengholt: Regarding data historization, how do you manage that? Do you partition data or process it into SCDs, for example?

Sascha Saumer: In some of our landing zones, we use SCDs, typically of type 2, where we simply add new records to preserve history. In terms of historization, many zones focus on keeping only the most recent version of data in the Silver layer. However, in other landing zones where there's a need to maintain a complete historical record, we store the entire history in the Silver layer and sometimes even into the Gold layer. This approach is particularly useful when we need to analyze how data changes over time.

Piethein Strengholt: Moving on to the Gold layer, what processes occur there?

Sascha Saumer: In the Gold layer, we typically focus on integrating multiple data sources. This includes tasks like joining data, calculating key performance indicators (KPIs), and performing initial aggregations. We also create views on different subsets of the raw data to manage access permissions and simplify virtualization. Generally, reporting tools like Microsoft Power BI connect to the Gold layer to visualize the data.

Piethein Strengholt: Are the views created in the Gold layer intended for the semantic layers? And is it primarily the Import mode that's used in Power BI?

Gert Christen: The situation with the Gold layer can become quite complex. As you know, we primarily implement the Medallion architecture on our main eVA 3.0 data mesh platform. However, there is an ongoing discussion about whether the data products we publish and make available for consumption on eVA 3.0 truly belong in the Gold layer or if they should be categorized in the Silver layer. This is due to a significant amount of modeling still occurring on the Power BI side, which could arguably place those models in the Gold layer as well. Therefore, the boundaries can be a bit blurry. But yes, we primarily use the Import mode in Power BI. Additionally, we employ direct query scenarios when we need more real-time data access or are dealing with very large data models.

Data Products and Sharing

Piethein Strengholt: Can you explain the concept of a data product and how you see that?

Markus Morgner: To simplify, a data product is something that serves a specific purpose, directly linking to value or a particular use case. The technical implementation of a data product can vary greatly—it could be a dashboard, an API, or a table. The key aspect is that it serves a defined purpose and ideally adds value. While we don't have this setup everywhere, our goal is to associate OKRs with each data product to track its effectiveness and impact.

Piethein Strengholt: How is data shared between different teams? Could you elaborate on that?

Sascha Saumer: Sharing data between teams is always a lively topic. We don't have a completely finalized concept yet, but we're actively working on it. Currently, the method of sharing depends on the specific use case and the technology being used.

For instance, in a classic batch use case, where data is shared once nightly, there are both push and pull options available. Teams can either pull data from an endpoint using SQL or a REST API, or we can push data to them, typically in a backend file format.

For real-time scenarios, we often set up data update subscriptions, where teams receive many small event updates rather than one large batch.

Technically, we frequently use Microsoft Purview for managing connections and permissions. In cases specific to Azure Databricks, we use Unity Catalog to share assets across multiple instances or our data landing zones. This approach allows for flexibility and adaptability in our data sharing processes.

Piethein Strengholt: You mentioned having two catalogs: Unity Catalog and Microsoft Purview. Are these integrated with each other?

Sascha Saumer: Actually, it's more complex than that. We have three catalogs currently. The enterprise data catalog will be based on Collibra. Previously, it was Informatica, but the Collibra-based catalog is still being developed and isn't production-ready yet. We use Microsoft Purview for some management tasks within our platform and the Unity Catalog specifically for Databricks-related tasks. Currently, there's no integration between Purview and Unity Catalog, nor between Purview and Collibra, although integration is planned.

Gert Christen: And it gets even more complicated. Aside from source-aligned and aggregate domains on eVA 3.0, we also have consumer-aligned domains, such as what occurs on the Power BI side. Data sharing from eVA 3.0 data products to Power BI is currently gateway-based because our data products on eVA 3.0 are VNET protected, and Power BI can't access them otherwise.

With Power BI and the forthcoming Microsoft Fabric, we are introducing the Fabric Catalog. This built-in catalog encompasses the entire Fabric scope and introduces data discovery and sharing capabilities.

To enhance organization, we are exploring a *catalog of catalogs* approach. Our primary catalog at the moment is Collibra, which we aim to integrate with the Unity Catalog, Fabric Catalog, and any future catalogs. This integration is still in progress.

Piethein Strengholt: On the earlier point about data sharing, I've heard that some enterprises use data contracts to share data between domains or platforms. Do you also implement this approach?

Sascha Saumer: We've considered data contracts on a conceptual basis and have conducted some proofs of concept, but currently they are not implemented or in use. So, it's something we plan to do, but we're not there yet.

Piethein Strengholt: Knowing where you are today, are there things you'd like to do differently or improvements you foresee for the future?

Markus Morgner: We're looking at enhancing our data catalog management by integrating various metadata repositories and organizing data across different platform areas into a catalog of catalogs. This unified business catalog would provide comprehensive visibility of all data assets, ownership, transformations, and lineage across platform instances. It would also facilitate authorization requests, access management, and linkage to the business glossary, thereby improving data transparency and observability across our data universe. These changes are crucial as SAP remains a major data source and will continue to be so in the future.

Piethein Strengholt: On the data transformation point, is there any integration with a data modeling capability?

Markus Morgner: Yes, we've explored integrating data modeling capabilities, particularly through common data models. We've experimented in specific areas, like our device sector, where we aimed to consolidate various data sources into a single model. This would allow us to access all data in one place, regardless of whether it comes from SAP CRM, Salesforce, or directly from the devices. However, creating a common data model is a substantial task, and we haven't fully achieved it yet. It's still a work in progress.

Recommendations and Best Practices

Piethein Strengholt: Do you have any recommendations for readers of the book?

Markus Morgner: When we initially embraced data mesh principles, we recognized the importance of data governance but lacked the capabilities to fully implement it. We started with the technology aspect, which might have been premature. Now, we're seeing the need to circle back because data governance requires clear segregation of duties, defined roles and responsibilities, and a conceptual framework for slicing and dicing domains and sharing responsibilities.

Policy definition is also critical, along with policy automation, to ensure policies move at the same pace as the platform development. Initially, we had robust policies on paper, and everyone agreed on how data should be onboarded and used. However, the technical means to enforce these policies in real life were lacking, which is where data contracts will play a crucial role in the future. Data contracts will technically represent what you are allowed to do with the data, what the data product is supposed to do, when to scramble or delete data, and what quality level you can expect.

We aim to automate these definitions along with the data catalog integration, though additional components might be necessary since the data catalog may only reference, but not build, the data contract. Automating these policies is essential to ensure ongoing compliance and data processing checks.

For those considering a data mesh approach, I advise not to dive straight into the technology. Take a holistic view, set clear boundaries, and ensure everything is well thought out. Remember, there is no one-size-fits-all solution. You must assess your organization's specific needs and carve out your own path to adoption.

Piethein Strengholt: Gert, do you have any recommendations for readers about Power BI, reporting, and semantic models? Any best practices you could suggest?

Gert Christen: Honestly, I don't have many specific recommendations because Power BI has mainly developed from a self-service concept within our company. This typically involves small departments and data analysts who may not be deeply involved in advanced architectures. They might inherently use certain practices without recognizing them as part of a formal architecture like the Medallion architecture.

However, the scenario will change with the introduction of Fabric. In theory, Fabric allows setting up end-to-end scenarios. In our context, we use the eVA 3.0, our Azure data mesh, for source-aligned and aggregate domain activities. This means the base data products—already at the Bronze and Silver layers, and possibly Gold—are created there. Then, we positioned Fabric for the consumer-aligned side, where we might do additional transformations for reporting, AI, or other purposes. It's worth noting that we just entered the "gated release" phase with Microsoft Fabric, expecting to have a full-service release in 2025 H2.

Furthermore, we're still discussing whether it's necessary for data already at the Silver layer to pass through all three layers again on the consumer side. We're exploring whether a two-stage process might be sufficient: using already curated data products, applying transformations, and then moving directly to the Gold layer, effectively skipping the Bronze layer.

Piethein Strengholt: Sascha, could you share your thoughts on the process of multiple environments and how it relates to managing data in layers like Bronze, Silver, and Gold within a large organization like yours?

Sascha Saumer: In our setup as a large organization, we often face the challenge of having multiple stages before reaching an end-to-end environment. This could start with a source-oriented data landing zone from which we pull data and then start the process over again. A recurring question is how often we need to implement the Bronze, Silver, and Gold layers in a chain when looking at the entire data flow.

This issue raises broader considerations. One significant area is the balance between standardization versus flexibility and customization. While we try to enforce some standards, there's always a need for custom solutions. This leads to ongoing discussions about how much to enforce, especially in areas that aren't as straightforward as security, where enforcement is more clear-cut.

Another key point is self-service. As a platform, we aim to automate common scenarios and make them available for self-service. However, it's crucial to regularly reevaluate these assumptions to ensure they align with what is actually being used. In a large organization like ours, implementing self-service can be complex due to dependencies on other departments or areas that may not yet operate in a self-service mode. This complexity can make the implementation of self-service quite challenging.

Piethein Strengholt: Gert, could you expand on the challenges you see in governance, particularly with the eVA platform and Fabric?

Gert Christen: Absolutely, we're tackling some significant governance challenges. On the eVA platform side, we've established a robust initial governance framework. This involves connecting teams with security, compliance, and data privacy groups, ensuring a well-governed setup from the start. However, the challenge arises when the environment evolves. After the initial setup, people begin adding new elements, and currently, we don't have a strong concept to govern these ongoing changes within eVA 3.0 or Fabric.

Fabric's complexity is heightened because it allows users a high degree of freedom. Users might start with simple reporting tasks and gradually move to more complex processes like machine learning without clear oversight. Detecting such transitions and the activities being performed becomes difficult.

In both scenarios, what becomes crucial, as also recommended in the data mesh literature, is the concept of computed governance. This involves having mechanisms in place to scan and monitor what's happening on the platform and identify any undesirable patterns. Unfortunately, we currently lack the capabilities to fully implement this level of governance. We need to find some intermediate solutions until we can develop fully these capabilities.

Piethein Strengholt: Can I summarize your strategy as enabling teams to develop data products up to the Silver or even Gold layer? Essentially, teams handle the onboarding of large enterprise data onto the eVA 3.0 platform and proceed to develop and publish data products in source-aligned and aggregate domains. For consumer-aligned domains, there's the flexibility to use either eVA 3.0 or Fabric. In this setup, existing eVA 3.0 data products should serve as the source. Does this accurately capture your approach?

Gert Christen: Yes, that's correct. In terms of governance, we're improving and clarifying the terminology. Initially, there was a distinction between data products and data assets, but now we refer to everything as data products. We're working on defining *global data products* and *local data products*.

Global data products are intended for company-wide sharing and require rigorous governance because they impact everyone. This aligned to the source-aligned and aggregate domain activities on the eVA 3.0 platform side. Direct onboarding of enterprise data to Fabric is currently not a desired pattern. However, it can occur with smaller and/or infrequently used data sources where eVA 3.0 onboarding and data product sharing would not bring any value.

On the other hand, local data products might be used by smaller departments for their internal reporting and don't require such strict central governance. In that case, we allow for federated governance for "local data products" that are shared within departments or business units. This reduces the need for central involvement.

Piethein Strengholt: Thank you so much for your answering all these questions. Readers will be inspired by your insights and experiences. I appreciate your time and the detailed explanations you provided.

Markus Morgner: Thank you for the opportunity to share our journey. We hope our experiences can help others navigate the complexities of data management and governance.

## PART IV

Scaling, Governance, and the Future of Medallion Architectures

Understanding the complexities of scaling and governance within the Medallion architecture is crucial for organizations striving to meet increasing demands while maintaining control over their data environments. Many organizations find these areas particularly challenging, yet mastering them is essential for sustainable growth and regulatory compliance. Building on previously discussed concepts, such as data domains and data products, this part provides deeper insights and practical solutions for building scalable, secure, and future-proof Medallion architectures.

Chapter 11 provides a comprehensive guide on how to effectively scale Medallion architectures and manage multiple instances within the same organization. It discusses best practices, common pitfalls, and strategies for ensuring that the architectures can grow with the company.

Chapter 12 delves into the critical aspects of governance and security within the Medallion architecture. It explores the challenges and opportunities of implementing robust governance and security measures to protect data assets and ensure compliance with regulations.

Chapter 13 explores the future of Medallion architectures, particularly in relation to generative artificial intelligence. It concludes with a reflection on the evolving landscape of data architectures.

## CHAPTER 11

Scaling the Medallion Architecture

In Parts I and II, we focused on constructing a single Medallion architecture. Yet, in the real world, organizations often manage multiple Medallion architectures to meet the diverse needs of various teams and data domains. This isn't just speculation; it's a fact well-known to anyone with hands-on enterprise experience. As organizations expand, they must scale their data management to support more data, more users, and more varied use cases. Thus, it's common for enterprises to have decentralized architectures rather than a one-size-fits-all centralized solution.

However, there's a debate out there. Some experts push for full decentralization across every aspect of technology, organization, and governance. But that's not necessarily the best approach. Decentralization has its complexities, especially in managing processes and oversight. The key is to strike the right balance, as the degree of decentralization will differ between organizations. To delve deeper into this subject, we'll explore the following two topics:

1. Scaling through decentralized data management using multiple Medallion architectures.

2. Scaling through Medallion inner architecture variations, which includes topics such as master data management (MDM) and enterprise data models.

By the end of this chapter, you will have a clear understanding of how to scale the Medallion architecture effectively and manage multiple Medallion architectures within the same organization. This sets the stage for Chapter 12, where we'll discuss data governance, data contracts, and data security in a federated architecture.

Decentralization of Data Management

In Chapters 1 and 6, we introduced the concept of a data mesh. This design pattern focuses on decentralizing data ownership and architecture. It emerged as a solution to the challenges organizations face when managing data at larger scale. It shifts responsibilities from a central IT department to business units, allowing them to manage their data more effectively. This operational shift is illustrated in Figure 11-1.

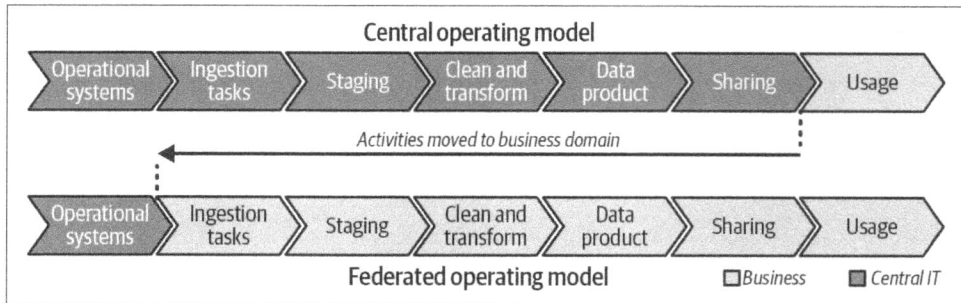

Figure 11-1. Implementing data mesh implies shifting responsibilities from central IT to business

In the top part of Figure 11-1, you can see the traditional central operating model. Here, central IT handles all stages of data management, including managing operational systems, ingestion tasks, staging, cleaning, transforming data, producing data products, and sharing. Meanwhile, the business is only responsible for data usage.

The lower part of Figure 11-1 highlights the federated operating model, which embodies the essence of data mesh. In this model, business units or business domains take on more responsibilities, especially in ingestion tasks, staging, cleaning, transforming data, and creating data products. Central IT still plays a crucial role but focuses on maintaining complex operational systems and providing central data management services to business domains. This setup ensures business domains have the tools they need to manage data as a product.

Flexibility in Federation

In this federated model, organizations can make trade-offs between the degree of centralization and decentralization. Some aim for a fully decentralized model, where business domains handle everything from managing operational systems to data usage. Others might adopt a hybrid approach, where central IT remains only responsible for tasks like operational system management, ingestion, and staging. Business domains then take over the rest of the data management process. This flexibility allows organizations to tailor their data management approach to fit their specific needs.

There is overlap with another book I have written. If you want to connect the dots and see the bigger picture, I encourage you to check out *Data Management at Scale*, 2nd ed. (O'Reilly).

The extent of federation between business domains within the same organization can vary. Not all business domains may manage their data with the same level of independence. Some might need more support from central IT, while others could be more self-sufficient.

So, bottom line: data mesh must not be viewed as a rigid concept; it's a spectrum of possibilities adaptable to unique circumstances, which influences the design of your data architecture. What does this mean for the Medallion architecture? Let's dive in.

Medallion Mesh

As the concept of data mesh gained popularity, market trends shifted, and vendors noticed. Technology providers began adjusting their strategies to align with data mesh principles, developing tools and platforms that support decentralized data management. This change sparked innovations in data governance and interoperability, making it easier for different business domains to share and manage data. For instance, data platforms such as Azure Databricks and Microsoft Fabric have adopted data mesh principles, allowing domain teams to independently manage their data using specific domains and workspaces.

Within the Medallion architecture, applying data mesh principles can help scale the architecture across various business domains, teams, or data domains. By adopting a mesh-like approach, organizations can deploy multiple data platforms tailored to specific business needs while maintaining centralized governance. An example of this is illustrated in Figure 11-2.

Let's dive a bit deeper into Figure 11-2. When we discuss the Medallion mesh,[1] we are referring to a network of Medallion architectures within the same organization, capable of sharing data with each other. In this setup, multiple teams work side-by-side, with each team operating its own Medallion architecture using the three *classic* layers: Bronze, Silver, and Gold. In this context, using Unity Catalog (pattern 1 in Figure 11-2) and Delta Share (pattern 2 in Figure 11-2) is considered a best practice for data sharing between Azure Databricks environments.

---

1 The term *Medallion mesh* was coined by Franco Patano and is described in the article "The Emergence of the Medallion Mesh" (*https://oreil.ly/nFHtn*).

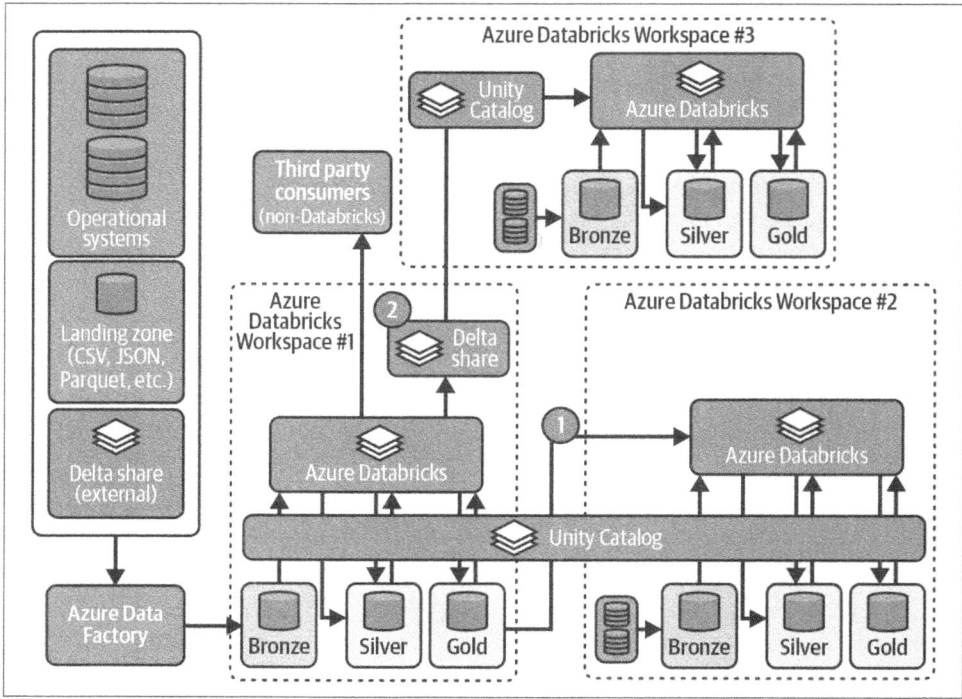

Figure 11-2. A Medallion mesh using Azure Databricks

> Microsoft Fabric allows you to create a network of multiple Medallion architectures, where each domain has its own Medallion architecture with a logical data lake. These logical lakes are stored together in a shared OneLake, providing numerous benefits such as improved governance and easier data sharing. This deviates from the "pure" data mesh, where each domain has its own dedicated infrastructure.

When constructed correctly, the mesh setup enables seamless data flow between different Medallion architectures, facilitating easier collaboration and teamwork. This enhances the scalability of data management, improves data quality, and brings data closer to business units for effective decision making.

However, with this approach, the complexity of the Medallion architectures increases as there are different patterns and designs to consider. First, let's examine the number of Medallion architectures, assuming each architecture shares the same layers and structure. Next, we'll delve into collaboration and data sharing through the data product layers. After that, we'll explore how to adjust the inner structure of the Medallion architecture to fit different settings and requirements.

Number of Medallion Architectures

When planning for scalability, you need to clearly define the boundaries or demarcation lines within your architecture, including the number of domains and platform instances. Here, a platform instance represents a deployment based on the Medallion architecture. There must be good alignment between these elements in a way that domains and platforms don't overlap. Without clarity about the architecture, you invite chaos and lengthy debates about the number of platforms, architecture principles, and similar issues. Enterprise architects play a crucial role in guiding the organization.

A common initial question is how many domains and Medallion architectures are needed. In this context, a "domain" refers to either a business unit or a specific area of expertise within an organization. For more details, see "Clarifying the Ambiguity of Domains" on page 226. For now, let's assume that each domain operates its own Medallion architecture, which is managed within a dedicated workspace—a logical container within the overarching data platform. We will explore nuances to this assumption later when zooming into the inner architecture.

The number of Medallion architectures you require depends on many drivers. There is no one-size-fits-all answer, as the number of domains can vary significantly based on the organization's size, structure, maturity, and data needs. Here are a few things to consider:

Organizational size

> The size of the organization and number of domains play a very important role in determining the number of Medallion architectures and workspaces you need. For instance, a very small organization with a handful of engineers might typically only need one Medallion architecture and a small number of workspaces for development, testing, and production.
>
> A somewhat larger organization might need a central domain for onboarding and managing all ingestion and integration processing pipelines and a few separate domains for different business units or projects. This scenario could require several Medallion architectures.
>
> A very large organization might define a domain for each business unit or project, and a few domains for shared services, like MDM, centrally managed enterprise data, and so on. Here, you could end up needing many Medallion architectures to meet your needs.

In large organizations where fine-grained domain alignment is used, data products play a crucial role in managing inter-team dependencies. By relying on data products, teams can operate independently of each other to a large extent. This is because they do not need to worry about the internal workings of other teams. Instead, they can focus on the interface provided by the data products, which details what data is available and how it can be accessed.

Organizational maturity

The maturity of an organization significantly influences the size and number of its domains. In more mature organizations, you typically see a larger number of smaller, more specialized domains. These organizations have refined their processes and systems, allowing them to break down their operations into specific areas of expertise. This specialization means that boundaries are precisely defined, targeting fewer systems and applications. In this case, each application team might operate its own Medallion architecture, with each domain focusing on a specific area of expertise.

On the other hand, less mature organizations might have fewer but larger domains. These broader domains often encompass multiple functions or areas due to a less developed structure. Consequently, these larger domains cover more context. In this case, you might see a lower number of Medallion architectures aligned to larger domains. As these organizations grow and mature, they often split these large domains into smaller, more focused ones, improving their data management and operational efficiency.

Security and compliance requirements

Different departments might be subject to varying regulatory requirements, necessitating stricter data controls. This could lead to the creation of separate domains to ensure compliance with regulations.

Cost tracking and budgeting

Separate workspaces can facilitate more precise tracking and attribution of costs to specific departments or projects. So, if budget control and cost allocation are a top priority, you might consider creating separate workspaces. Here, the focus shifts from the number of Medallion architectures to breaking down the architecture into smaller units for better cost management and budgeting.

Research and development

If your organization has a strong focus on research, development, data discovery or prototyping, you might need separate workspaces for different research projects. This separation can help maintain data integrity and prevent unwanted data movements or integration between projects. The implementation of this pattern can be done in different ways, which potentially could drive up the number of Medallion architectures.

Regional boundaries

> If your organization operates in multiple regions, you might need separate domains and workspaces for each region. This often happens for two reasons: 1) to comply with local data regulations and ensure data sovereignty, and 2) to ensure that data is processed and stored close to where it is used, reducing latency and improving performance.

The number of domains within an organization is not carved in stone; rather, it must evolve organically based on the changing needs and growth of the organization. You need to manage the evolution. So, start small and grow as needed. It's progression over perfection. This means the architecture will evolve with the requirements and maturity of the organization.

If you grow too fast, you'll likely have several backpedaling exercises because costs, technology proliferation, and labor-intense processes can no longer be controlled. Furthermore, it's a central authority, a central team, that oversees and sets standards and guidelines for the domains and workspaces, ensuring they align with the organization's overall data strategy and architecture. In addition, while growing, it is crucial to maintain optimal performance, cost-efficiency, and compliance. Governance and automation are key to managing the complexity. We'll connect back to these to areas later in this chapter.

From these sections, we can conclude that the number and size of domains vary greatly between organizations. Some aim for many highly mature, fine-grained domains, while others are content with a few larger ones. This choice impacts your overall architecture's design and the number of Medallion architectures required. The challenge lies in finding the right balance that aligns with your organization's needs and objectives.

Building on our understanding of data mesh and our discussion on determining the number of domains, we can now delve into the nuances previously mentioned and explore how to adapt the Medallion architecture to suit various settings.

Medallion Inner Architecture Variations

In the next sections, we'll look at various ways to scale the Medallion architecture using variations of the inner architecture. We'll start with scaling the architecture by implementing a specific layer for managing data products. Next, we'll explore Medallion variations, including provider- and consumer-aligned models, Bronze conglomerate models, and extra Gold layers for specific scenarios and consumers. We'll also discuss managing the Medallion architecture with enterprise data modeling and

MDM. By the end of this section, you'll see that scaling isn't about adding more architectures or layers; it's about finding the right nuances. Let's dive in.

Separate Data Product Layers

A decentralized model affects your data model, turning it into an interface model—what is now called data products. To execute this well, you must pay close attention to data modeling, data quality, and data governance. For best practices and considerations, refer to "Data Products" on page 222.

For turning your data model into an interface model, take, for example, a scenario where multiple domain teams own their operational applications and analytical data. Each team handles data ingestion, processing, and the curation of data products. To scale the Medallion architecture in this setting, you could introduce an additional layer dedicated to data product design and distribution. This extra layer helps differentiate the team's internal data consumption from the data they share with other teams—a crucial distinction since reusable, generic data products often don't meet specific use case requirements. You can see an example of this setup in Figure 11-3.

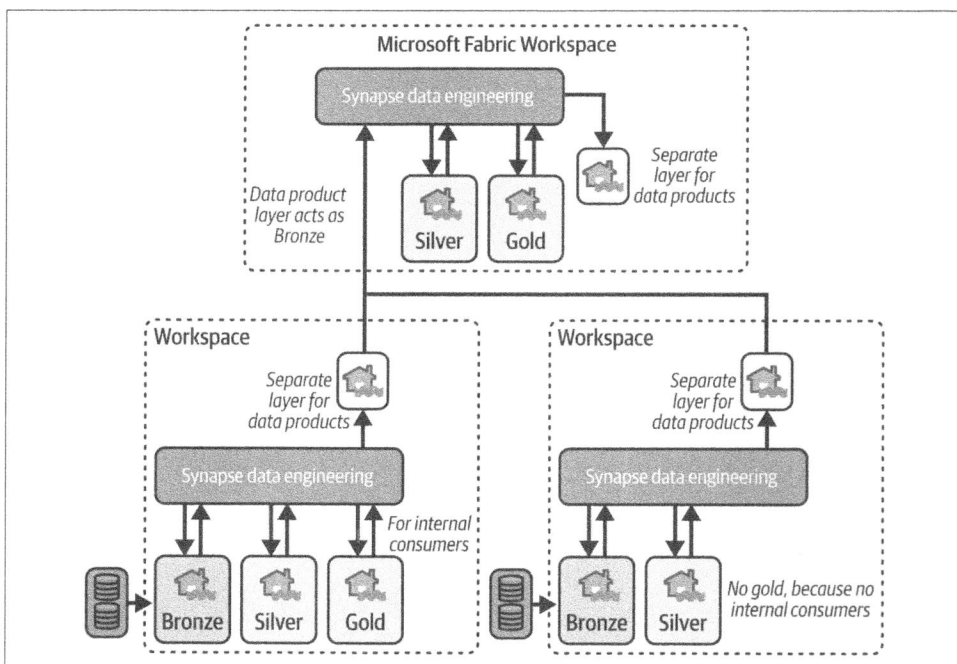

Figure 11-3. This Microsoft Fabric-based architecture design uses two separate layers for consumption: a Lakehouse entity (Gold layer) for use-case specific data and a Lakehouse entity (data product layer) representing data that is ready for consumption by other domains

In practical terms, within the Medallion architecture, this could mean splitting either the Silver or Gold layer into two distinct layers. One layer would handle stable "data product" data, which is usually cataloged with care, promoted to other teams, and always has clear ownership attached to it. The other layer would manage dynamic "domain- or use case-specific" data used by the team's applications. This split, which is commonly seen across more mature organizations, allows teams to independently manage their data products while still aligning with the Medallion architecture's core principles.

> Metadata and interoperability standards, including the promotion of open table formats, are essential for distributing data on a large scale. To achieve this effectively, robust data governance practices are necessary. These practices ensure that all domains within an organization adhere to the established data standards.

Scaling the Medallion architecture effectively hinges on adopting data mesh principles and decentralizing data ownership and governance. By empowering teams to manage their data independently, organizations can enhance data management capabilities, improve data quality, and expedite data-driven decision making. Next, let's explore some variations of the Medallion architecture that can help organizations scale their data initiatives more effectively.

Tailored Medallions Architectures

Not all domains require the same layering. Especially in a data mesh setup, where multiple Medallion architectures are used, the requirements for each domain can differ significantly. Requirements often vary and range from complex integration and distribution needs to simple data consumption.

A frequently encountered scenario involves creating isolated environments for different teams or business units that need to access and utilize data managed by other teams. For instance, a team might operate within a workspace that comprises a single layer (one lakehouse) with read-only shortcuts to data managed by another team. You can see an example of this setup in Figure 11-4 along with other variants, which we will discuss later in this section.

In another interesting scenario, consider handling two Medallion architectures—one tailored to the source system and the other to consumption. Here, the interaction between layers becomes crucial. You could argue that the Gold or data product layer in the source-aligned architecture effectively acts as the Bronze layer in the consumption-aligned architecture. This approach creates a leaner architecture by eliminating the need to duplicate the data product layer in the Bronze layer in the consumption setup.

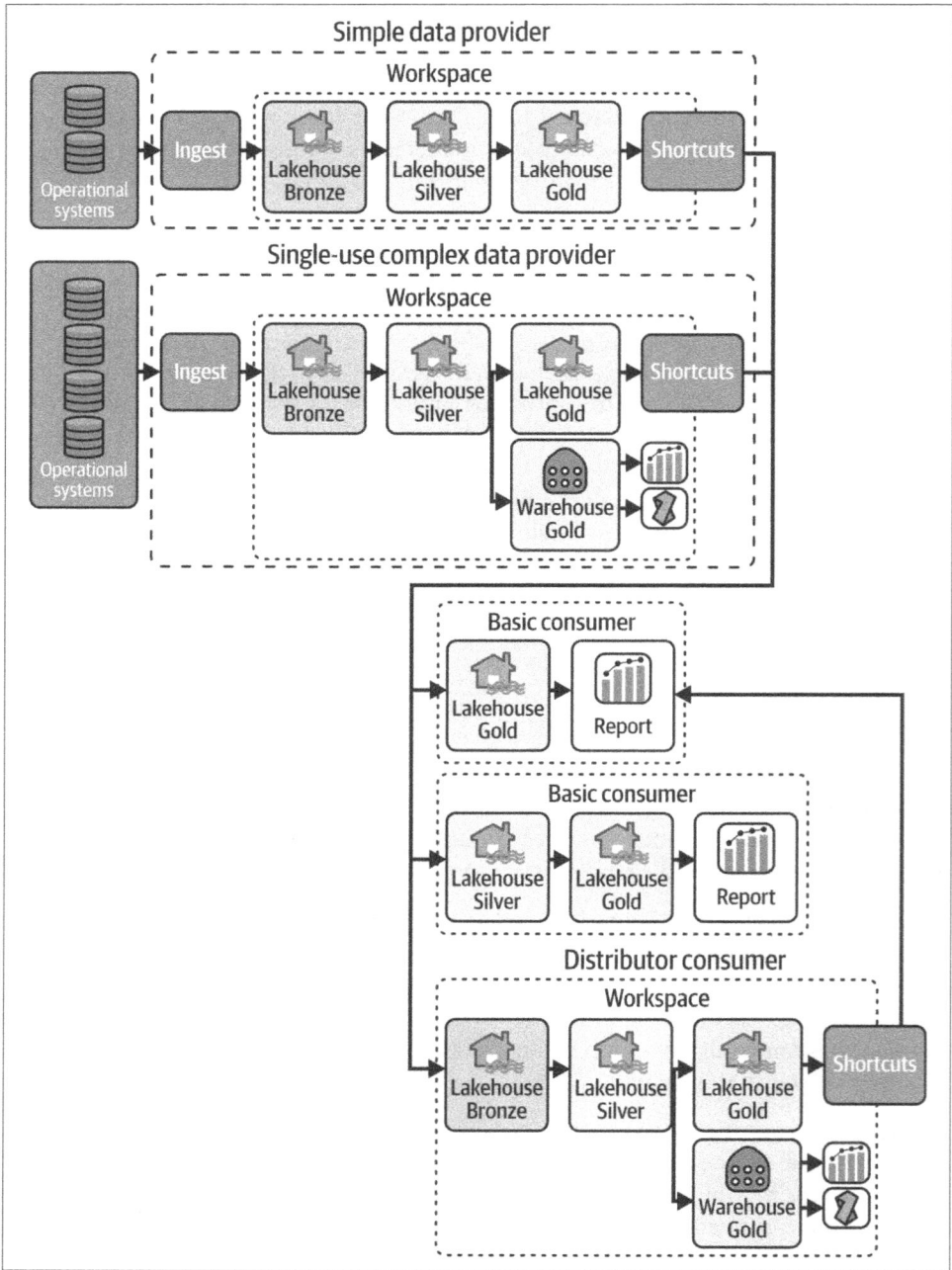

Figure 11-4. Different architecture styles: two basic consumers, a simple data provider, a single-use complex provider, and a distributor consumer

Building complex Medallion architectures using data mesh principles can get tricky, especially when many teams are involved, each needing to access data from others. In such scenarios, you might consider setting up separate Medallion architectures for each team, complete with their own Bronze, Silver, and Gold layers. Designing several tailored solution patterns for these situations can be beneficial. Here are some examples to guide you:

Simple data provider

> If you're a data provider with just a few sources and you're not consuming your own data for specific use cases, you might only need two or three layers (e.g., Bronze and a data product layer).

Single-use complex data provider

> As a provider handling numerous sources but only using this data internally for your purposes, a three-layer or four-layer setup could suffice, e.g., Bronze, Silver, and Gold.

Multi-use complex data provider

> If you're dealing with many sources and using this data for various internal projects, consider implementing at a minimum four or five layers.

Basic consumer

> If your role is primarily consuming data without complex processing, you might operate effectively with just one layer, or potentially none (e.g., reporting directly on layers from other domains).

Integrated consumer

> As a consumer who needs to integrate data from multiple sources for your own projects, a two- or three-layer structure would be appropriate.

Distributor consumer

> If you're integrating data from various sources for your own use and further distributing it to other domains, you might require several layers to manage this complexity effectively (e.g., Bronze, Silver, Gold, and a data product layer).

Consumer provider

> If you are solely a consumer of data for the purpose of providing it to others, and not for personal use, you may require a more complex setup with multiple layers to effectively manage the data.

What we've seen and learned is that scalability doesn't require sticking to one rigid design pattern. Instead, you can tailor Medallion architectures to fit your organization's unique needs, ensuring efficient and effective data management. Each pattern is designed to address different complexities and data integration needs, ensuring efficiency and clarity in your data architecture.

For example, consider the consumer provider pattern, which is frequently used in large enterprises to streamline integration efforts. In this model, multiple consuming domains delegate integration responsibilities to a providing domain, which is made accountable for organization-wide harmonization. This domain integrates and harmonizes enterprise sources, such as shared customer and product administrations, to produce flattened *golden data products* for consumption. This approach, also known as the use of aggregates, significantly reduces the repetitive integration tasks required on the consuming side. We will revisit this concept in "Enterprise Data Models" on page 313.

In another scenario, the integration process can be optimized through a delegation model, for instance, by using Unity Catalog. In this setup, each domain, aligned with its source systems, creates data products within its own context and then promotes them to individual catalogs. Additionally, there is a central catalog that outlines how these local data products should be consolidated into a unified view. Such a framework supports a delegation model, where providing domains map their local data products to centrally managed and harmonized data products, further simplifying data management across the enterprise.

For all the various designs, it's crucial to standardize and formalize these design patterns to streamline data management and enhance data quality across the organization. I recommended providing guidance on the design of each solution pattern, its layering, and data product management, as discussed in "Data Products" on page 222. This will help teams structure their architecture and seamlessly integrate data products into various designs. In this section, we've talked about boosting flexibility by adding or removing layers.

So far, we have focused on scaling and designing Medallion architectures by adding or removing layers. However, we can also scale or optimize a Medallion architecture by introducing variations within the layers themselves.

Adaptability of the Bronze Layer

You can divide the Bronze layer to manage different data ingestion flows effectively. Take, for example, a variation of the Bronze layer where it functions like a conglomerate of various pools of data. In this Microsoft Fabric-based setup, which is seen in Figure 11-5, various Lakehouse entities within the Bronze layer manage various data pools.

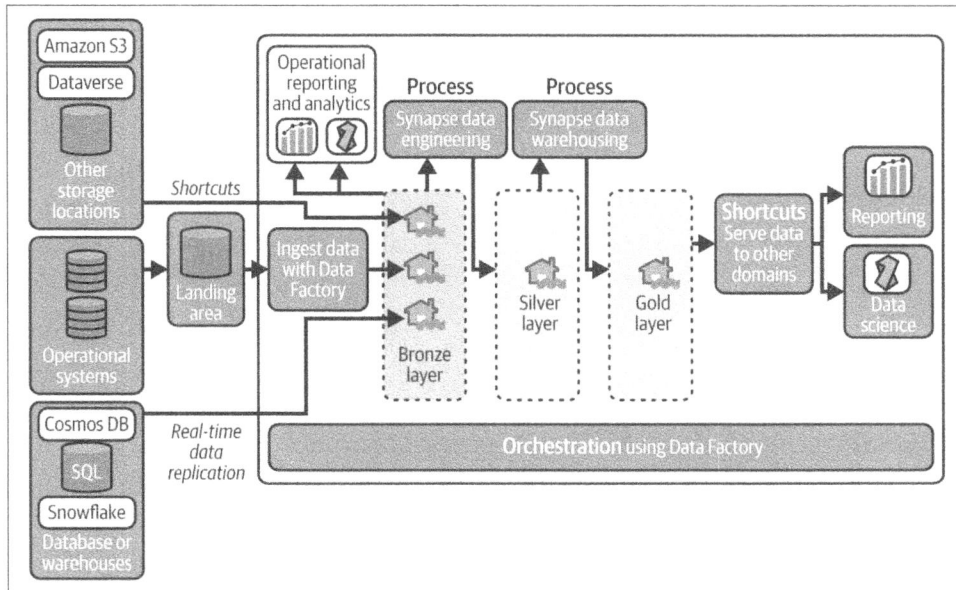

Figure 11-5. The Bronze layer is operating as a conglomerate of Lakehouses that use physical copies, shortcuts, and replication

In this model, different ingestion patterns operate in parallel. Here is what Figure 11-5 illustrates:

Shortcuts

For data that doesn't require extensive processing,[2] you might create shortcuts to the data in the Bronze layer. This approach is useful for data that's already in a compatible format (e.g., Delta Lake or Iceberg) and doesn't need technical data transformations.

Physical copies

In this scenario, you might ingest data from various sources into the Bronze layer, creating physical copies of the data. This setup is ideal for data that requires extensive processing or transformation before being used in the Silver or Gold layers.

---

2 Virtualized data, such as shortcuts, can encounter bottlenecks, particularly with large datasets. In such cases, creating a physical copy of the data is a better option.

Replication

Real-time synchronization, such as mirroring or CDC, is another option for data that needs to be replicated across different domains. This setup ensures data is always up-to-date and available for use in various applications.

In this example, the Bronze layer is split into different pools to align with various ingestion methods.

However, splitting can also be considered to align with different application teams. For instance, imagine a scenario in which different teams would like to ingest data from different sources into the Bronze layer of a larger domain, but these teams aren't allowed to see the data from other teams. In this case, you could introduce extra lakehouse entities within your Bronze layer to manage data ingestion for each team separately. This setup ensures that data is kept separate and secure, preventing unauthorized access to sensitive information.

So, what did you learn? You can tailor specific layers for separate data flows, ensuring concerns are separated effectively. So, even within a single layer, you can introduce variations to manage different data ingestion flows.

Another key aspect of architecture is optimizing it to handle complex processing needs. Let's shift our focus to the Silver layer, where we'll discuss variations and scaling options. After that, we'll explore the Gold layer.

Silver Layer Variations

The Silver layer serves as an essential intermediary, designed primarily to decouple the ingestion processes in the Bronze layer from the consumption patterns in the Gold layer. This decoupling facilitates smoother data management and transformation workflows, ensuring that variations in the Silver layer generally do not affect the provision of data from source systems to external consumers directly. So, in this layer, you can introduce variations to optimize data transformation and processing workflows.

However, to maximize efficiency and maintain clarity in data ownership and governance, it is advisable to consider some alignment in the inner structure of the Silver layer with the Bronze layer. This alignment helps in maintaining consistency in data handling and transformation rules across these layers, thereby simplifying the management and evolution of the data pipeline over time.

Gold Layer Variations

The Gold layer is all about delivering business value. You can tailor it to meet specific needs by introducing variations. For instance, some organizations might add extra layers to help distribute data across various platforms or teams. This could involve selecting and pre-filtering data for particular scenarios and storing it in newly created layers. We've seen this approach already when discussing the architecture of AP Pension in Chapter 8.

Moreover, if your organization requires different governance policies for different types of data, consider splitting the Gold layer into multiple sublayers, each with its own set of policies. This is particularly useful in large domains where, for example, one engineering and business team operates a larger Medallion architecture. Ensuring clear ownership of different parts of the Gold layer can be achieved by dividing it into sublayers, each managed by a designated owner responsible for the data's quality, security, and governance. This model is commonly used in large financial institutions that need to report on various parts of the business while maintaining a shared data model. With a larger team, it's crucial to establish clear processes, communication channels, and training to ensure everyone is aligned and working effectively toward the same goals.

The Gold layers are particularly notable for adhering to enterprise-wide standards. Despite the complexity and time-consuming nature of enterprise data modeling, many organizations embrace some kind of enterprise-wide data harmonization to ensure data reusability and standardization. This process of organizing and managing data to make it easier to integrate with is also referred to as data curation.

Enterprise Data Models

In the Medallion mesh approach, enterprises often establish additional domains for this integration or curation purpose. These domains manage complex and large data models to ensure conformity to enterprise-wide standards. From these (data) domains, newly created data products are distributed to other domains. This approach, often referred to as building aggregates—which is similar to the consumer provider scenario we discussed earlier—helps organizations to scale their data management effectively. Additionally, consumers benefit from the flexibility to switch between Silver, Gold, or aggregate layers based on their specific needs. This approach is seen in Figure 11-6.

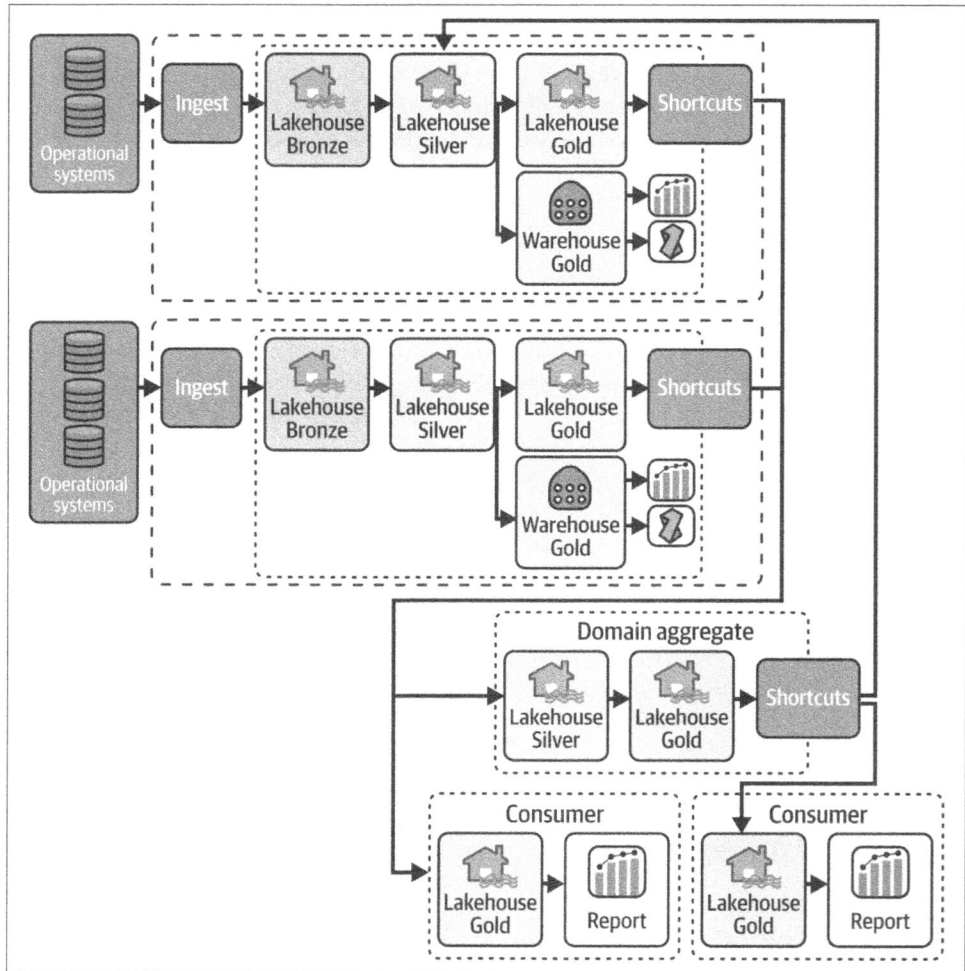

Figure 11-6. Domain aggregates enabling business units to perform seamless integration without extra integration efforts

Typically, a central team either manages or oversees these domain aggregates, focusing on maintaining data quality, governance, and compliance. These aggregates are not ready-to-use data products for specific use cases; instead, their primary role is to pre-integrate and distribute data across different domains. This ensures that all teams have access to the same high-quality data. The result is a neatly organized data product that seamlessly flows into other domains. It's worth noting that these consuming domains might even be the producing domain on the left side of the architecture, as depicted in Figure 11-6. This strategy prevents each business unit from duplicating integration efforts, thereby streamlining processes across the company.

You might be wondering, how do I know what data to pre-integrate or aggregate? How to strike a balance by only modeling what is critically important? In a federated architecture with vast amounts of data, determining which data overlaps and should be pre-integrated can feel daunting. Here's a strategic approach to tackle this task:

First, identify the most critical data domains and understand the relationships between them and their underlying source systems. Next, engage early with stakeholders to find out which datasets they frequently use together. This helps you prioritize integration based on data that provides the most value when combined, such as customer data from different sources or financial data across departments.

Additionally, use metadata from your data catalog to map and track data usage patterns. This helps identify common data intersections and high-demand datasets. Furthermore, explore your old legacy data warehouses if they still exist. These systems have already combined and pre-integrated a lot of data and can serve as a good starting point for your data curation efforts.

By focusing on high-value, frequently used data and leveraging tools to understand data relationships, you can efficiently decide what data to pre-integrate without overwhelming your engineering teams.

The approach for MDM is quite similar to data curation, as both play crucial roles in data management, though they serve different purposes. Let's explore the differences in the next sections.

Master Data Management

MDM and curated data creation both aim to streamline data usage within large organizations. They use common techniques such as ETL (extract, transform, load), data cleansing, data science, and metadata management. This includes capturing lineage and describing data models. However, MDM has a unique focus—it strives to establish a single, accurate, and authoritative source of truth for essential business data, often known as master data. Essentially, MDM is a data quality practice that ensures everyone can depend on consistent and current master data across different systems and business units. Note that in highly regulated industries, such as finance or healthcare, MDM is crucial for maintaining compliance and ensuring data accuracy. So, it's a necessity, not an option.

In the context of multiple Medallion architectures, MDM takes a specialized approach. It designates specific domains, which can be either centralized or decentralized, to handle the management of harmonized (mastered) entities. Other domains then utilize these standardized entities, which you typically find in the Silver and Gold layers. For a practical illustration of this setup, refer to Figure 11-7.

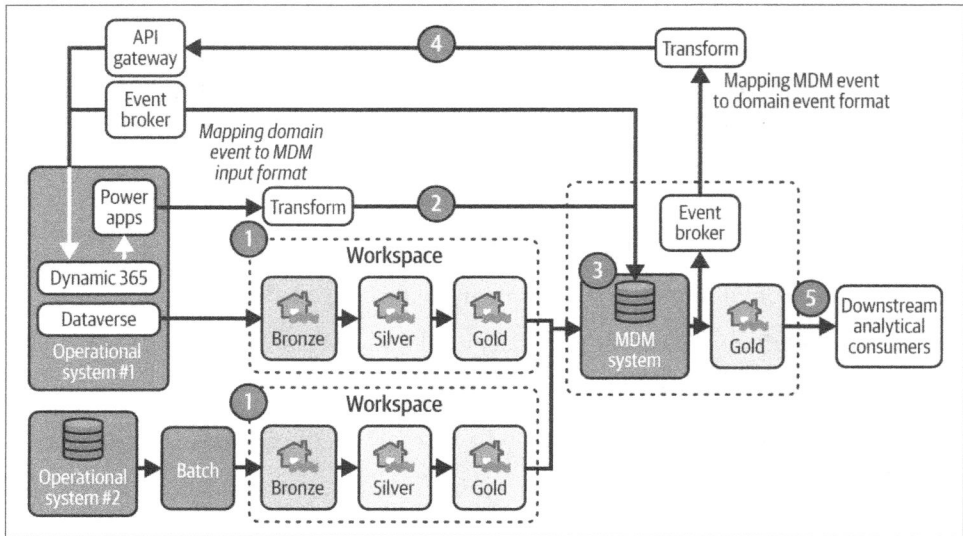

Figure 11-7. An illustrative architecture that outlines how data moves between source systems and the MDM system

In this setup, Dynamics (a CRM system) (*https://oreil.ly/UVJyF*), another source system, and MDM collaborate within a data ecosystem. Let's break down the process:

1. Domain data is initially extracted from various source systems, such as Dynamics, and delivered to different workspaces. The data then moves through stages—Bronze, Silver, Gold—to ensure its quality and integrity. In larger architectures, domains usually handle this process themselves.

2. Dynamics and Power Apps (*https://oreil.ly/N32JY*) use data from Dataverse (*https://oreil.ly/F3rG0*), a common data service. These components might generate domain events, which are then transformed to match the MDM input format before being sent to the MDM system. This pattern embodies the real-time data flow between source systems and the MDM system.

3. The MDM system stores and processes the data from different applications. It consolidates this data into a single and unified view using complex merge and match algorithms. Typically, a central team manages this system.

4. The MDM system can also generate events as needed. These events are transformed to align with domain event formats and can be sent back to Dynamics or used elsewhere.

5. Finally, the high-quality data processed by the MDM system is shared across different domains, ensuring everyone has access to consistent and reliable data.

In essence, master data generated by MDM domains finds its way back to other domains in various ways. One effective method is distributing it as (mastered) data products, as detailed in Chapter 7. To achieve this, you might want to leverage technologies from your Medallion architecture.

Additionally, sharing this refined and accurate data back to the original source systems significantly enhances their performance. This redistribution, known as the coexistence pattern, often occurs through events or API calls, as illustrated in Figure 11-7. This approach ensures seamless collaboration between old and new systems, facilitating a smooth and efficient digital transition.

Reference Data Management

Unlike master data, you can manage reference data within specific domains because it doesn't need to be compared across different domains. Reference data is vital for defining, classifying, organizing, grouping, or categorizing other types of data. It often encompasses value hierarchies, such as the relationships between product types and geographic locations. Reference data also plays a vital role in data security and access management. User authorization models frequently rely on reference data to determine access rights. This makes reference data essential for maintaining clarity and structure in data management.

To ensure reference data remains consistent across various domains, teams must synchronize their data distribution processes within each Medallion architecture with centrally managed reference data. Common examples include currency codes, country codes, and product codes, which can all be centrally published in an MDM system. Using identifiers from the MDM reference data for classification or reference is essential when domains distribute their data products to others. This alignment enables other domains to quickly recognize and integrate with the enterprise reference data. Automating this integration within the Medallion architecture ensures that the reference data stays up-to-date and consistent across all domains.

When you need your domains to align their data products with enterprise reference data, consider these approaches:

- Offer central services that enable domains to discover, understand, select, and integrate enterprise reference values into their data products. For instance, you could push reference data directly to the domains to facilitate their data product development.

- Offer a central MDM service to manage the alignment from local to enterprise levels, or employ a catalog to assist domains in mapping their data product columns to those in the central reference datasets. In this case, when a data product is published in the Gold layer, initiate a post-processing activity like a data quality lookup job to identify and resolve any inconsistencies.

Ensuring data consistency and quality across various domains is crucial for effective reference data management. By aligning reference data with enterprise standards, you guarantee that all data products are accurate, current, and consistent, regardless of the originating team.

Conclusion

We've seen that you can customize configurations to suit specific business needs while following certain standards for ensuring consistency and reliability in all your data operations. Yet, standardization does not mean a rigid, one-size-fits-all approach. You have the flexibility to select various levels of standardization and choose between centralized and decentralized approaches. These options can coexist, giving you the adaptability needed in your data management strategy. For example, you might choose coarser domains in your source system architecture and finer, more mature domains on the consumer side. You could implement a centralized MDM system for master data, while allowing individual domains to manage and map their specific reference data, such as country and currency codes. This flexibility ensures your architecture is tailored for an ever-evolving business landscape.

The control aspect is equally important as flexibility. Without careful control, these scaling practices can lead to increased costs and technology proliferation. For instance, if teams independently decide on their data quality frameworks, comparing metrics across domains becomes challenging. Similarly, without a unified transformation framework, tracking lineage across domains is difficult. The best strategy is to start small, building a solid foundation for one domain before organically expanding the architecture with more domains. This gradual approach helps maintain scalability and manageability.

In large organizations, the enterprise architecture department plays a crucial role in aligning the architecture with business objectives. The enterprise architecture team must guide the organization in transitioning toward a federated model while striking a balance between centralized data governance and decentralized flexibility.

As we move toward a decentralized yet controlled data environment, the importance of data governance and data security intensifies. In Chapter 12, we'll explore these subjects, as well the concept of data contracts in a federated architecture.

## CHAPTER 12

Medallion Governance and Security

In Chapter 11, we explored the nuances of decentralization and federated models within Medallion architectures, which are increasingly relevant in large, complex organizations. In Chapter 12, our focus will shift toward robust governance and security protocols. The importance of these aspects cannot be overstated.

This chapter provides a comprehensive overview of the governance and security aspects necessary for effectively managing federated models. We begin with a detailed discussion on governance, highlighting the use of Unity Catalog as a best practice. Then, we address data contracts and their role in the secure and efficient sharing of data across different domains. We will examine methodologies for implementing data contracts within a data catalog, using metastore configurations, and deploying YAML templates along with Git for version control and collaboration.

We conclude with an in-depth look at data security and access management. This section will focus on securing data platforms such as Microsoft Fabric and Azure Databricks, ensuring that access to data is tightly controlled and in accordance with established security protocols.

By the end of this chapter, readers will have a solid understanding of the essential governance and security measures required to manage Medallion architectures effectively, ensuring data remains both a valuable and protected asset.

Data Governance

Data governance in a large federated architecture is complex. It requires a structured approach to ensure data quality, integrity, and security is managed accordingly across all domains. To achieve this, you need to establish clear guidelines for managing data effectively within each Medallion architecture instance. This involves defining roles, setting boundaries, and managing data across the Bronze, Silver, and Gold layers.

Let's further explore how to implement data governance effectively in a Medallion architecture and look into the specifics of managing data within each layer. After that, we will discuss Unity Catalog, a critical component for data governance in Medallion architectures.

Governance Within a Medallion Architecture

To begin implementing data governance principles, it's recommended to start by examining the source system aspect of the architecture because it is where data originates. Here, begin by identifying which source systems generate and hold authentic data. Then, assign roles for application and data ownership. The application owner tackles data collection issues, while the data owner focuses on data quality and decides what data to share with the data platform.

Next, map out the boundaries within your application landscape. Group applications that work closely together and support the same business objective. Once you define these boundaries, appoint a domain owner for each domain. This appointed "persona" will act as the primary contact for that domain.

> Personas represent different roles within an organization, and it's common for the same individual to take on multiple roles depending on the domain's structure. For example, an employee might serve as both the application owner and the data owner. This multiple role flexibility allows for versatile participation in various aspects of data governance, adapting to the needs of each domain.

After you establish domain boundaries on the source system side, determine the granularity of each Medallion architecture and how it correlates with the application domains identified earlier. Decide if multiple application teams should share a single platform instance or if each team requires a dedicated Medallion architecture. Refer to the number of Medallion guidelines to assist in making these decisions. Typically, the size and maturity level of an organization will influence how applications align with platform instances. In highly mature organizations, you often see a fine-grained alignment, where smaller groups of applications share the same Medallion architecture. Conversely, less mature organizations may prefer a coarser alignment, with larger groups of applications sharing the same platform instance.

Once you've established the domains and the number of platform instances, focus on managing data within each Medallion architecture instance, starting with ingestion and the Bronze layer. It's crucial to implement strict access controls to prevent unauthorized data access. Additionally, set clear guidelines on how data can move from one layer or domain to another. For example, restrict data from the Bronze layer to within its domain; only allow certified datasets from the Silver layer or data from the Gold layer to be shared externally.

In the Bronze layer, maintaining tight feedback loops with the sourcing application teams is essential. If issues with technical validation or ingestion arise, the application teams responsible for the source systems must address these issues promptly. This ensures that data management remains efficient and secure throughout the process. Furthermore, ensure security measures are in place right from the point of data collection or ingestion. So, (automatically) label and classify data as soon as it enters the architecture. Optionally, symmetric encryption frameworks can be used to protect PII or other sensitive data. Therefore, it is crucial to define organization-wide sensitivity labels and classification schemas beforehand to ensure consistent protection of PII and other sensitive data.

Moving on to the Silver and Gold layers, your governance should prioritize integrity, consistency, and usability. Develop rules to standardize data modeling: data formats, naming conventions, transformations types, and so on. Such rules ensure uniformity across various datasets. It's also crucial to align with any enterprise data and master data management standards, especially if the same data is heavily used across multiple domains. For the Silver layer, avoid integrating data across sources to better align data ownership with your application teams. Additionally, conducting regular audits is vital to ensure compliance with these standards. This approach will help maintain the quality and reliability of your data as it moves through the advanced stages of your architecture. For the Gold layer, select data models that best suit your organization's needs. Focus on nuances rather than absolutes. You should transform your data model into an interface model optimized for intensive data consumption.

Having discussed the ingestion and processing up to the Gold layer, we can now summarize the discussion at this point with Table 12-1, which provides a quick glance at the most important data governance objectives for each layer.

Table 12-1. Medallion layers governance overview table

Layer	Governance-related objectives
Bronze	• Report issues with technical validation • Label and classify data • Optionally encrypt data • Define access controls for raw data
Silver	• Report functional data quality issues • Avoid integrating data sources • Conduct regular audits • Apply MDM • Ensure inclusion of security metadata • Define allowance of operational usage • Ensure alignment with Bronze layer • Sign-offs for operationally aligned data products

Layer	Governance-related objectives
Gold	• Focus on nuances for usage • Ensure uniformity across datasets • Transformation of your data model • Sign-offs for data products

With the creation of data in the Bronze, Silver, and Gold layers, the next step is to focus on the consuming side of the architecture. This side is facilitated by the Gold layer, where you'll notice significant variation depending on the requirements of different domains and use cases. Instead of over-provisioning resources by repeatedly delivering the same platform, consider offering your teams flexible solution patterns tailored to their specific needs. Additionally, it's crucial to manage the portfolio of all consuming use cases effectively. You want to avoid the unnecessary proliferation of new platform instances.

For instance, manage the onboarding of each new use case with care. First, identify any overlapping requirements. Then, consider setting up consumer providing domains for areas that require the same data to be pre-integrated. This strategy streamlines processes and ensures that data integration is efficient and tailored to meet the specific needs of various domains. Remember, it's about progression, not perfection. Evolving into a large-scale architecture doesn't happen overnight. It involves organic growth, where areas such as data governance, data culture, change management, and data architecture must develop equally and gradually.

To effectively support all your activities, you need a strong data governance framework. This framework should include well-defined policies, procedures, and tools to manage your data efficiently. It should also clearly establish who is responsible for what, ensuring that everyone knows their part in keeping data accurate and secure. It should spell out what metadata is critical to manage and how teams can contribute and maintain the quality of metadata management. To achieve this, you must focus on continuous education and foster a community where new ideas and insights are freely exchanged. A collaborative environment is crucial for keeping up-to-date and for improving data governance practices continually.

It's vital to integrate the principles of your data governance framework into your data catalog. This integration ensures consistency, while at the same time, it promotes central oversight, enhances team collaboration, and improves data discoverability. A data catalog offers a centralized view of all data assets, showing their lineage, key metadata, insights on data quality, and details about data ownership. With such a tool, you can quickly find, understand, and access data assets throughout your organization. This transparency is essential for maintaining data quality and complying with regulations. Data catalogs are also important for managing data contracts and ensuring data security and access. Let's delve deeper into the role of data catalogs by examining Unity Catalog.

Unity Catalog

In Chapter 1, we explored the Hadoop ecosystem, focusing on a critical component: the Hive Metastore. Initially, the Hive Metastore played a vital role in Hadoop and later the Databricks platform as the metadata repository for managing data objects and enabling queries. While it was effective for some time, it lacked flexibility and ease of use. A major drawback was that each workspace required its own metastore for configuration management, which necessitated either painful replication or the implementation of a broader-scoped external metastore. Imagine you're trying to manage permissions for tens or hundreds of workspaces that all must share one security model. Managing this consistently across multiple workspaces was quite cumbersome.

To address these challenges, Databricks revamped its approach to managing access control, auditing, lineage, and data discovery across workspaces. This overhaul led to the creation of the Unity Catalog. This centralized catalog manages data assets across multiple workspaces, simplifying data management significantly.

As the Unity Catalog began to gain widespread adoption, Databricks decided to make it open source.[1] This decision was a game-changer, allowing organizations to utilize the catalog's features across various platforms. The Unity Catalog has now become a crucial component of an open source ecosystem. Figure 12-1 shows what the open source Unity Catalog looks like.

With the catalog now open source, it offers a universal interface that supports a variety of data formats and computing environments. It supports table formats like Delta Lake, Iceberg, and Hudi through Delta Universal Format (UniForm) (*https://oreil.ly/ I-7Pr*), which automatically generates Iceberg metadata asynchronously, allowing clients to read Delta tables as if they were Iceberg or Hudi tables. Notable clients include Microsoft Fabric (*https://oreil.ly/kx_Sm*), Snowflake (*https://oreil.ly/RTN2O*), DuckDB (*https://oreil.ly/XZ94d*),[2] Apache Spark (*https://oreil.ly/0IsnK*), Trino, and Dremio (*https://oreil.ly/0F4cd*).

Furthermore, Unity Catalog supports external access via Credential Vending API (*https://oreil.ly/hYmcY*) and standards like the Iceberg REST Catalog and Hive Metastore interface. This direction marks a promising future for collaboration around metadata standards for Lakehouse Tables and an open catalog.

---

1 When Unity Catalog was made open source, not all features of the Unity Catalog were made available in the open source version. However, it is expected that more features will be added in the future. For the most up-to-date information, refer to the official Unity Catalog documentation (*https://docs.unitycatalog.io*).

2 Kyle Weller demonstrates the versatility of the Unity Catalog in his blog post, "Unity Catalog OSS with Hudi, Delta, Iceberg, and EMR + DuckDB" (*https://oreil.ly/B88jJ*).

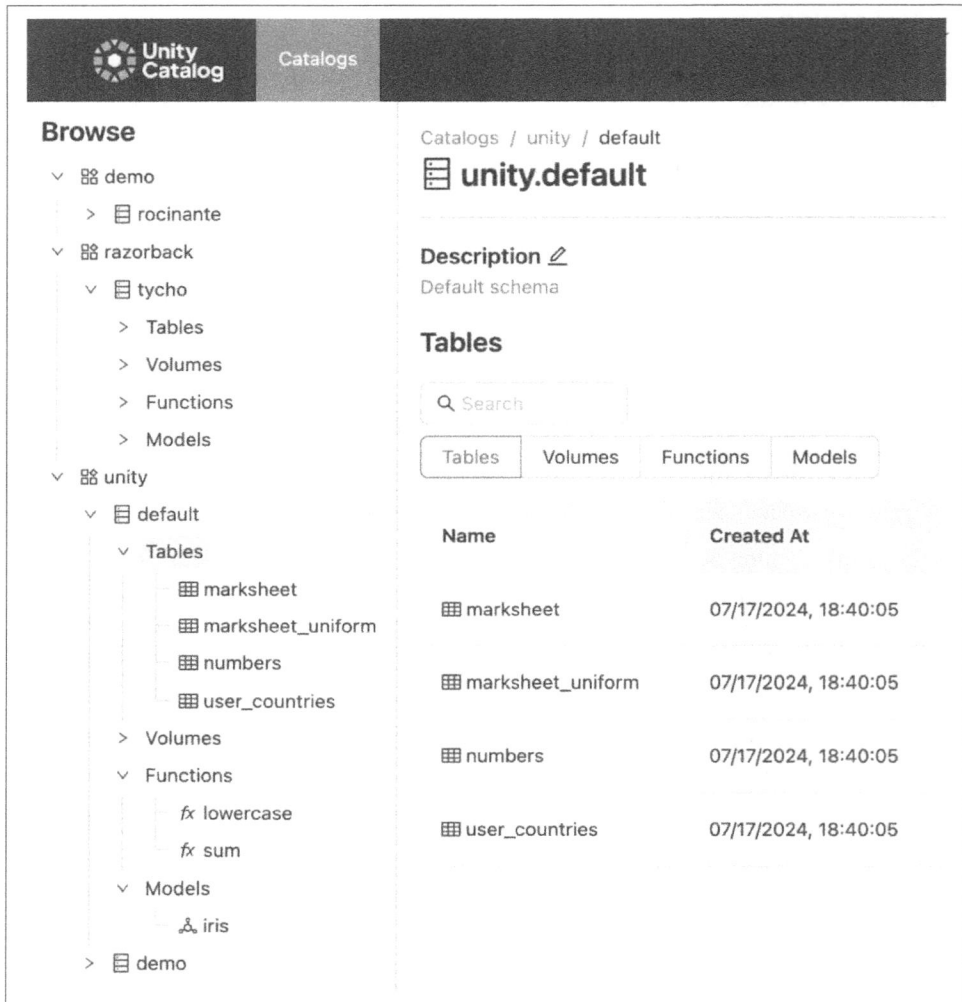

Figure 12-1. The UI of Unity Catalog open source software, providing a comprehensive view of various catalogs, schemas, tables, and properties

Open Source Data Catalogs

The trend of making data catalogs open source is gaining momentum, as evidenced by several emerging projects in the tech community. Unity Catalog (*https://unitycatalog.io*), Project Nessie (*https://projectnessie.org*), Apache Polaris (*https://polaris.apache.org*), and Apache Gravitino (*https://gravitino.apache.org*) are prime examples of this movement. These platforms aim to democratize data access and governance, making it easier for developers and organizations to manage data at scale.

This shift could significantly disrupt the market by lowering the barriers to entry for utilizing data cataloging solutions, potentially leading to more competition or standardization.

How does Unity Catalog fit into the Medallion architecture? Let's explore that next.

Medallion Architecture with Unity Catalog

Particularly in a Medallion architecture setup, Unity Catalog is not just an option but a necessity for robust operational governance. It provides a cohesive view of data assets and promotes collaboration among different workspaces. It provides numerous benefits, which we will explore in detail.

One of the key features of Unity Catalog is its enhancement of the namespace hierarchy. Traditionally, data management systems use a two-level structure denoted as `schema_name.table_name`. Unity Catalog introduces a third layer, adopting a three-layer format: `catalog_name.schema_name.table_name`.

An illustrative example of how this can be practically applied can be seen by setting up separate catalogs for different teams or data domains, each labeled with prefixes such as `dev`, `test`, and `prod` to address different CI/CD concerns effectively. Within each catalog, you can incorporate the Medallion architecture layer into the schema name, using prefixes like `bronze`, `silver`, or `gold`. For instance, a table for the sales team using AdventureWorks data might be named `prod_sales.silver_adventure works.clean_customer`. This naming strategy not only facilitates seamless data retrieval across various environments but also clarifies the stage of data transformation, with Bronze and Silver layers typically being source-oriented, and the Gold layer being more aligned with the needs of consuming applications or data products.

The naming conventions process plays a pivotal role in ensuring scalability and consistency. A centralized team, often a center of excellence, is responsible for setting human-readable and intuitive naming standards. This team also plays a crucial role in publishing shared catalogs that adhere to these standards. Importantly, this uniformity in naming conventions is also vital for future AI applications, as it aids in more effectively locating and integrating data, thereby enhancing overall system efficiency and intelligence.

> You can limit catalog access to specific workspaces through a feature known as workspace-catalog binding. This feature is particularly useful when you want to restrict access to specific objects within a catalog. For more information on limiting catalog access to specific workspaces, see the Databricks documentation (*https://oreil.ly/61PgB*).

But there's more to implementing catalogs for table management. Unity Catalog also acts as a security gatekeeper, as each object in the catalog can be individually secured. These privileges are assigned by the object's owner, typically the creator of the data asset. In this context, Unity Catalog also integrates with identity providers, such as Microsoft Entra ID. This allows you to assign access to different Entra ID groups, such as catalogs and schemas. For example, if you want to grant a group of users access to a specific table in Unity Catalog, you can use the following SQL syntax:

```
GRANT USE CATALOG ON CATALOG <catalog_name> TO <group_name>;
GRANT USE SCHEMA ON SCHEMA <catalog_name>.<schema_name>
TO <group_name>;
GRANT
SELECT
  ON <catalog_name>.<schema_name>.<table_name>;
TO <group_name>;
```

In the Unity Catalog security model, the hierarchical and object-level security measures are not only complementary but also synergistic. This integrated approach ensures a robust and flexible security management system. When privileges are assigned at a higher level in the hierarchy, such as a catalog or a schema, these privileges are inherited by all subordinate objects, including tables and views. This flexible setup allows for the application of different rules at each level as needed, adapting to various requirements effortlessly.

For more best practices, I recommend the article "Unity Catalog Best Practices" (*https://oreil.ly/pkgs1*). Here are some of the other key benefits that make Unity Catalog an effective tool for data governance:

Centralized data governance
Unity Catalog acts as a centralized platform for managing data assets across an organization. It oversees all workspaces, allowing you to track data lineage, manage metadata, and ensure data quality and governance throughout your data landscape. It also features a search interface that exposes metadata while restricting access based on user privileges.

Access controls
Effective access control is essential for robust data governance. Unity Catalog offers fine-grained access controls, enabling organizations to specify access rights down to the catalog, schema, or object level (table, column, or row level). This setup enhances both flexibility and security. We'll discuss more about access controls in "Data Security and Access Management" on page 333.

Data lineage and auditability
You can use Unity Catalog to capture runtime data lineage across queries run on Databricks. Lineage is supported for all languages and is captured down to the column level. Lineage data includes notebooks, jobs, and dashboards related to the query.

Data classification and tagging

To aid governance and compliance, Unity Catalog allows for the classification and tagging of data based on sensitivity, usage, or other criteria. These tags help enforce governance policies, such as restricting access to sensitive data or implementing specific data retention rules. We'll revisit data classification and tagging in "Data Security and Access Management" on page 333.

Data sharing

Unity Catalog offers the ability to share objects with others, both inside and outside your organization, through Delta Sharing (*https://oreil.ly/SXfQU*). Here's how it works: first, you create a "share" and add objects to it. Next, you add recipients and give them the necessary access. Once this is set up, a URL is generated. Recipients can use this URL to download a profile file. This file contains the URL of the Delta Sharing server and a bearer token, which recipients use to access the shared objects. This feature isn't just limited to Databricks; it also works with other technologies like Power BI, Spark, and pandas, making it versatile.

How do these features align with the distributed data governance model principles discussed earlier? What strategy should you adopt?

In aligning with the principles of a distributed data governance model, the initial step involves identifying distinct domains within the organization by using the guidance from Chapter 11. Following this, each domain should have its own dedicated workspaces, catalog, or set of catalogs, overseen by a designated domain owner. This owner is tasked with managing all assets and ensuring effective governance within their domain.

To further enhance organization and clarity, it's advisable to create specific catalogs for each team and purpose. For instance, distinct catalogs like `dev_sales`, `test_sales`, and `prod_sales` can be established for easily promoting artifacts between environments. Using descriptive names for these catalogs, as well as for their schemas, tables, and columns, makes it easier to understand and manage their contents. This approach not only keeps the data well-organized but also enhances security and simplifies management.

Let's talk about permissions within a domain itself. Table 12-2 outlines an example access model.

Table 12-2. Table-level grants

	Development catalog	Test catalog	Production catalog
Developers	Select and modify	None	Select or none
Test service principal	None	Select and modify	None
Production service principal	None	None	Select and modify

In this model, managing access within domains is strategically important to maintain both security and functionality. For instance, developers should have write access to the development catalog where they can freely test and adjust code, and read-only access to the production catalog. This read-only access is crucial for debugging purposes, allowing developers to view but not alter production data, thereby preventing unintended disruptions to the live environment.

Additionally, the introduction of a test catalog warrants the assignment of a dedicated service principal. This service principal is designed specifically for automated testing processes, such as continuous integration (CI) testing. It should have write access to the test catalog to enable active testing scenarios but must be restricted from accessing the production and development catalogs to maintain a strict separation of environments. This segregation ensures that automated tests do not interfere with development work or impact production stability.

By carefully structuring access permissions in this way, the organization can foster a secure and efficient workflow, supporting development practices without compromising the integrity of the production environment.

Effective identity management within the Unity Catalog is also vital. It is advisable to create groups with specific permissions, such as INSERT, UPDATE, or DELETE, tailored to a particular schema or catalog. These groups must then be linked to individual users. Reflect the diverse roles within your organization in these groups—developers, data scientists, and business analysts, for example—and grant them appropriate rights to different catalogs. For instance, data scientists might have access rights to the prod_sales catalog and schemas using a silver_prefix, where they can analyze data. This structured approach not only safeguards data security but also enhances operational efficiency. Note that we'll revisit this subject in "Data Security and Access Management" on page 333.

To conclude: Unity Catalog significantly enhances data management and governance in Databricks and other open source ecosystems. It serves as an operational catalog, streamlining tasks like data engineering, security, lineage, and monitoring. However, when Unity Catalog is part of a broader data infrastructure, pairing it with another catalog such as Microsoft Purview can be advantageous. In this setup, Unity Catalog focuses on the operational aspects of data governance within Azure Databricks. On the other hand, Microsoft Purview acts as a "referential catalog" or "catalog of catalogs." Using both catalogs together promotes a unified data management strategy across different platforms, improving data handling efficiency.

In the next section, we'll delve into data contracts, a crucial aspect of data governance in a decentralized data management environment.

Data Contracts

Manual data security and governance are things of the past. Today, we need a computational governance layer that automates and orchestrates the entire data platform. Data contracts play a crucial role by automatically enforcing policies. These contracts transform manual workflows into programmable ones while keeping the necessary guardrails in place. This evolution streamlines processes and enhances security across the board.

Essentially, a data contract is a formal agreement between a data provider and a data consumer that outlines the terms and conditions for sharing and using data. It specifies details such as data format, quality, availability, and security policies, as well as the responsibilities of each party involved. While the data product pertains to the definition and content of the data itself, the data contract focuses on the data's interface, aiming to formalize the expectations and responsibilities associated with data sharing.

Keep in mind that the term *data contract* can be ambiguous, much like *data products*. Different people might understand it in different ways, and there's no standardized definition in the industry. Therefore, it's crucial to define data contracts clearly within your organization to avoid misunderstandings and ensure that everyone is on the same page.

In the Medallion architecture, leveraging data contracts helps manage data distribution across multiple Medallion architectures within the same organization. This practice sets guidelines for data delivery, sharing, and consumption, which, in turn, bolsters data quality and governance and accelerates data-driven decision making. We'll begin with exploring how to set data contracts up in a data catalog, then move on to using a metastore. Next, we'll check out how YAML templates and Git can be useful in this process. We'll also touch on some other approaches you might want to consider.

Contracts Within a Catalog

Organizations often implement data contracts or data sharing agreements using data catalogs and governance tools like Microsoft Purview and Unity Catalog. These tools serve as centralized repositories to store and manage data contracts. Figure 12-2 shows an example of requesting a data product in Microsoft Purview. Once you have requested access to a data product, a workflow is triggered, and the owner of the data resource or a manager can grant you access to the data product. You could argue that this is a form of a data contract.

The agreements captured in Microsoft Purview are currently only loosely connected to other data services. Microsoft Purview tracks data requests and facilitates contract creation through a self-service workflow. However, it does not yet enforce or share the data itself. For that, you need to integrate with HTTP connector (*https://oreil.ly/FN5dA*) or other tools, such as ServiceNow (*https://oreil.ly/P2c73*).

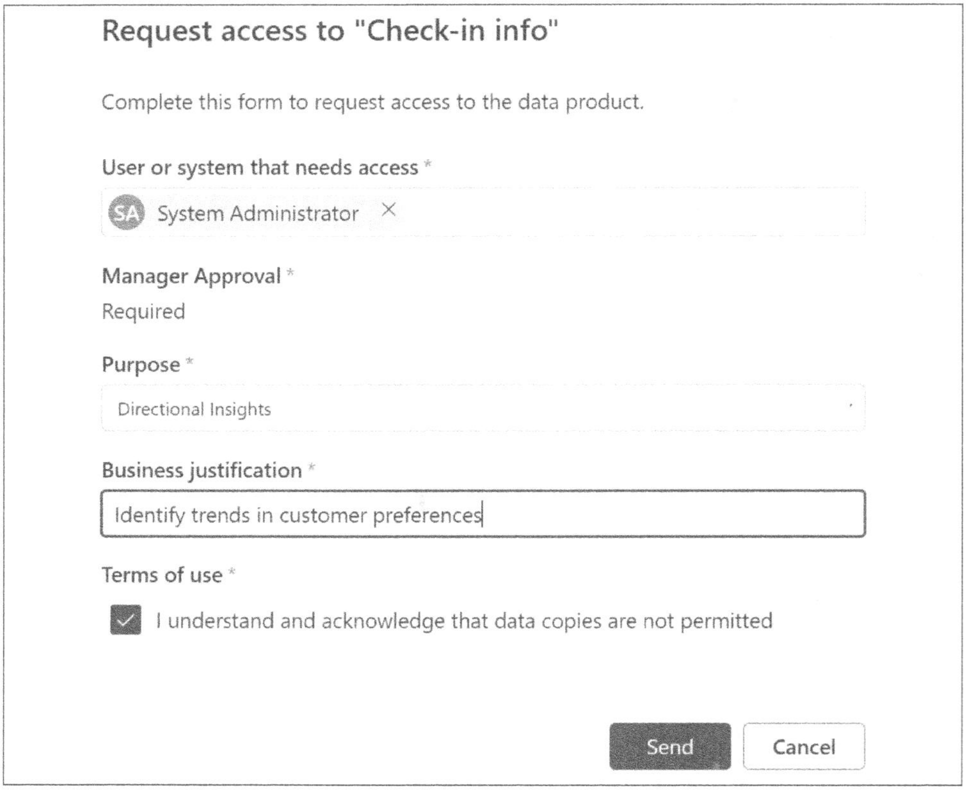

Figure 12-2. A data product being requested in Microsoft Purview

Using services like Microsoft Purview to quickly build and manage data contracts certainly has its perks. However, there is a downside: it could make you too dependent on a specific platform. This dependency might cause difficulties if you need to extend usage or integrate with technologies that aren't fully compatible. Moreover, such services might restrict your ability to customize or adapt the data contracts for particular needs that fall outside the predefined scope of the service.

So, let's shift to more generic approaches. We'll begin by exploring the use of a custom metastore to streamline and enhance data contract management. This method provides more flexibility and expands the capabilities of your data management processes. Afterwards, we'll delve into managing data contracts using YAML files and GitOps.

Contracts Within a Metastore

Using a metastore can significantly support the building and managing of data contracts in several ways. First, it provides a clear and consistent view of all data assets, a subject you learned more about in "Implementation of the Metadata Store" on page 152. Additionally, a metastore can automate some aspects of data governance, such as access controls and auditing, ensuring that data contracts are adhered to consistently across the organization. For instance, you can enhance your metastore by adding extra tables. Say you already have a metastore for describing schemas; you could extend this approach by adding more information about what is sensitive information, information about where and how data is stored, access rules, audit logs, and so on. This setup helps store crucial information about data contracts.

A practical solution design for a metastore could involve several key components to handle different aspects of data contract management efficiently. As we discussed in Chapter 6, you could opt for using Azure SQL as a metastore for managing the contracts. On top of that, you could integrate a web app to visualize these contracts, making it user-friendly and accessible for stakeholders to review and understand the agreements in place.

To streamline the approval process, you could employ a Logic App (*https://oreil.ly/ cRcjW*), which allows for automated workflows that manage the approval sequences, ensuring that contracts are reviewed and authorized according to predefined rules and criteria.

Finally, incorporating Azure Functions (*https://oreil.ly/YSihc*) could be a smart move to trigger the provisioning process. For example, after the contract is approved, the Microsoft Fabric OneLake Shortcuts REST APIs (*https://oreil.ly/AVb1N*) can be invoked for setting up the data access.

This customized approach not only ensures the secure management of data contracts but also offers the flexibility to tailor the process to specific needs. A widespread practice in many organizations is that the user permissions are controlled based on their group memberships. By tailoring your own solution and integrating it with Microsoft Entra ID, you can effectively manage scenarios where, for example, individual user permissions hinge on group membership, and application permissions depend on service principals. This adaptability is crucial for maintaining both security and functionality in dynamic environments.

Remember, the solutions described here are just one way to go about it. There are other methods available that might shift the balance between governance and self-service to better suit your needs. Let's look another approach that combines YAML files with GitOps to manage data contracts.

Data Contracts Using YAML Files and GitOps

Managing data contracts using YAML files combined with a GitOps process can be effective too. With this approach, you would start by defining your data contracts in YAML files, which are both human-readable and easy to track. These files can then be checked into a version-controlled system like Git using pull request workflows. This approach is more aligned with the discussion we had earlier about "YAML or JSON Configurations" on page 139.

For example, when you need to consume and verify a dataset's data, you start by preparing a data contract YAML file. This file serves as a formal description of the data. In the data contract, you specify details like the dataset, the filter SQL statements, and the dataset owner. Here's a simplified example of what a data contract YAML file might look like:

```
owner: piethein@oceanicairlines.internal
purpose: To analyze customer behavior and sales trends.
use_case:
  description: Tailored for targeted campaigns in New York.
workspace_id: 92187CE0-B7EB-4FDF-80CE-EFF76639EED8
dataset_location: https://onelake.dfs.fabric.microsoft.com/<workspace>/<item>
dataset: dim_customer
filter_sql: customer_state = 'New York'
columns:
  - name: first_name
  - name: last_name
  - name: birthdate
```

Note that in a real-world scenario, you would include additional details in the YAML file, such as data retention policies and the method of distribution.

Once you've created the data contract, there are several ways to validate and approve it. One effective method is to use the metastore. You can validate, approve, and then load the contract directly into the metastore.

You could also incorporate verification into a CI/CD workflow to ensure the YAML template adheres to the specified data standards of the platform. Once integrated, the data contract within the pull request can be reviewed and approved by the data governance team. Following approval, you can trigger a release pipeline that utilizes the data contract to assign the appropriate rights within the platform through the provided REST APIs. This approach helps preserve data integrity and ensures compliance with organizational standards.

Other Data Contract Specifications

Some data practitioners choose to use a data contract specification. This formal document details the terms and conditions for sharing and using data.

The Open Data Contract Standard (*https://oreil.ly/aIQtR*) and Data Contract Specification repos (*https://oreil.ly/sHcPp*) offer examples of open source data contract specifications. These specifications are technology-neutral, making them compatible with any data platform. Specifications are typically written in languages like YAML or JSON. For a practical example of implementing data contracts, consider reading "How To Build a Data Product with Databricks" (*https://oreil.ly/uxnu_*). This article dives into using CI/CD with Databricks and Azure DevOps to craft a data product based on data contracts. Another resource worth exploring is the Data Contract CLI (*https://oreil.ly/QSIEu*), which is an open source implementation of issuing data contracts with a command-line interface and support for Unity Catalog.

Another way that data contracts are approached is by focusing on a dataset (data product) always having a predefined and guaranteed structure. For example, dbt refers to these guarantees as a "contract." This contract outlines expectations for the data produced by a model, including the schema, column types, and data constraints. It's a strategy to maintain consistency and reliability in the data. Unlike data quality tests, if the model's logic or input data doesn't match the contract, the model won't build. To dive deeper into dbt's approach to data contracts, check out their guide on model contracts (*https://oreil.ly/c5GPi*).

Lastly, data contracts sometimes come into play during data ingestion. When data is ingested, it must adhere to a predefined contract outlining the data format, schema, and quality requirements. If the data doesn't meet these standards, it's rejected. This approach is similar to a service-level agreement in software development, where the data provider agrees to specific terms and conditions for sharing data with the platform.

These contracts must be fit to the specific needs of the organization for all of the custom implementations. Data contracts aren't universally applicable. Typically, data contracts manage the flow of data and are implemented as metadata records within a data platform. They might oversee data integrity and quality. Additionally, contracts often link back to data products owned by domains. In this context, there must be a close relationship between data contracts and their protection and enforcement. This leads us into the critical area of data security and access management on data platforms. Here, the rules set forth in data contracts come to life, ensuring data is used properly and shielded from unauthorized access.

Data Security and Access Management

Managing data access—who can see what data, when, and under which specific conditions—can be quite intricate, particularly in large organizations with detailed divisions of roles and responsibilities. Additionally, various platforms each have their unique security features and requirements. Therefore, it's crucial to implement security correctly across multiple layers within a data platform. To enforce what has been stated in a data contract, you likely need to combine security measures and access management strategies.

This section delves into data security and access management, focusing on platforms like Microsoft Fabric and Azure Databricks. Keep in mind that security is critical, yet also quite complex. For Microsoft Fabric, see this security whitepaper (*https://oreil.ly/X-mBQ*). For Azure Databricks, I recommend the "Security and Compliance" guide (*https://oreil.ly/nJvbw*).

You can provision data access in various ways, controlling who can view or use certain data. These approaches vary in complexity and precision, from broad to very granular levels of access control. Let's a have a look at some common options. After that, we draw conclusions using a reference diagram:

Network security basics
Isolating your network is key for network security. Start by blocking public access, using VNET injection (*https://oreil.ly/tyx5E*), and deploying Spark workloads within isolated virtual networks. Use private endpoints (*https://oreil.ly/UrNYd*) to limit access exclusively to trusted services. Implement firewall-enabled storage accounts (*https://oreil.ly/rLo-u*) to further secure your data. Establish workspace identities to verify trusted access consistently, and use key vaults to manage your security keys safely and efficiently. By taking these steps, you fortify your network against potential threats and ensure that your data remains protected.

Furthermore, consider using safe landing zones. Instead of letting your data platform (insecurely) communicate to public endpoints, you can use isolated Azure Data Factory self-hosted integration runtime (*https://oreil.ly/FQxLT*) instances to transfer data from (external) sources to an intermediate storage location. This way, you can ensure your data platform only interfaces with trusted sources.

Single sign-on (SSO) and multi-factor authentication (MFA)
SSO and MFA are fundamental security measures that help protect your data platform. SSO allows users to access multiple applications with a single set of credentials, simplifying the login process. MFA adds an extra layer of security by requiring users to provide two or more verification factors before gaining access. This could be a one-time code sent to their phone or authentication app. Together, SSO and MFA help prevent unauthorized access to your platform services.

Audit everything
Auditing is a critical aspect of data security. By auditing all activities with services like diagnostic logs (*https://oreil.ly/bJ4wx*), Storage Analytics logs (*https://oreil.ly/hiBc4*), network security group (NSG) flow logs (*https://oreil.ly/qLh07*) and track user activities (*https://oreil.ly/H1zM1*), you know who is taking what action on

which item. This helps in making your architecture secure and fulfilling requirements such as meeting regulatory compliance and records management regulations.

Implement point-in-time recovery

Point-in-time recovery is a crucial security measure that allows you to restore your data to a specific point in time. This feature is particularly useful in case of accidental deletions, data corruption, or security breaches, such as ransomware attacks. René Bremer has published a great article about securing your Azure Data Lake with Azure Databricks or Synapse Analytics (*https://oreil.ly/7EByo*). For securing Microsoft Fabric, see Nicholas Hurt's best practices and considerations for planning your business continuity and disaster recovery strategy (*https://oreil.ly/heWxx*).

Workspace roles and permissions

Microsoft Fabric and other platforms, such as Azure Databricks and Synapse Analytics, come with a set of built-in roles that you can assign to users or groups to specific workspaces. These roles determine what actions users can perform and what objects they can access. You can also create custom roles tailored to your organization's specific needs. For example, you might have a role for viewing all content in a workspace and another for administration. Once you've defined the roles, you can assign them to the relevant users or groups.

These workspace roles and permissions apply solely to workspace objects. For data access, it is recommended to use fine-grained data permissions through tools like Unity Catalog. This approach ensures that data management is both effective and secure.

Item-level permissions

Item-level permissions function similarly to workspace roles and permissions but offer a more precise, coarse-grained access control mechanism for individual items. Platforms like Microsoft Fabric and Azure Databricks provide the ability to set permissions on specific items, such as a pipeline or data science project. This feature allows for more precise control over access to individual data assets within workspaces. In Azure Databricks, you can use access control lists (ACLs) (*https://oreil.ly/ZvXqs*) to set permissions for workspace-level objects. Meanwhile, in Microsoft Fabric, item permissions (*https://oreil.ly/dT0zW*) let you determine who can view, modify, and manage individual items within a Workspace.

To assign these permissions, you typically follow a workflow that involves "create" and "wait for completion" tasks to manually set roles and permissions for users or groups. Alternatively, tools like ServiceNow can manage access requests and permissions. Once approved, you can apply built-in roles to grant specific permissions for Workspaces or items. Assign these roles to the appropriate users or groups to ensure that only authorized individuals can access data and artifacts.

Sharing items with Microsoft Fabric

Still at the levels of workspaces and item-level security, there is also a way to collaborate with team members who don't have a role in the Workspace. For this, you can share items directly with other users. See "Share Items in Microsoft Fabric" (*https://oreil.ly/D8Zvm*) and "Collaborate Using Databricks Notebooks" (*https://oreil.ly/2Ra16*) for more information.

Using sensitivity labels

Another great way to boost security is by using sensitivity labels on all your data and artifacts. Let's say you're using Microsoft Fabric and Microsoft Purview together. You can set up a policy within the information protection manager that automatically tags data with sensitivity labels based on its content. For instance, if any document contains customer personal information like credit card numbers, social security numbers, or passport numbers, it can be marked as Highly Confidential automatically. Once labeled, you can enforce strict access policies. Only users with the right permissions can view this highly confidential information. This approach ensures sensitive data stays protected and only reaches those who truly need to see it. For more information about setting up sensitivity labels, see Microsoft Purview's protection policies (*https://oreil.ly/3N666*), "Protected Sensitivity Labels in Fabric and Power BI" (*https://oreil.ly/8IyY-*), and the YouTube video, "Microsoft 365 Information Protection and How it Really Works!" (*https://oreil.ly/-UVmG*).

Using Unity Catalog in Databricks

For a more detailed level of data access management across various schemas and their associated data structures, using Unity Catalog in Databricks is a good strategy. With Privileges in Unity Catalog, you can control who accesses what catalogs, tables, views, and other objects. You can assign privileges to users or groups, allowing them to perform specific actions on these objects. Databricks has more information about Privileges in Unity Catalog (*https://oreil.ly/pr2od*).

Additionally, you can set up an attribute-based security model using tags and rules to classify data and enforce policies. For instance, you can tag data with a pii:ccn tag and create a rule that users will see this data masked with a regular expression rule replacing all numbers with X values. This way, you can ensure that sensitive data is not exposed to users who have over-privileged access. You can find more information about setting up tags and rules in this video demonstration (*https://oreil.ly/OxaPa*).

Setting up access control lists (ACLs) in Azure Data Lake Storage (ADLS)

This approach is not recommended as a best practice but is sometimes seen among enterprises: implementing ACLs in ADLS for security management. Typically, this results in coarse-grained permissions that can be difficult to manage precisely. It can pose significant risks by providing extensive access to all underlying data.

Granting access via shortcuts in Fabric

In Microsoft Fabric, you can share data directly by using shortcuts. With shortcuts, you can grant access to data without sharing the item itself and without moving the data. When using shortcuts, the combination of permissions from both the shortcut path and the target path determines access levels. The most restrictive permission between the two paths is applied when a user accesses a shortcut. More information can be found in the Microsoft documentation (*https://oreil.ly/C868Z*).

Implementing fine-grained data access controls

You can enhance security by limiting access to data using row-level security (RLS), column-level security (CLS), and object-level security (OLS). Let's say you have a table with sensitive data, and you want to restrict access to certain rows or columns. You can use RLS and CLS to control who can view or modify specific rows or columns. OLS, on the other hand, allows you to restrict access to specific objects, such as tables or views. This approach is especially useful when you need to manage access to sensitive data at a granular level. For Microsoft Fabric, see "Security for Data Warehousing in Microsoft Fabric" (*https://oreil.ly/_3aSR*) and "OneLake Role-Based Access Control (RBAC)" (*https://oreil.ly/9yTZC*). For Azure Databricks, see "Filter Sensitive Table Data Using Row Filters and Column Masks" (*https://oreil.ly/QbCf5*).

Identifying sensitive data

To manage sensitive data effectively, you need to identify it first. You can use tools that automatically detect and classify sensitive data based on predefined patterns or rules. A couple of the most popular tools today are Presidio (*https://github.com/microsoft/presidio*) and Data Profiler (*https://github.com/capitalone/DataProfiler*).

Securing data with masking or encryption

In some cases, you might want to secure data right from the point of ingestion by either masking or encrypting any sensitive information. This process essentially requires metadata accompanying the data, which helps in identifying sensitive data elements. Masking or encrypting data ensures that confidentiality is maintained while processing or storing data. This method is particularly effective in preventing unauthorized access and ensuring that sensitive information remains protected across all stages of data handling.

Power BI security

In Power BI, users can either import data into the platform or connect directly to a data source. When importing data, the user's credentials are used for the initial connection and then consistently by Power BI to refresh the data. The imported data can be viewed in reports and dashboards without further accessing the original source. Power BI supports single sign-on (SSO) for certain data sources, which allows the semantic model owner's credentials to be used during the data connection.

For direct connections, preconfigured credentials or SSO can be used. With preconfigured credentials, all users access the data source using the same set credentials. With SSO, the individual user's credentials are used, enhancing security by potentially allowing the implementation of RLS and OLS on the data source.

When integrating Power BI with Azure Databricks, you have a couple of methods to choose from. One option is to import data directly from Databricks using a service account. Alternatively, you can opt for direct querying through Databricks SQL, which is best done using Microsoft Entra pass-through authentication. This approach leverages the end user's identity within Unity Catalog. When you send an authentication request to the Databricks SQL warehouse, it verifies data access privileges via Unity Catalog before returning the query results. For both methods, it's essential to establish fine-grained access control policies in Unity Catalog (for users directly consuming through Databricks SQL) and in Power BI. To dive deeper into this integration and understand the nuances of setting it up, check out the technical articles "Publish to Power BI Online from Azure Databricks" (*https://oreil.ly/gg1Li*) and "Access Control and Networking Security with Power BI and Databricks" (*https://oreil.ly/N7zp9*).

Integrating across platforms like Azure Databricks and Microsoft Fabric, which includes Power BI, requires maintaining consistent security policies across both platforms. Given that each platform has its unique security model and access control mechanisms, aligning them can be challenging. This alignment involves configuring roles, permissions, and data access controls across the two systems. Additionally, effective data governance relies on consistent and well-managed metadata. When operating across platforms, ensuring synchronized and accurate metadata that reflects data structures, usage, and provenance is crucial, potentially necessitating extra tools or manual processes to align metadata between the two platforms. The same applies to data contracts, which must be consistent and up-to-date across all platforms to ensure that data is shared securely and accurately.

Moreover, a comprehensive architecture protects data by combining various security mechanisms at every level. Let's take a closer look in Figure 12-3, which shows an example security architecture of Azure Databricks.

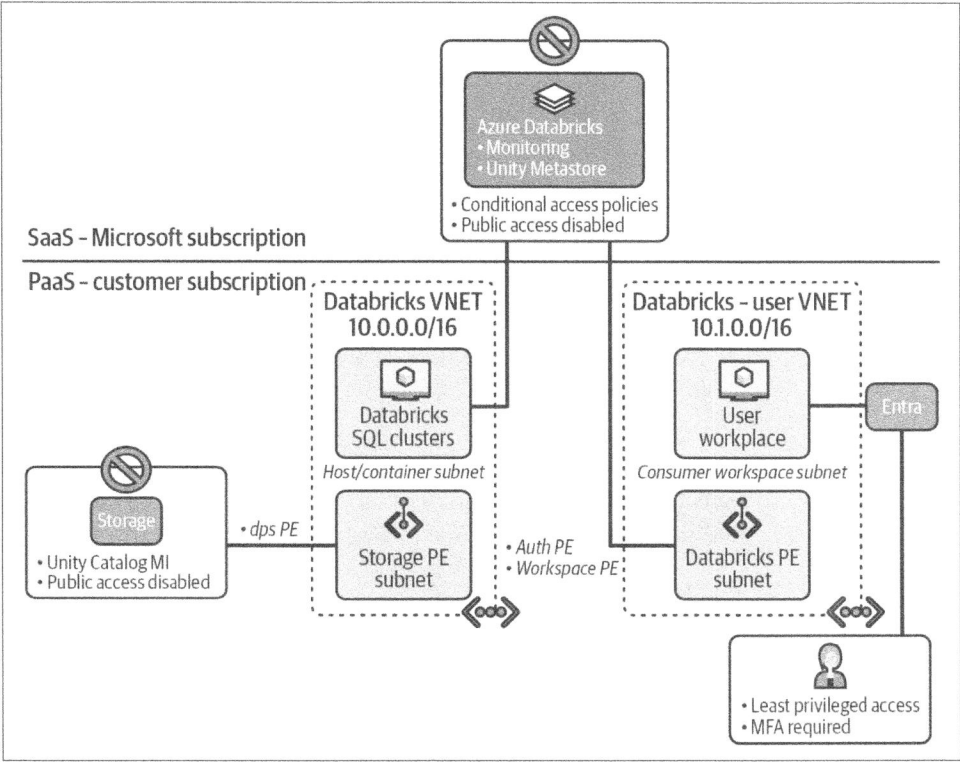

Figure 12-3. An Azure Databricks network architecture that follows the recommended security best practices

Starting at the foundational level, network security is essential. You can significantly enhance security by segregating compute clusters from user workplaces and controlling both inbound and outbound network access between these virtual networks. Implementing measures such as disabling public internet access, using private endpoints, granting access only to trusted workspaces, enforcing conditional access, and maintaining IP access lists ensures that only authorized traffic accesses the network. This not only protects data from unauthorized access from the outset but also acts as your primary line of defense.

> René Bremer has written an extensive blog post (*https://oreil.ly/0MMRg*) about securely connecting Microsoft Fabric to Databricks SQL. It contains several architecture diagrams using secure VNETs and gateways.

Next comes authentication and access control. By working with enterprise identity providers, such as Entra ID, and implementing SSO, MFA, and requiring VPN-only access, the system blocks unauthorized access right from the start. Once access is granted, the focus shifts to authorization. This stage is all about defining roles and permissions. Administrators set specific rules determining which data users can access and the actions they can perform. These could involve access to workspaces and items, or the ability to perform actions such as viewing notebooks and executing specific jobs.

Next up is data security, a critical layer of the architecture. The data access control model uses detailed rules to specify which applications, users, and groups can access data. To enhance this model, consider using user-defined functions, tags, or sensitivity labels to classify data and enforce policies. These controls set the boundaries on who can view data and how they interact with it.

The final piece of the puzzle is monitoring and compliance. This involves tracking usage patterns and ensuring that all operations comply with regulatory standards. This continuous monitoring helps maintain the integrity and security of the entire system.

Over the top of all this is a governance framework that ensures all these measures are implemented and processes are followed. This framework includes policies, procedures, and guidelines that govern how data is accessed, used, and protected. It also includes regular audits to ensure the system is secure and compliant. This framework is supported with a catalog for overseeing tags, classifications, lineage, and other metadata, such as information about data ownership and data quality.

Is this all? No, there is even more. In a federated model, security metadata and reference data play a vital role in data access management within the Medallion architecture. This metadata includes details about data access, classification, and protection, ensuring that data usage aligns with organizational policies and regulations. It's especially crucial when dealing with data contracts that touch upon sensitive information, such as personal or financial data.

In the Medallion architecture, you can manage security metadata using various tools and techniques. One effective method is embedding security metadata directly into data products. This approach ensures that access controls and classification information travel with the data wherever it goes.

Remember the AdventureWorks database you worked with in Part II? In the customer table, you have a column called SalesPerson. Let's say you want to restrict access to this table based on the SalesPerson column. You can create a security policy using a user-defined function (*https://oreil.ly/RM8JS*) to enforce this restriction. In the following example (*https://oreil.ly/Eh3kh*), you see a code snippet for restricting access to the SalesLT.Customer table based on the SalesPerson column:

```
CREATE SCHEMA Security;
GO

-- Creating a function for the SalesPerson
-- We presume no names in the system exceed 50 characters but this could vary
CREATE FUNCTION Security.udf_securitypredicate(@SalesPerson AS varchar(50))
    RETURNS TABLE
WITH SCHEMABINDING
AS
    RETURN SELECT 1 AS udf_securitypredicate_result
    WHERE @SalesPerson = USER_NAME() OR IS_ROLEMEMBER('manager') = 1;
GO

-- Using the function to create a Security Policy
CREATE SECURITY POLICY SalesFilter
ADD FILTER PREDICATE Security.udf_securitypredicate(SalesPerson)
ON SalesLT.Customer
WITH (STATE = ON);
GO
```

This policy ensures that only users who match the `SalesPerson` column value or belong to the `manager` role can access the data. For this policy, it's essential to embed this metadata within the data itself. Thus, if stored in the Bronze layer, this metadata must also be present in the Silver and Gold layers to remain effective.

Note that data security and access management go hand in hand with data governance because they both aim to protect and manage data effectively. Think of data governance as the rulebook that outlines the processes of how data should be stored, handled with metadata and classifications, approved, and accessed.

Conclusion

As we wrap up our discussion on scaling with data governance, data contracts, and data security, I've emphasized the importance of catalogs and metadata in managing and controlling data distribution. However, there's more to the story. Effective data security involves more than just setting up catalogs or data contracts. It's about automation and building a solid data governance framework. This means defining roles, setting up clear processes, creating efficient workflows, writing policy documents, and training users comprehensively. It's a holistic approach that requires more than just the deployment of a tool.

To scale efficiently and maintain a robust, compliant data architecture, prioritizing data governance, strategic planning, and organizational alignment is crucial. These elements are the foundation of any data architecture. It's critical that these different focus areas develop together. For example, even if you have a perfectly designed data platform, it's useless without governed data because you can't trust the data. On the other hand, a high mature data governance organization is ineffective if it lacks a stable data platform, as you can't trust the data processing. So, to successfully scale the Medallion architecture, make sure all areas equally grow and mature in parallel.

In Chapter 13, we will delve into the integration of emerging technologies such as AI into Medallion architectures. The potential of AI to automate complex data tasks, enhance analytical capabilities, and foster smarter decision making holds thrilling possibilities for the evolution of these architectures.

Future Medallion Architectures with Generative AI

To conclude this book, we explore how the evolving Medallion architecture is increasingly intertwined with generative artificial intelligence (GenAI).[1] Traditionally focused on structured data within its Bronze, Silver, and Gold layers, this architecture must now accommodate unstructured data to enhance AI application readiness. This chapter addresses two pivotal questions: 1) is it practical to have a unified Medallion architecture for managing structured, semi-structured, and unstructured data? 2) Additionally, how can large language models (LLMs) be integrated into the existing processes associated with the Medallion architecture?

Let me lay my cards on the table: I firmly believe that managing structured and unstructured data holistically holds immense value, paving the way for more comprehensive and effective data- and AI-driven insights. Furthermore, LLMs are transforming data management tasks such as cleansing and integration, prompting a reimagining of traditional paradigms. They are expected to impact how engineers and data scientists interact with data, making it more accessible and actionable.

To delve deeper into this transformation, we will begin with an overview of the challenges and opportunities presented by unstructured data in modern AI contexts, highlighting the role of the retrieval-augmented generation (RAG) pattern in using such data effectively. Following this, we will outline the specifics of each layer in the Medallion architecture as it relates to AI, detailing processes from data collection and cleaning to advanced refinement and indexing for AI-driven searches and applications.

---

1 GenAI is a subset of artificial intelligence focused on creating new content, such as text, images, or video, by learning patterns from existing data.

Furthermore, the chapter will discuss the synergistic potential of integrating LLMs within the Medallion architecture, illustrating through practical scenarios how these models enhance data transformation, cleaning, and enrichment processes. We will also consider the future trajectory of data management technologies, anticipating the integration of GenAI and other advanced tools, which promise to revolutionize the way we handle, process, and leverage data in business and technology landscapes.

By the end of this final chapter, you will not only have gained a deep understanding of the Medallion architecture but also be equipped with actionable knowledge to implement or enhance this framework within your own AI and data management strategies. This conclusion serves as a capstone, synthesizing the insights and strategies discussed previously, and puts everything into perspective for a final reflection.

Unstructured Data Processing

In today's landscape, the Medallion architecture has been predominantly focused on structured data, which is well-organized and easily searchable by using open table formats, such as Delta Lake or Iceberg. This structured approach facilitates straightforward processing and analysis but fails to address the complexities of managing the unstructured data that modern systems frequently require.

LLMs primarily engage with content that is stored in semi-structured and unstructured data formats, encompassing diverse forms like JSON and XML files as well as PDF documents, emails, social media content, or speech and images. These data types, characterized by their richness and complexity, requires robust and flexible architectures to be managed effectively. To address this need, let's start by examining the RAG pattern, a key framework for LLMs to work with unstructured data. After that, we'll delve into managing unstructured data and its alignment with the RAG pattern. Then, finally, we draw conclusions.

Retrieval-Augmented Generation

RAG is a crucial framework in the realm of generating more precise and relevant responses with modern AI and LLMs. The RAG pattern, which is visualized in Figure 13-1, is a method that enhances language model outputs by incorporating external knowledge. Thus, instead of relying solely on the foundational model's source knowledge, RAG allows you to provide additional context to the model, enabling it to generate more precise and relevant responses.

To implement RAG, the process begins by gathering data relevant to a particular use case and dividing it into smaller, manageable pieces, or chunks. These chunks are then transformed into vector embeddings, which are numerical representations designed to capture semantic meanings. In this setup, shorter distances between vectors signify a higher degree of similarity. The numerical formats and content are subsequently stored in a vector database.

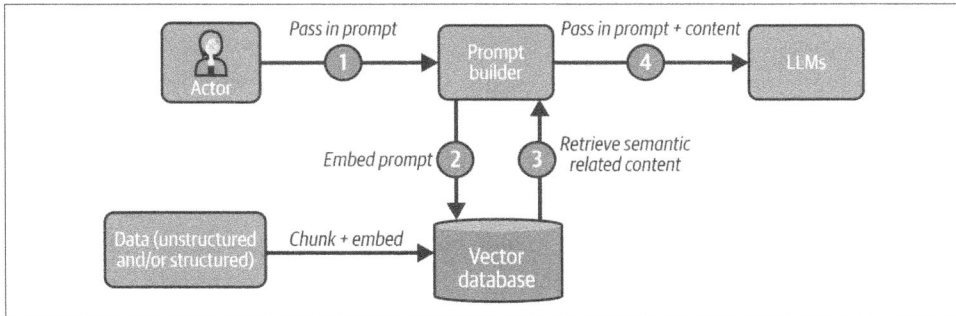

Figure 13-1. The RAG pattern

RAG is also capable of processing data tables, not just unstructured data. It can handle inputs from various enterprise data sources, such as enterprise resource planning (ERP) and CRM systems, whether they are structured or unstructured.

Once the vector database is populated, the RAG system enhances its effectiveness by augmenting the initial prompt with supplementary content. Here's how it works: when a user or an application inputs a prompt (step 1 in Figure 13-1), this prompt is transformed (step 2) into a vector using the same embedding model previously employed to populate the database. Using this embedded prompt, the system retrieves (step 3) the vectors closest to it from the database, which represent the most pertinent information. This content is then integrated (step 4) with the original prompt and processed by an LLM to generate a response that is both contextually richer and more precise.

To maximize the effectiveness of the RAG pattern, it's essential to ensure the data is well-structured and organized. Here are some typical steps involved:

1. *Capture the raw documents*
   Extract data from both structured and unstructured sources, categorizing them by source, date, or business process.

2. *Generate document metadata*
   Generate and extract metadata such as creation date, document titles, page numbers, URLs, or other relevant information.

3. *Organize and standardize documents*
   Rearrange the documents in a structured manner using a standard format. Standardizing documents during this process ensures high reusability.

4. Chunk documents
   Break down the documents into smaller, more manageable parts for efficient processing by the LLM.

5. Embed chunks
   An embedding model transforms each chunk into numeric vectors.

6. Index chunks in a vector database
   Load the vector representations of the chunks, along with the chunk's text, into a vector database.

To effectively manage and leverage the potential of unstructured data within AI systems, it is pivotal to align architectural layers. Here, we've already outlined the Medallion architecture, consisting of three critical layers: Bronze, Silver, and Gold, each tailored to refine the data progressively. Let's explore how the layers align with the RAG pattern to optimize data handling and LLM integration. After that, we'll look at more complex scenarios.

Bronze Layer

The Bronze layer marks the initial stage in the unstructured data stack, with a stark focus on data extraction and ingestion. In this setup, the Bronze layer serves the same purpose as it does for capturing and organizing structured data. In the context of unstructured data, the focus is on capturing, extracting, and optimizing raw data for storage and processing. This foundational layer is essential for collecting unstructured data from various sources, such as log files, social media platforms, customer feedback forms, emails, and scientific research documents.

To extract unstructured data, organizations typically use techniques such as upload forms, web scrapers, API integration, and file parsers. Depending on the types of data and the accuracy needed, they may either develop custom extractors or utilize prebuilt ones, such as LlamaParse (*https://github.com/run-llama/llama_parse*) and Tensorlake (*https://github.com/tensorlakeai*) to ensure high accuracy rates in data extraction. These extractors are also useful in the Silver and Gold layers, where they allow customization with parsing rules and patterns to better suit specific data extraction needs. We'll come back to this point in the next section.

After extracting the data, organizations transfer data in its original file format, such as PDF, DOCX, or TIFF, to a raw data storage system, often a data lake service like Azure Data Lake Storage. During this transfer, additional metadata is often generated to provide more context about the data, such as its source, its format, the person who uploaded the document, the creation date, and so on. This metadata is usually stored in a data catalog or alongside the unstructured data, ensuring a clear record of the data's origin and history.

To generate metadata, organizations can use small language models (SLMs). These models are more efficient and optimized for specific tasks compared to their larger counterparts. SLMs excel in classifying, labeling, identifying sensitive and PII, performing entity extraction, and summarizing, making them ideal for handling metadata generation efficiently. The metadata generated by SLMs is crucial for the subsequent layers of the Medallion architecture, as it provides context and additional information about the unstructured data. It's also expected that this metadata is passed forward to the subsequent layers. For example, sensitive data or PII labels generated by SLMs in the Bronze layer can be used to enforce data access policies in the Silver and Gold layers.

> SLMs are also highly effective for generating metadata for structured data. Aligning the management of both unstructured and structured data is considered a best practice, enhancing consistency and coherence across data systems. To effectively scale and manage this metadata, invest in a robust metastore or data fabric solution is essential.

Another objective for the Bronze stage is the initial sorting of data, setting the groundwork for later processing. This objective parallels the organization of structured data in the Bronze layer, where the primary goal is to preserve its raw form while maintaining accessibility. To organize the data, organizations often set up folders or containers that mirror business processes or data origins, such as Teams channels or SharePoint folders. This approach helps maintain order, making it easier to access and process data later. Furthermore, organizations frequently use a partitioning strategy, such as organizing by date, to implement time-based versioning for different documents. This method transforms unstructured data into an archive, much like the Bronze layer when it is used with structured data, preserving its raw form.

In this data lake structure, it's essential to maintain strong links to the schema definitions, parsers, and extraction scripts. Concretely, in the Bronze layer, you organize by data source, project, or business process. Within each folder or container, there are subfolders for raw data, intermediate data, and metadata. Within this metadata, you maintain references to schema definitions (for semi-structured documents), parsers, and scripts, typically housed in a code repository. This arrangement allows you to trace every data piece back to its origin, ensuring you have all the necessary information for processing and analysis in later stages.

To conclude: the Bronze layer, in the context of unstructured data, is essential for capturing data in its most authentic and raw form, providing a detailed snapshot for further refinement. It is crucial to maintain clarity about the data's origin throughout this process. For the effective identification and sorting of unstructured data, LLMs and SLMs can be used to generate metadata, adding a structured layer of information to the otherwise unstructured data. This metadata plays a critical role in the subsequent layers of processing.

Silver Layer

Ascending to the Silver layer, the emphasis shifts towards refining and stabilizing the data to make it functional for AI-driven use cases. An important aspect at this stage is ensuring the data's reusability. This not only benefits RAG applications but also serves future fine-tuning models, a topic that will be discussed later in "Training and Fine-Tuning LLMs" on page 357.

At this stage, it becomes essential to partition the previously raw data into logically organized units based on semantically meaningful contexts. This involves a detailed process of restructuring, labeling, and cleaning the data to ensure its consistency and usability. This involves techniques such as noise detection and duplicate identification, which help filter out irrelevant or erroneous information that could compromise the accuracy of AI outputs. Note that LLMs are also instrumental in this phase, as they can help identify and correct errors in the data, ensuring that the information is accurate and reliable.

Regarding the quality of unstructured data, it is highly subjective and can even be biased due to the collection process. Therefore, it is imperative for organizations to establish their own quality assessment frameworks. Consider utilizing an LLM as a judge to oversee this framework.

After the unstructured data has been checked for quality, cleaned, and partitioned, it is then often formatted into a structured, machine-readable format. Employing markup languages, particularly Markdown, is recognized as a best practice due to its lightweight and readable syntax. Using Markdown simplifies the documents, making them more programmatically accessible and easier to handle for AI systems, thereby enhancing their compatibility with various analytical tools and platforms. The simplicity of Markdown helps AI models to more effectively parse and comprehend the content, which is crucial for tasks such as information retrieval, classification, and summarization.

Frameworks like MarkItDown (*https://oreil.ly/pLnsJ*) and PyMuPDF (*https://oreil.ly/OzrQ0*) are instrumental at this stage because they standardize the output and prepare the data for more sophisticated analytical tools. The clean and clearly formatted data is then ready for deeper analysis and insights extraction. The straightforward nature of Markdown minimizes potential errors associated with complex formatting, ensuring the data remains pristine and consistent.

Francesco Fava has published an end-to-end showcase on how to use Markdown for data processing and LLM consumption (*https://oreil.ly/uYxzE*).

During this data transformation phase, extra metadata is often generated to help AI systems better understand the context of the data. Key activities for the Silver layer include the following:

- Summarizing extensive documents concisely.
- Breaking down complex documents into smaller, more manageable parts. This may also involve extracting images and tables within the documents and storing them separately with references. Note that this process isn't part of the chunking strategy, which is typically deferred to later stages when the unstructured documents are refined for specific AI applications.
- Translating different languages to the same organizational language for consistency (with the help of LLMs).
- Creating classifiers and labels for the sensitivity of the data. For example, you could apply a classification of "Confidential" based purely on content type, and assign a sensitivity label indicating "Low Risk" based on access controls or the potential impact of data exposure.
- Classifying and categorizing text.
- Recognizing and extracting entities, such as using an LLM to identify and organize critical information like party names, contract dates, and obligations into a structured database for quick reference.
- Modeling topics and analyzing trends.
- Handling sensitive data within documents by breaking up markup files into different parts, allowing for more fine-grained access and control.
- Storing the metadata in a structured format, such as a catalog or a metadata store, or alongside the unstructured data in the data lake.

To support these activities, selecting the appropriate data processing engines is crucial. These engines differ based on various factors, such as their design for structured or unstructured data and whether they operate on a single node or in a distributed environment. Additionally, the data stored in the Silver layer can be accessed by other upstream applications. For instance, a knowledge graph tool could tap into the entities and other metadata present in the Silver layer.

After reading this section, you might question why there is so much emphasis on standardizing and stabilizing unstructured data in the Silver layer. Operationalizing language models and training models depends on stable and predictable data to yield reliable outcomes, and the Silver layer serves a similar purpose. It prepares data for rapid deployment of new RAG applications and fine-tuning LLMs for specific tasks. Therefore, specific chunking strategies will need to be deferred. Once the data is appropriately processed, it becomes primed for further utilization in advanced AI applications in the Gold layer.

Gold Layer

Transitioning to the Gold layer, the data refinement reaches a stage where it is tailored to meet the specific demands of particular applications. This layer focuses on enhancing the precision and specificity of the data to ensure it aligns perfectly with the intended use.

For teams leveraging unstructured data for applications like RAG, the process begins with selecting the most relevant documents or objects for the specific use case, based on specific criteria, such as keywords, topics, or entities. Again, you could draw a parallel to the structured data process, where generalized data is selected and refined for specific analytical use cases.

After selecting data, typically another data preprocessing step is included to enhance the data for the specifics of the use case. Techniques like data augmentation could make the data more representative, accurate, and diverse. This step is crucial for ensuring the data is well-suited for the intended application, such as training an LLM for a specific task or the embedding process. Again, language models could play a role in this step, as they can generate additional data points and context, or refine existing ones to enhance the dataset.

The next critical step involves chunking data and generating embeddings—this is where embedding models come into play to represent text as vector strings, encapsulating the semantic meanings of the data. This takes us back to the earlier conversation about the RAG pattern, where the data is transformed into numerical representations and stored within a vector database. It's hard to generalize this process for all use cases because each application has its unique requirements, such as what data is required, the chunking strategy, and the choice of embedding model. While the tasks of chunking and embedding are distinct, they are interdependent:

Chunking strategy

This approach involves breaking down large documents into smaller, manageable pieces, or "chunks," before processing them with an embedding model. The strategy is crucial because embedding models often have a limit on the input size they can handle effectively. For example, in question-answering applications, documents are typically chunked into sizes like paragraphs, ensuring that each chunk contains enough context to answer potential questions. Furthermore, models have token limits, beyond which their performance may degrade, or they might not process the input at all. Therefore, chunking is essential to ensure that the data is processed effectively and accurately.

Embedding models

Embedding models play a crucial role in transforming text into numerical representations that capture the semantic meaning of the content. The choice of an embedding model can affect how well the semantic relationships in your text are captured and preserved. Different models have varying capabilities in terms of capturing context, handling different languages, and encoding domain-specific knowledge. For example, a low-dimensional embedding model is tailored for efficiency and minimal resource consumption, making it suitable for real-time environments such as chatbots. On the other hand, a high-dimensional embedding model offers intricate representations ideal for tasks that demand thorough analysis and precision, such as detailed academic research. Therefore, it is crucial to choose an embedding model that aligns with the specific needs of your application.

To facilitate efficient retrieval of semantically correlated data by LLMs, it is imperative that the data is vectorized, stored, and indexed in a manner that allows for rapid and effective search capabilities. Choosing the right storage solutions, such as vector databases or data lakes, is crucial at this stage to manage the volume and variety of unstructured data effectively. In the Gold layer, the aim is to refine unstructured data into a form that is not only structured but also meticulously curated for specific applications. Consequently, the data transcends its original unstructured state to become highly targeted and fit for purpose.

Database engines like Pinecone (*https://pinecone.io*) and Azure AI Search (*https://oreil.ly/SxKj8*) are often employed to ensure that the data is not only accessible but also organized in a way that supports decision-making processes and enhances AI applications. So, for the Medallion architecture, this effectively means the data is provided through a serving layer that is optimized for AI applications.

Looking ahead, future Medallion architectures with engines, such as Spark, are expected to better support operations on vector embedding columns, such as exact or approximate nearest neighbor searches and range searches. Currently, these engines struggle with handling lots of vector data, often forcing users to depend on open source databases like LanceDB (*https://lancedb.com*) or distributed vector query engines such as Quokka (*https://github.com/marsupialtail/quokka*) for big data vector search tasks. However, this situation is likely to improve. Future developments might enable you to perform complex operations on vector data directly within the Spark engine, eliminating the need to transfer data to specialized vector databases. This advancement will streamline processes and unify data handling capabilities within one single unified architecture.

Robust data governance practices are indispensable across all layers of the Medallion architecture. These practices help maintain compliance with regulations and ensure the security of data. Establishing stringent policies for data access, usage, and privacy is crucial to protect sensitive information while promoting a data-driven culture within organizations. Additionally, managing the relationship to the catalog and incorporating semantic contextual information about the data and documents is essential. This extra discipline ensures that data is well-organized, easily discoverable, and contextually understood, further supporting effective data management. This strategic approach not only safeguards data but also enhances confidence in deploying AI applications across various departments or organizational units.

LLMs and API Management

When developing LLM applications, it's crucial to recognize the significant overlap with API management. To effectively manage this, you must enhance the Medallion architecture by incorporating a connectivity layer. This integration harmonizes various data structures like APIs, data products, and events into a cohesive framework, which is pivotal for the versatile consumption of data by intelligent applications, including LLMs.

Designing a solid application integration solution is a complex task, given that there may be multiple possible "right" and complementary solutions. It's often a trade-off between different dimensions: performance, maintainability, flexibility, cost, resilience, and so on. These considerations may require you to have a deep understanding of the business problem you're trying to solve. Therefore, it's crucial to collaborate closely with your application integration engineers. This teamwork ensures the chosen solution and patterns are in perfect alignment with your organization's goals and objectives.

Having completed the unstructured data processing journey, we can confidently say that the prescriptive labels of the Medallion architecture can be effectively reused to manage the complexities of unstructured data. By leveraging its layering, you can separate concerns in managing unstructured data. Moreover, utilizing LLMs to generate metadata enhances the management of both structured and unstructured data. Therefore, adopting a unified Medallion architecture for handling both types of data is advantageous, as it aligns diverse disciplines for improved outcomes.

With these considerations for managing unstructured data in mind, let's delve into how AI, particularly LLMs, can be combined with Medallion architectures by discussing some practical examples.

Integration of LLMs and Medallion Architectures

In Chapter 6, we explored how AI, particularly through the use of LLMs, can enhance data integration by enriching data. These models excel in natural language processing, allowing machines to understand human language and generate new content. They efficiently handle both structured and semi-structured data, extracting insights, reorganizing data, and creating new content, which is crucial for data integration tasks.

It's important to consider how LLMs can be integrated into existing Medallion architecture processes, or conversely, how the Medallion architecture can enhance LLM workflows. Combining these two unlocks new possibilities for data processing, scalability, and application capabilities in AI-driven environments. Figure 13-2 shows three example scenarios where the Medallion architecture can be combined with LLMs to optimize data handling and application integration.

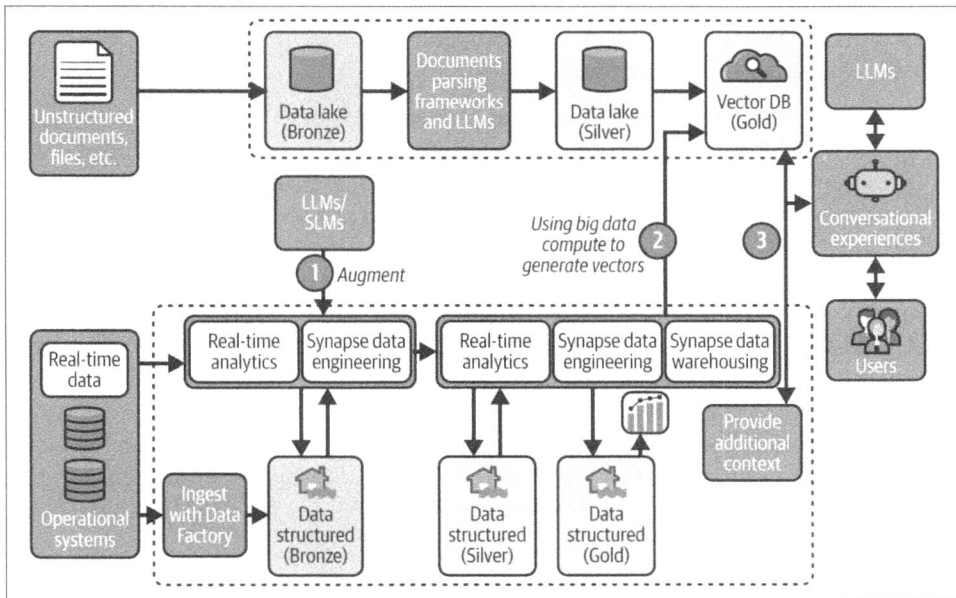

Figure 13-2. Three scenarios where the Medallion architecture integrates with LLMs to optimize data handling and enhance application integration across diverse AI-driven environments

Here's an expanded discussion of the three scenarios outlined:

Enhancing data transformation, cleaning, and enrichment through LLMs
    LLMs excel in transforming complex semi-structured and unstructured datasets that traditional methods often struggle with. As shown as scenario number 1 in

Figure 13-2, LLMs and SLMs can parse intricate data formats, such as extracting crucial information from texts mixed with numerical data found in log files, emails, or reports. For example, consider an organization dealing with numerous XML files coming from different sources, each with its unique structure. Traditional data integration methods struggle with these variably structured XML files because they rely on predefined schemas. Here, a language model can make a significant difference. It doesn't need prior knowledge of the XML's structure. It can dynamically interpret each file's unique layout and content. For instance, if the organization needs to extract specific details like transaction data or customer information from thousands of different XML documents, the LLM can be used to locate and extract this information, no matter where it appears in the files.

Another significant advantage of LLMs is their capability in data enrichments, preprocessing, or feature engineering. Take, for example, Marvin (*https:// github.com/prefecthq/marvin*). It shines in handling sentiment analysis, data structuring, and multi-label classification. These LLM-based frameworks improve datasets by filling in gaps, expanding data points, and fixing errors like misspellings or inconsistencies.

In addition to these LLMs, foundational models like Nixtla's TimeGPT-1 (*https:// github.com/Nixtla/nixtla*) demonstrate the power of complex data processing in the domain of forecasting by analyzing sequential (time-series) data, which is invaluable for industries reliant on predicting trends and patterns. For instance, an airline operator could use TimeGPT-1 to analyze historical data on flight bookings and cancellations to predict future passenger volumes. This model not only forecasts future trends but also enhances the dataset by detecting seasonal variations and potential disruptions, such as those caused by holidays or weather conditions. Unlike traditional machine learning approaches that require extensive initial training with organization-specific data, these foundational models come pre-trained on a wide array of datasets, allowing them to provide immediate insights. This simplifies the process of integrating models into existing data architectures, making it easier to leverage AI capabilities for data enrichment and preprocessing.

Using big data for large-scale document processing

The powerful big data processing capabilities of the Medallion architecture, as seen in scenario number 2 from Figure 13-2, offer a robust way to dissect data or documents into meaningful chunks. These chunks can be enriched with metadata, tags, or other (structured) data. With both structured and unstructured data stored within the same architecture, more complex enrichments and combinations become possible. After augmentation, they can be transformed into high-dimensional vectors and stored in a specialized vector search database like Azure AI Search (*https://oreil.ly/hIThb*). This approach to using big data processing for chunk embedding can take away the limitations of traditional embedding techniques, eliminating issues such as scalability constraints and inefficiencies in handling diverse data types.

Direct data serving from Medallion layers to LLMs

Directly serving data from the Medallion layers to LLMs can greatly enhance the way AI applications can be implemented. This approach is demonstrated in pattern number 3 in Figure 13-2. Consider an intelligent customer support application as an example. Before sending a query to an LLM, the application first collects structured data, like customer details, from a layer of the Medallion architecture. Next, the application revises the prompt to let the LLM respond effectively. By chaining and combining these types of data, the LLM can generate responses that are not only accurate but also highly relevant to the user's specific context.

For simplicity, I've left out complex application integration topics like using an API gateway from this discussion. In real-world applications, achieving these integrations often involves some overlap with API management strategies, as we've touched upon earlier.

By integrating Medallion architecture with LLMs and application integration patterns, organizations can fully leverage their data, enhance operational efficiency with automation, and provide more personalized, responsive AI-driven services. This approach not only maximizes the utility of existing data but also paves the way for sophisticated applications that seamlessly interact with and adapt to user needs in real time.

Projecting into the future, AI is set to reshape the design of Medallion architecture significantly, creating possibilities for more advanced scenarios. This evolution will be marked by the increasing role of autonomous agents, which will enhance the architecture's ability to dynamically interact with and process complex data structures.

Role of Agents

Currently, the focus of the Medallion architecture is on handling tabular data, but thanks to advancements in GenAI, there's a growing interest in managing unstructured data like documents in landing and subsequent layers. In the future, this process might become a best practice for managing, for example, the Silver layer, as this layer is meant for preserving data in its authentic context. AI-powered search tools and LLMs will then interact with these vector databases, as depicted in Figure 13-3.

Let's imagine how the Medallion architecture could reshape the future with more complex, AI-driven applications. Take an airline company that wants to boost its customer service with intelligent agents using a framework like CrewAI (*https:// github.com/crewAIInc/crewAI*) or LangChain (*https://github.com/langchain-ai*). In this scenario, several agents collaborate, leveraging the Medallion architecture with SQL or RAG patterns. Each agent focuses on a specific dataset, such as passenger itineraries, frequent flyer profiles, flight schedules, or buying behavior. They employ tailored prompts to retrieve the relevant data, which is likely a mix of processed structured and unstructured information.

These agents don't just stick to static data; they also bring in real-time updates from air traffic control, taxi services, and traffic reports. This mix of patterns helps the AI tailor its responses to the current situation and give practical advice. For instance, if a passenger's flight gets delayed, one agent could suggest compensation options while another rearranges their travel plans to the hotel. Meanwhile, a third agent could put all this information together into a clear, friendly update for the passenger. This collaborative approach enables the airline to provide top-notch, responsive service. This layered approach ensures the response is both empathetic and practical, greatly enhancing the passenger's experience. In this scenario, the Medallion architecture serves as the crucial data foundation, enabling a seamless and personalized interaction.

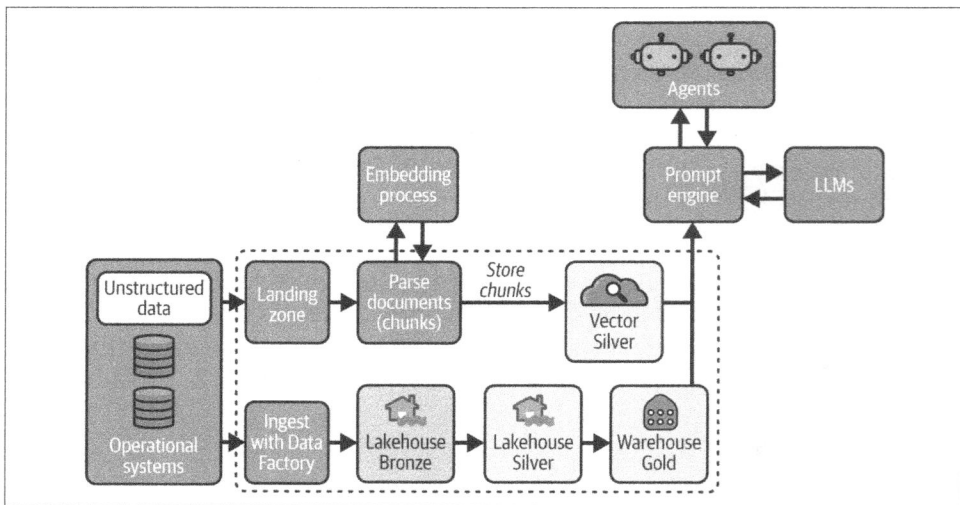

Figure 13-3. The roles of vector databases and LLMs within the Medallion architecture

Despite some skepticism, AI agents are quickly becoming more popular.[2] According to LangChain's State of AI Agents survey (*https://langchain.com/stateofaiagents*), which included 1,300 respondents, 51% of the companies surveyed already have agents in production, and 78% have active plans to implement agents into production soon. So, the scenario we've just discussed is not far-fetched; it's a reality that's already taking shape.

---

2 Sanjeev Mohan demystifies AI Agents in a Q&A: "FAQ on Demystifying AI Agent"s (*https://oreil.ly/eIGow*).

In summary, by combining the Medallion architecture with LLMs and application integration patterns, you can unlock new possibilities for AI-driven environments. This approach not only maximizes the utility of existing data but also paves the way for sophisticated intelligent applications that seamlessly interact with and adapt to user needs in real time. Let's now explore how the Medallion architecture can be used for training and fine-tuning LLMs.

Training and Fine-Tuning LLMs

Fine-tuning LLMs involves refining pre-trained models using smaller, task-specific datasets to enhance their performance for particular applications. This process transforms general-purpose models into specialized models, ensuring that the language model closely aligns with human expectations and the distinct needs of specific tasks.

The fine-tuning of LLMs is a supervised learning process. It utilizes a dataset of labeled examples, consisting of prompts and completions provided during training, to update the model's weights. Typically, this dataset should include thousands to tens of thousands of examples, reflective of the real-world scenarios where the model will operate. For instance, if fine-tuning a model for customer self-care support, the dataset should include common customer inquiries paired with the ideal responses.

To fine-tune a model, such as those provided by OpenAI, you begin by selecting appropriate prompts from your training dataset. These prompts are inputted into the LLM, which then generates completions. These examples should be formatted, for example in JSON, with each example comprising a <prompt, completion> pair. The process continues when you choose a base model and both training and validation datasets, with the model then being fine-tuned on the training set. The final step involves evaluating the model's performance on the validation data, which could involve comparison against outputs generated by a more powerful model or human-created responses to ensure high-quality performance.

In terms of data management using the Medallion architecture, it is crucial to adhere to established best practices across the Bronze, Silver, and Gold layers. The Bronze layer focuses on capturing raw documents and generating metadata. The Silver layer emphasizes organizing, standardizing, and preparing documents, while the Gold layer is dedicated to assembling the datasets used in the fine-tuning process. By adhering to these practices, you ensure proper separation of concerns and promote efficient reuse of data.

Fine-tuning LLMs is a powerful method to adapt pre-trained models to meet the specific requirements of different tasks or domains, significantly boosting their effectiveness and relevance. By leveraging the Medallion architecture, you can customize LLMs to deliver precise and contextually appropriate responses, perfectly suited to the unique challenges of your business. As we continue to explore the impact of AI, the future of Medallion architectures and their role in shaping data management looks promising. Let's look into some related trends before we conclude the book.

Future of Medallion Architectures

As of 2025, GenAI is transforming data management by making it more accessible and efficient. It streamlines data engineering, enhances governance, and offers clearer insights into business impacts. This technology accelerates processes and broadens participation due to its capability of handling complex data structures and metadata. Here's how advancements, such as AI, are poised to enhance Medallion architectures:

Data enrichment with AI
> As of 2025, AI is transforming the way you can clean and enhance data. For instance, AI can analyze a company's name and identify its industry, translate languages, classify customer support issues, locate the nearest store, determine the level of urgency, and much more. As demonstrated in Chapter 6, this technology is on the verge of changing the way you can enrich data. It will make the process faster, more precise, and easier to access.

The rise of generative business intelligence (GenBI)
> GenAI is poised to transform business intelligence by streamlining the creation of dashboards and reports. This innovative technology allows users to pose questions in natural language and receive precise, data-driven responses. It simplifies the process of creating visualizations and reports, eliminating the need for manual coding or design. Looking ahead, this technology could eventually make traditional reports obsolete. Rather than designing a report, you could simply generate one from a saved prompt.
>
> However, it's essential to recognize that GenBI will require extensive metadata to function effectively. It must have access to business terms and definitions, popular datasets, frequently used reports, relationships between datasets, and more. This metadata is crucial for the AI to understand business context and generate accurate reports.

AI-based data quality assurance
> AI is transforming data management with intelligent data quality solutions. Using sophisticated machine learning algorithms, AI can quickly sift through vast amounts of data to spot anomalies and inconsistencies. This marks a significant improvement over traditional manual methods, which are slower and more error-prone. For instance, Microsoft Purview utilizes machine learning and GenAI to propose new data quality rules based on existing metadata.

Streamlining data integration with AI
> Traditional data integration can be labor-intensive, requiring manual mapping and transformation. AI helps automate this by understanding data patterns and

relationships, which leads to more accurate and efficient integration. Tools like Prophecy (*https://prophecy.io*) use AI to help users build and manage data pipelines more effectively, enhancing both AI applications and analytics. The future of data integration will likely involve semantic information about the data to automatically identify and integrate data by cross-correlating what business relationships exist. Or, GenAI could be wired into the data integration process to automatically generate the integration logic to transform data.

AI-driven data governance

AI is also set to play a crucial role in data governance, automating processes to meet regulatory standards and protect data assets. For example, machine learning could be used to enforce governance policies and monitor compliance risks in real time, reducing the likelihood of breaches. Or, GenAI could be used to automatically label and classify data. This technology extends to metadata management too, improving data discoverability and usability.

Enhancing developer productivity with AI

GenAI tools like GitHub Copilot, Copilot in Microsoft Fabric, and Databricks Assistant help developers and data professionals boost their productivity. These tools provide code suggestions and answers, helping to speed up the development process and improve code quality. By working alongside these AI assistants, users can ensure the accuracy and relevance of the generated outputs.

Chatting with data

The ability to interact with data through conversation is likely to be seen in the future. GenAI can now interpret specific datasets, facilitating quicker data retrieval and more timely decision making, giving businesses a competitive edge. This innovation is similar to GenBI, but it operates seamlessly without the use of traditional dashboards.

Building AI skills

Creating conversational Q&A systems on platforms like Microsoft Fabric allows users to get accurate, data-driven answers simply by asking questions. By training the AI with specific instructions and examples, it can better understand the context of your organization, making this technology more effective and broadly applicable. For more information, see "AI Skill Example with the Adventure-Works Dataset (Preview)" (*https://oreil.ly/laZJS*).

Vector search

A dynamic capability that enhances the way items that share similarity in semantics can be found within any dataset.[3] The underlying technique is based on

---

3 Cosine similarity is a metric used to measure how similar two vectors are, irrespective of their size. Mathematically, it calculates the cosine of the angle between two vectors projected in a multi-dimensional space.

vector databases, which store data in a format optimized for similarity searches. These databases are particularly useful when dealing with complex data types like images, text, or products in an ecommerce catalog. By converting data into vectors—mathematical representations in a high-dimensional space—vector search allows for querying items that are similar to the query. This capability is invaluable for numerous applications, such as product recommendation systems, image retrieval, or document search, enhancing user experience and creating more value from existing data.

GraphRAG

An approach that combines graph databases with the RAG pattern to enhance data retrieval and generation. By leveraging the relationships between entities in a graph database, GraphRAG can provide more contextually relevant responses to queries. This approach is particularly useful in scenarios where data is interconnected, such as news sources, research papers, or knowledge bases. More information about this subject can be found in Microsoft's research paper, "GraphRAG: Unlocking LLM Discovery on Narrative Private Data" (*https://oreil.ly/rNr1d*).

Let's wrap up by revisiting our initial questions: is there value in managing structured, semi-structured, and unstructured data as a whole? And does integrating LLMs into the Medallion architecture add value? The answer to both is a resounding yes.

Managing all types of data together brings significant benefits, unlocking more comprehensive and effective insights. Additionally, LLMs are revolutionizing tasks like data cleansing and integration, pushing us to rethink traditional methods. Although these technologies are still being adopted, their potential to reshape organizational processes is both immense and thrilling.

Let's review the key takeaways from our exploration and conclude our journey through the Medallion architecture.

Conclusion

It's clear that designing and building these architectures is a complex process filled with vital decisions. We began by exploring the layers of Medallion architectures in detail in Part I and learned that the typical three-tier structure isn't always going to be the best fit. Instead, it should be customized to suit the specific needs of an organization and the nature of its data. A practical approach is to align sublayers with the Bronze, Silver, and Gold layers, ensuring each implemented layer matches its corresponding Medallion classification. Guiding your teams to understand what type of activities belong in each layer is crucial for maintaining a clear and consistent architecture. Developing an organization-wide Medallion layering standard is recommended to ensure that everyone is on the same page.

Throughout Part II, we bridged the gap between theory and practice with a practical implementation of Medallion architectures using services like Microsoft Fabric and Azure Databricks. We learned that creating a queryable Bronze layer can be a challenging task that requires a robust data ingestion process that must be tailored to the unique specifics of the source systems. By delving into the technical details of deploying and managing data pipelines, notebooks, and data products, we learned how to navigate this multifaceted challenge.

In the Silver layer, we saw that data transformation plays a critical role in the overall pipeline. We covered the importance of putting the activities of data cleansing, denormalization, data enrichments, and historization in the correct sequence to ensure a smooth process. By simplifying the approach and including metadata-driven approaches, we made sure that data transformation is a breeze.

The Gold layer is where we explored the importance of creating easily accessible, understandable, and actionable data products. We saw how to build a data product that provides value to the business and how to ensure that it's well-documented and maintained. We also learned that building a data product is a collaborative effort that requires a long set of guiding activities.

In Part III, we delved into the obstacles faced by various enterprises and the valuable lessons they've learned. Every organization has its own distinct challenges and chances for growth, and the key to success is recognizing and addressing these unique factors with tailored architecture. Our exploration demonstrated how Medallion architectures can be used in a flexible way to promote business innovation, enhance decision making, and streamline operations. We discovered that Medallion architectures are most successful when implemented alongside robust data governance and a deeply ingrained data engineering culture.

In Part IV, we looked at Medallion architectures in federated and distributed environments, where multiple architectures operate simultaneously. We encountered a challenge: the possibility of overly fragmented data products scattered across numerous domains. The remedy lies in establishing robust standards and a central authority to oversee data product creation. This requires setting standards for data modeling and coordinating changes and data delivery. Admittedly, these tasks are daunting, so strong security and governance frameworks are crucial. Tools like data catalogs can help organizations manage and oversee their data products and business concepts more effectively and efficiently. Finally, we concluded there is value in incorporating LLMs and holistically managing both structured and unstructured data using a single framework, such as the Medallion architecture.

In conclusion, our exploration of building Medallion architectures reveals a flexible framework for managing and processing data. It highlights the importance of viewing their layers as logical structures rather than physical ones. There is no one-size-fits-all rule; the need for three distinct tiers depends on the organization's specific goals and the complexity of its data. Even more important is that effective data modeling is the cornerstone of delivering success. Just as with traditional data warehouse systems, poor modeling leads to the deterioration of data integrity and utility. Therefore, organizations must prioritize developing their teams' data modeling skills to ensure that the Medallion architecture—or any data architecture—fulfills its intended purpose efficiently and effectively.

Managing a data journey effectively is just as crucial as having a strong data architecture in place. To embark on a transformation journey, you need to focus on communication, coaching, training, solid data governance, and alignment within the organization. These activities are essential, so don't underestimate their significance. You need competent leaders who can oversee and align different activities. They should have a clear vision and organize design and brainstorming sessions. They should also be practical and inspiring so they can motivate everyone to follow. You must develop a well-thought-out data transformation plan that includes a clear roadmap for delivering tangible results. The challenge lies in addressing different focus areas or streams simultaneously. You need to build and mature the technology architecture, establish data governance, provide skilling and training, foster cultural awareness, and ensure business alignment. All these areas must progress in parallel and mature equally over time. Though complex, this approach is essential for a successful data transformation journey.

Looking to the future, the integration of GenAI into data management opens exciting new possibilities. Although GenAI technology is still emerging, its potential to transform data management is immense and something to watch closely. It's expected to have a major impact on evolution of data architectures.

Index

About the Author

Piethein Strengholt is a seasoned expert in data management with significant experience in chief data officer (CDO) and chief data architect roles. He has a strong track record of collaborating with CDO executives at large enterprises, where he focuses on driving community growth and aligning strategies with business goals. Piethein is also a prolific blogger and a sought-after speaker who regularly addresses the latest trends in data management, including data mesh concepts, data governance, and scaling strategies. He resides in the Netherlands with his family.

Colophon

The animal on the cover of *Building Medallion Architectures* is a gray-breasted parakeet (*Pyrrhura griseipectus*). This endangered bird is found only in pockets of Brazil's northeastern forests at the time of this writing, though conservationists have made remarkable progress in protecting the species from poaching and deforestation.

Gray-breasted parakeets are small parrots—typically 8–9 inches from head to tail—and not sexually dimorphic. Both the males and females have green bodies, red and white faces, bright red tail feathers, and this bird's eponymous scalloped gray breast feathers. They are social birds, living in family groups of 4 to 15 individuals. They roost in the cavities of old growth trees.

The population of endangered gray-breasted parakeets is on the way up. Many of the animals on O'Reilly covers are endangered; all of them are important to the world.

The cover illustration is by José Marzan Jr., based on an antique line engraving from *Lydekker's Royal Natural History*. The series design is by Edie Freedman, Ellie Volckhausen, and Karen Montgomery. The cover fonts are Gilroy Semibold and Guardian Sans. The text font is Adobe Minion Pro; the heading font is Adobe Myriad Condensed; and the code font is Dalton Maag's Ubuntu Mono.

O'REILLY®

Learn from experts.
Become one yourself.

60,000+ titles | Live events with experts | Role-based courses
Interactive learning | Certification preparation

**Try the O'Reilly learning platform
free for 10 days.**

www.ingramcontent.com/pod-product-compliance
Lightning Source LLC
Chambersburg PA
CBHW080703220326
41598CB00033B/5297